Strikes: An Ess
Industrial Actic

C000221813

For Patrick and for Bernadette

Strikes: An Essential Guide to Industrial Action and the Law

Mary Redmond

B.C.L., LL.M. (NUI), Ph D (Cantab), Solicitor

Tom Mallon

Barrister-at-Law

Bloomsbury Professional

Published by
Bloomsbury Professional
Maxwelton House
41–43 Boltro Road
Haywards Heath
West Sussex
RH16 1BJ

Bloomsbury Professional
The Fitzwilliam Business Centre
26 Upper Pembroke Street
Dublin 2

ISBN 978 1 84766 548 5

© Bloomsbury Professional 2010

British Library Cataloguing-in-Publication Data
A catalogue record for this book is available from the British Library

Typeset by Marie Armah-Kwantreng, Dublin, Ireland
Printed and bound in the United Kingdom by Martins the Printers Ltd

Contents

FOREWORD

Industrial relations and strikes in particular, occupy a contested boundary area between economics, social policy, politics and the law. As this book valuably demonstrates, the factors which have influenced which of the competing sectors determines the legal framework in relation to industrial relations has varied over time. The initial judge made law which favoured employers, the political circumstances leading to the 1906 Act which, in substance, was designed to reverse that judge made law, the industrial difficulties of the 1970s and 1980s with resultant increased regulation of the circumstances in which industrial action could lawfully be maintained, are all examples of shifting dominance within that contested battleground. This book makes a most valuable contribution to many areas but not least amongst them is an understanding of the political, economic, social and legal history which has led to the law in relation to industrial relations generally, and strikes in particular, evolving in the way in which it did.

Most of the main developments occurred against a backdrop of fraught economic and social times with consequent pressure for political action and legal development. One might reasonably express the fear that we are about to enter another such time when a fraught industrial relations landscape is likely to lead to a testing of the boundaries of permissible industrial action. In that context, a book which addresses all aspects of the law relating to that most potent industrial relations weapon of the strike is more than timely.

One feature of this comprehensive work is the separate consideration of the various ways in which those who might argue that a particular strike is unlawful have and may continue to seek to make their case. The chapter headings are themselves a ready guide. The contract of employment may be said to be interfered with. There may be said to be a conspiracy or an economic tort. There may be said to be intimidation. All legislation and judicial interpretation in the field is faced with the difficult problem of attempting to find an appropriate balance between the rights of all concerned. That checklist and the analysis under each heading provides a ready guide to the battleground.

It might have been said that, in relatively recent times, there has been less recourse to the courts in the industrial relations context. In some three years in charge (for most of the time) of the Chancery 1 Monday List (in which almost all interlocutory injunction applications come to be heard), I can recollect only a very few cases in which injunctions arising out of industrial action were sought between 2005 and 2008. Whether that superficial view bears detailed scrutiny or not is one question. However, if it be accurate, the question is also raised as to whether that situation stemmed from the success of the 1990 Act in establishing the parameters within which strike action was to be permitted or whether, as one might suspect, the relative lack of action was a by-product of the boom now over. Which was the true cause may be revealed over the next number of years.

However, this book is much more than a theoretical and historical perspective on the evolution of the interaction between strikes and the law. It also provides a very practical guide to those who may be faced with advising clients on either side of the divide as to the legal implications of strike action. It provides, in addition to a lucid account of the law as it now is, a ready access to the important and relevant procedural questions that may arise. In this latter regard, a number of very helpful precedents are provided for the practitioner who may be faced with representing parties to court proceedings. Unfortunately, it may well be that those precedents will come to be used with increasing frequency in the weeks and months ahead.

It may be that the economic and social pressures which give rise to strikes will occur with increasing frequency over such a timeframe. If that be so, the courts will be faced with many more questions, both of specific and general application. Whether the current legal framework will be seen to be fit for purpose in those circumstances is not clear. Whether, for example, the Charter of Fundamental Rights of the EU, now recognised by the EU Treaties, will play any role is a matter that remains to be seen. That charter does not, of course, provide any new competence to the EU. However, the Charter is given the same legal weight as the Treaties and, in areas where the EU has competence, it is likely that the Charter will come into play. The Charter expressly recognises the right of collective action. It is possible to envisage at least some circumstances in which EU issues might arise in relation to strike action involving cross border business or the free movement of workers.

But any such considerations are for the future. This most valuable work will provide both legal practitioners and anyone else who has a responsibility for considering the legality or otherwise of actions taken in furtherance of trade disputes, with, as it says on the tin, an "essential guide" which will enable timely and effective advice to be given in what are, almost inevitably, fraught and urgent circumstances.

This book is truly "essential" for anyone involved in industrial relations.

Frank Clarke

The High Court

8th July, 2010

PREFACE

It seemed timely to write about the economic torts in trade disputes, and the Industrial Relations Act 1990. There are already some excellent books on industrial relations law, and on the Irish law of torts, but none concentrates on the discrete area of trade disputes law and the small number of sections that are relevant in Part II of the Act of 1990.

The authors were prompted in part by the current industrial relations climate which weekly contains threats of, or actual, strikes and industrial action, and for which all involved need to know about the law whether they are pursuing a statutory resolution procedure or not. But the need to write the book arose also from the fact that this area of the law is in a 'terrible mess'. Should an opportunity present itself to the superior courts to review the economic torts there is help at hand from a recent decision of the House of Lords, *OBG Ltd v Allan* [2008] AC 1, and the potential influence of this case features throughout. Although most cases under the Act of 1990 have been interlocutory, decisions under the Act's predecessor, the Trade Disputes Act 1906, are of valuable assistance where the statutory provisions are not inconsistent.

Employment law responds to the times. Practitioners in industrial relations very rarely needed to advise on the law of strikes and industrial action in recent decades. Now that has changed and it is hoped this book will provide a useful guide for them in what is a complex area of the law. Draft pleadings are included as helpful illustrations of the many nuances that can be expected.

This book could not have been written without the cheerful and expert help of Thérèse Broy, Librarian at Arthur Cox, to whom we offer our grateful thanks. Sinead Casey of the Employment Law Group at Arthur Cox did research on some knotty issues and we thank her also. Tom Mallon would like to thank the many colleagues in the Law Library who have discussed issues with him and pointed him in appropriate directions. We are most grateful to Amy Hayes of Bloomsbury Professional for her encouragement and patience at all times, and Marie Armah-Kwantreng for typesetting the book.

We would particularly thank Mr Justice Clarke for taking the time to read the book at pre-publication stage and for kindly agreeing to write the foreword.

For the faults and failings of the book, the usual disclaimer applies.

MARY REDMOND

TOM MALLON

Summer Solstice Day, 2010

TABLE OF CASES

TABLE OF STATUTES

TABLE OF STATUTORY INSTRUMENTS

TABLE OF EUROPEAN LEGISLATION

TABLE OF CONVENTIONS AND COVENANTS

TABLE OF CONSTITUTIONS

Chapter 1

FROM THE TRADE DISPUTES ACT 1906 TO THE INDUSTRIAL RELATIONS ACT 1990

INTRODUCTION

[1.01] For almost 80 years the Trade Disputes Act 1906 (the Act of 1906) was regarded as a statute of fundamental importance in Ireland. This landmark in the history of Ireland's labour law was repealed and replaced by the Industrial Relations Act 1990 (the Act of 1990). That the Act of 1906 was of fundamental importance is not attributable to any immutable foundations of principle in the Act itself nor to well debated theories at the time of its enactment. The birth of the Act of 1906 at Westminster was a muddle: the result of a combination of political pressure by the trade unions, the nascent Labour Party and the liberal Radicals, the retreat of the government from its own Bill for political expediency and the opposition's concern with other problems.[1] Kenny J in *Goulding Chemicals Ltd v Bolger*[2] referred to the 1906 Act as having been introduced:

> to redeem an election pledge of the Liberal Party to overrule the decision of the House of Lords in *Taff Vale* and there are many indications in it that it was hurriedly drafted and that its wording did not receive adequate consideration.

Parke J[3] stated in the same case that:

> the Trade Disputes Act of 1906 was the child of political expediency, hastily conceived and prematurely delivered. It has now survived more than the allotted span of life with all its inbred imperfections still uncorrected.

Yet the Act was fundamentally important because it took the law out of industrial relations and allowed a voluntary structure of collective bargaining to be created. It did so by continuing and entrenching the system of statutory immunities originating in the Conspiracy and Protection of Property Act 1875 for acts 'in contemplation or furtherance of a trade dispute' (a phrase which became known as 'the golden formula'). The system of immunities in tort for trade unions, their officials and members under the 1906 Act, which provided that certain acts in the particular context of a trade dispute would not attract civil law remedies for unlawful acts, survived in Ireland after Independence and its constitutional integrity has never been impugned by

---

1. Kidner, 'Lessons in Trade Union Law Reform: the Origins and Passage of the Trade Disputes Act 1906' (1982) *Legal Studies* 34. More generally, see Wallace, Gunnigle and McMahon, *Industrial Relations in Ireland* (3rd edn, Gill & Macmillan, 2004); Gibbs, 'Beyond Voluntarism in Collective Labour Law' (2005) 2 IELJ 3; Kerr, 'Industrial Relations Law' in *Employment Law* (ed Regan) (Bloomsbury Professional, 2009), ch 18.
2. *Goulding Chemicals Ltd v Bolger* [1977] IR 211 at 236.
3. *Goulding Chemicals Ltd v Bolger* [1977] IR 211 at 242.

the courts. The result is that in Ireland there is no right to strike as such. Lord Denning famously said:[4]

> Parliament granted immunities to the leaders of trade unions, it did not give them any rights. It did not give them the right to break the law, or to do wrong by inducing people to break contracts. It only gave them immunity if they did.

COMMON LAW AND LEGISLATIVE BACKGROUND TO THE TRADE DISPUTES ACT 1906

[1.02] During the nineteenth century UK governments were predominantly representative of interests hostile to organised labour. Trade unions trusted neither government nor the judges charged with the task of administering any laws which Parliament passed. Time and again the courts pronounced on the law in a manner hostile to trade unions. A legal game of battledore and shuttlecock developed. Repeatedly trade unions pressurised governments to change the law to remove the effect of a judicial decision only to see their success frustrated and undermined by a subsequent legal decision. The hostile attitude to trade unions flowed inevitably from *laissez-faire* capitalism, from the early years of the Industrial Revolution emphasising the free exchange of goods and services in a market with which nobody 'interfered.'

Common Law

[1.03] It is, and always has been, a fundamental principle of the common law that every person has the right to dispose of his capital or of his labour according to his will. The law was slow to accept the political, social, economic and industrial importance of trade unions. The essence of trade unionism is collective: the procurement of higher wages and better conditions of employment for members through the mechanism of collective bargaining. Prior to 1871 any group of workmen combining for the purpose of raising the rates of their wages was liable to be indicted for conspiracy.[5] Moreover, any contract or agreement between two or more persons to exercise the freedom to combine in such fashion was regarded by the law as against public policy, being in unreasonable restraint of trade. Large undertakings, monopolies and cartels were all intrinsically questionable and this wrongfulness of combinations extended to collectivities of workers.[6]

Parliament

[1.04] Repressive legislation by Westminster from the sixteenth century on did not prevent trade unionism flourishing in Ireland. Throughout the eighteenth century legislation was passed as often as 1729, 1743, 1757, 1763 and 1780. Following the Act of Union of Great Britain and Ireland 1800, the Unlawful Combinations (Ireland) Act 1803 was passed by the Parliament at Westminster. The long title of this Act stated that it was 'an Act to prevent Unlawful Combinations of Workmen, Artificers, Journeymen

---

4.   *Express Newspapers v McShane* [1979] ICR 210.
5.   See, eg, *R v Journeymen Tailors of Cambridge* (1721) 8 Mod 10.
6.   McCarthy, *Elements in a Theory of Industrial Relations* (Irish Academic Press, 1984).

and Labourers in Ireland.' The preamble declared that previous anti-combination laws in Ireland 'had been found to be inadequate to the suppression thereof'. Offenders were therefore to be brought to 'more speedy and exemplary punishment.'

[1.05] Trade unions in Ireland derive their legal status largely from the Trade Union Act 1871, as amended. The Act is often called 'the Charter of Trade Unionism' because it gave legal recognition to a trade union of workers or a trade association of employers. Trade unions were not, however, given an elaborate code of positive rights. Section 2 of the Act provided protection for *bona fide* union activities:

> The purposes of any trade union shall not, by reason merely that they are in restraint of trade, be deemed to be unlawful, so as to render any member of such trade union liable to criminal prosecution for conspiracy or otherwise.

The taint of illegality was thereby removed from trade unions. Although several trade union statutes were passed in Ireland from 1935 on, the Act of 1871 has never been repealed or significantly amended. It is still the principal Act dealing with trade unions and has featured in a considerable number of judicial decisions in this country and in Britain affecting the contractual or personal status of trade unions.

[1.06] The main effect of the Act of 1871[7] regarding trade disputes law was to relieve all trade unions and societies of traders from some of the civil and criminal disabilities under which they laboured as a result of the legal doctrine of restraint of trade.[8] Section 3 of the Act of 1871 provides that the purposes of a trade union shall not be unlawful so as to render void or voidable any agreement or trust.[9] Hence any contracts entered into by a trade union were not to be regarded as contracts which the law would not enforce. Because it is significant in trade disputes law, the definition of 'trade union' will now be examined.

Definition of Trade Union

[1.07] Trade unions are legal entities subject to the law and accorded a number of legal duties and privileges. The statutory definition of 'trade union' concerns both its

---

7. The other main objects were as follows: (i) To protect trade unions in their domestic disputes with their own members. Section 4 provides that nothing in the Act shall enable any court to entertain any legal proceedings instituted with the object of directly enforcing or recovering damages for the breach of certain domestic agreements made between trade unions and their members and between one union and another. (ii) To provide a system of voluntary registration of trade unions. Most unions in Ireland are registered. Generally certification or registration and authorisation are necessary to obtain various benefits under statute, but not always: see, eg, *NUJ and Irish Print Union v Sisk* [1990] ELR 177.
8. The common law doctrine being to the effect that 'it is the privilege of a trader in a free country in all matters not contrary to law, to regulate his own mode of carrying it on according to his own discretion and choice. If the law has regulated or restrained his mode of doing this, the law must be obeyed. But no power short of the general law ought to restrain his free discretion' *per* Lord Smith LC in *Mitchell v Reynolds* (1711) 1 P Wms 181.
9. 'Agreement' covers the rule book.

membership and its purposes. The Trade Union Act 1871, s 23, amplified by the Trade Union Acts 1876 and 1913,[10] defines a 'trade union' as any:

> combination whether temporary or permanent

and

> whose principal objects under its constitution [include] the regulation of the relations between workmen and masters, or between workmen and workmen, or between masters and masters, or the imposing of restrictive conditions on the conduct of any trade or business; and also the provision of benefits to members.[11]

A peculiar feature of this definition is that it deliberately did not give a trade union the status of incorporation as a limited liability company. In legal theory a trade union is an unincorporated association, although in fact it obtains most of the benefits and bears most of the burdens of incorporation. An unincorporated association does not exist as an entity separate from its members. It is an association of individuals bound together by contract, with the rule book providing the terms of the contract.

[1.08] A registered trade union (see s 6 of the Act of 1871) is anomalous in that, although consisting of a fluctuating body of individuals and not being incorporated as a limited liability company, it can own property, bring or defend an action at law to protect it and act by agents. It is capable of making contracts in its own name. All property belonging to the union is vested in trustees in trust for the union. Such unions possess many of the attributes of corporations.[12] The House of Lords permitted a trade union to be sued in its own name in *Taff Vale Railway v Amalgamated Society of Railway Servants*[13] although in doing so it did not (Lord Brampton excepted) see itself as conferring on the union any new juristic status by way of quasi-corporate personality.[14]

[1.09] The legal status of a trade union bears on the question of whether a trade union can be a proper party to a trade dispute for purposes of the statutory immunities, now found in the Industrial Relations Act 1990. Moreover, it affects both the perception and the outcome in law of the problem when the rights of a collectivity of workers are

---

10. In general see Kerr, *The Trade Union and Industrial Relations Acts* (3rd edn, Round Hall, 2007).

11. The proviso excludes any agreement between partners as to their own business; same between any employer and those employed by him as to such employment or same in consideration of the sale of the goodwill of a business or of instruction in any profession, trade or handicraft.

12. *R v Rathmines Urban District Council* [1928] IR 260.

13. *Taff Vale Railway v Amalgamated Society of Railway Servants* [1901] AC 426. See further para **1.16** below.

14. However, in *Bonsor v Musicians' Union* [1956] AC 104 some members of the House of Lords, in deciding that a member of a registered union could sue for damages, went further, but the overall result on the question of the precise juridical nature of the union was inconclusive.

examined. Where a collectivity of workers is exercising its own particular rights and freedoms, it is important to ascertain whether the collectivity is acting as a 'quasi-corporate' possessor of such rights and freedoms or whether one is dealing with the sum total of the exercise of these rights and freedoms by the individual workers who make up the collectivity.

[1.10] In relation to the definition of 'trade union' in the Act of 1871, as amplified, two observations may be made. The first relates to the description of the association as an 'organisation whether temporary or permanent.' This phrase is unclear as to the degree of stability an association must possess before it can be a trade union, eg must it have some degree of formality in its institution? Suppose a grouping of workers is a casual and 'temporary' one coming together in the context of a particular dispute – would this qualify as a 'trade union'? An 'ad hoc' association limited to a specific and temporary purpose is likely to be covered if it possesses a degree of formality. In *Frost v Clarke & Smith*[15] it was held that a joint works committee representing all the workers could not be an 'organisation' because it had no name and no rules. Contrariwise, in *Midland Cold Storage v Turner*[16] Donaldson J held that a committee of shop stewards from various unions was an 'organisation' since it had a name and at least a fairly basic structure in so far as it had a chairman and secretary. A broader approach is evident in *Butler Bros v NUFLAT*[17] where an informal but regular meeting of employers was held to amount to an employers' association by the UK Central Arbitration Committee.

[1.11] The second point to note arises in relation to the principal purposes of a trade union. They must include the regulation of relations between the social partners, or between either of these *inter se*. The Acts do not state that the principal purpose must be such regulation, only that that must be one of the principal purposes. While a shop stewards committee is an 'organisation' consisting of workers (the shop stewards being members), its objects do not include the necessary 'principal purposes': *Midland Cold Storage v Turner*[18] (see also *Midland Cold Storage v Steer*).[19] According to Donaldson J:

> Its most apparent activity seems to consist of recommending the taking or abandonment of industrial action ... Thereafter it does not seem to enter into negotiations with the employers but leaves this task to the established union machinery ... No body whose principal objects included [the regulation of relations between workers and employers] could fail at least to seek recognition from employers.

Thus organisations with limited objectives and those that have only an advisory function are excluded. It may be 'regulation' requires that the organisation must wish to affect relations between the employer and the workforce. However, it is uncertain whether the purpose must be to affect relations between particular employers and

---

15.   *Frost v Clarke & Smith* [1973] IRLR 216.
16.   *Midland Cold Storage v Turner* [1972] ICR 230.
17.   *Butler Bros v NUFLAT*, CAC award No 80/121.
18.   *Midland Cold Storage v Turner* [1972] ICR 230.
19.   *Midland Cold Storage v Steer* [1972] Ch 630.

workers or whether it is sufficient to have the aim of improving industrial relations generally. If one adopts the former view, bodies such as the Irish Congress of Trade Unions (ICTU) and the Irish Business and Employers Confederation (IBEC) could not be regarded as trade unions.

[1.12] Prior to the enactment of s 3 of the Trade Union Act 1913, the definition of 'trade union' for the purposes of the Act of 1906 was that in the Trade Union Act 1871, as amplified. In relation to three sections in the Act of 1906, a trade union was subject to restrictions imposed by the Trade Union Act 1941, s 11 (re-enacted by the Industrial Relations Act of 1990), namely a 'trade union' had to be an 'authorised' trade union which for the time being is the holder of a 'negotiation licence'.

An authorised trade union holds a negotiation licence. Statute places restrictions on the granting of such licences to avoid a multiplicity of trade unions. The various requirements are set out in the Trade Union Act 1971 (the Act of 1971) and depend on whether the union concerned is Irish or foreign based and whether it first applied for a licence before or after the Act of 1971. An authorised trade union may carry out collective bargaining and invoke the Industrial Relations (Amendment) Act 2001 (para **2.28**), and its members may benefit under employment statutes such as the Unfair Dismissals Act 1977, ss 1 and 6(2)(a) (dismissal for membership or activities of an authorised trade union deemed unfair). Most importantly for the present context, a trade union must be authorised for purposes of Pt II of the Industrial Relations Act 1990, which concerns trade disputes, and its members and officials may obtain the benefits of the immunities in ss 11, 12 and 13 of that Act.

THE CONSPIRACY AND PROTECTION OF PROPERTY ACT 1875 AND THE SYSTEM OF IMMUNITIES

[1.13] The Trade Union Act 1871 had serious defects. Parliament's reaction to harsh judicial decisions was to accord specific exemptions from the legal penalties which trade unionists automatically incurred at common law. The Conspiracy and Protection of Property Act 1875 – optimistically called the 'rock upon which the freedom to strike in Britain is built'[20] – introduced in s 3 an immunity from prosecution for criminal conspiracy. A system of immunities meant the common law was left intact, thus perpetuating a cause of continuing conflict between the courts and trade unions. Union rights depended on the strength unions could develop and assert themselves. The method of protecting the freedom to strike in the UK consisted in the enactment of immunities for taking industrial action, in the withholding of state intervention. The strike was seen as a corollary of collective bargaining, an industrial sanction. Ireland inherited the fruits of this historical tradition and, following a brief flirtation with the idea of a system based on rights rather than immunities in the 1980s (para **1.31**), the Industrial Relations Act 1990 continues and reinforces the tradition of immunities. Thus Ireland has no right to strike or to take industrial action. Civil and criminal wrongs may be committed by those organising or participating in industrial action.

---

20.   Wedderburn and Davies, *Employment Grievances and Dispute Procedures in Britain* (University of California Press, 1969), 8.

Outside of the wrongs for which statutory immunities are given lie significant areas of potential liability.

LEGAL ISSUES BEFORE ENACTMENT OF THE TRADE DISPUTES ACT 1906

[1.14] In the period before 1906 there were three principal areas of legal significance in Britain in relation to the conduct of trade disputes. Firstly, there was the legal liability of persons engaged in trade disputes, the focus of the present work. It concerns the limits of lawful picketing and the extent to which the common law torts of inducing breach of contract, causing loss by unlawful means, intimidation and conspiracy, may be used against those engaged in trade disputes. Secondly, there was the issue of immunity of trade union funds from actions for damages and thirdly, the extent to which arbitration and conciliation, whether compulsory or voluntary, should be the method of resolving disputes.

The legal liability of persons engaged in trade disputes before 1906

[1.15] Before the Criminal Law Amendment Act 1871 and the Conspiracy and Protection of Property Act 1875 the criminal law was most often used for the control of industrial disputes. The attention of the courts, and of employers, then turned to the civil law. Trade unions were concerned about the limits on lawful picketing, particularly in the wake of *Lyons v Wilkins*[21] (para **10.05** below) where the court, led by Lord Lindley, seems to have decided that any picketing for the purpose of persuading a person to do what he has a lawful right to do was a common law nuisance. That period of time also witnessed an era of great development for the economic torts, beginning in 1853 with *Lumley v Gye*[22] and ending in a wider tort of causing loss by unlawful means.[23] By 1905 union officials could be liable for inducing breaches of employment contracts[24] and of commercial contracts[25] and it was unlikely such action could be justified.[26] It seemed likely also that they could be liable for a wider tort of interfering with trade by unlawful means (**Ch 7**). A major area of concern was the tort of conspiracy in trade disputes (**Ch 5**). A move which failed in *Allen v Flood*[27] to control trade disputes by law succeeded in *Quinn v Leathem*.[28] The tort of civil conspiracy

---

21.   *Lyons v Wilkins* [1896] 1 Ch 811, [1899] 1 Ch 255.

22.   *Lumley v Gye* (1853) 2 E & B 216.

23.   The desire for expansion earlier mentioned was based on the individualist philosophy and *laissez-faire* economics of the judiciary, which called for a law that restrained unlawful interference with trade but fell short of developing a tort of unfair trade: see *Bowen v Hall* (1881) 6 QBD 333 *per* Brett LJ; and *Mogul Steamship v McGregor Gow* (1889) 23 QBD 598 at 617 *per* Bowen LJ.

24.   *Read v Friendly Society of Operative Stonemasons* [1902] 2 KB 88.

25.   *Temperton v Russell (No 2)* [1893] 1 QB 715.

26.   *Read v Friendly Society of Operative Stonemasons* [1902] 2 KB 88; *Glamorgan Coal Company v South Wales Miners' Federation* [1905] AC 239.

27.   *Allen v Flood* [1898] AC 1.

28.   *Quinn v Leathem* [1901] AC 495.

posed a great threat to unions. In almost every strike there was a conspiracy by the members and officials to injure the plaintiff for a purpose which the law might not recognise as justified.

Immunity of trade union funds before 1906

[1.16] A most serious problem facing the unions was exposure of their funds to legal action by employers and liability for the actions of their officials and members. Although *Taff Vale Railway Company v Amalgamated Society of Railway Servants*[29] (*Taff Vale*) was easily the most important case on the topic, it was not the first court decision to hold a union liable in its own name for the acts of others thus exposing union funds to actions, mainly by employers.[30] Until 1871 the legal liability of trade unions never arose because they were regarded as unlawful associations in restraint of trade and the courts would have nothing to do with them.

[1.17] After the Trade Union Act 1871 the problem was merely the procedural one of actions against unincorporated associations. Rather than try to resolve that problem, the House in *Taff Vale* affirmed that a registered union was not the same as other unincorporated associations because they had been given certain powers and duties in the 1871 Act. These rendered them more like corporations but at the same time no new juristic status was accorded to trade unions. To what extent should a union be liable for the acts of its officials and members? This issue arose out of *Taff Vale* and has been important ever since. The problem was not taken on board in *Taff Vale* because, albeit with some reluctance, the dispute was made official, but in 1904 the Court of Appeal decided that a union should be liable if the act of the official was done in the service of and for the benefit of the union, even though the act was *ultra vires*: *Giblan v National Amalgamated Labourers Union of Great Britain and Ireland*.[31] In 1906, however, under a Liberal Lord Chancellor, Lord Loreburn, the House decided that a union should not be liable for acts not authorised by the rules: *Denaby and Cadeby Main Collieries v Yorkshire Miners Association*.[32]

[1.18] *Taff Vale* threatened the whole structure of collective bargaining. Moreover, it meant that injunctions could be issued directly against unions, and their funds made available to pay damages for loss of profits brought about by the strike.

Arbitration and conciliation

[1.19] The third major factor in the debate on trade union law reform before 1906 was the proposal that arbitration and conciliation should be the basis of dispute settlement rather than collective bargaining and strikes. Legislative provisions for arbitration in

---

29.   *Taff Vale Railway Company v Amalgamated Society of Railway Servants* [1901] AC 426.

30.   In *Pink v Federation of Trade Unions* (1893) 8 TLR 216, 711 the plaintiff succeeded in injuncting the union on the grounds that they, the defendants, had issued a circular to co-operative society secretaries, urging them not to buy the plaintiff's pickles.

31.   *Giblan v National Amalgamated Labourers Union of Great Britain and Ireland* [1903] 2 KB 600.

32.   *Denaby and Cadeby Main Collieries v Yorkshire Miners Association* [1906] AC 384.

trade disputes, encapsulated in the Arbitration Act 1824, had become obsolete by 1856. After many years of discussion about arbitration, the Councils of Conciliation Act 1867 was passed. But the Act apparently was never used, partly because it needed the impetus of employers and workmen to set up a Council and partly because it had no jurisdiction over wages. The Arbitration (Masters and Workmen) Act 1872 provided for compulsory arbitration on voluntary agreements entered into under the Act. But by the time of the Royal Commission on Labour 1891–94 the statutory provisions for arbitration were a dead letter. The Conciliation Act 1896 enabled conciliation boards to register and gave powers of inquiry to the Board of Trade, but it too was of little consequence. Whatever might have been the merits of an increase in the use of arbitration and conciliation, in the event that issue was pushed to one side in favour of the view that immunity from liability was essential.

TRADE DISPUTES 1906 ACT IN BRIEF

[1.20] In the autumn of 1901 the immediate issue before the trade unions was how to counter the combined effects of extended civil liability and the exposure of union funds to legal action. This also raised the wider question of the political and legal status of trade unions. The Conservative government refused to entertain the lawfulness of trade dispute activities or suggestions for moderate reform. According to Kidner,[33] had the Conservatives of 1902 been more receptive to moderate trade unionism, the law might well have accepted the development of trade unions as part of the legal and political structure of the country. The argument for total immunity is based on the view that unions should not only have the power to use the independent sanction of the strike in order to support the collective bargaining system, but also that they must be free from interference by outside bodies in their control of such power. As Kidner puts it:

> By this means they are able to represent their members without regard to their relationship with the law or the government. Hence it is argued that they should not be corporate bodies, for that implies a licensing system by the state, nor should they be required to submit to government controls on their internal or external activities, for as free associations responsible to their members they would find difficulty in obeying both government controls and the wishes of their members.

[1.21] Under the Act of 1906, those organising or participating in trade disputes were granted immunity from certain forms of criminal and civil liability if they were acting 'in contemplation or furtherance of a trade dispute', provided the parties were proper parties and the subject matter constituted a 'trade dispute' as defined under the Act. The definition of 'trade dispute' in s 5 of the Act of 1906 was as follows:

> any dispute between employers and workmen, or between workmen and workmen, which is connected with the employment or non-employment or the terms of employment or the conditions of labour of any person.

---

33.   Kidner, 'Lessons in Trade Union Law Reform: the Origins and Passage of the Trade Disputes Act 1906' (1982) *Legal Studies* 41.

The first three sections in the 1906 Act conferred immunities on all persons, whether trade union officials or not, by protecting them from actions for damages in conspiracy (s 1), by legalising peaceful picketing (s 2) and by removing any liability on them for interfering with another person's business (s 3). The fourth section removed exposure of union funds to legal action in tort by conferring complete immunity on a trade union by prohibiting any action being taken against it in respect of any tort alleged to have been committed by or on behalf of the trade union. The fifth section contained the definitions of 'trade union', 'trade dispute' and 'workmen.' The text of the 1906 Act is set out in the **Appendix**.

[1.22] Two important additions were later made to the 1906 Act. Firstly, s 11 of the Trade Union Act 1941 provided that ss 2, 3 and 4 of the Act of 1906 should apply only in relation to authorised trade unions who for the time being were holders of negotiation licences, and members and officials of such unions, and not otherwise. Secondly, the Trade Disputes (Amendment) Act 1982 amended s 5 of the Act of 1906 by substituting a new definition of 'workmen', deleting the requirement that they be employed 'in trade or industry'.

[1.23] The bulk of Irish collective labour law, including the Trade Disputes Act 1906, derives from pre-Independence days. A significant divergence was introduced by the Irish Constitution in 1937 (see further **Ch 2**), which guarantees fundamental rights to individual citizens. Because it predated the Constitution, the Act of 1906 did not enjoy a presumption of constitutionality. This in theory rendered it more vulnerable to constitutional challenge.

Interpretation of the 1906 Act

[1.24] Not long after the Trade Disputes Act 1906 was passed, Lord Parker of Waddington gave this view in the House of Lords in *Larkin v Long*:[34]

> An Act of this sort ought, according to principles which have hitherto prevailed in construing Acts of the Legislature, to be construed with reasonable strictness and not to be given a meaning wider than the words used will justify.

On traditional principles, because the Act exempts from liability at common law, its boundaries are narrowly, rather than widely, construed. Judges in Ireland have adhered firmly to traditional principles.

In *B & I Steampacket Co Ltd v Branigan*[35] Dixon J was able to say that the phrase 'trade or industry' used in the Act had never been precisely defined but 'in several cases, there were *dicta* to the effect that the Act should be given a somewhat strict construction.' These *dicta* were referred to with approval by Kingsmill Moore J in *Smith v Beirne*[36] where other members of the majority of the court adopted a similar approach to the Act. [37]

---

34.   *Larkin v Long* [1915] AC 814 at 832–3.

35.   *B & I Steampacket Co Ltd v Branigan* [1958] IR 128 at 103.

36.   *Smith v Beirne* 89 ILTR 24 at 35.

37.   Dixon J reiterated this view in *The Esplanade Pharmacy Ltd v Larkin* 62 ILTR 149 at 150.

[1.25] Gavan Duffy J in *Cooper v Millea*[38] lamented the fact that judges have to resolve difficult employer-labour problems in the 'milky way of the common law.' Few judges have uttered such notes of warning as Maguire CJ (diss) in *Educational Co of Ireland Ltd v Fitzpatrick*:[39]

> In all these cases it is of the utmost importance that the Court should keep in mind the fact that it is not to consider questions of policy, or whether the conduct of employees on the one hand or their representatives on the other hand is considered wise or expedient. The sole duty of a judge is to consider whether the act complained of is lawful or unlawful.[40]

Significance of immunities

[1.26] In general statutes are norm-creating. They prescribe that in certain circumstances behaviour of a specified type ought, can or may be indulged in by persons of a particular class. The 'rules' in the Act of 1906 and the Industrial Relations Act 1990 are not normative or prescriptive in this sense. They provide a series of immunities for actions that would otherwise be unlawful at common law. It might be said that persons engaging in industrial action are free to act within the immunity-providing formulae but the rules do not guide and serve as standards for behaviour. They are neither norm-creating nor prescriptive.

[1.27] Legislation on trade disputes has been described by McCarthy[41] as creating a normative chasm by not recognising that the strike and other industrial action are collective phenomena. The problem is compounded by the fact that the common law adopts an individualist point of view, placing almost complete emphasis on fundamental rights. This view is copper-fastened by the Constitution (see **Ch 2**). Judicial interpretation is generally arrived at through the doctrine of precedent and established legal canons of construction. The position of trade unions under the Constitution is weak. The common law, which is the main source of judicial interpretation, contains guarantees to individual citizens in relation to collectivities. This, as McCarthy noted, 'is the very heart of the normative conflict.'

[1.28] By and large commentators on the Act of 1906 in Ireland criticised the interpretive role of the courts of common law. Yet the root problem on another view, such as McCarthy's, lies within the raw material of the statute (retained by the Industrial Relations Act 1990).

---

38. *Cooper v Millea* [1938] IR 749 at 755.
39. *Educational Co of Ireland Ltd v Fitzpatrick* [1961] IR 323 at 378 endorsed by Hamilton J in *Reg Armstrong Motors Ltd v CIE* (2 December 1975, unreported), HC.
40. See too *White v Riley* [1921] 1 Ch 1 at 80 *per* Peterson J.
41. McCarthy, *Elements in a Theory of Industrial Relations* (Irish Academic Press, 1984). Some have suggested, however, that the negative protection afforded by the statutory immunities ought to be regarded as equivalent to a right to strike, eg Lord Weddenburn, 'Industrial Relations and the Courts' (1980) 9 ILJ 65.

FROM 1906 TO 1990: COMMISSION OF INQUIRY ON INDUSTRIAL RELATIONS

[1.29] In 1978 a Commission of Inquiry on Industrial Relations was established to come up with agreed recommendations on industrial relations law but the endeavour failed after the withdrawal of the ICTU representatives following a motion at their Annual Delegate Conference instructing them to do so until legislation had been enacted which would give legal protection for strikes to workers in all sectors of the economy. The Second National Understanding (a national agreement on pay agreed between the government and the social partners) in October 1980 contained, *inter alia*, the following provisions under the heading 'Industrial Relations':

> 13. The Minister for Labour will, at an early date, introduce legislation to extend the provisions of the Trade Disputes Act 1906 as sought by the Irish Congress of Trade Unions and after consultation with both sides of industry, introduce such other legislative changes as may be necessary to achieve a more satisfactory application of the Act.

> 14. It would be the intention of the Minister to deal with all of these issues, if possible, in a single piece of legislation at an early date.

The *Report of the Commission of Inquiry on Industrial Relations*, published in May 1981, recommended a significantly enlarged role for the law in industrial relations. In a statement on the report, the Minister said:

> Because the representatives of the Irish Congress of Trade Unions withdrew from the Commission, the Government has taken no decisions on the recommendations of the Report. Any decisions or proposals for reform of industrial relations will only be taken after the views of the Irish Congress of Trade Unions have been made known.

[1.30] ICTU got its wish in 1982 when the Trade Disputes (Amendment) Act was passed, extending the Act's protection to workers in all sectors of the economy (para **1.22**). The fact that it was passed almost 30 years after the issue was first raised in the courts was an indication of the difficulties encountered in making progress. Reference is made in this book to some recommendations of the Commission of Inquiry. They should be read always with the caveat that their formulation lacked input from ICTU.

Statutory right to strike and to take industrial action

[1.31] In 1983 the Minister for Labour announced that he had invited the Federated Union of Employers (FUE), as IBEC was then styled, and ICTU to discussions on the reform of industrial relations. The Labour Minister was of the view that the law on picketing and the definition of a trade dispute were defective and urged that consideration be given to establishing consensus as to what forms of picketing would be given legal protection and to a more developed notion of what constituted a trade dispute.

Two years later, the Department of Labour published proposals on industrial relations reform, committing it, in conjunction with the social partners, to examine the form and content of all aspects of trade disputes law. This examination was to 'actively explore the feasibility of replacing the system of immunities itself by a system which would give workers a positive right to strike.' In other words, the Act would be either modernised or replaced by legislation incorporating a positive right to strike. This was the first time serious political consideration in Ireland was given to change from an immunities- to a rights-based code. It was also proposed that a Labour Relations Commission charged with statutory responsibility for the promotion of good industrial relations should be established as an independent agency.

[1.32] In January 1986 the Department of Labour published a package of proposals on new trade dispute and industrial relations legislation. It acknowledged that:

> In no other area of labour law, perhaps, are differences so marked, apprehensions so prominent and confusions so evident. This may well be demonstrated in the responses to the current proposals.

It also pointed out that part of the problem was that analysis of the adequacy of the law tended to begin and end with the text of the 1906 Act. Of critical importance was liability outside the Act, at common law and under the Constitution.

The 1986 package detailed proposals for the repeal of the Trade Disputes Act 1906 and its replacement by new legislation which would include a right to strike and to take industrial action as well as limitations on that right. Where the right to strike and to take industrial action was exercised in accordance with the legislation, workers would enjoy a 'complete defence' in all civil legal proceedings arising therefrom. The package also included proposals on picketing, secret ballots and injunctions. In the end, however, the proposals to strike were added to Ireland's archives of 'Suggestions for Change'.

[1.33] On one view, a network of immunities precariously serves as a substitute for a general principle, and such a network runs the risk of becoming a labyrinth. Ireland opted to re-enact the network of immunities in 1990, and the labyrinth which inevitably accompanies it.[42]

THE INDUSTRIAL RELATIONS ACT 1990

[1.34] The Industrial Relations Bill 1989 was presented by the Minister for Labour in Dáil Éireann on 5 December 1989 and became law on 18 July 1990. The successor to the old Act of 1906 is found in Part II, the full text of which is in the **Appendix**. The Second Schedule repeals the Trade Disputes Act 1906 in its entirety.

---

42. Note that a right to strike subject to limitation is variously provided for in international law. Egg UN International Covenant on Economic, Social and Cultural Rights, art 8.1.d; European Social Charter, art 694; International Convention on Economic, Social and Cultural Rights, art 8; Charter of the Fundamental Rights of the EU, art 28; Community Charter of the Fundamental Social Rights of Workers 1989, Point 13. The ILO Governing Body's Committee on Freedom of Association has frequently reiterated that although there is no express reference to strike action in its Conventions, they impliedly guarantee such a right, cf *Freedom of Association: Digest of Decisions of the Freedom of Association Committee of the Governing Body of the ILO* Geneva 1972, paras 240, 292. See para **2.52** on the potential for a right to strike under the European Convention on Human Rights.

[1.35] Part II of the Industrial Relations Act 1990 in the main re-enacts the immunities of the 1906 Act, although the sections bear new numbers. In addition, it amends the law on trade disputes in five ways. First, it removes civil immunity from picketing a person's home and from disputes involving only one worker where proper procedures have not been followed (ss 9(2) and 11); second, it confines the immunity of trade unions to acts done in contemplation or furtherance of a trade dispute (s 9); third, it clarifies and tightens the law on secondary picketing (s 11); fourth, it requires trade union rule books to contain a rule providing for secret ballots before industrial action (s 14) and fifth, it restricts the granting of injunctions in trade disputes (s 19). It is important for the non-legal reader to be aware that judicial decisions under the Act of 1906 which concern the same or similar subject matter in the Industrial Relations Act 1990, while no longer binding on courts in this jurisdiction, will be highly persuasive, eg where the same words or phrases are used. They therefore have an important role in this book.

[1.36] The Industrial Relations Act 1990 contained significant changes designed to provide a better framework for collective bargaining and dispute settlement (para **1.47** *et seq*) and to help create conditions favourable to employment-generating investment. In particular, it provided for the establishment of a Labour Relations Commission (LRC) with a general remit to promote good industrial relations, to provide conciliation and advisory services and to prepare codes of practice. The LRC monitors and carries out research into developments in industrial relations. Although the topic is outside the scope of the present book, the succeeding paragraphs provide a synopsis of the role of the LRC and the Labour Court. Knowledge of the law on trade disputes and the potential liability of those taking part is critical to the negotiating strength of the parties engaging in voluntary disputes settlement.

[1.37] Under 38(2), where the Minister for Enterprise, Trade and Innovation is of the opinion that a trade dispute is of special importance, he may request the LRC or the Labour Court or another person or body to conduct an enquiry into the dispute and furnish a report. This power has been used three times: in the Dublin Airport baggage handlers' dispute in 1998, the TEAM Aer Lingus dispute in 1994 and the electrical contracting industry dispute in 2009.

Voluntary disputes settlement involving the Labour Relations Commission or the Labour Court

The Labour Relations Commission

[1.38] Under s 24 of the 1990 Act, the LRC (http://www.lrc.ie) was established on 21 January 1991. The Labour Court (http://www.labourcourt.ie) had been responsible for providing a conciliation service since 1946 and a Rights Commissioner Service since 1969. The 1990 Act changed the role of the Labour Court and re-assigned these services to the new body.

Trade disputes are normally referred to the LRC and its services in the first instance and the Labour Court will not investigate a dispute unless it receives a report from the LRC that it has been unable to resolve the dispute. Exceptions to this are: (a) where the LRC waives its conciliation function and the parties request that the Labour Court investigates the dispute, and (b) where the Labour Court, after consulting the LRC, is of the opinion that there are exceptional circumstances.

The Minister for Enterprise, Trade and Innovation may refer a dispute to the LRC or the Labour Court with a view to its resolution or to conduct an inquiry on the dispute and furnish a report.

[1.39] Section 25(1) of the 1990 Act sets out the functions of the LRC.[43] It also provides that the LRC may, at the request of the parties or on its own initiative, offer the parties its services with a view to bringing about a settlement and may also provide, on request or on its own initiative, advice on any matter associated with industrial relations to employers, employers' associations, workers and trade unions.

[1.40] Conciliation is a voluntary process used to resolve disputes between parties. The LRC's conciliation service assigns an Industrial Relations Officer from the LRC as mediator to attempt to reach agreement between disputing parties. There are two possible outcomes of the conciliation process: resolution of the dispute or continuing disagreement. If no settlement is reached in conciliation, the parties may refer the dispute to the Labour Court. Referrals to the LRC conciliation service in the first nine months of 2009 grew by over 100 per cent in comparison with the same period in 2008. The referrals concerned pay restructuring and redundancy-related disputes.

In late 2009 the LRC called for the use of voluntary binding arbitration if necessary in dealing with disputes in a challenging industrial relations climate.[44]

[1.41] The Rights Commissioner Service is an independent service of the LRC. Resort to this service grew in 2008 by 21 per cent and continued to grow in 2009. Rights Commissioners investigate disputes, grievances and claims made mostly by

---

43.   Industrial Relations Act 1990, s 25(1) provides that:

'The Commission shall have general responsibility for promoting the improvement of industrial relations and shall—

   (a) provide a conciliation service;
   (b) provide an industrial relations advisory service;
   (c) prepare codes of practice relevant to industrial relations after consultation with unions and employer organisations;
   (d) offer guidance on codes of practice and help to resolve disputes concerning their implementation;
   (e) appoint equality officers of the Commission and provide staff and facilities for the equality officer service;
   (f) select and nominate persons for appointment as rights commissioners and provide staff and facilities for the rights commissioner service;
   (g) conduct or commission research into matters relevant to industrial relations;
   (h) review and monitor developments in the area of industrial relations;
   (i) assist joint labour committees and joint industrial councils in the exercise of their functions.'

44.   *Labour Relations Commission Annual Report 2008*; (2009) *Irish Times*, 29 October.

individuals or small groups of workers under various statutes, including the Industrial Relations Acts 1969 to 2004. A party to a dispute may object to a Rights Commissioner's investigation where the case has been referred under the Industrial Relations Acts, 1969 to 2004. The applicant may then request that the Labour Court hears the case. A party may also appeal a Rights Commissioner's decision in relation to a dispute under the Industrial Relations Acts 1969 to 2004 to the Labour Court.

The Labour Court

[1.42] The Labour Court[45] was established in 1946 (following the enactment of the Industrial Relations Act 1946), *inter alia*, to adjudicate in trade disputes and to provide a conciliation service. There have been many changes to its structure and functions since then, following the amendments to the Industrial Relations Act in 1969, 1976, 1990, 2001 and 2004, and the enactment of other employment legislation.

The mission of the Labour Court is:[46]

> To find a basis for real and substantial agreement through the provision of fast, fair, informal and inexpensive arrangements for the adjudication and resolution of industrial disputes.

---

45. The Labour Court consists of nine full-time members: a Chairman, two Deputy Chairmen and six Ordinary Members, three of whom are Employers' Members and three of whom are Workers' Members. The Chairman and the two Deputy Chairmen are appointed by the Minister for Enterprise, Trade and Innovation. The Employers' Members are nominated by IBEC and the Workers' Members are nominated by ICTU.

46. The main functions of the Labour Court under the Industrial Relations Acts 1969 to 2004 are:

   (a) to investigate industrial relations disputes and issue recommendations for their settlement;

   (b) to investigate, at the request of the Minister for Enterprise, Trade and Innovation, trade disputes affecting the public interest, or conduct an enquiry into a trade dispute of special importance and report on its findings;

   (c) hear appeals of Rights Commissioners' recommendations under the Industrial Relations Acts;

   (d) establish Joint Labour Committees and decide on questions concerning their operation;

   (e) register, vary and interpret employment agreements;

   (f) register Joint Industrial Councils;

   (g) investigate complaints of breaches of registered employment agreements;

   (h) investigate complaints of breaches of codes of practice made under the Industrial Relations Act 1990 (following consideration of the complaint by the LRC);

   (i) give its opinion as to the interpretation of a code of practice made under the Industrial Relations Act 1990; and

   (j) investigate disputes (where negotiating arrangements are not in place) under the Industrial Relations (Amendment) Act 2001 as amended by the Industrial Relations (Miscellaneous Provisions) Act 2004.

[1.43] Industrial relations disputes may be referred to the Labour Court in a number of different ways:

(a) if the parties to the dispute have availed of the conciliation services of the LRC but have failed to reach agreement and the LRC at the request of the parties refers the case to the Labour Court;

(b) if the LRC has waived its conciliation function in the dispute;

(c) if the Labour Court determines that exceptional circumstances prevail in the dispute and, following consultation with the LRC, invites the parties to the dispute to avail of its services;

(d) if the Minister for Enterprise, Trade and Innovation refers a dispute to the Labour Court;

(e) if a worker, or workers, in a trade dispute, or a trade union on his/her/their behalf, or all the parties, agree in advance to accept the Labour Court's recommendation, they can bring their case directly to the Labour Court under s 20(1) of the Industrial Relations Act 1969; or

(f) if a case has been heard by a Rights Commissioner and a recommendation has been issued, either party to the dispute may appeal the recommendation to the Labour Court within six weeks of the Rights Commissioner's recommendation.

[1.44] Due to the voluntarist nature of the industrial relations machinery, Labour Court Recommendations for the resolution of trade disputes are not legally binding.[47] However, as the Labour Court is a court of last resort in the industrial relations process, it is expected that the parties come to that process in good faith and are prepared to accept the outcome of the process. Similarly, where the recommendation of a Rights Commissioner in an industrial relations case is appealed to the Labour Court, it is expected that the parties will abide by the court's decision on the appeal.

[1.45] Figures from the Central Statistics Office (CSO) for 2008 show that there were just 4,179 days lost to industrial disputes in 2008, compared with 6,038 in 2007. There were a total of 12 industrial disputes in 2008 compared with six in 2007. These statistics appear in the *Annual Report of the LRC* for 2008 which notes at the same time that the official CSO dispute data does not tell the full story on industrial conflict. Significantly, disputes are included in CSO figures only if they involve a stoppage of work lasting for at least 1 day and total time lost is ten or more person-days. Many forms of industrial action fall outside this definition, such as short, sharp stoppages, protests, work to rules and so forth. There are no figures yet for 2009 but it is certain that they will be markedly different for that year, and indeed for 2010. The economic climate in Ireland has changed dramatically. Industrial action has moved centre stage, particularly in the public sector, as government measures to combat the country's

---

47.   *State (St Stephens Green Club) v The Labour Court* [1961] IR 85.

financial crises are unveiled. The air traffic controllers' dispute in early 2010 led to calls for a ban on strikes in essential services or the introduction of a code of practice for such disputes.[48]

SCHEME OF THE BOOK

[1.46] The relationship between unions and employers is in some respects like that between states. States frequently resolve their differences by making a treaty. Many union-employer disputes are settled by following agreed disputes procedures.[49] At national level, successive agreements on pay have been critical to Ireland's economic stability. Sometimes the peaceful method of resolving differences fails and industrial action is taken, or industrial action is taken against the backdrop of ongoing national pay talks, as happened in this country in the spring of 2010.

[1.47] This book is not about how trade disputes in industry are settled day in, day out. It charts the lawfulness and unlawfulness of strike and industrial action. **Chapter 2** looks at the effects of Ireland's fundamental law, the Constitution of 1937, on trade disputes. This effect is significant, as will be seen, both in the theory and practice of industrial relations. **Ch 3** considers the contract of employment, which plays a central role in determining the lawfulness of industrial action and which in turn is affected by it in different ways. Following these important areas of preliminary consideration, **Ch 4** examines the so-called industrial economic torts in an overall way and then **Chs 5–8** analyse the individual torts of conspiracy, inducing breach of contract, causing loss by unlawful means and intimidation. The extent, if any, to which the Industrial Relations Act 1990 provides immunity from liability in respect of these torts is considered in each chapter. The parties, context (acts in contemplation or furtherance of a trade dispute) and the subject matter of trade disputes are considered in **Ch 9**. **Chapter 10** considers picketing, the criminal and civil wrongs that may be committed by pickets, and the protections afforded by statute. The important changes to the labour injunction introduced by the Industrial Relations Act 1990 form the subject matter of **Ch 11** where the statutory requirements as to balloting before industrial action are also considered.

[1.48] Where the line between lawful and unlawful industrial action should be drawn is an important subject for public debate; there are disagreements about the part the law

---

48. See Code of Practice on Dispute Procedure (Declaration) Order 1992 (SI 1/1992), an initiative which was largely a failure through lack of interest to agree a local code. The 1992 codes were agreed in only three state companies. *Sustaining Progress* (the Social Partnership Agreement 2003–2005) stated that voluntary codes of practice for the maintenance of essential services were to be agreed by September 2003. Codes of practice were introduced in late 2003 across the public service – the health service, local authorities, the civil service, education – to comply with the industrial peace/ modernisation terms under *Sustaining Progress*, implementation being a precondition for payment of the second phase of benchmarking. See further IRN 4/2010.

49. See the Code of Practice on Voluntary Dispute Resolution 2004, in the **Appendix**.

should play as well as about where the balance of power should lie.[50] The challenging times we live in have revived this debate and it is hoped that this book, amongst other things, will contribute to this debate.

---

50.   Tucker, 'Renorming Labour Law: Can We Escape Labour Law's Recurring Regulatory Dilemmas?' (2010) ILJ 99.

Chapter 2

TRADE DISPUTES AND THE CONSTITUTION

INTRODUCTION

[2.01] All laws, decision-making practices and procedures must be consistent with the Constitution.[1] Neither statute nor common law can stand against an opposing right guaranteed by the Constitution: *Meskell v CIE*.[2] The Constitution is significant in the theory and practice of Ireland's trade disputes law. The personal rights to basic fairness of procedures[3] and of access to the courts[4] could be said to support the treatment of injunctions in the Industrial Relations Act 1990.[5]

[2.02] The Fundamental Rights provisions in Art 40 of the Constitution contain the rights most likely to affect trade disputes. Most important of these is the freedom of association in Art 40.6.1°iii of the Constitution, which reads:

> The state guarantees liberty for the exercise of the following rights, subject to public order and morality ...
>
> iii The right of the citizens to form associations and unions. Laws, however, may be enacted for the regulation and control in the public interest of the exercise of the foregoing right.

Subsection 2 provides that:

> Laws regulating the manner in which this right ... may be exercised shall contain no political, religious or class discrimination.

In addition to the rights expressed in Art 40, there are 'unspecified rights' under Art 40.3 such as the right to work,[6] the right to strike (para **2.39** *et seq*), and the right to basic fairness of procedures. The Directive Principles of Social Policy in Art 45 may

---

1. A fuller account of the effect of the Constitution is found in Redmond, *Dismissal Law in Ireland* (Bloomsbury Professional, 2007), ch 8. Although it concentrates on dismissal, much of the chapter is relevant to labour law generally.

2. *Meskell v CIE* [1973] IR 121. The case concerned dismissal. It was held that if an employer dismisses a worker because of the latter's insistence upon exercising his constitutional right, the fact that the form of notice of dismissal is good at common law does not in any way lessen the infringement of the right involved or mitigate the damage which the worker may suffer by reason of his insistence upon exercising his constitutional right.

3. See *In re Haughey* [1971] IR 217, 263; *The State (Healy) v Donoghue* [1976] IR 325.

4. eg *The State (Quinn) v Ryan* [1965] IR 70.

5. Constitutional issues may be raised at the *ex parte* stage: *The State (Shatter Gallagher & Co) v de Valera (No 2)* (26 January 1987, unreported), HC. See more relaxed attitude of the courts procedurally where constitutional issues are raised: *Shannon v Ireland* [1985] ILRM 449.

6. *Murphy v Stewart* [1973] IR 97.

also be relevant to the enumeration of unspecified personal rights. In *Murtagh Properties Ltd v Cleary*[7] picketing to compel an employer to dismiss female staff was held unconstitutional and therefore outside the protection of s 2 of the Trade Disputes Act 1906. Constitutional rights may be relied on in injunction proceedings by an employer or worker not only against the State but also against private citizens.[8]

[2.03] A constitutional argument might be raised in a trade dispute whether the industrial action takes the form of picketing, inducing breach of the contract of employment, intimidation, or conspiracy. If the object of the action is to coerce others or to penalise them in relation to the exercise of a constitutional right, those taking part cannot avail of the statutory immunities. The usual range of actions and orders are available for breach of a constitutional right; what is appropriate depends on the circumstances. In many cases the remedies sought will be a declaration that the breach has taken place, an injunction restraining the breach and damages.

[2.04] This chapter begins by looking at an important decision involving trade disputes and Art 40.6.1°iii of the Constitution guaranteeing freedom of association: *Educational Company of Ireland v Fitzpatrick (Educational Company).*[9]

The Industrial Relations Act 1990 enjoys a presumption of constitutionality,[10] which its predecessor lacked when *Educational Company* was decided. The chapter then considers the issue of conflicting constitutional rights and whether in a trade dispute there can be an incidental breach of a constitutional right. It ends by querying whether the system of immunities is constitutionally unassailable.

FREEDOM OF ASSOCIATION AND TRADE UNIONS

[2.05] *Educational Company* gave as its legacy the right to all involved in trade disputes to question the validity of any statutory immunity allegedly protecting the strike or industrial action, on the basis that the 'protected action' violates a constitutional right. *Educational Company* gave overriding force to the constitutional guarantee of freedom of association in Art 40.6.1°iii of the Constitution against the immunity for picketing in s 2 of the Trade Disputes Act 1906 (now s 11 of the Industrial Relations Act 1990).

In *Educational Company* the Plaintiff company employed 45 clerical workers of whom 16 belonged to a trade union. The union members tried to persuade 9 other members of the clerical staff to join the union. When the 9 refused, the union attempted to force the

---

7.   *Murtagh Properties Ltd v Cleary* [1972] IR 330.

8.   As Budd J pointed out in *Educational Company v Fitzpatrick* [1961] IR 345, 368–9. See too *Attorney General (Society for the Protection of the Unborn Child (Ireland) Ltd) v Open-Door Counselling Ltd* [1987] ILRM 447; *Hosford v John Murphy & Sons* (unreported, 24 July 1987), HC.

9.   *Educational Company of Ireland v Fitzpatrick (Educational Company)* [1961] IR 345.

10. *East Donegal Co-Operative Ltd v Attorney General* [1970] IR 317; *Brennan v Attorney General* [1983] ILRM 449, 479.

employer either to dismiss the men or to compel them to join the union. The employer refused to comply, a strike was called and picketing began. The company sought an injunction in the High Court restraining the picketing as unlawful and unconstitutional. The defendants relied on s 2 of the Trade Disputes Act 1906 to protect the picketing. The Supreme Court (Kingsmill Moore, O Dálaigh and Haugh JJ; Maguire CJ and Lavery J dissenting) upheld Budd J in the High Court and found, *inter alia*, that s 2 of the Act of 1906 was void as being inconsistent with the Constitution in so far as it authorised a trade dispute to coerce persons to join a union against their will. This was not tantamount to declaring the section unconstitutional.

[2.06] The freedom of association[11] is one of the Fundamental Rights in Arts 40–44 of the Constitution (sub-titled, 'Personal Rights'). At times, the language of these provisions refers solely to individuals and at others, while still referring to individuals, it embraces a collective context. For example, in Art 40.3.1°–2°, concerning Personal Rights, the guarantee is accorded to 'the citizen.' Likewise in Art 40.4 no citizen may be deprived of his personal liberty and in Art 40.5 the dwelling of 'every citizen' is inviolable. There is no equivocation about the individualist nature of the guarantee.

[2.07] The language changes in Art 40.6, however, where 'the State guarantees liberty for the exercise of the following rights, subject to public order and morality.' With the introduction of public order and morality, the setting ceases to be a wholly individual one (borne out in *Aughey v Ireland*[12] where the High Court held that the close connection of the Garda Síochána with the security of the State necessitated their accepting limitations on freedom of association). The right of the citizens to express freely their convictions and opinions in Art 40.6.1°i is qualified by reference to the organs of public opinion not being used 'to undermine public order or morality or the authority of the State.' The right of the citizens to assemble peaceably and without arms in the following sub-s 1°ii is qualified in relation to meetings. The right of assembly arises in a collective context: by definition it involves more than one person. Similarly with the freedom of association in Art 40.6.1°iii. The 'right of the citizens to form associations and unions' is qualified by reference to laws which may be enacted in the public interest to regulate and control the exercise of the right. The Constitution refers to 'associations and unions' thereby implying that a 'union' is a type of association worthy of particular mention, and that the guarantee extends beyond trade unions.

[2.08] The Constitution is a political instrument as well as a legal document and is not to be read with the exactness of a taxing statute, as Costello J remarked in *Attorney*

---

11.   See Whyte, 'Industrial Relations and the Irish Constitution' (1981) vol XVI *Irish Jurist* 35; von Prondzynski, *Freedom of Association and Industrial Relations: A Comparative Study* (Mansell Publishing, 1987); Kerr and Whyte, *Irish Trade Union Law* (Professional Books, 1985).

12.   *Aughey v Ireland* [1989] ILRM 87. Members of the Garda Síochána have representative bodies established under the Garda Síochána Act 1924, as amended by the Garda Síochána Act 2005 which act as a kind of trade union. There are comparable bodies for the Defence Forces.

General and Minister for Posts and Telegraphs v Paperlink Ltd[13] (and Gavan Duffy J before him, in *National Union of Railwaymen v Sullivan*).[14] Nonetheless, the shift in emphasis away from individually guaranteed rights against the State in the early paragraphs of Art 40 to rights expressed plurally and to be regulated on the basis of public order and morality in Art 40.6, suggests that an exclusively individual exercise of the right is not envisaged.[15]

[2.09] In common sense the right to form associations or unions has meaning only if one person wishes to associate with another or others. It is plainly more than the exercise of rights by 'a collectivity.' It is an individual right which, if it is to have any meaning, requires or demands the exercise of the same right in concert by others.

Balancing Collective and Individual Interests

[2.10] The principal purpose of labour law is 'to regulate, to support and to restrain the power of management and the power of organised labour.'[16]

The collective interest can rarely be absent from any rule, constitutional or otherwise. 'Collective' here refers to the interests of a group such as a trade union, not to the 'social' or 'public' interest, which relates to the good of society as a whole.[17] There may be conflict between individual and collective interests in relation to freedom of association but the tension thereby produced cannot be settled by calling exclusively in aid the dogma of individual freedom or of collective security.

[2.11] Courts in Ireland, no less than elsewhere, have not dealt satisfactorily with this paradox. By and large, they have construed Art 40.6.1°iii in an exclusively individualist sense. No conflicting rights or interests appear to be taken on board to assess 'public order and morality'. There are competing constructions, however, as between majority and minority judgments. Minority judges have tended to base their decisions on an understanding of freedom of association from a collective standpoint. For example, in the Supreme Court, Maguire CJ in the *Educational Co* case said of Art 40.6.1°iii:[18]

> When our Constitution was enacted there can have been few voters who were unaware of the aims and objects of trade unions. It must have been well known to most intelligent voters that the trade unions had won recognition of their right, when engaged in collective bargaining, to use the weapon of the strike and the right to picket in furtherance of a trade dispute.

---

13.   *Attorney General and Minister for Posts and Telegraphs v Paperlink Ltd* [1984] ILRM 373 at 385.

14.   *National Union of Railwaymen v Sullivan* [1947] IR 77 at 87.

15.   For a European perspective, see von Prondzynski, 'Freedom of Association and the Closed Shop: the European Perspective' [1982] Camb LJ 256.

16.   Davies and Freedland, *Kahn-Freund's Labour and the Law* (3rd edn, Stevens, 1983) at 15.

17.   See Kidner, 'The Individual and the Collective Interest in Trade Union Law' (1976) ILJ 90; Pound, 'A Survey of Social Interests (1943) 57 Harv LR 1.

18.   At 379–80.

In relation to Art 40.6.1°iii, the Chief Justice said:

> I have no doubt that it was trade unions which the framers of the Constitution
> and those who enacted it had principally in mind.

The *Dáil Debates* in 1937 support this: at the time, the memory of ultra-restrictive,
anti-union legislation was still alive.[19]

[2.12] There are those for whom the decision in *Educational Co* came as a body blow
and those for whom it was a vindication of individual liberty. Regrettably, majority and
minority judges respectively failed to explore the freedom's parameters or to resolve
the conflicts within it. At the time it could be said that the courts were still embedded
in difficulties produced by earlier attempts at common law to regulate the activities of
trade unions. In order to protect not only the interests of capital but the interests of
dissenting workers against the demands of trade unions, the courts traditionally
embraced freedom of contract.[20] By the time courts in Ireland came to interpret
Art 40.6.1°iii, the judicial mould had been set and freedom of contract was taken to be
a social fact.

Statutory regulation of industrial relations and freedom of association: *NUR v Sullivan*

[2.13] Case law on the freedom of association began almost a decade after the
Constitution came into effect. The Supreme Court held unconstitutional a statutory
attempt in the Trade Union Act 1941 (the Act of 1941) to confer on specified unions
the right to organise and to represent workers in a specific union, to the exclusion of
other unions: *National Union of Railwaymen v Sullivan*.[21] The Act of 1941 was
designed to tackle trade union multiplicity in Ireland, a problem perceived as a threat to
efficient industrial relations. Part III provided for the setting up of a 'trade union
tribunal' empowered on the application of any trade union claiming to have organised,
for negotiation purposes, a majority of the workers of a particular class, to grant or
refuse, in the public interest, a determination that the applicant union alone (or two or
more specified unions alone) should have the right to organise workers of that class.

The then styled Irish Transport and General Workers Union (ITGWU) applied for the
sole right to organise workers in the road passenger services of Córas Iompair Éireann
(CIE). Before the hearing of the application, the National Union of Railwaymen
(NUR), a rival union, issued proceedings in the High Court claiming that Pt III of the
Act of 1941 was unconstitutional.

[2.14] The Act's attempt to prescribe which union workers were entitled to join, the
Supreme Court held, was an attempt not to regulate or control the right to form unions
but altogether to abolish its exercise. The court's decision was – and still is – seen by

---

19.   Volumes 67–8, 11 May 1937, in particular cols 127 (Lavery) and 158 (MacEntee).
20.   Kidner, 'The Individual and the Collective Interest in Trade Union Law' (1976) ILJ 91.
21.   *National Union of Railwaymen v Sullivan* [1947] IR 77.

the trade union movement as an example of judicial interpretation overgenerously favouring individual rights or interests.[22]

In coming to its decision, the Supreme Court (Maguire CJ, Murnaghan, Geoghegan, O'Byrne and Black JJ) overruled Gavan Duffy J in the court below who had regarded freedom of association as a freedom the exercise of which was primarily in the interests of trade unions. In Gavan Duffy J's view the Constitution enabled the State to enact laws for the regulation of this freedom 'in the public interest.' Such regulation involved policy aims. He emphasised that a regulating law cannot please everybody. To regulate means 'to subject to guidance and restrictions.' Consequently, if an Act might incidentally deplete the membership of unprivileged unions it could not be unconstitutional, and a regulating law did not cease to regulate because it was designed to make some trade unions stronger than others. The judge would have been prepared to hold the regulation went too far, no doubt, had the right to associate been *denied* to *all* members of trade unions. His decision might also have been different if the policy purportedly being adopted by the legislature was leading to head-on confrontation with another constitutional right, such as the right not to be discriminated against in a political, religious or class sense. The NUR attempted to argue political discrimination inasmuch as a trade union obtaining an organising monopoly for a class of workers under the Act might lawfully apply part of its general funds to the furtherance of its political objects. But the judge was clear that there was 'no trace of political discrimination in the enactment.'

[2.15] The Supreme Court acknowledged that the Act of 1941 purported 'to limit the right of the citizen to join one or more prescribed associations'.[23] But the court looked upon the freedom of association as concerning a distinctly personal and individual experience. It declared that the limitation in the Act of 1941 'does undoubtedly deprive the citizen of a free choice of the persons with whom *he shall associate* [emphasis added].'[24]

Murnaghan J in *NUR v Sullivan*[25] said:

> Both logically and practically, to deprive a person of the choice of the persons with whom he will associate is not a control of the exercise of the right of association, but a denial of the right altogether.

The NUR submitted that the Act was *ultra vires* because, the argument ran, it virtually compelled workers of a particular class to join a privileged union, thus depriving them of the liberty to associate with whom they pleased. Their argument succeeded

---

22. See *Report of the Committee on the Constitution* (1967), paras 116–122 inclusive; McCarthy, *Trade Unions in Ireland 1894–1960* (Institute of Public Administration, 1977), 486; contrast the foreword by Walsh J to Kerr and Whyte, *Irish Trade Union Law* (Professional Books, 1985), vi–vii.

23. *Per* Murnaghan J at 99.

24   At 102. An interesting speculation that might encourage disapproval of the NUR case by a future court is that it is difficult in principle to distinguish between the effect of Pt III of the Trade Union Act 1941 and Pt II of the same Act, as amended by the Trade Union Act 1971 (Pt II hinders the creation of new unions). (contd .../)

notwithstanding that Art 40.6.1°iii does *not* guarantee a right to join a particular trade union, privileged or otherwise.

[2.16] The Act of 1941 attempted to channel the exercise of the right to apply to belong to a trade union in such a way as to limit the number of trade unions involved in particular bargaining contexts. Whatever else it did, it did not 'deprive a person of his choice of the persons with whom he *will associate*' [emphasis added]. Kelly suggested in *The Irish Constitution*,[26] that in a suitable future case, *NUR v Sullivan* may be disapproved by a 'new' Supreme Court bearing in mind the consequences of the decision itself, a proliferation of trade unions.

With all its imperfections, however, the *NUR* case continued to influence subsequent constitutional decisions.

Trade disputes and freedom of association: *Educational Co v Fitzpatrick*

[2.17] *Educational Company v Fitzpatrick*[27] extended the *NUR* case to circumstances outside of statutory regulation, a trade dispute involving trade union membership. The facts are summarised at para **2.05**.

The Court of Appeal had held in 1921 that a dispute about trade union membership attracted the protection of the Trade Disputes Act 1906 being in essence a dispute concerning the terms upon which a non-unionised member or members should continue in the employment of the employer: *White v Riley*.[28] This approach was not uniformly adopted in Britain[29] but it seems to have been regarded as correct by the Irish High Court on at least two occasions.[30] In 1950 the Circuit Court enforced a post-entry closed shop agreement, taking the view that it did not violate the provisions of

---

24.   (contd) See Whyte, 'Industrial Relations and the Irish Constitution' (1981) vol XVI *Irish Jurist* 57. Likewise it might be contended by analogous reasoning that s 11 of the Act of 1941, not repealed but re-enacted in the Industrial Relations Act 1990, s 9(1), which restricted the protection of the Trade Disputes Act 1906 to unions granted a negotiation licence is *ultra vires* in that it virtually compelled an individual to join a 'privileged' union. It was on this ground that the Committee of Independent Experts on the European Social Charter continued to find the Irish Republic in breach of its Social Charter. (See eg *Council of Europe, Committee of Independent Experts on the European Social Charter* Conclusions I, Strasbourg 1969–70 at 288.) This conclusion was later reiterated: see O'Higgins, 'The Right to Strike – Some International Reflections' in *Studies in Labour Law* (ed Carby-Hall) (1976) 110 at 115. In *Attorney General v Southern Industrial Trust* 94 ILTR 161, Davitt P drew attention to the logical consequence of the Supreme Court's ruling in the *NUR* case: 'It could be reasoned similarly that to deprive a person of any part of his property, is not a delimitation of the exercise of his rights over his property, but a denial of those rights altogether.'

25.   *NUR v Sullivan* [1947] IR 77 at 102.

26.   *The Irish Constitution* (2nd edn, Butterworths, 1984) 597.

27.   *Educational Company v Fitzpatrick* [1961] IR 345.

28.   *White v Riley* [1921] 1 Ch 1.

29.   eg *Valentine v Hyde* [1919] 2 Ch 129; *Hodges v Webb* [1920] 2 Ch 70.

30.   *Riordan v Butler* [1940] IR 347; *Maher v Beirne* 93 ILTR 101.

Art 40.[31] But *Educational Company* in the early 1960s, through the mechanism of the Constitution, reversed this view.

[2.18] In *Educational Company* Budd J[32] construed Art 40.6.1°iii according to the judgment of the Supreme Court in *NUR v Sullivan*:

> ... wherein Murnaghan J states that the language of the Article means that 'each citizen is free to associate with others of his choice.' Since he has the choice he can surely exercise it so as not to associate with those he does not want to associate with.

Maguire CJ, whose dissenting judgment was referred to at para **2.11** above, regarded the *NUR* case as distinguishable (a matter of particular significance as he sat in the Supreme Court which decided it). There was a clear dissimilarity, he said, between the sort of provision in a statute of the Oireachtas and the action of the trade union in the case before him.

[2.19] But the majority in the Supreme Court held there was an implicit guarantee in the Constitution that citizens shall not be coerced *to join associations or unions* against their will. Kingsmill Moore J[33] was clear that:

> The Constitution does not give such a guarantee in express terms, but I think it does so by necessary implication. The right to express freely convictions and opinions, guaranteed by Article 40.6.1(i), must include the right to hold such convictions and opinions and the right not to be forced to join a union or association professing, forwarding, and requiring its members to subscribe to contrary opinions. The undertaking in Article 40.3.2, to protect the property rights of every citizen may perhaps include an undertaking to protect his right to dispose of his labour as he wills, and would include impliedly a right not to be forced against his will into a union or association which exacts from him a regular payment. Moreover I think a guarantee of a right to form associations and unions is only intelligible where there is an implicit right to abstain from joining such associations or unions or, to put it another way, to associate and unite with those who do not join such unions.

Casey[34] has observed that whether or not the guarantee is intelligible only in the context of an implicit right to abstain from joining depends on the purpose and policy of the guarantee in Art 40.6.1°iii, and no such implication is necessary, he suggests, if the guarantee is a positive affirmation of the right of trade unions to exist.

[2.20] Apart from the Supreme Court's failure to disentangle conflicting rights, its reasoning demonstrates a logical fallacy. The right to associate and unite with those who do not join unions was found to be implicit in the very different right, namely the right to *form* associations and unions. Only if we assume that the last-mentioned

---

31. *Buckley v Rooney* [1950] Ir Jur Rep 5. See Whyte, 'Industrial Relations and the Irish Constitution' (1981) vol XVI Ir Jur 47, at 54.

32. At 364–5.

33. At 395.

34. Casey, 'Some Complications of Freedom of Association in Labour Law: A Comparative Study with Special Reference to Ireland' (1972) 21 ICLQ 699, at 707–8.

includes a right to join trade unions, does the correlative make sense. It patently does not include this right, and judges faced squarely by the issue have not thought so either.[35] Moreover, Kingsmill Moore J fell into the trap of confusing rights and liberties.[36] By referring initially to a 'right' he proceeded to find a correlative duty or obligation. If A has a right to join a union, B (supposedly) is obliged not to interfere. Yet A has no such right.

[2.21] Haugh J, the third member of the majority, took a different approach and contributed a second *ratio decidendi* to the Supreme Court decision. He saw the non-unionists as exercising a positive constitutional right: they were associated together to stay out of the union.

[2.22] The dissenting Maguire CJ[37] challenged the logic of the majority's position:

> If the contention is right that action which aims at persuading non-union men to join a union is a denial of the rights given by Article 40.6.iii [sic], it would seem to me that each step taken with this end in view is an infringement of the Article. The demand upon the employer that men shall be dismissed if they do not join the union, the threat of a strike to support this demand and, above all, the strike itself would seem to me just as much a derogation of the right of the non-union workmen as the placing of a picket on the premises. Yet it is conceded that none of these steps does violence to the constitutional rights of the non-union workmen or of their employers.

Kingsmill Moore J responded to this[38] by saying that the claim to picket and the claim to strike seemed to him to involve very different considerations (he did not say what they were):

> The right to dispose of one's labour and to withdraw it seems to me a fundamentally personal right which, though not specifically mentioned in the Constitution as being guaranteed, is a right of a nature which I cannot conceive to have been adversely affected by anything within the intendment of the Constitution. But the matter does not arise for decision in this case.

Industrial action to enforce a closed shop

[2.23] Suppose employees in a particular employment are represented by several trade unions. Suppose further they agree with the employer that all contracts of employment should be terminated and employees be re-employed immediately on the same terms as before but with an additional new condition that each employee should agree to be 'at all times' a member of one of the trade unions concerned. This happened in *Meskell v CIE*.[39] Meskell received the appropriate notice of termination from CIE but refused to

---

35. *Tierney v Amalgamated Society of Woodworkers* [1959] IR 254.
36. See further by Redmond, 'Towards an Hohfeldian View of the Rights and Freedoms in the Irish Constitution' (1979–80) DULJ 52. And see Kelly with Hogan and Whyte, *The Irish Constitution* Supplement to 2nd edn, 140.
37. At 381–2.
38. At 397.
39. *Meskell v CIE* [1973] IR 121.

accept the new condition which was in effect a post-entry closed shop condition. He had at all times prior to dismissal been a member in good standing of a trade union. He sought damages for conspiracy (para **5.74**) and a declaration in the High Court that his dismissal was a violation of his rights under the Constitution. His claims were dismissed in that court. On appeal, however, the Supreme Court reaffirmed that the right of citizens to form associations and unions necessarily implied a correlative right of dissociation, to abstain from joining associations and unions.

[2.24] Applying *Educational Company*, Walsh J in the Supreme Court emphasised that action may be *ultra vires* whether it operates directly or indirectly: directly when it involves infringing another's constitutional rights or coercing him into abandoning them or waiving them (in so far as that may be possible); indirectly in so far as such conduct constitutes the means towards an end which is not in itself unlawful. Here the means were unlawful and an agreement to employ such means constitutes a conspiracy.

In such circumstances, the withdrawal of labour and any other act taken with a view to influencing the employer would almost certainly be unconstitutional. The only way in which this prediction might change would be if a 'right to strike' were recognised as having constitutional protection (on which, see further para **2.39** *et seq* below).

[2.25] The view was expressed by Henchy J in *Becton Dickinson and Co Ltd v Lee*[40] that a pre-entry closed shop requiring an employee to belong to a trade union before he is employed would ordinarily be a matter of free contractual choice for a prospective employee. A dispute about a pre-entry closed shop would therefore constitute a 'trade dispute' under the Industrial Relations Act 1990. Such a pre-condition may be unlawful, however, if the trade union has a monopoly in a particular area of work: *Murphy v Stewart*,[41] or if it is indirectly discriminatory: *Nathan v Bailey Gibson*.[42] Notwithstanding the view in *Becton Dickinson*,[43] applying the views of the ECt HR as set out in the recent case of *Sorensen and Rasmussen v Denmark*,[44] and having regard to the mandatory obligations of the European Convention on Human Rights Act 2003, it is strongly arguable that an Irish court would now be obliged to hold the pre-entry closed shop incompatible with the provisions of the Convention. Moreover, an Irish court would not be in a position to provide the statutory immunities and protections to picketing or other industrial action if it were for the purpose of enforcing a pre-entry closed shop.

Taking part in decision-making processes of union and statutory secret ballots

[2.26] It would appear that there is a constitutional right to take part in the democratic processes of a trade union, and in particular to take part in the decision-making processes within the rules of the trade union. Action by a union which violated this

---

40.   *Becton Dickinson and Co Ltd v Lee* [1973] IR 1.

41.   *Murphy v Stewart* [1973] IR 97 at 116.

42.   *Nathan v Bailey Gibson* [1996] ELR 114 SC, [1998] ELR 51, Labour Court.

43.   Mallon and O'Sullivan, 'Are Pre-Entry Closed Shop Agreements Permissible under the ECHR?' (2009) Vol 1 *Employment Law Review*.

44.   *Sorensen and Rasmussen v Denmark* [2008] 46 EHRP 572.

constitutional right, regarded as 'a necessary corollary of the right to join and become a member of a trade union,' as Finlay P in the High Court loosely put it in *Rodgers v ITGWU,*[45] would be *ultra vires*. A later case described this right as one which trade union members enjoy to fair procedures when their union takes a decision materially affecting their interests: *Doyle v Croke*.[46] Costello J found the right to fair procedures in Art 40.6.1°, in Art 40.3 (which guarantees Personal Rights) and the common law. Concerning freedom of association, he said:[47]

> It seems to me that if the constitutional right of citizens to form associations and unions is to be effective the Article in which it is to be found should not be construed restrictively as the right would be of limited value if it did not protect individual members against procedures which might be unfair to them.

The right could be relevant regarding the provisions on secret ballots in the Industrial Relations Act 1990 (**Ch 11**). Members affected by strike or other industrial action are accorded a right to ballot on the proposed industrial action and union rule books are deemed to so provide (s 14). If members are not balloted, they could rely perhaps not only on the statute but on the Constitution.[48]

No right to recognition

[2.27] The principal function of trade unions, to engage in negotiations for fixing wages and other terms and conditions of employment, is recognised by the Trade Union Act 1941.

The Constitution, however, does not oblige an employer to recognise a trade union or association seeking to represent its employees (nor does the common law). In *Association of General Practitioners & Ors v Minister for Health*[49] O' Hanlon J said:

> I do not consider that there is any obligation imposed by ordinary law or by the Constitution on an employer to consult with or negotiate with an organisation representing his employees or some of them when the conditions of employment are to be settled or reviewed.

> The employer is left with freedom of choice as to whether he will negotiate with any organisation or consult with them on such matters and is also free to give a

---

45. *Rodgers v ITGWU* [1978] ILRM 51. Reactions to this case cover rejection of the right enunciated: Whyte, 'Industrial Relations and the Irish Constitution' (1981) vol XVI Ir Jur 64–66, to seeing the decision as impliedly supporting the doctrine of waiver of constitutional rights, Kerr, 'Employment – The Constitution – Rights to Work and Fair Play' (1978) DULJ 61, 63.

46. *Doyle v Croke* (6 May 1988, unreported), HC (1988) 7 JISLL 150.

47. *Doyle v Croke* (6 May 1988, unreported), HC (1988) 7 JISLL 150 at 159.

48. The earlier decision of *Darby and Others v AGEMOU* (26 July 1972, unreported), SC is strengthened by the right in *Rodgers v ITGWU* [1978] ILRM 51.

49. *Association of General Practitioners & Ors v Minister for Health* [1995] 2 ILRM 481 at 489; also *Abbott & Whelan v ITGWU* [1982] 1 JSLL 56, HC; *Dublin Colleges of Academic Staff Association v City of Dublin VEC* (31 July 1981, unreported), HC; *Irish Municipal Public and Civil Trade Union & Others v Ryanair* [2007] 1 ILRM 45.

right of audience to one representative body and refuse it to another, if he chooses to do so.[50]

[2.28] A dispute about trade union recognition is a valid trade dispute for purposes of the Trade Disputes Act 1946 and Pt II of the Industrial Relations Act 1990 and may be referred to the Labour Court under s 20 of the Industrial Relations Act 1969. Following the high degree of notoriety achieved by some recognition disputes, and the advocacy of ICTU, a High Level Group on the topic was set up, which reported in 1999.[51] The Group proposed two routes for trade union recognition: the first voluntary and the second a 'fall back' procedure. The first is now found in the LRC's Enhanced Code of Practice on Voluntary Dispute Resolution declared a Code of Practice for the purposes of the Industrial Relations Act 1990 in 2004 and the text of which is in the **Appendix**.[52] The second was given effect by the Industrial Relations (Amendment) Act 2001, which in turn was substantially amended by the Industrial Relations (Miscellaneous Provisions) Act 2004.[53]

[2.29] The 'fall back' mechanism arises where an employer refuses or fails to avail of the voluntary option or, having availed of it, the issues remain unresolved. Section 2(1)(a) of the Act of 2001, as amended, permits the Labour Court, at the request of a trade union or excepted body, to investigate a trade dispute, among other things, where the Labour Court is satisfied that it is not the practice of the employer to engage in collective bargaining negotiations and the internal dispute resolution procedures (if any) normally used by the parties have failed to resolve the dispute. Although the Chairman of the Labour Court said in *IMPACT v Ryanair Ltd*[54] that the Act of 2001 provides 'a measure of protection to employees where pay and conditions are not freely determined by collective bargaining,' following the Supreme Court decision in

---

50. See similarly *Wilson and Palmer* [2003] IRLR 128 (para **2. 34** *et seq*) in which the ECt HR said: 'Compulsory collective bargaining would impose on employers an obligation to conduct negotiations with trade unions. The Court has not yet been prepared to hold that the freedom of a trade union to make its voice heard extends to imposing on an employer an obligation to recognise a trade union. But a union and its members must be free in one way or another to seek to persuade the employer to listen to what it has to say on behalf of its members. Nevertheless it is of the essence of the right to join trade unions for the protection of their interests that employees should be free to instruct or permit the union *to make representations* to their employer or to take action in support of their interests on their behalf.' See Ewing, 'The Implications of *Wilson and Palmer*' (2003) ILJ 1.
51. *Industrial Relations News* (1999) IRN 11, 18 March.
52. SI 76/2004. See too Industrial Relations Act 1990 (Code of Practice on Victimisation) (Declaration) Order 2004, which provides the procedure for addressing complaints of victimisation arising from an employee's membership or non-membership, activity or non-activity on behalf of a trade union or excepted body, or a manager discharging his managerial functions, or any other employee where negotiating arrangements are not in place and collective bargaining fails to take place. The text is set out in the **Appendix**.
53. Ryan, 'Leaving it to the Experts-In the Matter of the Industrial Relations (Amendment) Act 2001' (2006) 3 (4) IELJ 11.
54. *IMPACT v Ryanair Ltd* [2005] ELR 99, 105.

Ryanair Ltd v Labour Court[55] it would appear the Act is of little effect in achieving the aims of the trade union movement. In *Ryanair* the Supreme Court was not prepared to give the term 'collective bargaining negotiations' the meaning it would normally bear in industrial relations. Definitions peculiar to trade union negotiations could not be imposed on non-unionised companies. Thus Geoghegan J:[56]

> If there is machinery in Ryanair whereby the pilots may have their own independent representatives who sit around the table with representatives of Ryanair with a view to reaching agreement if possible, that would seem to be 'collective bargaining' within an ordinary dictionary meaning.

[2.30] In *Towards 2016 Review and Transitional Agreement 2008* the government, responding to union demands arising out of *Ryanair*, committed itself (at paras 9.1–9.3) to set up a six-month process in which the issue of employee representation and the appropriate legislative framework would be reviewed, with a view to the enactment of necessary legislation. As a result, a Review Group on Employee Representation has been set up. In late 2009 Fine Gael announced it would propose new legislation recognising the rights of workers to bargain collectively if elected to government, relying on Art 28 of the Charter of Fundamental Rights guaranteeing the right to bargain. No doubt any legislative proposal will be scrutinised to ensure no inconsistency with the constitutional rights of employers.

Trade disputes concerning individual contracts of employment

[2.31] Freedom of association could influence trade disputes law where the cause of industrial action concerns an individual's contract of employment. The Industrial Relations Act 1990 goes some way towards alleviating the disturbance that can accompany a trade dispute about dismissal (para **9.26**). But what if the strike or other industrial action infringed the *employer's* constitutional right to freedom of association?

There is nothing in Art 40.6.1°iii to limit the freedom of association's application to individuals, trade unions and their members.[57] As the freedom protects a range of activities which, not being unlawful, are therefore inferentially lawful, the freedom might be capable of being invoked by an employer in the context of the employer-employee relationship.[58] Like the relationship between a trade union member and his union, this too is based on contract.

---

55. *Ryanair Ltd v Labour Court* [2007] 4 IR 199. Doherty, 'Union Sundown? The Future of Collective Representation in Irish Law' (2007) 4(4) IELJ 96.

56. At 218.

57. This is illustrated by, eg, *Attorney General (Society for the Protection of the Unborn Child (Ireland) Ltd) v Open-Door Counselling Ltd* [1987] ILRM 477; *Private Motorists' Provident Society Ltd v Attorney General* [1983] IR 339; *Norris v Attorney General* [1984] IR 36 and *Loftus v Attorney General* [1979] IR 221.

58. See the doubt surrounding the constitutionality of the remedy of reinstatement in the Unfair Dismissals Act 1977, *Seanad Debates*, Vol 86 cols 40–41; Robinson and Temple Lang, 'The Constitution and the Right to Reinstatement after Wrongful Dismissal' *Gazette of the Incorporated Law Society of Ireland* (1977) May–June, 78.

[2.32] If the freedom allows the exercise of a personal right to choose one's associates, an employer must have a right to contract, or not to contract, with an employee subject only to constraints imposed by law (eg under the Employment Equality Act 1998). And just as an employee has no right to join a particular trade union, there can be no right to be employed by a particular employer or to be reinstated after an employer has unequivocally terminated the contract of employment. Each citizen is free to associate with others of his choice: 'Since he has the choice he can surely exercise it so as not to associate with those he does not want to associate with', as Budd J said in *Educational Company*.[59] No employee can force a contract of employment upon an employer without contravening the employer's freedom of association. This cuts both ways: an employee cannot be forced by an employer to enter into a contract of employment with him.

[2.33] The circumstances in which this application of *Educational Company* could be developed include industrial action designed to coerce an employer to reinstate a dismissed worker or workers (whatever the reason for dismissal, including redundancy) or to employ a particular worker or workers. And as the freedom embodies a positive and negative aspect, it might also be invoked where industrial action attempted to coerce an employer to dismiss. The individual nature of the freedom, as interpreted, could be essential in the context of employee representation. As the law stands, there is no right to be represented by a particular trade union. If that were to change, depending on the details of any proposal, it might be possible for an employer to argue that as he is constitutionally entitled not to associate with those with whom he does not want to associate, *a fortiori* he cannot be coerced into recognising those he does not want to associate with for bargaining or any other purpose.

Freedom of Association and the European Convention on Human Rights

[2.34] Freedom of association is guaranteed to everyone under Art 11 of the European Convention on Human Rights which was incorporated into Irish law by the European Convention on Human Rights Act 2003. Section 3 obliges State organs to perform their functions in a manner which is compatible with the State's obligations under the Convention. Article 11(1) and (2) provide:

> Everyone has the right to … freedom of association with others, including the right to form and to join trade unions for the protection of his interests.

> No restrictions shall be placed on the exercise of these rights other than such as are prescribed by law and are necessary in a democratic society in the interests of national security or public safety, for the prevention of disorder or crime, for the protection of health or morals or for the protection of the rights and freedoms of others. This Article shall not prevent the imposition of lawful restrictions on the exercise of these rights by members of the armed forces, of the police or of the administration of the State.

Whether the right in Art 11 involved a correlative not to associate formed the basis of the claims in *Young and James v The United Kingdom* and *Webster v The United*

---

59.   *Educational Company* [1961] IR 364 at 365.

Kingdom.[60] Under UK legislation at the time, an employee could refuse to join a union in a closed shop situation on the grounds of religious objection. The applicants so objected and, because they refused to join the appropriate railway union, were dismissed by British Rail. In all three cases, at the time employment began, there was no requirement for a British Rail employee to be a member of a specified trade union. The European Court of Human Rights (ECt HR) by 18 votes to 3 decided that there had been a breach of Art 11. The majority held that the requirement to join a particular union which had not existed when the applicants were engaged amounted to an infringement of their right as employees to join an association of their choice – the sanction of dismissal being, for practical purposes, compulsive. The ECt HR also held that compulsion to join a particular union contrary to the employees' convictions was an infringement of Art 11.[61] Until recently, the jurisprudence of the ECt HR on cases under this article has been unexciting. In a number of decisions it acknowledged that trade unions must have the right to represent the interests of their members but, the court said, the article did not guarantee any particular means by which this could be done. Freedom of association did not imply a right to be consulted by an employer, a

---

60.   *Young and James v United Kingdom* and *Webster v United Kingdom* [1981] IRLR 480. Noted Whyte, 'The right of workers to choose their collective bargaining agents' (1981) 75 *Gazette of the Incorporated Law Society of Ireland* 237.

61.   The majority decision is not a model of clarity. It did not finally decide whether the positive freedom of association necessarily included the negative freedom not to associate. On the assumption that it did not, however, the court concluded that the freedom to associate involved an element of freedom of choice which must imply some limit on the power to compel membership of a particular union. A compulsive threat of dismissal involving loss of livelihood directed at those engaged before the introduction of the requirement struck at the very substance of the guaranteed freedom of choice. It was important, moreover, that the union membership requirement was a new arrival on the employment scene. At common law this would amount to an attempt unilaterally to vary the contract of employment. In the majority view the suggestion that the applicants could form any association they chose, provided they also joined the specified union, did not alter the degree of compulsion to join the specified union even if it was true that such action would not have led to their expulsion from the railway union. This compulsion in reality reduced any freedom to join another association to one of no practical value. It has been argued that the implications of this holding for industrial relations in Ireland are very significant (Whyte, 'Industrial Relations and the Irish Constitution' (1981) vol XVI *Irish Jurist* 57) but it is very doubtful whether the decision can be applied to protect other than existing non-union employees. Only seven members of the court went so far as to hold that the positive freedom necessarily involved a correlative negative freedom not to join an association. The court also added that Art 11 was part of a pattern of protection of freedom of thought, conscience and expression and this whole pattern was threatened by compulsion to join an association against one's convictions. Even if the applicants constituted a minority, it did not follow that the majority could insist that restriction of their freedom was necessary to protect the rights and freedoms of others. 'Necessary' means more than advantageous and there was no evidence that the railway unions could not have striven to protect their interests without power to compel membership of persons such as the applicants. Even had there been such evidence a balance must be struck to avoid the majority acting unfairly to the minority. The decision, in short, adds little to Irish law save a different approach.

right to bargain collectively, or a right to strike.[62] Ewing has described how the court, while failing to protect the rights of trade unionists and trade unions, was carefully crafting a right of indeterminate scope and content not to be a member of a trade union, even though there is no such right in the body of the Convention and even though it was the intention of those who drafted the Convention that there should be no such right.

[2.35] This 'debit balance' of Art 11 was significantly readjusted, however, following *Wilson and Palmer v The United Kindgom*[63] in which the court went 'a long way to restore confidence in Art 11'. In *Wilson and Palmer* one of the applicants received a letter from his employer (the *Daily Mail*) to advise that the company was not going to renew the recognition agreement it had with the NUJ. The letter continued by explaining that any worker who signed a new personal contract with the company before the expiry of the collective agreement would receive a 4.5% wage increase backdated three months. The applicant, then a lay official of his union (the NUJ) at the *Daily Mail,* refused to sign a new contract and did not receive the wage increase as a result. The applicants complained that British law was in breach of Arts 10, 11 and 14 of the ECHR by failing to ensure the applicants' rights to protect their interests through trade union membership and freedom of expression. The ECt HR acknowledged that although the alleged breach of Art 11 was by an employer and not by the State, the State was nevertheless liable. Although Art 11 does not encompass collective bargaining, the court held that nevertheless it is of the essence of the right to join trade unions for the protection of their interests that employees 'should be free to instruct or permit the union *to make representations* to their employer or to take action in support of their interests on their behalf.' Moreover, it was 'the role of the State to ensure that trade union members are not prevented or restrained from using their union *to represent* them in attempts to regulate their relations with their employer.' The court concluded that by permitting employers to use financial incentives to induce employees to surrender important union rights, the respondent State had failed in its positive obligation to secure the enjoyment of the rights under Art 11 of the Convention. On waiver of rights under the Irish Constitution, see para **3.26**.

[2.36] The right to collective bargaining was held to be an essential element of the right to freedom of association in Art 11 in the recent landmark decision of the ECt HR, *Demir and Baykara v Turkey.*[64] This involved a reversal of earlier jurisprudence of the Court. The ECt HR also held that the jurisprudence of the International Labour Organisation and of the European Social Charter are embedded in that right, regardless of whether the member state has ratified the relevant convention. The decision no doubt requires a re-examination of jurisprudence on trade union rights associated with

---

62. See respectively, *National Union of Belgian Police v Belgium* (1975) 1 EHRR 578; *Schmidt and Dahlström v Sweden* (1975) 1 EHRR 637; and *Swedish Engine Drivers' Union v Sweden* (1975) 1 EHRR 617.

63. *Wilson and Palmer v United Kingdom* [2003] IRLR 128.

64. *Demir and Baykara v Turkey* Application No 34503/97, 12 Nov 2008; Ewing and Hendy, 'The Dramatic Implications of *Demir and Baykara*' (2010) 39 ILJ 2.

collective bargaining but the pre-eminence of the Constitution in Ireland may mean that its significance is limited.

CONFLICT OF CONSTITUTIONAL RIGHTS

[2.37] Constitutional rights may conflict. There is no such thing as an absolute and unqualified fundamental right.[65] A constitutional right must be exercised with due regard to the rights of others. If it is exercised without regard to the harm that may be done to others, what is taking place is an abuse, and not the lawful exercise, of a right given by the Constitution. At times constitutional rights may appear to clash but the primary object of the exercise of one of the rights may be the promotion of the other. If so, there will be no unconstitutionality. One right cannot become the means of restricting or preventing the exercise of another. For example, freedom of association cannot be exercised in such a way as to deprive another of his right to work: *Murphy v Stewart*.[66]

[2.38] McMahon J in *Crowley v Ireland*[67] touched on the topic of conflicting constitutional rights:

> The character of an act depends on the circumstances in which it is done and the exercise of a constitutional right for the purpose of infringing the constitutional rights of others is an abuse of that right, which, in my opinion, can be restrained by the courts.

There are many potential candidates for a conflict argument in trade disputes, apart from the freedom of association. Depending on the circumstances, plaintiffs or defendants might cite, for example, the guarantee of basic fairness of procedures,[68] property rights,[69] the right to maintain a livelihood or the right to run a business.[70] Perhaps the most obvious candidate is the so-called right to strike or to take industrial action.

'Right to strike or to take industrial action'

[2.39] The freedom of association is arguably meaningless without the backup of the economic strike weapon. As Lord Wright acknowledged, 'the right of workmen to strike is an essential element in the principle of collective bargaining'.[71] The right has

---

65.   See eg *Murray v Ireland* [1985] IR 532.
66.   *Murphy v Stewart* [1973] IR 97, Walsh J at 117. However, the likelihood of there being such an abuse is rare. See *Nagle v Fielden* [1966] 2 QB 633 where Lord Denning perhaps overstepped himself. *Murphy v Stewart* does, however, provide an example of where a trade union might be forced to accept a member.
67.   *Crowley v Ireland* [1980] IR 102 at 110.
68.   See fn 3 of this chapter.
69.   See *Attorney General v Southern Industrial Trust Ltd and Simon* (1960) ILTR 161; *Central Dublin Development Association Ltd v Attorney General* (1973) 109 ILTR 69; *Moynihan v Greensmyth* [1977] IR 55; *Blake v Attorney General* [1982] IR 117; *Pine Valley Developments v Minister for the Environment* [1987] IR 23.
70.   See Kelly with Hogan and Whyte fn 36 above, at 150.
71.   *Crofter Hand Woven Harris Tweed Co Ld v Veitch* [1942] AC 435.

not been firmly proposed, still less recognised, in Ireland's jurisprudence. As it is not laid down explicitly, the right – if it exists – could be adduced only as a corollary to an express right such as the freedom of association or as a personal right under Art 40.3.

[2.40] There is little likelihood of this happening based on case law. For example, in the case of picketing, Art 40.6.1°iii guarantees liberty for the exercise of the right of citizens to assemble peaceably and without arms. But no headway has been made in giving constitutional protection to picketing. In *Educational Company* Kingsmill Moore J[72] said that picketing as 'ordinarily conducted' was a 'murderous weapon' and that even if carried out with scrupulous avoidance of any express threats:

> its inevitable effect was to intimidate customers and to cause such a conditional reflex in all trade unionists as inevitably to interfere with the business of the party picketed and with the ordinary user and enjoyment of his property in such a way as to constitute a common law nuisance.

A *prima facie* candidate in the Constitution for a right to strike corollary is Art 40.6.1°iii, which guarantees the right to freedom of association. In practical terms, however, given the way in which the freedom has been construed, it is unlikely a right to strike will be derived from the freedom of association.

[2.41] Potential green shoots recognising the right are few. In *Brendan Dunne v Fitzpatrick*[73] Budd J suggested the Constitution protected the right of the employer and employee 'to deal with and dispose of their property and labour as they will without interference unless such interference be made legitimate by law'. In *Educational Company v Fitzpatrick*[74] Kingsmill Moore J referred *obiter* to the right to dispose of, and to withdraw, one's labour. The context, in which the judge emphasised the individual nature of the right, may be recalled (para **2.19**). The 'suspension theory' of strike action (**para 3.12** *et seq*) adopted by Irish judges in *Becton Dickinson & Co v Lee*[75] could be said to support a constitutional right to strike.

[2.42] But Irish courts appear unwilling to legitimise any form of the so-called right to strike or to take industrial action. Two decisions of the superior courts could be said to confirm this, albeit that as precedents neither concerned a concerted right to withdraw labour, ie strike action. In so far as they insist that the right to withdraw labour, if it exists, must not be exercised for the purpose of frustrating, infringing or destroying the constitutional rights of others, they proclaim nothing new.

[2.43] The first case is *Crowley and Others v Ireland and Others*.[76] As a result of a directive incorporating a decision taken by the Irish National Teachers Organisation (INTO), all the teachers, with one exception, in the three national schools in Drimoleague, Co Cork, absented themselves from work on strike. The INTO's directive resulted in teachers in neighbouring schools refusing to accept or teach

---

72.   *Educational Company v Fitzpatrick* [1961] IR 345 at 390–1.

73.   *Brendan Dunne v Fitzpatrick* [1958] IR 29 at 34.

74.   *Educational Company v Fitzpatrick* [1961] IR 345 at 397.

75.   *Becton Dickinson & Co v Lee* [1973] IR 1.

76.   *Crowley and Others v Ireland and Others* [1980] IR 102.

children from Drimoleague. The teachers from outside Drimoleague had no direct grievance with their employers. The plaintiffs were children on the rolls of the three national schools in Drimoleague affected by the strike. They did not challenge the right of the INTO members to withdraw their labour from the Drimoleague schools. They claimed instead that the circular issued by the INTO was an unlawful interference with their constitutional right to obtain free primary education elsewhere, as guaranteed by Art 42.4. It was submitted that the injury to the children's constitutional rights by the teachers in neighbouring schools was merely incidental to the exercise by INTO members of their constitutional rights.

[2.44] In the High Court McMahon J[77] responded thus:

> I think it is doubtful whether the refusal of members of the INTO to enrol children from the Drimoleague schools can be treated as a partial withdrawal of labour and the exercise of a constitutional right. If it is not the exercise of a constitutional right, there is no answer to the children's claim because as Walsh J pointed out in *Meskell v CIE* [1973] IR 121, 135, it is no answer to a claim based on an infringement of a constitutional right to say that the defendant was exercising a common law right ... Assuming, without so deciding, that INTO members were exercising a constitutional right in refusing to enrol the children from Drimoleague schools, it does not follow that the interference with the constitutional right of the children is not actionable. Mr Justice Walsh in his judgement in *Murphy v Stewart* [1973] IR 97 117, adverted to the possible abuse of a constitutional right which might require the intervention of the Courts ... The character of an act depends on the circumstances in which it is done and the exercise of a constitutional right for the purpose of infringing the constitutional rights of others is an abuse of that right which, in my opinion, can be restrained by the Courts.

The teachers' refusal to enrol Drimoleague pupils was not 'primarily' done for the purpose of exercising their right to work or their right to choose the conditions under which they would work, according to McMahon J. The primary purpose was to exert pressure in a situation of industrial dispute. This amounted to unlawful means to deprive the Drimoleague children of their constitutional right and was therefore actionable at the suit of the children. Later McMahon J said that 'the claim of the Plaintiffs against the INTO is for damages alleged to have been suffered by the Plaintiffs by reason of a conspiracy on the part of the INTO to deprive the Plaintiffs of their constitutional rights.' Conspiracy, therefore, lay at the heart of the case. From this aspect of his judgment there was no appeal to the Supreme Court although the Minister for Education and the Attorney General appealed in other respects.

In the Supreme Court O'Higgins CJ[78] (who dissented from the majority finding, Parke J concurring) was doubtful, as McMahon J had been, that the teachers had a constitutional right to do what they did:

> However, if they had any such right so to refrain from teaching it was not a right which could be exercised for the purpose of frustrating, infringing or destroying the constitutional rights of others.

---

77. At 110.
78. At 125.

[2.45] None of the judgments clarify the right which the teachers may have been exercising: was it the right to dispose of their labour as they wished, or the right to work or to take industrial action, or to choose their conditions of work? Only by an unjustifiable extension of the constitutional provision could it be alleged that the teachers in nearby schools owed any duty to the Drimoleague children and thereby breached the latter's rights. The children's rights were not enforceable against teachers at large or against neighbouring teachers but solely against the State, represented by the Minister for Education.

[2.46] The wrong itself, in respect of which damages were awarded, is ambiguous: *Hayes v Ireland.*[79] Carroll J's description of the wrong ranged from 'breach of the constitutional right to free primary education' to 'unlawful interference ... with the constitutional right' and she also said 'this is not an action based on tort' *pace* McMahon J in the High Court in *Crowley.* In *Conway v INTO*[80] Finlay CJ, while equating an action for breach of constitutional rights with an action in tort, did not speak in terms of constitutional torts. The immunity from suit for licensed trade unions regarding claims for common law torts in s 13 of the Industrial Relations Act 1990 (replacing s 4 of the Trade Disputes Act 1906) does not lie in respect of constitutional wrongs.

[2.47] The view that to exert pressure in a situation of industrial unrest is unconstitutional emerges also from *Talbot (Ireland) Ltd v Merrigan.*[81] The dispute concerned redundancy. A number of employees at Talbot (Ireland) Ltd occupied the company's premises. An injunction was issued to restrain the occupation and picketing started. The union concerned, the Amalgamated Transport and General Workers Union (ATGWU), decided to increase pressure on the company by seeking the support of other unions. It announced an embargo on Talbot products. The executive council of ICTU endorsed the decision to effect an embargo. All members of trade unions affiliated to ICTU were asked not to permit the importation of Talbot cars, spare parts and other components, not to handle them within the country and not to permit services to be carried out in connection with the company's activities.

[2.48] The company succeeded in restraining the general secretary of the ATGWU, and ICTU, by interlocutory injunction. The general secretary ignored the restraining order and was committed to prison for contempt of court. The contempt order was not implemented so that an appeal could be taken to the Supreme Court. The Supreme Court endorsed the lower court and the boycott was called off. Henchy J described the

---

79. *Hayes v Ireland* [1987] ILRM 651.

80. *Conway v INTO* [1991] 2 IR 305.

81. *Talbot (Ireland) Ltd v Merrigan* (30 April 1981, unreported), SC, cf McMahon and Binchy, *Cases and Materials on the Law of Torts* (3rd edition, Tottel Publishing, 2005), 863. Kerr, 'Trade Disputes Economic Torts and the Constitution – The Legacy of Talbot' (1981) 16 Ir Jur (ns) 241. Generally, see Kerr, 'Industrial Action: Rights of Immunities' 1986 JISLL 7; Forde, 'Bills of Rights and Trade Union Immunities: Some French Lessons' 1984 ILJ 40 where he raised the intriguing possibility that immunity may fall foul of the European Convention.

embargo as 'no mere empty request but an implemented direction which in effect had procured the breach of many contracts between the company and third parties'.

Henchy J commented that, irrespective of the existence of a trade dispute, trade unions had to operate 'within the constitutional framework and the constitutional guarantees in Art 40.3.2' and went on to declare *obiter*, that:

> *Innocent persons cannot be damnified at will* by the law [emphasis added] – in other words, they must be protected from 'unjust attack.'

When he spoke of 'innocent persons', he was not referring to the union or the company:

> but to persons such as dealers who had no dispute with anybody, owners of the vehicles who have no dispute with anybody, but who, because of this embargo, cannot get their vehicles serviced – a service they are entitled to under their contract.

[2.49] *Talbot* appeared to drive a coach and four through the protections in the Trade Disputes Act 1906 but its influence may be doubted. There is no approved transcript and as it is an oral judgment, it is difficult to cite as an authority. The decision was made in circumstances of urgency, as Henchy J later told the *Sunday Tribune*.[82] It was an application for an interlocutory injunction; the court relied on affidavit evidence. There were no written averments from the defendants on the constitutional implications of the embargo.

The case does not bear on strikes, all-out strikes or pickets. To Henchy J, the impugned action went 'far beyond any legitimate industrial action.' Griffin J agreed with him and Kenny J, while also agreeing, added that the Trade Disputes Act 1906 was 'not relevant to any matter in this case.'[83]

[2.50] As the law now stands, the lawfulness or otherwise of industrial action depends upon two things: firstly, the majority of the Supreme Court has affirmed that if strikers give such notice as would validly terminate their contracts of employment, this will 'suspend' the contract and render the strike legitimate (*Becton Dickinson v Lee*).[84] Secondly, there is the known will of parliament in the Act of 1990. The constitutional provision cited by Henchy J, Art 40.3.2, refers to 'unjust attack.' Such attack, arguably, involves only action that is outside the 1990 Act. The Industrial Relations Act with its presumption of constitutionality could be described as removing the threat of *Talbot* from action enjoying immunity and as embodying Parliament's considered regulation of the right to withdraw labour. This is not to say, however, that there will be no future legal challenge on the basis of an alleged constitutional right to strike or to take industrial action.

---

82. (1981) *Sunday Tribune*, 2 August.

83. See McMahon and Binchy, *Irish Law of Torts* (3rd edn, Tottel Publishing, 2000), 437 and von Prondzynski and McCarthy, 'Is the law above trade unions?' (1981) *Irish Times*, 18 May.

84. *Becton Dickinson v Lee* [1973] IR 1.

[2.51] The ECt HR consistently took the view that, although the right to strike is not protected *per se* by Art 11, it is one of the means by which trade unions may promote the interests of their members. For example, in *UNISON v United Kingdom*[85] it was recognised – despite the fact that the right to strike is not formally protected by Art 11 – that the prohibition of the strike in that case must be regarded as a restriction on the ability of the union to protect the interests of its members and therefore disclosed a restriction on the freedom of association guaranteed by Art 11. In the *Wilson and Palmer* case[86] (paras **2.34–36**), the right to strike was raised in a different context, by the British government, as a defence to the action against it, on the ground that the right to strike existed as one of the ways by which trade unions could represent and promote the interests of their members. Having considered the matter, the ECt HR agreed with the government that:

> the essence of a voluntary system of collective bargaining is that it must be possible for a trade union which is not recognised by an employer to take steps including, if necessary, organising industrial action, with a view to persuading the employer to enter into collective bargaining with it on those issues which the union believes are important for its members' interests.

Ewing asks the following question:[87] if industrial action is to be seen as a means available to trade unions in a voluntary system to promote the interests of their members, is it compatible with that right that employees can be dismissed for taking part in a strike? The case thus raises the question whether the risk of dismissal is consistent with the court's agreement with the British government.

[2.52] In April 2009 the ECt HR recognised for the first time that Art 11 protects the right to strike and that State interference must be justified in accordance with Art 11(2).[88] The ruling is regarded as having potentially very significant implications for UK law; indeed:

> it is a decision of one of the most important courts in the world, a decision that in principle will have direct implications for the law in at least 47 countries of the Council of Europe in which some 800 million people live.[89]

The ECt HR held that the right to collective bargaining is 'an essential element' of the right to freedom of association in Art 11 and embedded the jurisprudence of the International Labour Organisation and the European Social Charter into that right.

---

85.   *UNISON v United Kingdom* [2002] IRLR 497.

86.   *Wilson and Palmer* [2003] IRLR 128.

87.   Ewing, 'The Implications of *Wilson* and *Palmer*' (2003) ILJ 1.

88.   *Enerji Yapi-Yol Sen v Turkey* Application No 68959/01, 21 April 2009. Noted in Dukes, 'The Right to Strike under UK Law: Not Much More than a Slogan?' (2010) 39 ILJ 82.

89.   Ewing and Hendy, 'The Dramatic Implications of *Demir and Baykara*' (2010) 39 ILJ 2, 47. The authors consider the apparent collision between trade union rights established by the ECt HR and trade union liabilities under EU law by the *Viking* and *Laval* judgments.

Both of these recognise a right to strike. Should the ECt HR, in future cases, interpret the substance and nature of the right to strike under Art 11 by reference to these sources and this jurisprudence, Irish law may be challenged in a number of respects.[90]

INCIDENTAL INFRINGEMENT OF CONSTITUTIONAL RIGHTS

[2.53] Direct and indirect infringement of constitutional rights were mentioned by Walsh J in *Meskell* (above, para **2.24**). Action involving either will be *ultra vires*. The question of incidental infringement arose in *Gannon v Duffy*[91] where an interlocutory injunction was refused employees in a dispute between four bricklayers and officers of the Ancient Guild of Incorporated Brick and Stonelayers and Allied Trade Unions (the Guild). The employees obtained employment on terms alleged by the Guild to contravene a Registered Employment Agreement under Pt III of the Industrial Relations Act 1946 made by the Construction Industry Federation (CIF). The employer belonged to the CIF as did the Guild and some other trade unions. The Guild sought to restrain the employer from acting in breach of the Agreement. A picket was placed on the employer's site. The employees sought to restrain this activity, which was directed at their employment on the site. Three days later the employer lawfully terminated their contracts of employment.

[2.54] McWilliam J (High Court) expressed the view that once there was a genuine trade dispute and that the action was taken in contemplation or furtherance of it, it was not 'material' that action taken in furtherance of the dispute brought additional advantages to the defendants or disadvantages or hardships to the plaintiffs. He distinguished a situation where defendants act for the sole purpose of imposing these disadvantages or hardships on plaintiffs. This suggests that the incidental infringement of constitutional rights, in the course of the exercise of other lawful rights, may not be actionable.

[2.55] Kerr and Whyte disagree.[92] Relevant case law indicates that, in general, courts proceed on the basis that once there are any infringements of constitutional rights, established remedies will follow irrespective of the mental element involved.[93] The authors suggest that the system of providing immunities against common law liabilities to those who organise or participate in industrial action is in danger of being undermined by plaintiffs, whether employers, employees or members of the public at large, claiming that their constitutional rights are being infringed by industrial action. This process would be accelerated if violation of constitutional rights were actionable without proof of a specific mental element.

---

90. See *Metrobus v Unite The Union* [2009] EWCA Civ 829, in which counsel for the defence tried unsuccessfully to convince the Court of Appeal of the merits of *Demir and Baykara*.

91. *Gannon v Duffy* [1983] IEHC 46.

92. 'Labour Law, Trade Disputes and the Constitution' (1984) 6 DULJ (ns) 187.

93. They cite cases re exclusion of evidence eg *Peo (AG) v O'Brien* [1965] IR 102; and re conflicts of constitutional rights eg *Crowley v Ireland* [1980] IR 102.

If the process is to be checked, Kerr and Whyte[94] suggest that it should not be done by watering down the status of constitutional rights but rather by raising the status of what the defendants are doing, an argument not canvassed in *Gannon v Duffy*. Instead of holding that to be actionable a violation must be deliberate, defendants should be viewed as exercising constitutional rights, whether a right to assemble, to strike, or so on. The courts would then have to balance conflicting rights.

CONSTITUTIONALITY OF IMMUNITIES

[2.56] This chapter ends by raising the Industrial Relations Act 1990's constitutional health. In his *Foreword* to Kerr and Whyte's *Irish Trade Union Law*[95], Walsh J wrote:

> It is clear that in many respects trade unions enjoy a privileged position under the law. Some of their activities are prevented from being unlawful, as they would be if they had been engaged in by other persons or bodies of persons. Certain immunities against suit are available which are not available to other persons or bodies. Ireland has a written Constitution which in general leans against inequality and discrimination. Consequently there must be a question mark over the idea that any person or body of persons can be above the law. This is particularly so in respect of activities which would bring any other person or body of persons into conflict with the criminal law.

In *White v Ireland*[96] the plaintiff challenged the constitutional validity of ss 3 and 4 of the Trade Disputes Act 1906. He claimed that s 3 was inconsistent with Art 40.1 (Equality before the Law)[97] and Art 40.3 (Personal Rights).[98] He also claimed that s 4, which prohibited actions in tort against trade unions, was inconsistent with the said Articles and with Art 34.3, which invests the High Court with full original jurisdiction in and power to determine all matters whether of law or fact, civil or criminal. His contention was that the Act of 1906, and in particular ss 3 and 4 thereof, ceased to be of effect on the coming into operation of the Constitution. In the end the proceedings were settled before the High Court hearing and there can be no doubt that s 13 in the Industrial Relations Act 1990 was directly influenced by this threat to the Act of 1906.

[2.57] Not long afterwards, Forde in *Constitutional Law of Ireland*[99] says it is 'conceivable' that s 4 is justified by the freedom to have trade unions, especially in the light of judges' inventiveness in discovering new heads of tortious liability, and because the immunity does not apply to a union's officers, agents or employees.

---

94. Kerr and Whyte, 'Labour Law, Trade Disputes and the Constitution' (1984) 6 DULJ (ns) 187.

95. (Professional Books, 1985).

96. *White v Ireland* (1989, unreported), HC.

97. See *Quinn's Supermarket v Attorney General* [1972] IR 1; *McMahon v Attorney General* [1972] IR 69; 105 ILTR 89; Temple Lang, 'Private Law Aspects of the Constitution' (1971) *Irish Jurist* 237; Forde, 'Equality and the Constitution' (1982) *Irish Jurist* 295; Beytagh, 'Equality under the Irish and American Constitutions: a Comparative Analysis' (1983) *Irish Jurist* 36.

98. Para **2.02** above.

99. Forde, *Constitutional Law of Ireland* (First Law).

Moreover, statute law contains a large number of provisions which 'discriminate' between persons, 'no doubt in the main on grounds which the second sentence of Art 40, s 1 might justify'. For instance, the Diplomatic Relations and Immunities Act 1967 accords immunities to diplomatic representatives.

[2.58] The threat of challenge remains. The notion that trade disputes legislation accords 'privileges' to trade unions and their representatives implies an element of unfair advantage in their favour, or at any rate an inequality. Legislation that discriminates unfairly and oppressively against the interests of either employers or employees would not survive challenge before the ordinary courts. But imbalances can be reduced by 'discrimination' where there are differences of capacity and of social function.

Chapter 3
STRIKES AND THE CONTRACT OF EMPLOYMENT

INTRODUCTION

[3.01] So much of trade disputes law concerns the effect of industrial action on the contract of employment (see in particular s 12 of the Industrial Relations Act 1990) that it is essential to say something about it as a separate issue. Irish law on the effect of strike action on the contract of employment drew no comment from the Commission of Inquiry on Industrial Relations in 1981 (para **1.29**), although there could not be a more central concern in trade disputes law. The issue has rarely been discussed judicially.

[3.02] The common law in Ireland has formulated a doctrine of 'suspension', that is, provided strikers give notice of at least the length to terminate their contracts, their employment rights and obligations are suspended and there is no breach. The implications of this are uncertain and the doctrine is limited in the range of situations to which it applies.

The doctrine of suspension may have been motivated by a desire to meet the inadequacies of the Trade Disputes Act 1906 in that the tort of intimidation was not protected at the time of its formulation. But its genesis is suspect and its existence seems to have escaped the notice of the Oireachtas. Both the Unfair Dismissals Act 1977 and the Industrial Relations Act 1990 proceeded as though the doctrine did not exist.

[3.03] This chapter begins by looking at traditional common law principles regarding strike action and asks, when does a breach of contract take place? This question is relevant in circumstances where the suspension doctrine does not apply. It then examines Irish and English case law concerning the suspension doctrine. Whether a no-strike clause could have the effect of ousting the implied term to suspend receives separate consideration, and this discussion leads to the topic of waiver. The doctrine of suspension raises several questions to which there are no ready answers, eg regarding the law on unfair dismissal of strikers. To the extent that it is still an authoritative doctrine in Ireland, it is capable of producing unwanted and unwarranted consequences in common and statute law. The chapter ends by highlighting the potential importance of the wording and context of strike notice to the liability of those participating in such action.

TRADITIONAL COMMON LAW PRINCIPLES IN RELATION TO STRIKES AND INDUSTRIAL ACTION

[3.04] Contract law may not provide the best, or even a rational, basis for distinguishing legitimate industrial action. Nonetheless, the contract of employment is, and is likely to remain, an important starting point in all cases of industrial action. When considering industrial action, whether in the form of a strike, or action short of a strike, it is important to know what an employee's rights and obligations are. Normally a lawyer will be advising on a claim against the organisers of industrial action. They may be employees of the claimant company but they are frequently full-time trade union officials who are not in the claimant's service. The claimant will be asking questions with a view to proceeding in tort but in trade disputes law contract and tort (not to mention other branches of the law) necessarily intermingle. The most relevant heads of tort liability require the tort to have been committed by unlawful means and the lawyer will look to the contract of employment to see whether there has been any breach by those taking the industrial action. If there has, this will be the most likely source of unlawful means. The effect of statute on this will form the next stage of the lawyer's enquiry.

[3.05] Civil servants are deemed to be employees for purposes of the Unfair Dismissals Acts 1977–2007 and are eligible to challenge dismissal (unless they fall into the category of civil servants dismissed by the government).[1] For the purposes of these Acts, a 'contract of employment' means 'such arrangements as are made by the Minister for Finance under s 17 of the Civil Service Regulation Act 1956, together with such further terms and conditions of service which apply to the civil servant concerned, made in respect of a particular Department … which extend or alter the arrangements under the said s 17.'[2]

'Strikes'

[3.06] The Court of Appeal described the term 'strike' in *Tramp Shipping Corporation v Greenwich Marine Inc*[3] as a concerted stoppage of work done with a view to improving the wages or conditions of workers or to give vent to a grievance or make a protest about something or to support or sympathise with others in such endeavours. For the purposes of the Industrial Relations act 1990, Pt II, 'strike' is defined in s 8 (the definition is found also in the Payment of Wages Act 1991) as follows:

> A cessation of work by any number or body of workers acting in combination, or a concerted refusal or a refusal under a common understanding of any number of workers to continue to work for their employer done as a means of compelling their employer or any person, or to aid other workers in compelling their employer, to accept or not to accept terms or conditions of or affecting employment.

The legal meaning of the term for the purposes of this chapter is not limited to this definition. The effect of strike action on the contract of employment is explored in para **3.09**.

---

1. Unfair Dismissals Act 1977, s 2(1)(h).
2. Unfair Dismissals Act 1977, s 2A(3). See Redmond, 'Accountability and Dismissal in the Civil Service' *Journal of British and Irish Law Librarians* (OUP, 2005) reprinted in (December 2005) IELJ, and Redmond, 'New Civil Service Disciplinary Code' (2007) 4(2) IELJ 42.
3. *Tramp Shipping Corporation v Greenwich Marine Inc* [1975] 2 All ER 989. See generally, Brannick, Doyle and Kelly, 'Industrial Conflict' in Murphy and Roche (eds), *Irish Industrial Relations in Practice* (2nd edn, Oak Tree Press, 1997), pp 299–325; Wallace, Gunnigle and McMahon, *Industrial Relations in Ireland* (3rd edn, Gill & Macmillan, 2004), pp 213–237.

'Industrial action'

[3.07] 'Industrial action' is separately defined in s 9 of the Act of 1990 and, in contrast to its definition in the Unfair Dismissals Act 1977, s 1(1) (para **3.29**), is not confined to 'lawful' acts:

> Any action which affects, or is likely to affect, the terms or conditions, whether express or implied of a contract and which is taken by any number or body of workers acting in combination or under a common understanding as a means of compelling their employer, or to aid other workers in compelling their employer, to accept or not to accept terms or conditions of or affecting employment.

The effect of industrial action on the contract of employment can assume considerable legal importance. Ewing has said:

> [A]lmost all forms of industrial action (with the possible exception in some cases of a refusal to work voluntary overtime) will be a breach of contract by the individuals concerned, for so wide will be the powers of the employer under the express and implied terms of the contract of employment.[4]

A refusal to work overtime or effect new work changes may or may not be unlawful: all will depend on whether a duty to work overtime or carry out the changes existed in the contract of employment.[5] This in itself may be contentious between the parties, particularly if the term is implied rather than express. But breaches of contract will almost certainly be committed in circumstances involving withdrawal of co-operation,[6] a work to rule,[7] go-slow[8] and 'blacking' or secondary picketing.[9] Where an employee is engaged in industrial action in breach of contract, there is English authority that the employer is not obliged to pay wages or salary during the period of the breach.[10] The implied obligation of mutual trust and confidence which has developed in recent years

---

4.   Ewing, *The Right to Strike* (OUP, 1991) at 9.

5.   See *Power Packing Casemakers Ltd v Faust* [1983] 2 All ER 166; *Coates v Modern Methods and Material Ltd* [1982] 3 All ER 946; *Naylor v Orton and Smith Ltd* [1983] ICR 665; *Camden Exhibition and Display v Lynott* [1965] 3 All ER 28.

6.   See *Secretary of State for Employment v ASLEF* [1972] 2 All ER 949.

7.   *Secretary of State for Employment v ASLEF* [1972] 2 All ER 962.

8.   *Drew v St Edmundsbury Borough Council* [1980] ICR 513.

9.   Examples include *Stratford v Lindley* [1964] 3 All ER 102; *Torquay Hotel Company Ltd v Cousins* [1969] 1 All ER 522; *Heatons Transport (St Helens) Ltd v Transport and General Workers Union* [1973] AC 15; *Nolan Transport v Halligan & Others* [1995] ELR 1; see para **10.58** *et seq* further.

10   *Miles v Wakefield Metropolitan District Council* [1987] AC 529; *Wiluszynski v Tower Hamlets London Borough Council* [1989] ICR 493 followed in *Loftus v Ulster Bank* (1995) 10 JISLL 47; *Maher v AIB* [1998] ELR 209 and *O'Donovan v AIB* [1998] ELR 209. These decisions should now be reviewed in light of *Spackman v London Metropolitan University* [2007] IRLR 744, where Recorder Luba QC ruled that a 30% deduction could be made from the plaintiff's salary for periods when she had only given partial performance of her contract of employment. An employee engaging in collective industrial action takes the risk that she may be paid nothing at all even if she presents for work and does some or most of her ordinary duties. (contd .../)

has yet to be invoked in Ireland by an employer in circumstances of industrial action.[11] The implied term has the potential significantly to increase the unlawfulness of industrial action.

[3.08] Recent decades have seen novel forms of industrial action the lawfulness of which has not been the subject of a full hearing before the High Court. For example, during the Bank dispute in early 1992, a Directive issued from the Irish Bank Officials Association to its members that they were not to apply, collect or process fees, charges or commissions in respect of products or services listed in an accompanying circular. Earlier the union had initiated the first phase of their industrial action comprising the banning of all sales or referrals of assurance and insurance products in all banks and the banning of attendance outside the hours of 9:30 am and 5:45 pm each day.

Giving notice of industrial action short of strike cannot alter the legal consequences as to whether the action constitutes a breach or not.[12]

STRIKES: WHEN DOES A BREACH OF CONTRACT TAKE PLACE?

[3.09] Strike action may be preceded by some form of notice or by none. Notice may be given by or on behalf of the striking workers. When does a breach of contract take place? There will be no breach where the notice given is in terms of a notice to *terminate* the contract and is of the required length and the employee works out the notice before ceasing work. Here the contract is fulfilled according to its terms.[13]

[3.10] Where no or inadequate notice is given, a breach of the contract of employment occurs. If notice of intention to strike is given (not notice to terminate the contract) then whether it is shorter[14] or (possibly) longer than the notice required to terminate, there is likely *prima facie* to have been a breach. This derives from a straightforward

---

10.   (contd) Recorder Luba QC further ruled that *quantum meruit* could not realistically apply in the context of collective industrial action short of a strike. In *Cooper v Isle of Wight College* [2008] IRLR 744 the claimants took part in a one-day strike for which a deduction was made from salaries. The issue was the quantum. Blake J regarded the correct test as whether the employee could sue for wages withheld rather than the overall losses of the employer by reason of the partial non-performance. Strikers lose their entitlement to unemployment benefit or assistance: Social Welfare (Consolidation) Act 2005, ss 68 and 147 – a person who has lost employment by reason of a 'stoppage of work' due to a trade dispute at his or her place of employment is disqualified from receiving certain social welfare payments. Application may be made to the Social Welfare Tribunal, which may consider, *inter alia*, whether a person was deprived of employment 'through some act or omission on the part of the employer concerned which amounted to unfair or unjust treatment'. See also fn 47.

11.   See Redmond, 'The Implied Obligation of Mutual Trust and Confidence – A Common Law Action for "Unfair" Dismissal?' (2009) IELJ Vol 6 No 2, 36.

12.   *Bowes & Partners Ltd v Press* [1894] 1 QB 202.

13.   There are, however, attendant disadvantages. A worker who gives notice will lose the possibility of making a claim for redundancy or for unfair dismissal.

14.   As in *Doran v Lennon* [1945] IR 315.

application of general contract principles. Remedies for any such breach will include damages for breach of contract (for which strikers and trade unions have no immunity), rescission and/or deductions from wages.

[3.11] Most frequently a strike is organised without giving notice of termination of the contract of employment. Instead strike notice is given, ie notice of intention to withdraw labour upon a particular date unless by that time the employees' demands have been met. The length of strike notice may vary but, except in the case of a lightning strike, it is usual for some notice, though not usually a long one, to be given of the intention to strike. Only exceptionally has either side involved in a strike any expectation or wish that at the end of the strike, relations between them will have been severed. On one view the law of contract should give effect to the intention of the parties if that intention is not to break or terminate the contract for the period of the strike. Thus the Donovan Commission[15] in 1968:

> Where notice of a stoppage of work is given, not being a notice to terminate the contract, it is true that the employees concerned are in breach of the contract. Under that contract they are bound to go on rendering service until some event has occurred upon which it was agreed that the contract should end, as for example the giving of due notice to terminate it. Yet by ceasing to work without giving such a notice, the employees are not, it is argued, really intending to repudiate the contract altogether – they simply want it modified. Nor does the employer in such a case regard the cessation of work as a repudiation of the contract entitling him to rescind it. He really wants the contract to continue and he hopes to be able to come to terms over the modification which his employees are seeking. Only if this hope is finally dashed will questions of repudiation and consequent rescission arise.

> Similarly when due notice to end the contract is given prior to the strike the notice being to the effect that the employee will cease work on its expiry, neither side, it is said, really wishes to put an end to the contract. One party simply wants different terms; the other hopes to come to some agreement about them.[16]

These ideas, as we shall see, are reflected in Irish law.

THE SUSPENSION DOCTRINE

[3.12] In Ireland the doctrine of suspension was developed by a majority of the Supreme Court in *Becton Dickinson & Co Ltd v Lee*.[17] Becton Dickinson (the company) had provided by agreement that if a workman entered into employment with it he would have to be a member of a designated union. That might mean he could not remain a member of another union. Shortly after the commencement of employment the company requested that the six defendants transfer to the unions mentioned in their contracts. Instead of complying, the defendants authorised the Amalgamated Union of

---

15.   Donovan Commission Report Cmnd 3623 (1968).

16.   Paras 939–40.

17.   *Becton Dickinson & Co Ltd v Lee* [1973] IR 1.

Engineering and Foundry Workers (AEF) to represent them. A recognition dispute arose whereupon the AEF gave one week's notice of strike action to the company. At the end of the week, members of the union picketed the company's factory. The company sought a restraining injunction and although they were successful in the High Court, they failed in the Supreme Court where the defendants were held entitled to the protection of the Trade Disputes Act 1906.

[3.13] The company submitted that the strike was in breach of contract and therefore unlawful and not protected by ss 1, 2 or 3 of the Trade Disputes Act 1906 (Appendix). In support of this submission, they relied on cases analysed in later chapters, in particular *Cooper v Millea*,[18] *Riordan v Butler*,[19] *Rookes v Barnard*[20] and *Stratford v Lindley*.[21] To sustain their argument, the company had to establish a breach of contract by the strikers. Tangentially, if there was breach, the defendants would also have unprotected liability for threatening to strike in breach of contract; in other words, for intimidation. In Britain, following *Rookes v Barnard*,[22] in which the House of Lords developed the tort of intimidation (**Ch 8**), parliament extended the immunities to cover this wrong in the Trade Disputes Act 1965. The law in Ireland was not similarly amended until the Industrial Relations Act 1990. The existence of a wide open liability for threatening to strike in breach of contract may have been a factor influencing the suspension doctrine in *Becton Dickinson*.

[3.14] Walsh J reiterated that a contract is not discharged by unilateral breach unless the contract itself so provides or unless the aggrieved party chooses to and is able to terminate it upon that ground. O'Byrne J had indicated in *Riordan v Butler*[23] that if notice terminating the contract of employment had been given in the trade dispute before him, the result which the defendants had desired to achieve (dismissal of a particular employee) could have been lawfully achieved. Walsh J[24] did not think this should be taken as stating that the only way in which the defendants could have achieved their result lawfully was to have terminated the contract:

> I think his mind was really running on the question of adequate notice being given before such action was taken. ... It has long been recognised that strike action or threats of strike action ... in the case of a trade dispute do not involve any wrongful action on the part of employees whose service contracts are not regarded as being or intended to be thereby terminated. So much was stated by Lord Watson in his speech in *Allen v Flood* and has, as I believe, been since consistently followed – see eg per Lord Sterndale MR in *White v Riley*. The

---

18.   *Cooper v Millea* [1938] IR 749.

19.   *Riordan v Butler* [1940] IR 347.

20.   *Rookes v Barnard* [1964] AC 1129.

21.   *Stratford v Lindley* [1965] AC 269.

22.   *Rookes v Barnard* [1964] AC 1129.

23.   *Riordan v Butler* [1940] IR 347.

24.   *Becton Dickinson & Co Ltd v Lee* [1973] IR 1 at 32.

words of Donovan LJ to which Lord Evershed was referring appear in *Rookes v Barnard* [1963] 1 QB 623 at 482, as follows:

> There can be few strikes which do not involve a breach of contract by the strikers. Until a proper notice is given to terminate their contracts of service, and the notice has expired, they remain liable under its terms to perform their bargain. It would, however, be affectation not to recognise that in the majority of strikes no such notice to terminate the contract is either given or expected. The strikers do not want to give up their job; they simply went to be paid more for it or to secure some other advantage in connection with it. The employer does not want to lose his labour force; he simply wants to resist the claim. Not till the strike has lasted some time, and no settlement is in sight, does one usually read that the employers have given notice that unless the men return to work their contracts will be terminated, and they will be dismissed.

[3.15] In *Stratford v Lindley*[25] Lord Denning MR[26] dealt with the everyday case where there is no special contract forbidding a strike and where the threat to strike does not come from the prospective contract-breakers but from others on their behalf:

> Suppose that a trade union officer gives a 'strike notice.' He says to an employer 'we are going to call a strike on Monday week unless you increase the men's wages by £1 a week' – or 'unless you dismiss yonder man who is not a member of the union' – or 'unless you cease to deal with such and such a customer' … The 'strike notice' is nothing more nor less than a notice that the men will not come to work … In these circumstances it seems to me that the trade union officer by giving the 'strike notice' issues a threat to the employer; he threatens to induce the men to break their contracts of employment unless the employer complies with the demand. That is a threat to commit a tort. It is clear intimidation …

[3.16] Lord Denning MR developed the argument in *Morgan v Fry*.[27] He posed the question whether strike notice is a threat of a breach of contract. He pointed out that if there had been a full week's notice by the men concerned to terminate their employment altogether, it would not have been a threat to commit a breach of contract. Every worker was entitled to terminate his contract of employment by giving a week's notice. But in the case in question the strike notice was not a notice to terminate the employment but a notice that they would not work with non-unionists. It looked very like a threat of breach of contract and therefore intimidation, said the Master of the Rolls:

> But there must be something wrong … for if that argument were correct, it would do away with the right to strike in this country. It has been held for over sixty years that workmen have a right to strike (including therein a right to say that they will not work with non-unionists) provided they give sufficient notice beforehand; and a notice is sufficient if it is at least as long as a notice required to terminate the contract.

---

25.   *Stratford v Lindley* [1965] AC 269.

26.   At 285.

27.   *Morgan v Fry* [1968] 2 QB 710.

He concluded[28] that if the strike notice given is not shorter than the legal period for termination of the contract itself, the strike is not unlawful. As to the legal basis on which a strike notice of proper length is held to be lawful:

> I think it is this: the men can leave their employment altogether by giving a week's notice to terminate it. That would be a strike which would be perfectly lawful. If a notice to terminate it is lawful, surely a lesser notice, lesser in the sense of its objective, not duration, is lawful: such as a notice that 'we will not work alongside a non-unionist.' After all if the employer should retort to the men, 'we will not accept this notice as lawful, the men can say 'then we will give this notice to terminate.' The truth is that neither employer nor workmen wish to take the drastic action of termination if it can be avoided. The men do not wish to scatter their labour force to the four winds. Each side is therefore content to accept a 'strike notice' of proper length as lawful. *It is an implication read into the contract by the modern law as to trade disputes.* If a strike takes place, the contract of employment is not terminated. It is suspended during the strike and revived again when the strike is over. [Emphasis added.]

[3.17] In *Becton Dickinson* Walsh J agreed with the principle expressed by Lord Denning. There is to be read into every contract of employment an implied term that the service of a strike notice of a length not shorter than would be required for notice to terminate the contract would not in itself constitute a breach of the contract because the right to do so would be an implied term of it. The judge did not analyse the nature of the contract of employment during strike action. On the basis that he agreed with Lord Denning, we may take it Walsh J implied that the contract is suspended. But the legal treatment of rights and benefits relating to the contract of employment during a strike preceded by the correct notice is far from clear (para **3.27** *et seq*).

Walsh J in *Becton Dickinson* was speaking for two of his brethren while Lord Denning's was a lone voice in *Morgan*.

[3.18] The cases referred to above and the examples cited by judges involve strike notice being given – at times by the workers concerned, at times by the union on their behalf. Failure to realise that further questions may arise in the latter context is a criticism of these cases, yet to be addressed in Ireland. The chapter closes with the English case of *Boxfoldia Ltd v National Graphical Association*,[29] in which this distinction appears, a forerunner of what may appear in a future Irish case.

'NO-STRIKE' AND 'LOYALTY' CLAUSES

[3.19] An implied term to suspend the contract could not be read into an agreement containing an express provision to the contrary or where such a contrary provision would have to be read into it by necessary implication. This issue arose, though not decisively, in *Bates v Model Bakery Ltd*.[30] Following an unofficial strike, a document setting out an appeal procedure for resolving future grievances was drawn up between

---

28. At 728.
29. *Boxfoldia Ltd v National Graphical Association* [1988] IRLR 383.
30. *Bates v Model Bakery Ltd* [1993] 1 IR 359.

the employer and a shop steward. Under the agreement, no industrial action was to be taken until 14 days from the issue of a Labour Court recommendation. In the background was an ongoing dispute about arrears of wages. The general secretary of the plaintiffs' trade union wrote to the employer, after the agreement was signed, giving notice that if the moneys owed were not paid by close of business a fortnight later, the plaintiffs would commence industrial action. In due course a strike began. The company responded in writing alleging that the plaintiffs were in breach of the agreed disputes procedure and a further letter stated that the ongoing strike amounted to a frustration by the plaintiffs of their contract of employment. The bakery ceased business permanently and the plaintiffs claimed statutory redundancy before the Employment Appeals Tribunal. The Tribunal refused the claims, finding the plaintiffs had been in breach of the agreement. The High Court (Lardner J) allowed the appeal, holding that the plaintiffs had not frustrated their contracts of employment but had been dismissed on grounds of redundancy. The matter then went to the Supreme Court which upheld the court below and remitted the case to the Tribunal. The court found that the disputes procedure did not apply to the instant dispute which pre-dated the agreement. The agreement clearly referred to the resolution of future disputes. O Flaherty J, with whom the other members of the court agreed, noted that there was no attempt at the hearing before the Supreme Court to argue that the strike action was in any category of case within the doctrine of frustration of contract. Neither had there been any serious attempt to suggest the plaintiffs had repudiated their contracts of employment by going on strike. Such a proposition would be untenable, he remarked, in the light of *Becton Dickinson*.[31] Egan J recognised that 'to some extent' the Supreme Court in that case had been following the minority judgment of Lord Denning[32] in *Morgan v Fry*.[33] He reminded the court that Walsh J in *Becton Dickinson* had stated that the implied term:

> ... could not be read into a contract where there is an express provision in the contract to the contrary or where by necessary implication a provision to the contrary must be read into the contract.

But:

> Even if the 'agreement' could be read as containing any additional term to be added to the contract of employment it did not have this effect in regard to disputes which had pre-dated it.[34]

Employers, advertently or otherwise, have not tackled the potential of *Becton Dickinson*: witness the absence of clauses ousting the doctrine of suspension in industrial relations practice.

[3.20] As to the proper period of notice to terminate a contract of employment, the ordinary law of contract applies. Absent an express term of greater length in the

---

31. Quoting Walsh J at 35 and 36 of the judgment at *Becton Dickinson & Co Ltd v Lee* [1973] IR 1.
32. At 372.
33. *Morgan v Fry* [1968] 2 QB 710.
34. At 372.

contract, the minimum period of notice required of an employee who after 13 weeks' employment has been in continuous service for less than two years, is one week under the Minimum Terms and Conditions of Employment Act 1973, s 6. Periods of statutory minimum notice are not given contractual effect by the Act of 1973 although they are often incorporated expressly in individual contracts of employment.

A blanket period of 2 weeks' notice is generally given in strike notices. This may or may not satisfy the legal requirement of notice sufficient to terminate the relevant employees' contracts of employment. All will depend on the facts.

[3.21] The most obvious express term ousting the implied term permitting suspension would be a no-strike clause. *Rookes v Barnard*[35] is persuasive authority for the view that, when there is an express no-strike clause in a contract of employment, service of strike notice is a breach of the contract so long as the contract is in existence. Recently no-strike clauses have been mooted for employees working in essential services in Ireland (para **1.45**).

[3.22] In *Becton Dickinson* the contract of employment did not contain a no-strike clause. Nonetheless the company sought to oust the implied term of suspension by calling in aid other implied terms. They submitted that because of the express provision in the contract of employment to the effect that the defendant employees would join a designated union, it was an implied term of the contract that they would not take strike action to have that term varied or deleted and it was also to be implied that, on entering into such contracts, the defendants had agreed that they would not seek recognition for their own union, the AEF, or take any strike action or picket in support of a claim requiring the company to recognise the AEF. Walsh J declined to accept the first contention: because any particular term of a contract can be shown to be one without which there would have been no employment offered, did not mean there must necessarily be implied an agreement not to strike in respect of it:

> An express 'no strike' clause in a contract is itself such an unusual feature of a contract of employment and is such an apparent departure from the long established 'right to strike' that a court would be slow to imply it where it is not expressly included in the contract or where it is not a necessary implication; a court would probably only do so in cases where there was some particular provision for machinery dealing with disputes, the provision being so phrased as to give rise to the implication that it had been agreed between the parties that no other course would be adopted during the currency of the contract.[36]

[3.23] The judge expressly reserved his opinion on whether a withdrawal of labour in breach of contract, whether or not there is a no-strike clause in the contract, constitutes a 'trade dispute' within the meaning of s 5(3) of the Act of 1906 (now s 8 of the 1990 Act) and whether picketing in furtherance of it is or is not lawful within the meaning of s 2 (now s 11). Subsequent case law, albeit at an interlocutory stage, has borne out the judge's reservations. It is usual for an application for an interlocutory injunction to

35.   *Rookes v Barnard* [1964] AC 1129.

36.   At 38.

succeed where the defendant strikers have acted in breach of contract, whether by giving no or inadequate notice of termination or, for example, where agreed procedures have not been exhausted.[37] 'No-strike' clauses are generally found in collective agreements on disputes resolution. The clause must be capable of being incorporated into the individual contracts of employment of the workers affected by it in accordance with general principles. It must also have been consented to by the workers concerned (usually as a result of custom and practice) if they are to be bound by the terms of any such collective agreement.[38] See further para **9.73** *et seq.*

[3.24] Recent national agreements between the social partners and government, the *Programme for Competitiveness and Work 1994*, *Partnership 2000*, the *Programme for Prosperity and Fairness 2000*, *Sustaining Progress 2003* and *Towards 2016* all contain clauses precluding strikes or other forms of industrial action by trade unions, employees or employers in respect of any matters covered by the respective agreements, 'where the employer or trade union concerned is acting in accordance with the provisions of this Agreement'. None of these clauses, which are agreed by the social partners at national level, could be said to bind workers in a legally enforceable way and the legal principles in para **3.23** above apply to their implementation at local level.

[3.25] An employer faced by the prospect of industrial action or following same may request its employees to sign loyalty letters, ie letters of undertaking, variously worded, not to engage in industrial action. In *Chappell v Times Newspapers Ltd*[39] the question arose as to whether it was lawful to dismiss employees who refused to sign such undertakings. It was suggested that the relevant question is whether the workers' conduct 'evinces an intention no longer to be bound by their contracts of employment'.[40] If it does, then 'they could properly be said to be repudiating their contracts. But the failure to give such an undertaking might not, by itself, be sufficient.'[41]

---

37.   The High Court found the existence of a serious issue for trial concerning picketing in breach of contract, ie a registered agreement containing a no-strike clause, in *Daru Blocklaying Ltd and Another v BATU and Others* [2003] ILRM 227. The court adverted to the apparently differing views between on the one hand the Supreme Court in *Becton Dickinson & Co Ltd v Lee* [1973] IR 1, Kenny J in *Irish Biscuits Ltd v Miley* (3 April 1972, unreported), HC followed by him in *Merchants Warehousing Co v McGrath* (27 April 1974, unreported), HC (Kenny J) and in *Waltham Electronics Ireland Ltd v Doyle* (15 November 1974, unreported), HC (Kenny J), and the views of O'Higgins J (then a High Court judge) in *Kire Manufacturing Co Ltd v O'Leary* High Court 1974 No 551P, 29 April 1974. Other cases where picketing in violation of a disputes procedure have been found unlawful are *Kayfoam Wolfson Ltd v Woods* (4 June 1980, unreported), HC (para **9.74**) and *Acton and Jordan Ltd v Duff* (12 July 1982, unreported), HC.

38.   *Goulding Chemicals Co v Bolger* [1977] IR 211.

39.   *Chappell v Times Newspapers Ltd* [1975] 2 All ER 233.

40.   At 238.

41.   At 238.

WAIVER

[3.26] Suppose it were argued that a no-strike clause were itself unconstitutional as inconsistent with the right to withdraw labour, assuming the right ever becomes secure in constitutional law (para **2.39**); would it be possible by express contractual agreement to waive one's constitutional right?

In *G v An Bord Uchtála*[42] waiver of constitutional rights was referred to in the Supreme Court as a distinct possibility. Walsh J cautioned[43] that before anybody may be said to have surrendered or abandoned his constitutional rights it must be shown that he is aware of what the rights are and of what he is doing. Furthermore, the action taken must be such as could reasonably lead to the clear and unambiguous inference that such was the intention of the person who is alleged to have either surrendered or abandoned the constitutional rights.[44] On the assumption that the right to strike is constitutionally guaranteed (which is doubtful), any agreement containing a no-strike clause would have to subscribe to these standards.

DIFFICULTIES WITH THE DOCTRINE OF SUSPENSION

[3.27] The Donovan Commission in Britain reviewed the doctrine of suspension of the contract of employment as a result of strike notice.[45] It looked upon this doctrine as in practice creating a new right of unilateral suspension, since either side to the contract of employment could exercise the right without the consent of the other: the employee by striking, the employer by locking out. The Commission's report, which came too early to advert to the doctrine in *Morgan v Fry*, contended that considerable technical difficulties would follow if unilateral suspension became part of the law. For example:

(a)   To what strikes would it apply? To unofficial and unconstitutional as well as to official strikes? How would strikes be defined for this purpose?

(b)   Would it also apply to other industrial action such as a ban on overtime in breach of contract or to a 'go-slow'?

(c)   Would it apply to 'lightning strikes' or only strikes where at least some notice was given, though less than the notice required for termination of the contract? If so, what length of notice should be required?

---

42.   *G v An Bord Uchtála* (1979) 113 ILTR 25.

43.   At 48.

44.   Whether there is the requisite awareness and intention in a pre-entry closed shop will depend on the facts. See Redmond, 'Constitutional Law – Waiver of Rights' (1979–80) DULR 104; Temple Lang, 'Private Law Aspects of the Irish Constitution' (1971) Vol V, Ir Jur 237, 256. A pre-entry closed shop is likely to be incompatible with the European Convention on Human Rights (para **2.25**).

45.   Cmnd 3623, 1968, paras 936–952.

(d)   Would the new law apply to the gas, water and electricity industries, which are subject to the special provisions of s 4 of the Conspiracy and Protection of Property Act 1875?[46] What would be the position under s 3 of the same Act?

(e)   Would the employer still be allowed instantly to dismiss an employee for grave misconduct during the course of the strike?

(f)   Would 'contracting out' of the new law be permissible, eg in collective bargains or in individual contracts of employment?

(g)   Would strikers be free to take up other employment while the contract was suspended? If so, would any obligations of secrecy in the suspended contract be suspended too?

(h)   If all efforts to end the strike failed, upon what event would the suspension of the contract cease and be replaced by termination?[47]

The Commission emphasised that this list was not exhaustive. Should the doctrine extend to secondary and other types of strike action outside the immediate grievance context? Suppose union officials at plant A seek active support from trade unionists at plant B to bring pressure to bear on the employer at plant A who is in dispute with his workers at that plant. If the members employed at plant B take strike action in an effort to force their employer who is, let us suppose, a supplier to the employer in dispute and if they serve lawful strike notice, can we say they have suspended their contracts? If we can, then can we say the trade union officials at plant A are liable for procuring breaches of commercial contracts by unlawful means? It would seem we cannot. Or should one confine the doctrine of suspension to the primary parties in dispute? But why should the parties' intentions there be any different from their colleagues who are striking in support, when it comes to a desire to hold on to their employment? And the employer's intention must be the same in all cases, namely, not to scatter his labour force to the four winds.

[3.28] The Commission questioned the basis of the doctrine of suspension, namely, that it represents the true intention of the parties. When an employee goes on strike in breach of contract, it may well be that he does not intend finally to end his contract of employment. But this is true of many other breaches of contract. Where strikes are concerned, the parties will, as a rule, try to settle their differences. When notice is given pursuant to the contract to terminate it, again it may be true that the parties hope the employment relationship will not be impugned for good. But here there will be no choice at the end of the strike but to enter into another contract on new terms. There seems to be no justification for ignoring the plain terms of the notice.

---

46.   Para **6.03**.
47.   See Kerr and Whyte, *Irish Trade Union Law* (Professional Books, 1985) at 209 who believe that 'with the exception of the last question, all [of the questions in para **3.27**] can be satisfactorily answered'.

Moreover, there is the problem of rights or benefits that depend on continuity of service.[48] In particular, difficulties might be envisaged in regard to benefits provided for by the contract of employment itself. The Commission concluded:

> In our opinion a fundamental change in the law such as the creation by statute of a unilateral right to suspend a contract of employment should not be introduced except after prior examination of the whole problem and its possible repercussions by an expert Committee. The same Committee might also examine the question whether it would be practicable to enact that every notice given by an employee to cease work which was not less in length than a notice required to determine the contract should, in the absence of any intention clearly expressed, be regarded as a notice of termination of the contract rather than as a notice of intended breach.

Undoubtedly the doctrine has repercussions, which seem to have escaped the attention of parliament. Two will now be mentioned.

Unfair Dismissals Act 1977

[3.29] The first repercussion, in the Unfair Dismissals Act 1977, is highlighted by Redmond in *Dismissal Law in Ireland*.[49] Section 5(2) of the Unfair Dismissals Act, as amended by the Unfair Dismissals (Amendment) Act 1993,[50] provides that:

> The dismissal of an employee for taking part in a strike[51] or other industrial action[52] shall be deemed, for the purposes of this Act, to be an unfair dismissal, if—
>
> (a)   one or more employees of the same employer who took part in the strike or other industrial action were not dismissed for taking part, or

---

48.   As Irish law stands, the First Schedule to the Minimum Notice and Terms of Employment Act 1973 provides in para 11 that if in any week or part of a week, an employee is absent from his employment because he was taking part in a strike in relation to the trade or business in which he is employed that week shall not count as a period of service. Under para 13 if the strike was in a trade or business other than that in which he is employed that week counts as a period of service. There is no obligation to pay an employee engaged in industrial action: *Fuller v Minister for Agriculture, Food and Forestry* [2008] IEHC 95.

49.   Redmond, *Dismissal Law in Ireland* (Bloomsbury Professional, 2007), para 20.88. The reader is referred to paras 20.73–20.102 for full and comprehensive treatment of dismissal of those participating in strike or industrial action.

50.   See the question posed by Ewing as to whether a section such as the Unfair Dismissals Act 1977, s 5 is ECHR compatible (para **2.51**).

51.   The 'strike' in s 5(1) of the Unfair Dismissals Act 1977 is an industrial relations one:
       The cessation of work by any number or body of employees acting in combination or a concerted refusal or a refusal under a common understanding of any number of employees to continue to work for an employer, in consequence of a dispute, done as a means of compelling the employer or any employee or body of employees, or to aid other employees in compelling their employer or any employee or body of employees to accept or not to accept terms or conditions of or affecting employment.

52   'Industrial action' is defined in s 1 to mean:
       It is impossible to explain why 'lawfulness' should be required for industrial action and not for strikes (nor indeed for the definition of 'industrial action' under the Industrial Relations Act 1990). (contd .../)

(b)   one or more of such employees who were dismissed for so taking part were subsequently permitted to resume their employment on terms and conditions at least as favourable to the employees as those specified in paragraph (a) or (b) [of s 7(1) of the Act which deal with reinstatement and re-engagement respectively] and the employee was not.

[3.30] Section 5(2) of the Unfair Dismissals Act 1977 deems it unfair for an employer selectively to dismiss in an industrial dispute. To protect against potential misuse of collective dismissals of strikers, s 26 of the Protection of Employment (Exceptional Collective Redundancies and Related Matters) Act 2007 amended s 5 by inserting a new sub-s (2A),[53] which enables the rights commissioner, EAT or the Circuit Court, as the case may be, to have regard 'for that purpose only' to:

(i)   the reasonableness or otherwise of the conduct (whether by act or omission) of the employer or employee in relation to the dismissal;

(ii)   the extent (if any) of the compliance or failure to comply by the employer with the procedure referred to in s 14(1);[54]

(iii) the extent (if any) of the compliance or failure to comply by the employer or the employee with provisions of any code of practice referred to in s 7(2)(d);[55] and

(iv)   whether the parties have adhered to any agreed grievance procedures applicable to the employment in question at the time of the lock-out, strike or industrial action.

[3.31] As a result of *Becton Dickinson*[56], if a strike were preceded by notice of a length sufficient to terminate the contract with the result that, by virtue of an implied term, the contract was not actually terminated but was suspended, the strike would not be a

---

52. (contd) 'Lawfulness' may refer to the consequences of industrial action or to the acts *per se*. Several different branches of the law – criminal law, contract, constitutional law, tort – may be involved in assessing lawfulness. Statute law is frequently relevant. Given the increasing importance of implied rights and obligations in the contract of employment, no form of industrial action can safely be described as 'lawful' (para **3.07**). However, the limited meaning of 'industrial action' does not strike a complete blow to employees' rights, as dismissal for taking part in 'unlawful' industrial action could be dealt with under s 6(1) of the 1977 Act. In *Power v National Corrugated Products* [1980] UD 336 it was argued that the dismissed workers did not come within s 5 because their industrial action, namely a sit-in, constituted unlawful action, but the EAT seem to have turned a blind eye to this argument.

53. Following commitment between the social partners in *Towards 2016, Ten-Year Framework Social Partnership Agreement 2006–2015*.

54. Being the procedure the employer will follow before and for the purpose of dismissal.

55. Being any such procedure in s 14(1) or any code of practice relating to procedures concerning dismissal approved by the Minister. See Industrial Relations Act, 1990 (Code of Practice on Grievance and Disciplinary Procedures) (Declaration) Order 2000 (SI 146/2000).

56. *Becton Dickinson & Co Ltd v Lee* [1973] IR 1.

candidate for the 1977 Act at all. Dismissal under the Unfair Dismissals Act requires 'termination' of the contract of employment. A contract that is suspended would lie outside its jurisdiction. Can one end a relationship that by law is suspended? The argument could be made that, where lawful strike notice is given, an employer who purports to dismiss his workforce – selectively or otherwise – is in breach of the term implied by the Supreme Court in *Becton Dickinson*. He would not have terminated the contracts of his workers as such. If the workers decide to stay away from work in such circumstances, would this be constructive dismissal?

[3.32] Similar issues arise for the lock-out[57] from *Becton Dickinson*. Section 5(1) of the Unfair Dismissals Act 1977, as amended, deems a lock-out to be a dismissal (notwithstanding that a lock-out can be instituted without a breach of contract)[58] and deems the dismissal unfair if, after the lock-out is terminated, the employee was not permitted to resume his employment on terms and conditions at least as favourable as those specified in s 7(1)(a) and (b) (which describe reinstatement and re-engagement) and one or more other employees in the same employment were so permitted.

Suppose notice of strike action was given as described in *Becton Dickinson*. The contract by implication of law is suspended: no work, no wages. The employer recognises this and closes the premises. Although this behaviour would come within the definition above, it cannot be a lock-out because this is now deemed to be a dismissal and that would be contrary to the doctrine in *Becton Dickinson*.

None of the foregoing perplexities arise where strikers have not given notice sufficient to terminate the contracts of employment but the efficacy of unfair dismissals law should not depend on legalities.

Industrial Relations Act 1990

[3.33] Section 19 of the Industrial Relations Act 1990 deals with injunctions. As will be seen in **Ch 11**, where due notice of not less than one week has been given, it is a factor that weighs against an employer's power to obtain an injunction. But such strike action may not be injunctable if contracts are lawfully suspended. Presumably, too, the tort of procuring breach of the contract of employment cannot arise. Equally this tort cannot constitute unlawful means for other torts where unlawful means are an ingredient of the wrong. The same may be said of intimidation protected under s 12(b) of the Act of 1990. Can it be a threat to break his contract if what a worker is threatening is the exercise of an implied term to suspend?

---

57.   'Lock-out' is defined in s 5(5) of Unfair Dismissals Act 1977 to incorporate the 'golden formula' of trade disputes law:

'Lock-out' means an action which, in contemplation or furtherance of a trade dispute (within the meaning of the Industrial Relations [Acts 1946–2004]) is taken by one or more employers, whether parties to the dispute or not, and which consists of the exclusion of one or more employees from one or more factories, offices or other places of work or of the suspension of work in one or more such places or of the collective, simultaneous or otherwise connected termination or suspension of employment of a group of employees.

58.   *Express and Star Ltd v Bunday* [1987] IRLR 422 (CA).

Granted the 'one week requirement' in s 19(1) and (2) of the Act of 1990 is solely for the purposes of *ex parte* and interlocutory applications for an injunction and that the question of strike notice for the purposes of tortious liability is a separate matter. The questions posed here will arise where the notice served by the strikers and due notice of termination of their contracts of employment are one and the same.

MORGAN v FRY SIDESTEPPED IN BRITAIN

[3.34] It is not surprising that trenchant criticism of the suspension doctrine was delivered in Britain by Phillips J in *Simmons v Hoover Ltd*.[59] As the decision is one of the Employment Appeal Tribunal, *Morgan v Fry* was binding on the court and, to get round it, it was necessary to see precisely what the latter decided. Phillips J looked upon it as a case in which the court reached a desired outcome in order to avoid a particular result that would have been out of harmony by several months with the law on intimidation. Nor had there been a clear consensus between the judges. One member (Lord Denning MR) had been of opinion that the contract was suspended; another (Davies LJ) gave somewhat vague support to the view, but also thought that in some sense there was a threat to terminate the contract; and the third member (Russell LJ) found on a different ground and was of opinion that there was a threatened breach.

[3.35] The difficulties raised by the Donovan Commission (para **3.27**) could not, in the EAT's opinion, be adequately worked out except by legislation. Hence the Tribunal did not feel bound to hold that the effect of a strike, whether preceded by proper strike notice or not, was to prevent the employer from exercising the remedy which he formerly enjoyed at common law to dismiss an employee for refusing to work. The Tribunal did not wish to be taken as saying all strikes are necessarily repudiatory though usually they will be. Phillips J concluded:

> For completeness, it should be said that it was not contended by counsel for the strikers that there was here an implied term of the contract that it was to be terminated in the event of a strike. There are obvious difficulties in the way of implying such a term: cf *Cummins v Charles Connell & Co (Shipbuilding) Ltd* which, incidentally, tends to suggest that, in the absence of an express or implied term of the contract to the contrary, an employer, according to the law of Scotland may dismiss an employee who refuses to work because he is on strike.

[3.36] In *Wilkins v Cantrell and Cochrane (GB) Ltd*[60] Kilner-Brown J approved of the approach in *Simmons*. When a strike occurs:

> whatever legal description may be given to the situation the conduct of the employees gives to the employer a right to regard the conduct of the employee as a breach of the contract and to dismiss him.

In theory it is possible that strike notice could still suspend the contract if there were a term in the contract of employment giving employees the right to suspend irrespective of the length of the notice. Perhaps a collective agreement incorporated in individual contracts of employment requiring exhaustion of procedures before strike action might

---

59. *Simmons v Hoover Ltd* [1977] ICR 61.
60. *Wilkins v Cantrell and Cochrane (GB) Ltd* [1978] IRLR 483 (EAT).

entitle employees to strike without committing breach once the procedures had been exhausted. This, however, is conjecture.

Wording and context of strike notice

[3.37] This restoration of the traditional view received further refinement from the English High Court in *Boxfoldia Ltd v National Graphical Association*,[61] a case of potential importance for this jurisdiction.

The facts were that following a meeting of the NGA National Council, a national officer of the union wrote to the plaintiffs stating, 'I have been instructed to write giving the company 14 days' notice of withdrawal of all NGA members' labour from the company', a form not unfamiliar, it might be said, in dispute situations in Ireland. When the notice period expired, 39 employees failed to report to work. Later that day they were dismissed.

The plaintiffs claimed that the union induced the employees in question to break their contracts of employment and that, under the relevant British law, as this action was taken without the support of a ballot as required by statute, the union was liable in tort for damages. The NGA argued that the letter written to the employers gave contractual notice on behalf of the NGA members. Therefore it was contended that, as the contractual notice of termination for most of the employees concerned was two weeks, there had been no inducement of breach of contract for those employees.

[3.38] The judgment gives little comfort to trade unionists in dispute with an employer. Saville J held that a letter written by a national officer of the NGA to the employer giving 14 days' notice of withdrawal of all NGA members' labour could not be treated as having been written on behalf of the employees concerned giving contractual notice of the termination of their contracts of employment. There had therefore been wrongful inducement of breach.

The court held whether or not a strike notice is properly categorised as one giving notice of termination in accordance with the terms of the employment contracts depends on the meaning and effect of the words used in the context in which they were used. In considering the legal effect of a strike notice, there is no rule of law that it should be regarded as a notice of intended breach rather than a notice of contractual termination as that would presuppose that the party giving notice wished the contracts of employment to continue. The contrary view, in cases such as *Rookes v Barnard*,[62] *Stratford v Lindley*[63] and *Simmons v Hoover*[64], did not persuade the judge that there was some rule of law to be adopted in every case:

> ... for it presupposes that the party giving the notice wishes the contracts of employment to continue. To my mind this is not necessarily so, for in any given case the employees (or their union) may consider that by actually terminating the

---

61. *Boxfoldia Ltd v National Graphical Association* [1988] IRLR 383, see too *Ideal Casements v Shamsi* [1972] ICR 408; *Heaton Transport Ltd v TGWU* [1972] ICR 308.

62. *Rookes v Barnard* [1963] 1 QB 682–683, [1964] AC 1129.

63. *Stratford v Lindley* [1965] AC 269 at 285.

64. *Simmons v Hoover Ltd* [1977] ICR 61.

contracts on due notice, greater or more effective pressure can be put upon the employers, though, of course, by doing this the employees would ... lose certain unfair dismissal rights which would otherwise exist ... there is a distinction to be drawn between wanting to continue with existing but improved contracts of employment and wanting to continue (but with new contracts) the relationship of employer and employee.[65]

[3.39] In the case before the court, it was held that the NGA official's letter could not be categorised as a notice given pursuant to the termination provisions of the respective contracts of employment that the contracts would come to an end at the end of the stipulated notice period. To have this effect, the letter would have to be capable of being reasonably read and understood in its context as one written by the NGA as agent for the employees to implement the termination provisions and giving on their behalf the appropriate notice of termination. On its face the letter fulfilled none of those requirements. The letter did not purport to be written on behalf of, or as agent for, the employees[66] to bring their contracts to an end, and it did not purport on their behalf to give the appropriate termination notice stipulated in their contracts. On the contrary, the material part of the letter (extracted above) was written by the union official on the instructions of the National Council (not the employees) communicating the decision of that council (not the employees) to call an official strike on 14 days' notice.

[3.40] In calling an official strike, the union were not intending to bring the contracts of employment to a lawful end, but instead were intent upon calling the members out knowing that this would be in breach of their contracts of employment or at least being reckless as to whether or not that would result in a breach of those contracts. Hence the tort of wrongfully inducing or procuring breach had been established.

The union argued that as it had authority to call an official strike, it must have been implicit in the contract between the members and the union that it was 'authorised' by a member to take such a course. It also followed that the union was 'authorised' on behalf of its members to communicate the fact that a strike had been called, and thus (if it wished) to give to employers on behalf of its members contractual notice terminating their contracts of employment. In an *obiter* comment, the court rejected this argument:

> If the union is to act as the agent of the member in giving contractual notices under the employment contract of the latter, then authority – using this word as meaning the vesting of the union with power to act as agent for the member – cannot be established from the fact that the union is authorised in a different sense used above to instruct the member to strike or to take other forms of industrial action and to publicise that instruction.

A further important observation was made *obiter*:

> ... the doctrine of ratification should not extend so as to permit the retrospective validation of contractual termination notices of the kind under consideration, for

---

65.   *Boxfoldia Ltd v National Graphical Association* [1988] IRLR 383 at 385.

66.   It is a most exceptional occurrence for trade unions to act as agents: see *Goulding Chemicals Ltd v Bolger* [1977] IR 211, *Singh v British Steel Corp* [1974] IRLR 131.

to do so would mean that instead of being bound by the notice when given, the party concerned would be free at least during the notice period to ratify or not ...

[3.41] The relevance to Irish law of *Boxfoldia* lies both in the judge's eschewing of a rule of law on the legal effect of strike notice, which questions the Supreme Court's fundamental assumption in holding in favour of the suspension doctrine, and in his exposition of potential union liability in issuing strike notice. The issue whether or not a strike notice is categorised as one giving notice not less than would be sufficient to terminate the contract of employment will depend on the meaning and effect of the words used in the strike notice and on the context in which they are used. It would seem that notice must be worded so as to be capable of being reasonably read and understood in its context as one written by the union as agent for the employees to implement the notice provisions in their contracts and giving on their behalf the appropriate notice. Different employees may have different notice periods. Blanket notice of strike action by a union may result in the tort of wrongful inducement.

[3.42] The questions raised in this chapter suggest that the Supreme Court's endorsement of the suspension doctrine in *Becton Dickinson* merits serious reconsideration. If this does not take place, and the doctrine continues, it will be incumbent on the Oireachtas to examine it and its repercussions: otherwise judge-made and legislated solutions will be at variance with one another. The suspension doctrine is out of place in a system which does not recognise the right to strike, and particularly in a system espousing protection for unlawful action in the form of immunities.

Chapter 4

THE ECONOMIC TORTS

[4.01] In labour law, defining the economic torts has always been a challenge. Unlike other areas of the law where labels tend to be accurate, the so-called 'industrial torts' are often called one thing, but only when the liability alleged is analysed can one identify the tort involved and the authorities relevant to it. *Clerk and Lindsell on Torts*[1] use the headings 'conspiracy', 'inducing breach of contract,' 'unlawful interference' and 'intimidation'. This nomenclature is adopted in this book as a satisfactory basis for the industrial torts, the one difference being the substitution of 'causing loss by unlawful means' (the 'unlawful means' tort) for 'unlawful interference.'

[4.02] Litigation in commercial disputes has been responsible for important developments in economic torts. It is tempting for labour lawyers and trade unionists to refer to 'industrial torts' but the temptation should be avoided. It is precisely because economic torts often occur in circumstances of industrial action that judges' hostility to trade unions has led to legally undesirable extensions of liability, and to 'new' economic torts. Thus uncertainty and inconsistency have emerged as to, for example, intention, and the need to prove breach of contract, and it has adversely affected other areas of the law where the economic torts are relevant. The better approach is to see all of these torts as protecting against the infliction of economic harm, against a background of competition.[2] All of the economic torts inevitably limit the defendant's commercial behaviour.

'A TERRIBLE MESS'

[4.03] In the recent economic torts case of *OBG Ltd v Allan*[3] (*OBG*), Lord Nicholls observed:[4]

> These are much vexed subjects. Nearly 350 reported decisions and academic writings were placed before the House. There are many areas of uncertainty. Judicial observations are not always consistent, and academic consensus is noticeably absent. In the words of one commentator, the law is in a 'terrible mess'. So the House faces a daunting task ...

---

1. *Clerk and Lindsell on Torts* (19th edn, Sweet and Maxwell, 2005), ch 25.
2. Carty, *An Analysis of the Economic Torts* (OUP, 2001) at 3.
3. *OBG Ltd v Allan* [2008] 1 AC 1; [2007] UKHL 21 [2007] 2 WLR 90. The many articles on this case include Ryan and Ryan, 'Liability in Tort for Inducing a Breach of Contract' (2008) 2(4) Quarterly Review of Tort Law 7; O Sullivan, 'Intentional Economic Torts in the House of Lords' [2007] CLJ 503; McLeod, 'Offside Goals and Induced Breaches of Contract' (2009) 13 Edin LR 278; Lee, 'A Defence of Concurring Speeches' (2009) PL 305; Ong, 'Two Tripartite Economic Torts' (2008) JBL 723.
4. At 139. The law in relation to economic torts is described in *Clerk and Lindsell* as containing 'ramshackle elements' for they have 'lacked their Atkin': *Clerk and Lindsell on Torts* (19th edn, Sweet and Maxwell, 2006) 1492, para 25–01; see too Wedderburn, 'Rocking the Torts' (1983) 46 MLR 224 at 229.

Although the number of reported decisions and writings is nowhere comparable in this jurisdiction, the law might be described in the same uncomplimentary way. The *dicta* of Sir John Donaldson MR, criticising a particular statutory provision in *Merkur Island Shipping Corporation v Laughton*,[5] are apt:

> In industrial relations it is of vital importance that the worker on the shop floor, the shop steward, the local union official, the district officer and the equivalent levels in management should know what is and what is not 'offside.'

[4.04] The result of their Lordships' deliberations in *OBG* has been to bring a significant degree of clarity to this area of the common law and it is reasonable to assume, and to hope, that *OBG* will recommend itself to the Irish superior courts when an opportunity arises. It is expected[6] that *OBG* will have an influential and transformative effect on future claims in tort, and in particular on claims of inducing breach of contract and causing loss by unlawful means. The basic theme in their Lordships' decision is that there are two forms of economic liability, which ought to be kept distinct. During the twentieth century they became confused, and were undesirably conflated in the guise of a so-called 'unified' theory. The first is the liability for inducing breach of contract. The second concerns liability for intentionally causing loss by unlawfully interfering with the liberty of others. Inducing breach of contract is a stand-alone form of *accessory* liability, while wrongs involving intention may be regarded as constituting a category where liability is *primary*, comprising causing loss by unlawful means, intimidation and conspiracy. Regrettably, 'unlawful means' for the torts involved in the category of primary liability exhibit no consistent principle, with conspiracy being quite apart, although consistency in the 'intention' element of these torts is emerging. This chapter highlights the findings and influence of *OBG* – important requisites for the chapters to follow.

OBG LTD V ALLAN

[4.05] *OBG* concerned non-industrial conflict situations in three appeals principally concerned with claims in tort for economic loss caused by intentional acts. Briefly:

(a) In *OBG*[7] the defendants were receivers purportedly appointed under a floating charge which was admitted to have been invalid. Acting in good faith, they took control of the claimant company's assets and undertaking. The claimant argued this was not only a trespass to its land and a conversion of its chattels but also the tort of unlawful interference with its contractual relations. It claimed the defendants were liable in damages for the value of the assets and undertaking, including the value of the contractual claims, as at the date of their appointment. Alternatively, it said the defendants were liable for the same damages in conversion. By a majority, the Court of Appeal allowed the

---

5. *Merkur Island Shipping Corpn v Laughton* [1983] 2 AC 570, [1983] 2 All ER 189, [1983] ICR 490.

6. Eg Ryan and Ryan, 'Liability in Tort for Inducing a Breach of Contract' (2008) 2(4) Quarterly Review of Tort Law.

7. *OBG Ltd v Allan* [2005] QB 762.

receivers' appeal against the trial judge's decision upholding this claim. The House of Lords dismissed the appeal and held that the receivers did not intend to 'induce' OBG to break any of its contracts. Rather, the receivers honestly believed they were entitled to act on behalf of OBG in exercise of their powers as administrative receivers and so the tort of inducing breach of contract was of no relevance.

(b)   In *Douglas v Hello! Ltd (No 3)*[8] the magazine *OK!* contracted for the exclusive right to publish photographs of a celebrity wedding at which all other photography would be forbidden. The rival magazine *Hello!* published photographs which it knew to have been surreptitiously taken by an unauthorised photographer pretending to be a waiter or guest. *OK!* appealed against the rejection by the lower courts of their economic tort claims against *Hello! OK!* said there had been interference by unlawful means with its contractual or business relations or a breach of its equitable right to confidentiality in photographic images of the wedding. The House of Lords rejected their argument in relation to the first point but agreed on the second one. As to the unlawful means tort, the House held that whilst *Hello!* had the necessary intention to cause loss, they were not liable in tort because they had not interfered by unlawful means with the actions of the wedding couple. However, the appellants were successful in their appeal on breach of confidence.

(c)   In *Mainstream Properties Ltd v Young*[9] two employees of a property company, in breach of their contracts, diverted a development opportunity to a joint venture in which they were interested. The defendant, knowing of their duties but wrongly thinking they would not be in breach, facilitated the acquisition by providing finance. The company said he was liable for the tort of wrongfully inducing breach of contract. The Court of Appeal dismissed the claimant property developer's appeal against the rejection of its claim for interference with the employment contracts between the claimant and the two employees. The House of Lords also dismissed the appeal on the grounds that the defendant had honestly believed that assisting the employees with the joint venture would not involve them in breaches of their contractual obligations. The defendant had neither intended to induce a breach nor caused a loss by unlawful means.

OBG'S FINDINGS RE INDUCING BREACH OF CONTRACT AND THE UNLAWFUL MEANS TORT

[4.06] The claimants in these appeals relied on at least five different wrongs, or alleged wrongs, which they contended provided them with causes of action for economic loss: inducing breach of contract (*Mainstream*), causing loss by unlawful means (*'Hello!'*),

---

8.   *Douglas v Hello! Ltd (No 3)* [2006] QB 125.
9.   *Mainstream Properties Ltd v Young* [2005] IRLR 964.

interference with contractual relations (*OBG*), breach of confidence (*'Hello!'*) and conversion *(OBG)*. Regarding the economic torts, the House of Lords held:

> (1) That the unified theory which treated causing loss by unlawful means as an extension of the tort of inducing a breach of contract was confusing and misleading and should be abandoned; and that, accordingly, inducing breach of contract and causing loss by unlawful means were two separate torts, each with its own conditions for liability.[10]
>
> (2) That inducing a breach of contract was a tort of accessory liability, and an intention to cause a breach of contract was a necessary and sufficient requirement for liability; in order to be liable, a person had to know that he was inducing a breach of contract and to intend to do so with knowledge of the consequences; a conscious decision not to inquire into the existence of a fact could be treated as knowledge for the purposes of the tort; a person who knowingly induced a breach of contract as a means to an end had the necessary intent even if he was not motivated by malice but had acted with the motive of securing an economic advantage for himself; however, a breach of contract which was neither an end in itself nor a means to an end but was merely a foreseeable consequence of a person's acts did not give rise to liability; there could be no secondary liability without primary liability, and therefore a person could not be liable for inducing a breach of contract unless there had in fact been a breach by the contracting party.[11]
>
> (3) That causing loss by unlawful means was a tort of primary liability, and acts against a third party counted as unlawful means only if they were actionable by that third party if he had suffered loss; that (*per* Lord Hoffmann, Lord Walker of Gestingthorpe, Baroness Hale of Richmond and Lord Brown of Eaton-under-Heywood) unlawful means consisted of acts intended to cause loss to the claimant by interfering with the freedom of a third party in a way which was unlawful as against that third party and which was intended to cause loss to the claimant, but did not include acts which might be unlawful against a third party but which did not affect his freedom to deal with the claimant.[12]

Although most commonly described as the 'tort of procuring [or inducing] breaches of contract',[13] the tort has sometimes been described as one of 'interfering' with contract.[14] The difference between these two descriptions is significant as modern

---

10. *Lumley v Gye* (1853) 2 E & B 216, *Allen v Flood* [1898] AC 1, HL(E), *Quinn v Leathem* [1901] AC 495, HL(I), *GWK Ltd v Dunlop Rubber Co Ltd* (1926) 42 TLR 376 and *D C Thomson & Co Ltd v Deakin* [1952] Ch 646, CA considered.

11. *Emerald Construction Co Ltd v Lowthian* [1966] 1 WLR 691, CA and *Torquay Hotel Co Ltd v Cousins* [1969] 2 Ch 106, CA considered. *Millar v Bassey* [1994] EMLR 44, CA disapproved. *Merkur Island Shipping Corpn v Laughton* [1983] 2 AC 570, HL(E) not followed.

12. *Allen v Flood* [1898] AC 1, HL(E), *Quinn v Leathem* [1901] AC 495, HL(I), *JT Stratford & Son Ltd v Lindley* [1965] AC 269, HL(E), *Lonrho Ltd v Shell Petroleum Co Ltd (No 2)* [1982] AC 173, HL(E) and *Isaac Oren v Red Box Toy Factory Ltd* [1999] FSR 785 considered.

13. *Per Evershed MR in Thomson (DC) & Co Ltd v Deakin* [1952] Ch 646, 676.

14   See, eg, Roxburgh J in *British Motor Trade Association v Salvadore* [1949] Ch 556. (contd .../)

judgments, before *OBG,* extended liability to what in fact amounts to interference with, rather than procuring actual breach of, contract. The question of whether the tort is restricted to breach of contract, or covers interference with or prevention of, contract, is of fundamental importance. The trend of conflating these has led to the idea that there is a 'unified' tort of causing harm by unlawful means, under which procuring breach of contract is subsumed.

BEYOND CONTRACT BREACH

[4.07] The extended nature of the tort, and the idea of a unified tort, are considered in this chapter. It outlines the historical beginnings when the boundaries of the tort of inducing breach of contract began to be blurred, and the need for a breach of contract was gradually relaxed. Nearly 60 years ago, juridical pronouncements in England hinted at a tort of interference with, or prevention of, contract where no breach ensues. In *Stratford v Lindley,*[15] for example, Lord Reid said he did not have to consider:

> whether or how far the principle of *Lumley v Guy* covers deliberate and direct interference with the execution of a contract without that causing any breach.

Lord Donovan, however, was not of like mind.[16] To him:

> the argument that there is a tort consisting of some indefinable interference with business contracts, falling short of inducing a breach of contract, I find as novel and surprising as I think the members of this House who decided *Crofter Hand Woven Harris Tweed Co Ltd v Veitch* [1942] AC 435 would have done.

[4.08] Lord Denning regarded the point as open, however, in *Emerald Construction Ltd v Lowthian,*[17] and confirmed the existence of a tort of interference with contract by the time of *Daily Mirror Newspapers Ltd v Gardner.*[18] He revisited the theme in *Torquay Hotel Co Ltd v Cousins,*[19] where he was prepared to assume the defendant supplier would not have been in breach of contract but held nevertheless that the injunction would lie:

> The time has come when the principle should be further extended to cover deliberate and direct interference with the execution of a contract without that causing any breach.

---

14. (contd) The tort of interference with contract by unlawful means was unsuccessfully pleaded in *Malone and Another v McQuaid and Registrar of Titles* [1998] IEHC 86; and in a successful application for an interlocutory injunction Macken J found the defendant's barring of the plaintiff from driving a school bus 'may have interfered with or brought about or otherwise induced a breach of contract' between the parties: *Donohue v Bus Éireann* [1999] ELR 306.
15. *Stratford v Lindley* [1965] AC 269, 324.
16. At 340.
17. *Emerald Construction Ltd v Lowthian* [1966] 1 WLR 691 CA at 700–701.
18. *Daily Mirror Newspapers Ltd v Gardner* [1968] 2 QB 762.
19. *Torquay Hotel Co Ltd v Cousins* [1969] 2 Ch 106, 137–138.

In his view there were three requirements as to liability, namely:

(i)   an interference in the execution of a contract, extending to cases where the defendant 'prevents or hinders' performance (even though there is no breach) which is

(ii)   deliberate, ie done with sufficient knowledge and intention or recklessness, and is

(iii) direct.[20]

[4.09] *Clerk and Lindsell on Torts* took the view that the range of possible liability created by the extended tort made it incompatible with other authority.[21] Some subsequent judgments accepted the language of 'interference' when, before 1969, it had been regarded as little more than a shorthand way of describing inducement of breach. The principle enunciated a new tort of uncertain scope.[22] If mere hindrance can give rise to liability, it was inconsistent that the law should concern itself with issues such as whether inducing breach of a void or voidable contract, and so on, are tortious. Section 3 of the Trade Disputes Act 1906, now s 12 of the Industrial Relations Act 1990, provides immunity in the event of interference with 'trade, business or employment', all of which may involve contracts but it is generally accepted that Parliament included this clause in 1906 *in case* the law should extend liability in that direction. Two decisions, *Allen v Flood*[23] and *Quinn v Leathem*,[24] had earlier provided the Law Lords with opportunities to identify the boundaries between lawful and unlawful action. In *Allen v Flood*, a majority held that an otherwise lawful act did not become unlawful on grounds of disapproval of the motive behind it. By contrast, in *Quinn v Leathem*, the House of Lords unanimously decided what appeared to be the opposite, although for a majority the difference lay in the element of combination among the union defendants which led to liability for what is now styled simple conspiracy. These cases are fully discussed in the chapters which follow. The problem with the extended tort of interfering with contract was that it seemed to allow '*Quinn v Leathem* without the conspiracy'[25] – a malicious injury which was not, by reason of *Allen v Flood*, actionable unless unlawful means were used. This developing area was not helped by the fact that some judges referred to the tort of interference with business when plainly they were talking about inducing breach of contract.[26]

---

20.   Indirect interference is tortious only if 'unlawful means' are used. But see para **4.24**.

21.   *Clerk and Lindsell on Torts* (19th edn, Sweet and Maxwell, 2005), 25–33.

22.   See, eg, Lord Macnaghten in *Quinn v Leathem* [1901] AC 495, 510 but *per* Lord Herschell in *Allen v Flood* [1898] AC 1 at 120; the breach of contract was 'the essence of the action' in *Lumley v Gye*.

23.   *Allen v Flood* [1898] AC 1.

24.   *Quinn v Leathem* [1901] AC 495.

25.   *Per* Lord Devlin in *Rookes v Barnard* [1964] AC 1129 at 1215–16.

26.   Eg Caulfield J in *Messenger Newspapers Group Ltd v National Graphical Association* [1984] IRLR 397 at 405.

If the new tort did exist, *Clerk and Lindsell* suggested:

> that it goes no further than cases in which the defendant has deliberately brought
> about an event which would terminate the contract by reason of frustration; and
> even then the tortious liability may need further refinement.[27]

[4.10] Elias and Ewing[28] also regarded *Torquay Hotel Co Ltd v Cousins* as involving a change in the underlying principle of responsibility for the unlawful conduct of the third party. He is liable for his own conduct independently of third party liability. It also shifted the boundary line between *Lumley v Gye* and *Allen v Flood* and staked a larger claim for the former by protecting contractual expectations as well as contractual rights. The ramifications of this were very far-reaching, the authors suggested:

> For once contractual expectations are protected, how can it be lawful to persuade
> a party to a contract to terminate it lawfully, at least where the other party has a
> reasonable expectation that the contract will continue in force?

Elias and Ewing regarded the principle as 'highly dubious' and said it should certainly not be extended beyond protecting legitimate expectations in the manner of performing the contract. They adverted to the difficulty of confining any such tort: logically, why should the protection of expectations not extend, at least in some circumstances, to rendering it unlawful to persuade a person not to enter into a contract? Yet such an extension must be impossible if *Allen v Flood* is to retain any shred of authority.[29] If interference with expectations is unlawful, no employer could safely seek to tempt the employee of a competitor to work for him by persuading that employee lawfully to terminate his contract.

[4.11] In *OBG*, Lord Nicholls (he and Lord Hoffmann gave the leading opinions) described extending *Lumley* to 'prevention' cases, ie preventing performance of a contract or interference with contractual relations, as 'more troubled waters.'[30] Applying the *Lumley v Gye* tort to 'prevention' cases was unfortunate:

> There is a crucial difference between cases where the defendant induces a
> contracting party not to perform his contractual obligations and cases where the
> defendant prevents a contracting party from carrying out his contractual
> obligations. In inducement cases the very act of joining with the contracting
> party and inducing him to break his contract is sufficient to found liability as an
> accessory. In prevention cases the defendant does not join with the contracting
> party in a wrong (breach of contract) committed by the latter. There is no
> question of accessory liability. In prevention cases the defendant acts

---

27. *Clerk and Lindsell on Torts* (19th edn, Sweet and Maxwell, 2005), 25–35.

28. 'Economic Torts and Labour Law: Old Principles and New Liabilities', (1982) Camb LJ 321, 329.

29. It was confirmed that there could be no liability for interfering with future contracts in *Midland Cold Storage v Steer* [1972] Ch 630 (Megarry J).

30. At 59.

independently of the contracting party. The defendant's liability is a 'stand-alone' liability. Consistently with this, tortious liability does not arise in prevention cases unless ... the preventative means used were independently unlawful.[31]

The importance of the extended tort of interference with contract is significant in relation to the statutory immunities. If it exists, it is almost certainly not statutorily protected (para **6.89**).

[4.12] Not only was the tort extended as described but, no doubt as a result, gradually it was thought that *Lumley v Gye* covered *all* wrongful acts done intentionally to damage a particular individual and actually damaging him. This meant *Lumley,* and the tort of causing loss by unlawful means, were illustrations of one and the same principle, and could be regarded as unlawful ways of carrying on a dispute. The trouble with this was it ignored the centrality of contract rights to the tort of inducing breach of contract and the fact that this tort did not require 'extra' unlawful means, provided the defendant had induced the breach.

ONE SINGLE TORT?

[4.13] Is inducing breach of contract a single species of tort with distinct rules, or is it an example of a unified, innominate tort, a generic tort of causing harm by unlawful means 'whereunder the successful plaintiff must have been aimed at and hurt by a defendant using wrongful means in order to cause that harm.'[32] In Ireland, it seems there is recognition of a unified tort, although there has not yet been any analysis. For example, in *Bula v Tara Mines Ltd (No 2)*,[33] Murphy J observed that 'The well established tort of inducing breach of contract and the equally well recognised wrong of inflicting loss intentionally by means of a conspiracy[34] form part of, or have been extended into, a category of innominate tort which may be referred to as an unlawful interference with economic interests',[35] his view, and the plaintiffs' own admission, being that to seek such relief was 'to press the law to the limit of its existing frontier if not indeed to new ones.'[36]

---

31. At 60.

32. Weir, *Economic Torts* (OUP, 1997).

33. *Bula v Tara Mines Ltd (No 2)* [1987] IR 95.

34. The inclusion of conspiracy was novel here, the expected tort being causing loss by unlawful means.

35. Authorities cited in support of the contention were *Clerk and Lindsell on Torts* (15th edn, Sweet and Maxwell, 1982), 747, *Lumley v Gye* (1853) 2 E & B 216, *Quinn v Leathem* [1901] AC 495, *Sorrell v Smith* [1925] AC 700, *Cooper v Millea* [1938] IR 749, *Riordan v Butler* [1940] 347, *Sherriff v McMullen* [1952] IR 236, *Rookes v Barnard* [196] AC 1129, *Daily Mirror Newspapers Ltd v Gardner* [1968] 2 QB 762; *Torquay Hotel Co Ltd v Cousins* [1969] 2 Ch 106.

36. At 100. Cited by Laffoy J (High Court) in *Irish Municipal Public and Civil Trade Union & Others v Ryanair* [2007] 1 ILRM 45 at 57.

[4.14] In *Irish Rail v Holbrooke*[37] the High Court (O' Neill J) cited an earlier judgment of that court in *Armstrong Motors Ltd v CIE*[38] and approved and adopted Hamilton J's description of the ingredients of the tort of actionable interference with contractual relations 'otherwise known as the tort of procuring or inducing breach of contract' (having confused the nomenclature, the judge went on to focus on breach of contract):

> That the defendants did know of the existence of the contracts and intended to procure their breach

> That the defendants did definitely and unequivocally persuade the employees concerned to break their contracts of employment with the intention of procuring the breach of the contracts

> That the employees so persuaded, induced or procured did in fact break their contracts of employment

> That the breach of the contract forming the subject of interference ensued as a necessary consequence of the breaches by the employees concerned of their contracts of employment.

As will be seen (para **6.37**), the High Court was here describing the tort of 'indirect inducement' of breach of contract. In *Irish Municipal Public and Civil Trade Union and Others v Ryanair*[39] the High Court refused to strike out the plaintiffs' claims, which ranged from 'inducement of breach of contract' to 'intentional interference with contractual and commercial relations and their economic and commercial interests.' Counsel for the defendant, applying to strike out the proceedings, drew attention to the *dicta* of Murphy J above in *Bula*, but it was not clear to the judge that the plaintiffs' claim must fail.

From a survey of leading Irish authorities, it has been observed that:

> the tort of inducing breach of contract is regarded as part and parcel of a broader canvas of torts involving unlawful interference with economic interests.[40]

The clarity and analysis of the House of Lords in *OBG* is timely for Ireland. How did the idea of a unified tort begin?

[4.15] Lord Lindley in *Quinn v Leathem*[41] said of *Lumley* that:

> The principle which underlies the decision reaches all wrongful acts done intentionally to damage a particular individual and actually damaging him.

And Lord Macnaghten:

> I have no hesitation in saying that I think the decision [*Lumley*] was right, not on the ground of malicious intention – that was not, I think, the gist of the action –

---

37. *Irish Rail v Holbrooke* [2000] IEHC 47. The appeal to the Supreme Court [2001] 1 IR 237 was silent on this point.

38. *Armstrong Motors Ltd v CIE* (2 December 1975, unreported), HC, Hamilton J.

39. *Irish Municipal Public and Civil Trade Union and Others v Ryanair* [2007] 1 ILRM 45.

40. Ryan and Ryan, 'Liability in Tort for Inducing a Breach of Contract' (2008) 2(4) Quarterly Review of Tort Law.

41. *Quinn v Leathem* [1901] AC 495 at 535.

but on the ground that a violation of a legal right to interfere with contractual relations recognised by law if there be no sufficient justification for the interference.[42]

[4.16] The tort of causing loss by unlawful means has a different history from inducing breach of contract (see **Ch 7**). Cases such as *Garret v Taylor*[43] and *Tarleton v M'Gawley*[44] involved liability for the defendant, which was primary, for intentionally causing the plaintiff loss by unlawfully interfering with the liberty of others, and there was no other wrong for which the defendant was liable as accessory. These old cases were examined by the House of Lords in *Allen v Flood*[45] and their general principle approved. Because they involved the use of unlawful threats to intimidate potential customers, *Salmond on Torts*[46] classified them under the heading 'Intimidation' and the existence of a tort of this name was confirmed by the House of Lords in *Rookes v Barnard*[47] (**Ch 8**). But, as Lord Hoffmann pointed out in *OBG*,[48] 'an interference with the liberty of others by unlawful means does not require threats.' The act itself suffices. *Salmond*'s tort of intimidation was therefore only one variant of a broader tort, 'causing loss by unlawful means' recognised by Lord Reid in *JT Stratford & Son Ltd v Lindley*:[49]

> The respondents' action [in calling a strike] made it practically impossible for the appellants to do any new business with the barge hirers. It was not disputed that such interference with business is tortious if any unlawful means are employed.

[4.17] Lord Hoffmann went to considerable lengths to distinguish the tort of causing loss by unlawful means in *OBG* (Lord Nicholls referred to it as the tort of 'interference with the claimant's business by unlawful means') from the *Lumley* principle, as originally formulated. The torts differ in at least four respects:

(i)   Unlawful means is a tort of primary liability, not requiring a wrongful act by anyone else, while *Lumley v Gye* creates accessory liability, which is dependent upon the primary wrongful act of the contracting party.

(ii) Unlawful means requires the use of means which are unlawful under some other rule ('independently unlawful'), whereas liability under *Lumley v Gye* requires only the degree of participation in the breach of

---

42. *Quinn v Leathem* [1901] AC 495 at 510. Lord Macnaghten failed to include two important elements from the principle of *Lumley v Gye*, namely the need for inducement and the need for an actionable wrong.
43. *Garret v Taylor* (1620) Cro Jac 56.
44. *Tarleton v M'Gawley* (1794) Peake 270.
45. *Allen v Flood* [1898] AC 1.
46. *Salmond on Torts* (Stevens and Haynes, 1907).
47. *Rookes v Barnard* [1964] AC 1129.
48. At 19.
49. *JT Stratford & Son Ltd v Lindley* [1965] AC 269, 324.

contract which satisfies the general requirements of accesssory liability for the wrongful act of another person.[50]

(iii) Liability for unlawful means does not depend upon the existence of contractual relations. It is sufficient that the intended consequence of the wrongful act is to effect damage in any form, for example, to the claimant's economic expectations. Under *Lumley v Gye,* the breach of contract is of the essence: there is no primary liability and no accessory liability.

(iv) Although both are described as torts of intention (the pleader in *Lumley v Gye* used the word 'maliciously' but the court construed this as meaning only that the defendant intended to procure a breach of contract), the *results* which the defendant intended to procure are different. In unlawful means, the defendant must have intended to cause damage to the claimant (usually this will be a means of enhancing his own economic position). Because damage to economic expectations is sufficient to found a claim, there need not have been any intention to cause a breach of contract or to interfere with contractual rights. Under *Lumley v Gye,* on the other hand, an intention to cause a breach of contract is both necessary and sufficient. It is necessary because this is essential for liability as accessory to the breach. It is sufficient because the fact that the defendant did not intend to cause damage, or even thought the breach of contract would make the claimant better off, is irrelevant.[51]

[4.18] The Law Lords who formed the majority in *Allen v Flood*[52] showed a clear recognition that the *Lumley v Gye*[53] tort and causing loss by unlawful means were separate torts, each with its own conditions for liability. Lord Hoffmann noted[54] that some writers regret the failure of English law to accept bad motive as a ground for liability, as it is in the United States and Germany.[55] But he agreed with Weir[56] that it seems to have created a good deal of uncertainty in the countries which have adopted such a principle.

[4.19] *Quinn v Leathem,*[57] according to Lord Hoffmann, sowed 'the seeds of confusion.'[58] It suggested that the principle involved in *Lumley v Gye* cannot be confined to inducements to break contracts of service, nor indeed to inducements to break any contracts. Rather it reached *all* wrongful acts done intentionally to damage a particular individual and actually damaging him.[59] One reason, according to Lord

---

50. For the relevant principles see *CBS Songs Ltd v Amstrad Consumer Electronics plc* [1988] AC 1013 and *Unilever plc v Chefaro Proprietaries Ltd* [1994] FSR 135.

51. Cf *South Wales Miners' Federation v Glamorgan Coal Co Ltd* [1905] AC 239.

52. *Allen v Flood* [1898] AC 1.

53. *Lumley v Gye* (1853) 2 E & B 216.

54. *Allen v Flood* [1898] AC 1 at 22.

55. See eg Heydon, *Economic Torts* (2nd edn, Sweet and Maxwell, 1978), 28.

56. Forcibly expressed in his Clarendon Law Lectures on *Economic Torts* (OUP, 1997).

57. *Quinn v Leathem* [1901] AC 495.

58. *Allen v Flood* [1898] AC 1 at 22.

59. See Lord Lindley *Quinn v Leathem* [1901] AC 495, at 535.

Hoffmann, why it seemed to Lord Lindley, Lord Macnaghten, and others in *Quinn v Leathem*, that *Lumley v Gye* and the unlawful means tort were illustrations of the same principle, was that quite often, particularly in cases of torts committed in the course of commercial competition or industrial disputes, both could be regarded as unlawful ways of carrying on the competition or the dispute. But there is no single principle involved. And there is no reason, according to Lord Hoffmann, why the same facts should not give rise to both accessory liability under *Lumley v Gye* and primary liability for using unlawful means:

> If A, intending to cause loss to B, threatens C with assault unless he breaks his contract with B, he is liable as accessory to C's breach of contract under *Lumley v Gye* and he commits the tort of causing loss to B by unlawful means. The areas of liability under the two torts may be intersecting circles which cover common ground. This often happened in 20th century industrial disputes, where, for example, a union would use unlawful means (inducing members to break their contracts of employment) to put pressure upon the employer to break his contract with someone else who was the union's real target. Leaving aside statutory defences, this would make the union liable both under *Lumley v Gye* and for causing loss to the target by unlawful means. That does not make *Lumley v Gye* and unlawful means the same tort. But the close proximity of the circumstances in which they could be committed, particularly in industrial disputes, may explain why they were often thought to be manifestations of the same principle.[60]

[4.20] The seeds of confusion as to the tort of inducing breach of contract and a unified tort descended to 'muddle', according to Lord Hoffmann,[61] with *GWK Ltd v Dunlop Rubber Co Ltd.*[62] The GWK company made motor cars and the ARM company made tyres. GWK contracted to fit all their new cars with ARM tyres and to show them with ARM tyres at trade exhibitions. On the night before a motor show in Glasgow, Dunlop employees removed the ARM tyres from two GWK cars on the exhibition and substituted Dunlop tyres. The evidence showed that Dunlop knew of ARM's contractual right to have their tyres displayed. Lord Hewart CJ held Dunlop liable. Relying on the *dicta* of Lord Lindley and Lord Macnaghten in *Quinn v Leathem*[63] (para **4.15** above), Lord Hewart CJ said:[64]

> In my opinion the defendants ... knowingly committed a violation of the ARM company's legal rights by interfering, without any justification whatever, with the contractual relations existing between them and the GWK company, and [I think] that the defendants so interfered with the intention of damaging the ARM company, and that that company has been thereby damnified.

[4.21] In fact, said Lord Hoffmann, the case is a good example of intentionally causing loss by unlawful means. There was a finding of an intention to damage the ARM company (as a means of advancing the interests of the Dunlop company) and unlawful means were implied both by the reference to Lord Lindley's statement of principle and

---

60. *OBG Ltd v Allan* [2008] 1 AC 1 at 24.
61. *OBG Ltd v Allan* [2008] 1 AC 1 at 24.
62. *GWK Ltd v Dunlop Rubber Co Ltd* (1926) 42 TLR 376.
63. *Quinn v Leathem* [1901] AC 495.
64. *GWK Ltd v Dunlop Rubber Co Ltd* (1926) 42 TLR 376 at 377.

the separate finding of trespass to the goods of the GWK company. Lord Hewart, however, made no reference to the tort of causing loss by unlawful means 'possibly because the only form in which it was then recognised in the textbooks was *Salmond's* tort of intimidation.'[65] This was not a case of intimidation. Intended loss was caused by unlawful means used against a third party. Lord Hewart 'looked for a different pigeonhole'[66] and found it in Lord Lindley's extended definition of the *Lumley v Gye* tort. A 'unified theory' was well under way, according to his Lordship, and was adopted in *DC Thompson & Co Ltd v Deakin*[67] from which the judgment of Jenkins LJ directed the course of the law ever since. From the *dicta* in *Quinn v Leathem*[68] Jenkins LJ[69] deduced two propositions:

> First ... there may ... be an actionable interference with contractual rights where other means of interference than persuasion or procurement or inducement, in the sense of influence of one kind or another brought to bear on the mind of the contract breaker to cause him to break his contract, are used by the interferer; but, secondly, that (apart from conspiracy to injure, which, as I have said, is not in question so far as this motion is concerned) acts of a third party lawful in themselves do not constitute an actionable interference with contractual rights merely because they bring about a breach of contract, even if they were done with the object and intention of bringing about such breach.

Lord Hoffmann:

> [Jenkins LJ] fully adopted the theory, originating with Lord Lindley in *Quinn v Leathem* and supported (possibly unintentionally) by Lord Macnaghten's dictum in the same case, that the principle of *Lumley v Gye* extended to all interference with contractual relations by unlawful means. 'Direct persuasion or procurement or inducement applied by the third party to the contract breaker' was 'regarded as a wrongful act in itself' and constituted the 'primary form' of the tort: see p 694. But other forms of interference with contracts by unlawful means, such as *GWK Ltd v Dunlop Rubber Co Ltd* 42 TLR 376 ('a striking example') came within the same tort.[70]

Lord Diplock proclaimed that unlawful interference with trade was the *genus* economic tort in *Merkur Island Shipping Corporation v Laughton*,[71] other varieties of the general economic torts being but species of it. The idea of a *genus* tort was rejected unanimously by the House of Lords in *OBG Ltd v Allan*.[72] This, the authors suggest, is undoubtedly correct.

[4.22] In sum, the unified theory treated procuring breach of contract as one species of a more general tort of actionable interference with contractual rights at a time when

---

65. *OBG Ltd v Allan* [2008] 1 AC 1 at 24–25.
66. *OBG Ltd v Allan* [2008] 1 AC 1 at 25.
67. *DC Thomson & Co Ltd v Deakin* [1952] Ch 646.
68. *Quinn v Leathem* [1901] AC 45.
69. *DC Thompson & Co Ltd v Deakin* [1952] Ch 646 at 693.
70. *OBG Ltd v Allan* [2008] AC 1, Lord Hoffmann at 25.
71. *Merkur Island Shipping Corpn v Laughton* [1983] AC 570.
72. *OBG Ltd v Allan* [2008] AC 1.

there was an inadequate appreciation of the scope, posssibly even of the existence, of the tort of causing loss by unlawful means. One way or another, the unified theory gave rise to difficulties, to some extent of nomenclature, although as Lord Hoffmann said, 'it is not easy to point to cases which were wrongly decided because the court had adopted the unified theory rather than the two-tort analysis of *Allen v Flood*.'[73]

[4.23] There have been powerful voices supporting a unified theory. Weir, for one, would prefer *Lumley v Gye* to be subsumed under the tort of intentionally causing loss by unlawful means, treating the 'seduction' of the contracting party as a species of unlawful means and not distinguishing between interference with contractual rights and damage to economic expectation. According to Lord Hoffmann, the example of what Lord Atkins achieved for negligence in *Donoghue v Stevenson*[74] always beckons.[75] 'But this too is a form of seduction which may lure writers onto the rocks.'[76] The House of Lords unanimously held against the principle of accessory liability for breach of contract being subsumed in the tort of causing loss by unlawful means. Lord Hoffmann summarised, 'To induce a breach of contract is unlawful means when the breach is used to cause loss to a third party, as in *JT Stratford & Sons Ltd v Lindley* [1965] AC 269, but it makes no sense to say that the breach of contract itself has been caused by unlawful means.'[77] He endorsed Professor Peter Cane[78] who said that:

> The search for 'general principles of liability' based on types of conduct is at best a waste of time, and at worst a potential source of serious confusion; and the broader the principle, the more is this so. Tort law is a complex interaction between protected interests, sanctioned conduct, and sanctions; and although there *are* what might be called 'principles of tort liability', by and large, they are not very 'general'. More importantly, they cannot be stated solely in terms of the sorts of conduct which will attract tort liability. Each principle must refer, as well, to some interest protected by tort law and some sanction provided by tort law.

[4.24] The unified theory produced serious practical disadvantages and has been a source of confusion in more than one respect. One of the resulting disadvantages concerns the so-called version of the tort of 'indirect' interference with contract (para **6.37** *et seq*).

---

73.   *OBG Ltd v Allan* [2008] AC 1 at 26.

74.   *Donoghue v Stevenson* [1932] AC 562.

75.   Weir, *Economic Torts* (OUP, 1997) at 25.

76.   *OBG Ltd v Allan* [2008] AC 1, Lord Hoffmann at 27.

77.   Lord Hoffmann at 27. He appproved an article by Sales and Stilitz, 'Intentional Infliction of Harm by Unlawful Means'(1999) 115 LQR 411, 433, asserting that *Lumley v Gye* was 'founded on a different principle of liability than the intentional harm tort', it treated contractual rights as a species of property which deserve special protection, not only by giving a right of action against the party who breaks his contract but by imposing secondary liability on a person who procures him to do so. The unlawful means principle is concerned only with intention and wrongfulness and is indifferent as to the nature of the interest which is damaged.

78.   'Mens Rea in Tort Law' (2000) 20 OJLS 533, 552.

Lord Nicholls, who agreed with Lord Hoffmann, said that a regrettable consequence of treating 'preventing performance' as an extension of the *Lumley v Gye* tort had been to widen the ambit of the tort 'in an unprincipled fashion.'[79] In *Torquay Hotel Co Ltd v Cousins*[80] the judges 'were led astray by the width of Lord Macnaghten's observations made in 1901, long before the unlawful interference tort became shaped. The jurisprudence of the economic torts had not then been thought through.'[81] Lord Nicholls:

> I feel bound to say therefore that the ambit of the *Lumley v Gye* tort should properly be confined to inducing a breach of contract. The unlawful interference tort requires intentional harm effected by unlawful means, and there is no in-between hybrid tort of 'interfering with contractual relations.' In so far as authorities suggest or decide otherwise they should not now be followed. I leave open the question of how far the *Lumley v Gye* principle applied equally to inducing a breach of other actionable obligations such as statutory duties or equitable or fiduciary obligations.[82]

[4.25] According to Lord Brown in *OBG*, 'The whole area of economic torts has been plagued by uncertainty for far too long. Our Lordships now have the opportunity to give it a coherent shape. This surely is an oppportunity to be taken.'[83]

The welcome outcome of the House of Lords' decision in *OBG* is that there is now a sharp distinction between the two economic torts and a clearer understanding of each. The unified theory which treats causing loss by unlawful means as an extension of the tort of inducing breach of contract is confusing, and misleading. Inducing breach of contract is a tort of accessory liability for inducing a third party to commit an actionable wrong, notably a breach of contract and possibly some other actionable civil wrongs as well. The other tort, causing loss by unlawful means, imposes primary liability for intentional and unlawful interference with economic interests. In Ireland the restatement by the House of Lords should assist a more coherent development of the economic torts. This twofold structure substantially accords with the views of leading commentators.[84] A similar restatement in this jurisdiction may be hoped for. The implications for the statutory immunities are discussed in succeeding chapters.

CONSPIRACY

[4.26] The tort of conspiracy was largely unaffected by *OBG*. It was not referred to in any of the speeches. Conspiracy, as will be seen in **Ch 5**, takes the form either of

---

79.   At 61.

80.   *Torquay Hotel Co Ltd v Cousins* [1969] 2 Ch 106.

81.   At 62.

82.   *Ibid. Millar v Bassey* [1994] EMLR 44 was mistaken. *Merkur Island Shipping Corpn v Laughton* [1983] 2 AC 570 should not be followed so far as it holds that inducing an actual breach of contract is not a necessary ingredient of the *Lumley v Gye* tort.

83.   At 92.

84.   Including Carty, *An Analysis of the Economic Torts* (OUP, 2001), 271–276 and Weir, *Economic Torts* (OUP, 1997) reviewd by Oliphant (1999) 62 MLR 320, 322.

'simple conspiracy' and 'conspiracy to injure', or what is known as 'unlawful means conspiracy.' What falls within the scope of unlawful means remains unclear, but as Simpson points out, to the extent that the economic torts do or ought to rest on common principles, the ambit of unlawful means for the purposes of the unlawful interference tort ought to be a relevant if not decisive consideration.[85] In *Revenue & Customs Commissioners v Total Network SL*[86] the Court of Appeal felt constrained by authority to hold that the unlawful act relied on must be actionable at the suit of the claimant, but gave leave to appeal to the House of Lords. The House was not happy to introduce into unlawful means conspiracy a requirement that the unlawful means be independently actionable, thus perpetrating a distinction between conspiracy and other economic torts. See further para **5.36**.

ORDER OF QUESTIONS REGARDING CIVIL LIABILITY, AND IMMUNITY, FOR TRADE DISPUTES

[4.27] To determine whether a trade dispute involves civil liability for those organising or taking part therein, the questions to be asked by the legal or industrial relations practitioner should follow a particular order:

- Does the industrial action give rise to civil liability at common law?

- If so, is this liability removed because the wrongful act is protected by the statutory immunities in ss 10, 11 and 12 of the 1990 Act?

- If the act attracts immunity, are the parties the 'proper parties' within the 1990 Act, is there a 'trade dispute', and are they acting 'in contemplation or furtherance of a trade dispute'?

- If so, is immunity withdrawn for any reason? For example, is it a one-worker dispute within s 9(2) of the Industrial Relations Act 1990?

[4.28] The chapters that follow look separately at the tort of conspiracy, inducing breach of contract, causing loss by unlawful means, and intimidation. They tackle the first question in para **4.27** by examining the ingredients of the respective torts, they then consider the second question, namely, the extent, if any, to which the Industrial Relations Act 1990, protects liability. The third question is dealt with in **Ch 9**. It is most important, particularly in relation to the requirement that the defendants be members and officials of authorised trade unions (s 9(1) of the 1990 Act). The fourth question relates to one-worker disputes, and action contrary to the outcome of a secret ballot, and is detailed in **Ch 5**.

The overall immunity given to trade unions in tort acting within the golden formula is considered in **Ch 5**.

---

85.   Simpson, 'Economic Tort Liability in Labour Disputes: The Potential Impact of the House of Lords' decision in *OBG Ltd v Allan*' (2007) 36 ILJ 468 at 475.

86.   *Revenue & Customs Commissioners v Total Network SL* [2007] EWCA Civ 39; [2007] 2 WLR 1156; [2008] UKHL 19, [2008] 2 WLR 711. See para **5.36**.

The suggested order here may be ousted where circumstances clearly show, for example, that there is no trade dispute because the dispute is solely political or about business strategy.

Chapter 5
CONSPIRACY

INTRODUCTION

[5.01] The economic torts[1] raise questions of deep significance for each of the social partners. What forms of market or economic pressure should the law permit in trade disputes? Is it unlawful deliberately to harm the interests of another without justification? It is – and always has been – a fundamental principle of the common law that every person has the right to dispose of his capital or of his labour according to his will. As has been seen, it took a long time for the law to accept the political, social, economic and industrial importance of trade unions. Prior to 1871 any group of workmen combining for the purpose of raising the rates of their wages was liable to be indicted for criminal conspiracy. Moreover, any contract or agreement between two or more persons to exercise that freedom was regarded by the law as against public policy, being in unreasonable restraint of trade. Ch 1 detailed Parliament's hostility towards combinations of workmen throughout the eighteenth century. Following the Act of Union of Great Britain and Ireland 1800, the Unlawful Combinations (Ireland) Act 1803 was passed by the Parliament at Westminster. The long title stated that it was, 'an Act to prevent Unlawful Combinations of Workmen, Artificers, Journeymen and Labourers in Ireland.'

[5.02] The Combination Acts not only made it illegal in both England and Ireland for workmen to combine for the purpose of improving wages or conditions of labour, but also rendered it a criminal offence to organise or attend meetings for such purposes. Their repeal some 25 years later appeared to permit combinations of workers if the sole purpose was to negotiate their own hours or wages.[2] This Act, the Combination Laws Repeal Act Amendment Act 1825,[3] set out a number of widely phrased offences such as 'threats', actionable if they had the object of 'forcing' workmen and employers to operate in certain ways, notwithstanding that activities might be reasonably carried out in pursuit of a lawful dispute and in the interest of union members. The later Criminal Law Amendment Act 1871 made it a criminal offence to use violence, threats, intimidation, molestation or obstruction with a view to coercing an employer or workman to act in specified ways.

---

1. See Carey, 'The Tort of Conspiracy' (2001) 19 ILT 321, Burns, 'Civil Conspiracy: An Unwieldy Vessel Rides Judicial Tempest' (1982) 16 UBC Law Rev 229, Redmond *(sub nom* Mathews), 'The Tort of Conspiracy in Irish Labour Law' (1973) Ir Jur (ns) 252. Generally on the economic torts see McMahon and Binchy, *Law of Torts* (3rd edn, Bloomsbury Professional, 2000), ch 32.

2. See *R v Duffield* (1851) 5 Cox CC 404; *R v Rowlands* (1851) 17 QB 671; *Skinner v Kitch* (1867) LR 2 QB 393.

3. See similarly the Molestation of Workmen Act 1859. Both Acts were repealed by the Criminal Law Amendment Act 1871.

[5.03] Trade unions in Ireland derive their legal status largely from the Trade Union Act 1871,[4] as amended (para **1.07** *et seq*), which applied to Ireland as well as to Britain. It provided a measure of protection for *bona fide* activities of unions. Section 2 laid down that:

> The purposes of any trade union shall not, by reason merely that they are in restraint of trade, be deemed to be unlawful, so as to render any member of such trade union liable to criminal prosecution for conspiracy or otherwise.

A short time after 1871 defects began to come to light in so far as conspiracy was concerned. In *R v Bunn*,[5] for example, Brett J pointed out that the Act protected unions only when acting in restraint of trade, provided no coercion was thereby involved; otherwise there would be liability for criminal conspiracy. There could be a criminal conspiracy even though the acts threatened were not independently unlawful or illegal. Workers had threatened to go on strike unless a fellow worker, who had been dismissed, was reinstated. The resultant confusion in the law was alleviated by s 3 of the Conspiracy and Protection of Property Act 1875, which provided:

> An agreement or combination by two or more persons to do or to procure to be done, any act in contemplation or furtherance of a trade dispute shall not be indictable as a conspiracy if such act committed by one person would not be punishable as a crime.

Liabilities for conspiracy did not disappear, however. The courts went on to develop a new civil liability for conspiracy, thereby defeating the intention of Parliament.[6]

[5.04] In the late nineteenth century the tort of civil conspiracy entered the *dramatis personae* via a trilogy of legal actions. In *Allen v Flood*[7] the House of Lords did not appear prepared to go so far as to say that conduct otherwise not tortious would become so because it was carried out with the intention of deliberately harming the economic interests of another. The defendant union official threatened to call out boilermakers employed by the employer (without any breach of contract by the boilermakers) unless the plaintiff shipwrights also employed by the employer were dismissed (once more without breach of contract by the employer). An action by the shipwrights for malicious interference with employment failed. The union official had not done or threatened to do anything unlawful. The shipwrights also alleged that the union official acted partly as he did in order to punish them for past misconduct. But the House of Lords, reversing a unanimous Court of Appeal decision, dismissed the action, holding by a majority that malice or any other unjustified motive was insufficient to establish liability.

---

4.   See 'Jurisdiction of Courts under Trade Union Act 1871' (1921) 55 ILT & SJ 179.

5.   *R v Bunn* (1872) 12 Cox CC 316.

6.   Citrine, *Trade Union Law* (3rd edn, Stevens & Sons, 1967), pp 14–15.

7.   *Allen v Flood* [1898] AC 1.

[5.05] A differently constituted House of Lords decided the defendants had committed the tort of conspiracy in *Quinn v Leathem*.[8] There, the defendant union officials coerced the plaintiff (an Irish flesher) to dismiss non-unionists employed by him in his fleshing business. Upon his refusal to do so, the defendants approached a customer of his and persuaded him, under threat of a strike by his employees, not to deal with the plaintiff until he sacked the non-unionists. There was apparently no breach of contract involved. On the evidence, the jury found the defendants were motivated by malice in the sense of having no just cause for what they had done. Lord Lindley conceded that the defendants might well have been acting in what they perceived to be their own interests. Nevertheless their actions were not justifiable. Later attempts to reconcile *Allen v Flood* and *Quinn v Leathem* concentrated on the element of conspiracy in the latter. *Allen* involved a single trade union official, *Quinn* a group of trade unionists.[9]

[5.06] *Mogul Steamship Co Ltd v McGregor, Gow & Co Ltd*[10] was the third case of the trilogy (although the first in time). There the House of Lords held that an agreement among shippers to undercut a rival trader on a particular route in order to obtain a monopoly of it for themselves was not a tortious conspiracy. Alternatively, the House held that if it was a wrong, the defendants' acts were justifiable in that they were acting in pursuit of their own legitimate economic self-interests.

[5.07] Section 1 of the Trade Disputes Act 1906[11] added to s 3 of the 1875 statute an amendment designed to give protection for the tort of conspiracy. It provided that an act done in pursuance of a combination should not be actionable (ie as a tort) if done in contemplation or furtherance of a trade dispute, unless the act would be actionable if done without any such combination. The immunity is re-enacted with more detail in s 10 of the Industrial Relations Act 1990. It is not as protective as might be imagined (see para **5.48**).

This chapter begins by looking at the rationale of the tort of conspiracy[12] and at some of its key aspects, namely, the combination and the need for a causal link between it and the plaintiff's injury. It then examines separately the two forms of the tort: conspiracy to injure or 'simple' conspiracy and conspiracy to do an unlawful act or to use unlawful means.

---

8.   *Quinn v Leathem* [1901] AC 495.

9.   *Mogul Steamship Co Ltd v McGregor, Gow & Co Ltd* [1892] AC 25. This explanation is questionable in view of the doctrine of separate corporate personality, a point emphasised in *Lonrho Ltd v Shell Petroleum Co Ltd* [1982] AC 173. The more accurate contrast may have resided between the position of labour and that of capital, a view strengthened by *Mogul Steamship Co Ltd v McGregor, Gow & Co Ltd* [1892] AC 25 a case which, on the face of it, appeared irreconcilable with *Quinn v Leathem*.

10.   *Mogul Steamship Co Ltd v McGregor, Gow & Co Ltd* [1892] AC 25.

11.   The full text is reproduced in the **Appendix**.

12.   Salmond, *Law of Torts* (6th edn, Sweet & Maxwell, 1924), 576–78 suggested cases on conspiracy were effectively about intimidation: a perspective described as a 'leading heresy' by Lord Dunedin in *Sorrell v Smith* [1925] AC 700, 715.

RATIONALE OF THE TORT

[5.08] No one would dispute the words of Chief Baron Palles in *Kearney v Lloyd*:[13]

> The doctrine of conspiracy was, up to the commencement of the present century [the nineteenth], stretched far beyond its ancient limits; but notwithstanding this extension, no case can be found in which there was a conviction, as for an unlawful conspiracy, for a combination to effect an innocent purpose by innocent means.

Wiles J described the tort of conspiracy in *Mulcahy v R*[14] as comprising 'the agreement of two or more to do an unlawful act, or to do a lawful act by unlawful means.'

In this jurisdiction a *précis* of the tort was given by O'Neill J in *Iarnród Éireann v Holbrooke and Ors*:[15]

> The essential features of [the tort of actionable conspiracy] have long remained afflicted with some uncertainty, both in this jurisdiction and in England. However, the authorities in this jurisdiction and in particular the judgments of the Supreme Court in *McGowan v Murphy* unrep Supreme Court 19 April 1967 and *Meskell v CIE* [1973] IR at 121 and the judgment of Dixon J in the High Court in *Connolly v Loughney* 87 ILTR 49 at 51 establish the following essential features of the tort:
>
> 1.   The agreement or combination of two or more people, the primary or predominant object of which was to injure another is actionable even though the act done to the party injured would be lawful if done by an individual.
>
> 2.   An agreement or combination of two or more persons to carry out a purpose lawful in itself but by using unlawful means is actionable, in circumstances where the act in question might not be actionable against the individual members of the combination, as individuals.

There are two forms of the tort of conspiracy, considered separately at para **5.14** and para **5.24** respectively:

> *Conspiracy to injure or 'simple conspiracy'*: that is, where two or more persons combine for the purpose of injuring a third party rather than to serve their own *bona fide* and legitimate interests; and

> *Conspiracy to commit an unlawful act or to use unlawful means*: that is, where two or more persons combine to commit an unlawful act or use unlawful means.[16]

---

13.   *Kearney v Lloyd* [1890] 26 LR Ir 268.

14.   *Mulcahy v R* (1868) LR 3 HL 306 at 317.

15.   *Iarnród Éireann v Holbrooke and Ors* [2000] ELR 109 at 119. The evidence was held to fall short of establishing liability on the part of the defendants in respect of losses suffered by the plaintiff as a result of stoppages at Athlone and Cork but the judgment contains no detailed discussion of the tort's application.

16.   In the extract above (para **5.08**) describing the two forms of the tort, O Neill J did not mention that the second form of the tort of conspiracy may also comprise a combination to commit an unlawful act.

[5.09] In the twentieth century, the House of Lords consciously strove to curtail the limits of the tort. In *Lonrho Ltd v Shell Petroleum Co Ltd (Lonrho)*[17] Lord Diplock acknowledged that:

> regarded as a civil tort ... conspiracy is a highly anomalous cause of action. The gist of the cause of action is damage to the plaintiff; so long as it remains unexecuted, the agreement, which alone constitutes the crime of conspiracy, causes no damage; it is only acts done in execution of the agreement that are capable of doing that. So the tort, unlike the crime, consists not of agreement but of concerted action taken pursuant to agreement.

The tort of conspiracy has also been described as a combination of which the 'real purpose ... is the inflicting of damage on A as distinguished from serving the *bona fide* and legitimate interests of those who so combine.'[18]

In *Lonrho*, Lord Diplock recalled the 'chequered history' of the tort of conspiracy to injure or 'simple' conspiracy: it had attracted 'more academic controversy than success in practical application.'[19] The House had:

> an unfettered choice whether to confine the civil action of conspiracy to the narrow field to which alone it has an established claim or whether to extend this already anomalous tort beyond those limits that are all that common sense and the application of the legal logic of the decided cases require.[20]

Lord Diplock, with whom all the Law Lords agreed, was 'unhesitatingly' against extending the scope of the civil tort of simple conspiracy.

[5.10] It can be challenging to distinguish the boundaries between the two forms of the tort. Yet they are treated and regarded as different. Moreover, the courts' decisions on justification and on what constitute unlawful means, crucial elements in conspiracy, have not always been consistent or precise.

The combination

[5.11] The tort requires an agreement or combination between two or more persons. The word 'agreement' is generally not a preferred term, suggesting something of a contractual kind, whereas all that is required is a combination and common intention.[21] It is essential that there is a combination between the defendants; an uncommunicated intention or lack of overt acts may mean there has not been an effective conspiracy. Unlike the position in criminal law,[22] it is now accepted (at least in England) that

---

17. *Lonrho Ltd v Shell Petroleum Co Ltd* [1981] 2 All ER 456 at 463.
18. *Per* Viscount Simon LC, *Crofter Hand Woven Harris Tweed Co v Veitch* [1942] AC 435, 443.
19. *Lonrho Ltd v Shell Petroleum Co Ltd* [1981] 2 All ER 456 at 463/4.
20. *Lonrho Ltd v Shell Petroleum Co Ltd* [1981] 2 All ER 456 at 464.
21. *Clerk and Lindsell on Torts* (19th edn, Sweet & Maxwell, 2005), paras 25–119.
22. See UK Criminal Law Act 1977, s 2(2)(a); *Clerk and Lindsell on Torts* (Sweet & Maxwell, 1983), 763, fn 69.

spouses should not be treated as one person for the tort of conspiracy.[23] Tortious liability should not vary 'according to whether those who inflict it are casual acquaintances or are indissolubly conjoined in wedded bliss.'[24] A company being a separate entity can conspire with its directors or others.[25] In *Meskell v CIE*[26] the plaintiff was successful in alleging conspiracy wrongfully to interfere with his constitutional rights as between the defendant company and four trade unions.[27] Employees may conspire with their employer company.[28]

[5.12] It is generally a question of fact whether there has been a combination or not. Persons who have not participated in meetings which formed part of the combination and who played no active role will not be liable as conspirators.[29] In relation to conspiracy to threaten to break a contract, it seems immaterial whether a particular defendant was not a party to the contract concerned and therefore not in a competent position to threaten breach.[30] As the rationale of an action in respect of conspiracy to injure is the damage sustained, the existence of the combination itself is a matter of inducement or aggravation only:

> in an action upon the case in the nature of a conspiracy against the several defendants all but one may be acquitted [sic] and nevertheless the verdict and judgment against the one are good.[31]

Combination alone, or the fact of being a party to a combination, are not sufficient for liability. There must be a common design *and* the acts done by the conspirator must be 'in pursuance and furtherance' of that common design. In *Sandman v Panasonic UK Ltd*[32] Pumfrey J found no decision supporting liability in tort from mere association

---

23. *Midland Bank Trust Co Ltd v Green (No 3)* [1982] Ch 529 affirming [1979] Ch 496.

24. *Ibid* at 522 *per* Oliver J.

25. *Bank Gesellschaft Berlin v Makris* (22 January 1999, unreported), QB (Comm Ct).

26. *Meskell v CIE* [1973] IR 121. See, too, *Taylor v Smyth* [1991] IR 142 where the Supreme Court held an agreement to cause injury by unlawful means is an actionable conspiracy notwithstanding that parties to the agreement might be a person and a limited liability company under his control or two or more companies under the control of a single person. It had been doubtful whether a civil action could be maintained against a 'one-man' company alleging conspiracy between the company and its sole controller: *Gonlart v Trans-Atlantic Marine Inc* [1970] 2 Lloyd's Rep 389 (US).

27. See *Dillon v Dunnes Stores and Ors* (20 December 1968, unreported), SC, although the action for conspiracy was not successful.

28. *Generale Bank Nederland NV (formerly Credit Lyonnais Bank Nederland NV) v Export Credits Guarantee Dept* (1997) *The Times*, 4 August, noted (1997) 12 (11) JIBL N214.

29. *Morgan v Fry* [1968] 1 QB 521 *per* Widgery J (not affected by CA [1968] 2 QB 710).

30. *Rookes v Barnard* [1964] AC 1129.

31. *Per* Fitzgibbon J in *Molloy v Gallagher* [1933] IR 1 at 10 citing the following authorities: *Savill v Roberts* I Carth 417; *Muriel v Tracy* 2 Show 51; *Pollard v Evans* 5 Mod 169; *Skinner v Gunton* 1 Wms Saund 228. See, too, Oliver J in *Midland Bank Trust Co Ltd v Green (No 3)* fn 23 above at 523.

32. *Sandman v Panasonic UK Ltd* [1998] FSR 651 at 664.

with a group acting together, and concluded there must be evidence that the defendant was actually involved in furthering the common design – that he took part in the unlawful act.

The plaintiff's injury must result from the combination

[5.13] In conspiracy to injure another, the plaintiff must establish that the injury concerned was due to the combination between the defendants. In *Nunan v Amalgamated Society of Carpenters*,[33] a trade union or its officials were held not liable on a claim of conspiracy where there was no evidence to connect their action directly with a fellow worker's refusal to work with the plaintiff (thus preventing his employment). In *Molloy v Gallagher and Ors*,[34] the Supreme Court found the plaintiff's removal as assistant teacher in a national school was not brought about by the defendants – rather she had been removed solely on account of her own 'deliberate and prolonged insubordination.' The defendants' agreement, if agreement there was, had not produced the result alleged by the plaintiff. She had brought about her own injury.

Damage is an essential ingredient of the tort. Pecuniary loss must be shown.[35] Damages are at large and not limited to a precise calculation of the amount of the pecuniary loss actually proved.[36]

CONSPIRACY TO INJURE OR 'SIMPLE' CONSPIRACY

[5.14] Lord Cave LC offered the following definition of the first form of the tort, conspiracy to injure or 'simple' conspiracy, in *Sorrell v Smith*:[37]

> (1) A combination of two or more persons wilfully to injure a man in his trade is unlawful and, if it results in damage to him, is actionable.

> (2) If the real purpose of the combination is not to injure another but to forward or defend the trade of those who enter into it, no wrong is committed and no action will lie, although damage to another ensues.

Apart from the element of combination or concerted action, the defendants do not perpetrate a legal wrong. This form of the tort enables the decisions in *Allen v Flood*[38] and *Quinn v Leatham*[39] (paras **5.04–5.05**) to be reconciled. Subsequent rationalisation of these emphasised the element of combination in *Quinn v Leathem* thus enabling the law to be consistent in disavowing the imposition of liability for the deliberate infliction of economic harm on another without justification. The apparent justification for imposing liability in the circumstances is because the element of

---

33. *Nunan v Amalgamated Society of Carpenters* (1904) ILTR 202.
34. *Molloy v Gallagher and Ors* [1933] IR 1.
35. Considered in *Lonrho v Fayed (no 5)* [1993] 1 WLR 1489.
36. Dillon LJ in *Lonrho v Fayed (no 5)* [1993] 1 WLR 1489 at 1494.
37. *Sorrell v Smith* [1925] AC 700 at 712.
38. *Allen v Flood* [1898] AC 1.
39. *Quinn v Leatham* [1901] AC 495.

numbers is said to aggravate and to outweigh the impact of one person acting alone. Elias and Ewing describe this as 'a naïve assumption once the doctrine of separate legal personality for corporate bodies had been accepted into English law'.[40] And naiveté gave way to something far more serious with the development of large corporate organisations. Lord Diplock put the matter forcefully in *Lonrho*:[41]

> To suggest today that acts done by one street-corner grocer in concert with a second are more oppressive and dangerous to a competitor than the same acts done by a string of supermarkets under a single ownership or that a multinational conglomerate ... does not exercise greater economic power than any combination of small businesses is to shut one's eyes to what has been happening in the business and industrial world since the turn of the century and, in particular, since the end of the 1939–45 war.

However, he added:

> The civil tort of conspiracy to injure the plaintiff's commercial interests where that is the predominant purpose of the agreement between the defendants and of the acts done in execution of it which caused damage to the plaintiff, must I think be accepted by this House as too well established to be discarded, however anomalous it may seem today.

The tort of conspiracy to injure creates liability for abuse of the right to combine.[42]

Motive and intention

[5.15] In a conspiracy to injure, the most central distinction is where the object is the legitimate benefit of the combiners (hereafter called 'motive') and where the object is deliberate damage to the plaintiff without any justification (hereafter called 'intention').[43] Establishing an intention to injure the plaintiff is by no means an easy matter. An old and celebrated *dictum* of Brian CJ runs, '*Comen erudition est que l'entent d'un home ne sera trie, car le diable n'ad conusance de l'entent d'un home.*'[44]

A court of law has always encountered grave difficulty when dealing with evidence of intention. Moreover, it has not yet been established whether the concept of intention is the same for all the economic torts that require it. Intention may vary in meaning between different branches of the law. In contract law, for example, intention to create

---

40.   Elias and Ewing, 'Economic Torts and Labour Law: Old Principles and New Liabilities', (1982) Camb LJ 321.

41.   *Lonrho Ltd v Shell Petroleum Co Ltd (No 2)* [1982] AC 173, 188–89. See, similarly, Gatehouse J in *Metall and Rohstoff AG v Donaldson, Lufkin and Jenrette* [1990] 1 QB 391, 402–3.

42.   Elias and Ewing, fn 40 at 325.

43.   Salmond, *Law of Torts* (6th edn, Sweet & Maxwell, 1924), 358 prefer the terms 'purpose' and 'object' for 'motive' and 'intention'.

44.   Cited by O'Sullivan, 'It is common knowledge that a man's intention will not be tried, because the devil doesn't know what a man intends.' *The Spirit of the Common Law* (1965) at 74.

legal relations is not universally accepted as necessary evidence of the existence of contractual obligations: the common law test of consideration is believed sufficient to enable a determination of the boundaries of contract.

[5.16] In tort, 'intention' and 'motive' are frequently equated in a confusing way by writers and judges alike. The law of torts is generally not concerned with motives, whether selfish or altruistic, good or bad. A good motive will usually not transform an otherwise innocent act into a tortious one and a good motive likewise will not enable a defendant to escape liability for a tortious act committed by him.[45]

Tort law is, however, concerned with the weighing of an actor's interest against the interest of the person harmed by his act. Motive becomes a relevant consideration when it is related to some interest, for example, in trade relations. Where an actor possesses such an interest, the law balances his interest against that of the party injured by the act. So, as will be seen, a conspiracy resulting in injury to another *prima facie* may be excused if the motive of the combination is one that the law considers proper, for example, a desire to protect the joint economic interests of those who have combined. In such a case, where the motive is found to be proper or good, one speaks of the conspiracy as *justifiable* and there is no ensuing liability. In a tort action for conspiracy, therefore, it can be maintained that, although the defendants intended to injure the plaintiff, the motive behind their intention to injure was good, an argument paradoxical perhaps to the lay person.

[5.17] There is a clear need to distinguish between motive and intention in relation to conspiracy, to keep the substance of the words clear in spite of the form in which they appear.[46] Allen has described intention as 'a determination of the will to do or abstain from future action.'[47] The question why a man has determined to act in a particular manner may be answered in many ways, of which a 'motive answer' is but one. Motive answers may be detailed or general.

Heydon in his *Economic Torts*[48] enumerates some of the as yet unsolved problems arising out of the requirement of intention to injure the plaintiff. These problems include questions such as whether the defendant must know the plaintiff by name or whether he must merely intend to injure whoever is in the plaintiff's position. An Irish court would find these questions equally perplexing but is likely to follow the House of

---

45.   *Bradford Corporation v Pickles* [1895] AC 587.

46.   In *Sorrell v Smith* [1925] AC 700 Lord Sumner suggested the words stood in need of strict definition. See the earlier Irish case of *Kearney v Lloyd* (1890) 26 LR Ir 268 and the comment thereon by Andrews J in *Leathem v Craig* [1899] 1 IR 667 at 681 where 'object' (ie motive) and 'intention' are used as though synonymous. In *Sorrell* Viscount Cave LC referred to *Kearney v Lloyd* but did not feel called on to give his opinion of the case: *ibid,* 713.

47.   Allen, 'Motive and Intention' (1957) 73 LQR 512, at 513.

48.   Heydon, *Economic Torts* (2nd edn, Sweet and Maxwell, 1978).

Lords in *Lonrho v Fayed*[49] which said the combination must be aimed at or directed at the claimant.

Good motive or justification

[5.18] A defence of justification amounts to a claim by the defendant that he was motivated to protect some particular interest or right of his own. This right or interest must be regarded as legitimate by a court of law. Lord Bridge in *Lonrho v Fayed*[50] was clear (this textbook uses 'motive' for 'purpose', para **5.15**):

> Liability must depend on ascertaining the predominant purpose. If that predominant purpose is to damage another person and damage results that is tortious conspiracy. If the predominant purpose is the lawful protection or promotion of any lawful interests of the combiners (no illegal means being employed) it is not a tortious conspiracy even though it causes damage to another person.

In *Mogul Steamship Co v McGregor Gow & Co*[51] (para **5.06**), the House of Lords held that the plaintiff had no cause of action since the defendants had employed what were then lawful means and had acted with the lawful object of protecting their own trade interests. The case involved a conspiracy to ruin competitors by price cutting. Bowen LJ held that the right of traders to carry on trade freely to their own best advantage could be a justification for their acts, to be balanced against the right of the plaintiffs to be protected in the legitimate exercise of their trade.[52]

Mogul was followed by Dixon J in the Irish High Court in *Connelly v Loughney & McCarthy*.[53] The implementation of a policy of retail price maintenance that injured the plaintiff was held not to constitute an actionable combination. The purpose had been

---

49.   *Lonrho v Fayed (No 1)* [1992] 1 AC 448 at 465.

50.   *Lonrho v Fayed (No 1)* [1992] 1 AC 448 at 463–8 quoting Lord Simon in *Crofter Hand Woven Harris Tweed Co Ltd v Veitch* [1942] AC 435.

51.   *Mogul Steamship Co v McGregor Gow & Co* [1892] AC 25.

52.   See further *Boots Cash Chemist v Grundy* (1900) 82 LT 769. It is of historical interest that some years before *Mogul* the following extract appeared in the *Irish Law Times*: 'The life of trade though it be, competition forms the fiercest danger to be encountered in commerce nowadays, the most difficult to encounter judiciously and without entailing disaster no less lethal that any it is attempted to counteract. It becomes a war to the knife, in which the defendant's weapon may wound him worst. But, in the main, the antagonisms of force fructify in advantage, as Mr Justice Grove not long since ventured to demonstrate; and in point of public policy, competition too should be encouraged rather than checked': (1883) 22 ILT & SJ 465.

53   *Connelly v Loughney & McCarthy* [1953] 87 ILTR 49. See too *Baldwin v Left* (1 February 1973, unreported), HC and *Tru-valu Ltd v Switzer & Co* (10 March 1972, unreported), HC. The defence of justification is not more easily available to a public official than to an ordinary citizen. 'It cannot be within the performance of his public duty by a public official to conspire maliciously to injure a fellow servant and if a jury found upon the evidence so ... such a finding would negative the defence of statutory protection', *Molloy v Gallagher* [1933] IR 1, 9 *per* Fitzgibbon J (Supreme Court). (contd .../)

the legitimate promotion of trade interests and this was held sufficient to justify any apparent wrong the plaintiff had endured.

'Lawful interests' were considered in many cases since *Mogul*. For instance, the pursuit of business or similar interests were held to be legitimate interests in *Lonrho Ltd v Shell Petroleum & BP Ltd (No 2)*.[54] At times the lawfulness of the interests are dependent on the attitude adopted by judges. For example, *Sweeney v Coote*[55] would not be decided in the same way today upholding, as it did, religious discrimination.

[5.19] The obvious and compelling question in trade disputes law is whether the collective interest of workers constitutes a 'legitimate interest'. For decades after *Mogul* this interest was dismissed. For instance, in *Larkin and Ors v Long*[56] (the facts appear at para **9.36**) the House of Lords, on appeal from the Court of Appeal in Ireland, was unwilling to extend *Mogul* into the sphere of trade union interests. Sergeant Sullivan acting on behalf of the appellants tried to insist that it was quite legitimate for members of the Transport and General Workers Union in their own interests to pass a rule that they should not work for a stevedore who was not a member of the Stevedores' Union. They were not bound to work for him or for any other person for whom they did not choose to work and, 'in the legitimate promotion of their own interest', he argued they were entitled within *Mogul* to observe that rule though it might incidentally cause injury to those who desired to employ these workmen, but for whom they themselves did not desire to work. Lord Atkinson rejected this argument. His reasoning merits full citation:[57]

> It is undoubtedly true that the members of a trade union need not work for those for whom they do not desire to work. That is the right to personal freedom of action referred to in the well-known passages from the judgment of Lord Bramwell in *Regina v Druitt* 10 Cox CC 592, 600, and from the essay of Sir W Erle on trades unions (p 12). They have been many times approved of in your Lordships' House. But it is equally true that the members of trade unions are bound to respect the right of other workmen to work for whom they please, on what terms and at what times they please, so long as they do nothing illegal, and are also bound to respect the right of an employer to undertake any work he pleases to undertake, and to employ what workmen he chooses, on whatever terms they both agree to, unless there is something unlawful in this action. If,

---

53. (contd) At the time of this dictum in 1933, statutory protection was afforded to public officials under the Public Authorities Protection Act 1893; the Act was repealed by the Public Authorities (Judicial Proceedings) Act 1954.

54. *Lonrho Ltd v Shell Petroleum & BP Ltd (No 2)* [1982] AC 173, 189.

55. *Sweeney v Coote* [1906] 1 IR 428; [1907] 1 IR 233; (1907) ILTR 117. See 'Actionable Conspiracy' (1930) 64 ILT & SJ 193.

56. *Larkin and Ors v Long* (1915) ILTR 121. Before that case see *Gregory v Brunwick* (1843–44) 6 M & G 209, 953 (members of a theatre hissing an actor); *White v Riley* [1921] 1 Ch 1 (employer threatened with work stoppages by members of one union if he did not dismiss employee belonging to another union); *Sorrell v Smith* [1925] AC 700 (retail newsvendors against wholesale newsvendors); *Reynolds v Shipping Federation* [1924] 1 Ch 28 (exclusion from the industry of non-unionists).

57. *Larkin and Ors v Long* (1915) ILTR 121 at 124.

therefore, any two or more members of a trade union, whatever its rules may be, wilfully and knowingly combine to injure an employer by inducing his workmen to break their contracts with him, or not to enter into contracts with him, resulting in damage to him, that is an entirely different matter. That is an invasion of the liberty of action of others, and has no analogy to the action of the defendant in the *Mogul* case; for there, as Lord Halsbury pointed out in *Quinn v Leatham* [1901] AC 495, no legal right had been interfered with, no coercion of mind or will had been effected, all were left free to trade on what terms they willed, and nothing was done, except in rival trading, which could be supposed to interfere with the appellant's interest. The fact that members of a trade union are merely acting in obedience to a rule of their union believed by them to be for their benefit is no defence to an action for the breach of any contracts they have entered into: *Read v Friendly Society of Operative Stone Masons* [1902] 2 KB 88, 732, and still less is it a defence to the wilful and malicious infringement in combination of that legal right of personal freedom of action which they claim for themselves, but which others are entitled to quite as fully and as absolutely as they are.

[5.20] This was reversed, however, in *Crofter Hand Woven Harris Tweed Co v Veitch*[58] where it was held that 'lawful interests' covered those of workers as well as of traders:

> A perfectly lawful strike may aim at dislocating the employer's business for the moment but its real object is to secure better wages or conditions for the workers. The true contrast is, I think, between the case where the object is deliberate damage without any such just cause.[59]

This case was an essential counterbalance for *Mogul* in relation to trade union interests. In *Crofter,* a combination between trade union officials and employers (without unlawful acts on anyone's part) to prevent the handling by dockers in the union of supplies for the employer's trade competitors was held to be legitimate. The House of Lords did not define 'legitimate interests' in an exhaustive way. It is likely a *bona fide* belief will be sufficient to show a legitimate interest,[60] provided the action taken does not exceed what is necessary for the protection of that interest. In *Lonrho Plc v Fayed*[61] the Court of Appeal assumed the burden of proving justification is on the defendant. Lord Bridge noted that the 'predominant purpose' requirement in conspiracy to injure has 'no relevance to the second type of conspiracy which employs unlawful means'[62] where intention to injure, which is not predominant, is sufficient.

Mixed motives

[5.21] Some writers have criticised the defence of justification on the basis *inter alia* that it makes conspiracy to cause damage by lawful means a tort which is very difficult

58.   *Crofter Hand Woven Harris Tweed Co v Veitch* [1942] AC 435.

59.   *Per* Wright LJ at 469. For a discussion of this case in Ireland see *Meskell v CIE* [1973] IR 121, *passim, per* Walsh J (Supreme Court). A reference was made to it earlier in *Kearney v Lloyd* fn 46 above at 288 *per* Palles, CB.

60.   *Stratford v Lindley* [1965] AC 269, 323 *per* Lord Reid.

61.   *Lonrho Plc v Fayed (No 5)* [1993] 1 WLR 1489.

62.   *Lonrho v Fayed* [1992] 1 AC 448 at 464.

to commit. It amounts to giving a licence to any conspiracy the predominant motive of which is self-interest rather than malice.[63] In special reference to combined action against employers or non-unionists on the part of unionists, it has also been said that to ask the question whether they acted to defend their own trade interests or to injure their economic adversary for the time being, is equivalent to asking of a soldier who shoots in battle, whether he does so for the purpose of injuring his enemy or of defending his country.[64] The analogy is not altogether unsound, because combined strike action is usually undertaken both to harm the employer concerned, and to improve the conditions of the trade unionists.

People's motives are rarely solitary and obvious but complex and varied. The difficulties which arise out of this have mostly been resolved by the decision in the *Crofter* case, in which Lord Wright said:

> Cases of mixed motives, or as I should prefer to say, of the presence of more than one object, are not uncommon. If so, it is for the jury or judge of fact to decide which is the predominant object ... I may add that I do not accept, as a general proposition, that there may be a complete identity of interest between parties to a combination. There must, however, be sufficient identity of object, though the advantage to be derived from that same object may be the same ...[65]

[5.22] The greatest difficulty would be where there was an agreement to cause damage or loss with each of the parties seeking to carry out some object or satisfy some motive beyond the mere infliction of damage, one or more acting from a single object or motive, others acting solely from more than one single object or motive. This type of situation has not yet arisen in this country or in England but it has been analysed by the High Court of Australia, *obiter*, in *McKernan v Fraser*[66] and the views of Evatt J in that case are useful. Very briefly, he took an illustration where A, B, C, D, E and F agree to inflict damage on X. A and B agree because they desire to protect the standards of the professional body to which all belong and have no other object or quarrel, concealing this motive from the other parties to the agreement and from each other. C and D act with the motive of damaging X. E and F act from mixed motives: they genuinely wish to maintain the professional ideals of their body, but they also have a strong dislike of X, which they gratify when they enter into the agreement.

In the judge's opinion, A and B, not knowing of the various motives of C and D and of E and F are not liable. No question of agency can arise. Nor are C and D liable in his view, in the absence of, for example, a separate agreement between themselves to procure acts to be done by A, B, E, F and themselves, all in combination. The uncommunicated existence of an evil motive in C and D towards X does not make

---

63. 'English law ... has for better or worse adopted the test of self-interest or selfishness as being capable of justifying the deliberate doing of lawful acts which inflict harm': *per* Lord Wright in *Crofter's* case [1942] AC 435, 472.

64. *Per* Evatt J (quoting Sir Godfrey Lushington) in *McKernan v Fraser* (1931) 46 CLR 343 (High Court of Australia).

65. *Crofter Hand Woven Harris Tweed Co v Veitch* [1942] AC 435, at 478.

66. *McKernan v Fraser* (1931) 40 CLR 343.

them alone liable to X. Upon the same footing, E and F would not be liable, because no separate understanding between them is shown. In this illustration therefore, none of A, B, C, D, E and F would be liable for 'conspiracy to injure.'

[5.23] In the area of justification, the tort of conspiracy committed by lawful means differs significantly from the same tort committed by unlawful means. Where unlawful means have been employed, the defence of justification cannot operate. This is particularly important in cases alleging unconstitutional means. For example, in *McGowan v Murphy*[67] Walsh J said that:

> [If]the defendants combined to procure the expulsion of the plaintiff from the trade union and in so doing had as their sole or main purpose or object the injuring of the plaintiff and the plaintiff suffered damage by reason of it, the defendants would be guilty of the actionable tort of conspiracy, even if the expulsion was not in breach of the rules of the union. To that extent a combination of persons is in a less favoured position than an individual doing the same act ... If, however, the real purpose of the combination was not to injure the plaintiff but to defend the interests of the trade union by maintaining discipline then no wrong was committed and no action will lie even though damage to the plaintiff resulted *provided that the means used were not in themselves unlawful* [emphasis added].

Possibly the courts feel the enhanced power of a combination must be kept in check by imposing liability in such cases. The Supreme Court (McCarthy J) in *Taylor v Smyth and Ors*[68] did not hesitate to endorse and accept Walsh J's view above:

> In my opinion, if there be a combination to use unlawful means to achieve a particular aim, that is an actionable conspiracy, whether or not such means amount to an infringement of constitutional rights. I would emphasise that it is the very combination itself that strengthens the hands of the wrongdoers. It is entirely logical that what is actionable when done by unlawful means such as procuring a breach of contract, is actionable against an individual, even though his purpose be solely one of self-interest; it should not cease to be actionable when done in combination by a group with a like purpose. In my view the law is correctly stated in *McGowan v Murphy.*[69] If conspiracy be inchoate it is difficult to see how it can have caused damage, a necessary ingredient of every tort. If it be executed, then the cause of action derives from the execution whether it be because of the unlawful nature of the act done or the unlawful means used.

---

67.   *McGowan v Murphy* (10 April 1967, unreported), SC.
68.   *Taylor v Smyth and Ors* [1991] IR 142, 170.
69.   *McGowan v Murphy* (10 April 1967, unreported), SC. 'It would be hard to defend an outcome in which conspirators who have caused injury by unlawful means are allowed to escape liability for conspiracy if they show that they were predominantly motivated by intention to further their own interests but are caught if each conspirator is sued as an individual tortfeasor under the tort of unlawful interference in trade. It would be a strange reversal of the common perception that combination strengthened the hands of wrongdoers' (Eekelaar, 'The Conspiracy Tangle' (1990) 106 LQR 223, note re *Metall and Rohsroff v Donaldson, Lufkin & Jenrette* [1990] 1 QB 391).

CONSPIRACY TO DO AN UNLAWFUL ACT OR TO USE UNLAWFUL MEANS

[5.24] A useful statement of the essential elements of this form of conspiracy is to be found in the judgment of Nourse LJ in *Kuwait Oil Tanker Co v Al Bader & Ors*:[70]

> A conspiracy to injure by unlawful means is actionable where the claimant proves that he has suffered loss or damage as the result of unlawful action taken pursuant to a combination or agreement between the defendant and another person or persons to injure him by unlawful means, whether or not it is the predominant purpose of the defendant to do so.

In the same judgment,[71] Nourse LJ approved the following dictum of Oliver LJ in *Bourgoin SA v Minister of Agriculture, Fisheries and Food*:[72]

> If an act is done deliberately and with knowledge of its consequences, I do not think that the actor can sensibly say that he did not 'intend' the consequences or that the act was not 'aimed' at the person who, it is known, will suffer them.

[5.25] Whenever an act is itself tortious, a combination to do that act is tortious conspiracy: *Crofter* case above, *per* Lord Wright.[73] As damage is an essential element of the tort, a conspiracy to commit a tort, without more, will not be an actionable wrong. The House of Lords limited the scope of conspiracy to use unlawful means in *Lonrho Ltd v Shell Petroleum & BP Ltd (No 2)*[74] (para **5.09**). The House was determined to restrict liability, even in cases where the defendants' acts were crimes in breach of penal statutes.[75] Much reliance was placed on *Lonrho Ltd v Shell Petroleum & BP Ltd (No 2)*[76] and the Court of Appeal decision in *Lonrho Plc v Fayed*[77] in the Supreme Court in *Taylor v Smyth and Ors*.[78] It was argued that the defendants were solely motivated to protect their own interests, in this instance their financial interests and an intoxicating liquor licence, and that the damage caused, if damage was caused, was incidental to their conduct motivated in that fashion. McCarthy J's words will be recalled (at **5.23**):

> ... if there be a combination to use unlawful means to achieve a particular aim, that is actionable conspiracy, whether or not such means amount to an infringement of constitutional rights.

---

70. *Kuwait Oil Tanker Co v Al Bader & Ors* [2000] 2 All ER (Comm) 271 at 312.
71. At 315.
72. *Bourgoin SA v Minister of Agriculture, Fisheries and Food* [1986] QB 716 at 777.
73. *Crofter Hand Woven Harris Tweed Co v Veitch* [1942] AC 435 at 462.
74. *Lonrho Ltd v Shell Petroleum Co Ltd (No 2)* [1982] AC 173.
75. *Clerk and Lindsell on Torts* (19th edn, Sweet & Maxwell, 2005), opine at para 768 that although the conspiracy in *Lonrho* involved unlawful means of criminal offences under a penal statute, the House's ruling seemed to apply to the civil tort of conspiracy in all its forms. On *Lonrho* see Elias and Tettenborn, 'Crime, Tort and Compensation in Private and Public Law' (1981) Camb LJ 230.
76. *Lonrho Ltd v Shell Petroleum Co Ltd (No 2)* [1982] AC 173.
77. *Lonrho Plc v Fayed (No 1)* [1990] 2 QB 479.
78. *Taylor v Smyth and Ors* [1991] IR 142. See analysis by Kerr, (1990) 12 DULJ 166.

There is no requirement of predominant motive or purpose to injure the plaintiff, which the House of Lords, in *Lonrho Plc v Fayed*[79] decided after *Taylor*, made clear.

[5.26] This is reflected in recent English cases. In *Colliers CRE Plc v Pandya and Ors*[80] Seymour J accepted the House of Lords decision in *Revenue and Customs Commissioners v Total Network SL*[81] on the role of motive in the second form of this tort:[82]

> Where, however, unlawful means are employed by the conspirators to achieve their object and their object involves causing harm to the victim, the intent to cause that harm does not have to be the predominant purpose of the conspiracy. This difference between the torts of lawful means conspiracy and unlawful means conspiracy is sometimes described as anomalous. In my opinion it is not. The difference reflects and demonstrates the essential flexibility of the action on the case. It is not all conduct foreseeably likely to cause, and that does cause, economic harm to another that is tortious. Nor should it be. The circumstances must be such as to make the conduct sufficiently reprehensible to justify imposing on those who have brought about the harm liability in damages for having done so.

His attention had been drawn to the decision of Newman J in *The Mayor and Burgesses of the London Borough of Tower Hamlets v Chavda*:[83]

> Of the two types of actionable conspiracy referred to by the Court of Appeal, [the plaintiffs] allege a conspiracy to injure by unlawful means. As a result, before finding the claim proved, the court must be satisfied that the defendants intended to injure the claimant, but injury to the claimant need not have been the predominant purpose. The claimant must prove that it has suffered loss or damage as a result of the unlawful action taken pursuant to the conspiracy. It is not necessary to show that there is anything in the nature of an express agreement, whether formal or informal. It is sufficient if two or more persons combine, albeit tacitly, to achieve a common end. The task of the court is to scrutinise the acts which are relied upon to see what inferences can be drawn as to the existence or otherwise of the alleged conspiracy.

---

79. *Lonrho Plc v Fayed (No 1)* [1992] 1 AC 448.

80. *Colliers CRE Plc v Pandya and Ors* [2009] EWHC 211 (QB). See too *Meretz Investments NV and Anor v ACP Ltd and Ors* [2007] EWCA 1303, CA, held on the facts that the requisite intention for the tort had not been made out. The court also held that although *OBG* was not in terms a case about conspiracy, but rather about the closely related torts of inducing a breach of contract and causing loss by unlawful means, nonetheless, the dicta about intent to injure were fully applicable to conspiracy to injure by unlawful means. This approach was repeated in *Bank of Tokyo-Mitsubishi UFJ Ltd, KBC Bank NV v Baskan Gida Sanayi Ve Pazarlama AS and Others* [2009] EWHC 1276 (Ch), para 833.

81. *Revenue and Customs Commissioners v Total Network SL* [2008] 2 WLR 711.

82. Paragraph 56 of the speech of Lord Scott of Foscote at 733–734.

83. *Mayor and Burgesses of the London Borough of Tower Hamlets v Chavda* [2005] EWHC 2183 (QB), paras 18 and 19.

On the burden of proof, he said:

> I remind myself that the burden of proof rests on [the plaintiffs] and that, although the standard of proof in this case is the same as that which applies in all civil proceedings, namely proof on the balance of probabilities, the court should require cogent evidence commensurate with the seriousness of the allegation before it considers itself justified in finding the case proved.

A tort to agree a tort

[5.27] Whether there is a separate tort to agree to commit a tort was once doubtful, following *Dillon v Dunnes Stores and Ors*.[84] In that case the plaintiff, a shop assistant, was instructed to go to an upstairs office. She was then transferred to another office where she was questioned by members of An Garda Síochána who were also detectives. Eventually she signed a statement purporting to confess to having stolen goods and money belonging to the company, crimes of which she afterwards said she was innocent. Her questioning lasted for two hours. She was later questioned by one of the directors and suspended from her employment. The plaintiff claimed damages for false imprisonment, wrongful dismissal, defamation of character, injurious falsehood and conspiracy to: (a) injure, (b) defame, (c) falsely imprison and (d) maliciously prosecute. In her statement of claim she alleged only conspiracy (a) to injure and (b) falsely to imprison. The questions eventually left to the jury dealt with two only of the alleged causes of action – conspiracy to imprison unlawfully and unlawful (or false) imprisonment.

The Supreme Court found on the evidence that the plaintiff's case for false imprisonment failed against the company and its directors. As there was no evidence, the allegation of conspiracy to imprison was held to fall also – '*agreement* and *conspiracy* are one and the same thing.'[85] It was submitted on behalf of the directors and the company that conspiracy to commit a tort is not an independent tort. The Supreme Court responded positively: if one considers the difference between conspiracy in criminal law and the tort of conspiracy, said O Dálaigh J, it becomes clear why there is no room in civil law for the independent tort of conspiracy to commit a tort.

The judge noted that Lord Denning (as he then was) had expressed 'the same idea' in *Ward v Lewis*[86] when he said that, if the court sees a charge of conspiracy as well as an actually committed tort (the object of the agreement), it will strike out the allegation of conspiracy 'on the simple ground that the conspiracy adds nothing when the tort has in fact been committed.'[87]

---

84. *Dillon v Dunnes Stores and Ors* (20 December 1968, unreported), HC.
85. *Per* O Dálaigh J at 9 (his emphasis).
86. *Ward v Lewis* [1955] 1 WLR 9, 11. Burns, 'Civil Conspiracy: An Unwieldy Vessel Rides a Judicial Tempest' (1982) 16 UBC Law Rev 229, at 245.
87. This was questionable at the time in the light of *O'Keeffe v Walsh* [1903] 2 IR 681.

[5.28] In the circumstances of *Dillon,* it was not necessary for the Supreme Court to 'express a concluded view' on the matter. However, in *Kuwait Oil Tanker Co SAT v Al Bader*[88] the Court of Appeal expressed a contrary view:

> The claimants had to show an intention to injure but not that that was the defendants' predominant purpose. The intention to injure could be inferred from the acts themselves. The fact that the unlawful acts in this case were tortious did not mean that the conspiracy merged in the torts and did not prevent the claimants alleging both the conspiracy and the torts. The claimants had to prove the nature of the agreement, the unlawful means alleged, each unlawful act relied on as causing loss and the fact that each act was carried out pursuant to the conspiracy.

These words were cited with approval by McCarthy J in the Supreme Court in *Taylor v Smyth and Ors*[89] who extracted the following comment from a review of *Dillon* by McMahon and Binchy in their *Irish Law of Torts*[90]:

> In the light of subsequent decisions in which proceedings for conspiracy have been litigated without any discussion as to the existence of the tort, it is safe to assume that the view tentatively favoured by the Supreme Court in *Dillon*'s case has been quietly interred.

Knowledge

[5.29] What knowledge must the conspirators have for purposes of liability in the second form of the tort? In *Colliers CRE Plc v Pandya and Ors*[91] counsel for the defendants submitted that the court should follow Harman J in *Huntley v Thornton*[92] who said:

> No doubt it is not necessary that all the conspirators should join at the same time, but it is, I think, necessary that they should know all the facts and entertain the same object.

He further cited as a correct statement of the law Viscount Dilhorne on the knowledge required for criminal conspiracy in *R v Churchill (No 2)*:[93]

> The question is, 'What did they agree to do?' If what they agreed to do was, on the facts known to them, an unlawful act, they are guilty of conspiracy and cannot excuse themselves by saying that, owing to their ignorance of the law, they did not realise that such an act was a crime. If, on the facts known to them, what they agreed to do was lawful, they are not rendered artificially guilty by the existence of other facts, not known to them, giving a different and criminal quality to the act agreed upon.

---

88. *Kuwait Oil Tanker Co SAT v Al Bader* [2000] 2 All ER (Comm) 271.
89. *Taylor v Smyth and Ors* [1991] IR 142 at 168.
90. McMahon and Binchy, *Irish Law of Torts* (3rd edn, Butterworths, 2000).
91. *Colliers CRE Plc v Pandya and Ors* [2009] EWHC 211 (QB).
92. *Huntley v Thornton* [1957] 1 WLR 321, 343 *per* Harman J.
93. *R v Churchill (No 2)* [1967] 2 AC 224, adopted by the Court of Appeal for civil cases of conspiracy (see *Belmont Finance Corp v Williams Furniture Ltd (No 2)* [1979] Ch 250 at 271 and *Pritchard v Briggs* [1980] Ch 338, 414).

[5.30] In *Meretz Investments NV and Anor v ACP and Ors*,[94] Arden and Toulson LJJ went further by requiring, as a condition of liability, that the defendant knows that the claimant's loss was to be caused by the use of unlawful means:[95]

> Just as the tort of conspiracy to induce breach of contract is not committed if the defendant believes that the outcome sought by him will not involve a breach of contract (the *Mainstream* case [2005] IRLR 964) so a defendant should not be liable for conspiracy to injure by unlawful means if he believes that he has a lawful right to do what he is doing. This is consistent with Lord Hoffmann's comment in the *OBG* case [2008] 1 AC 1 para 56, when considering the tort of causing injury by unlawful means, that the common law in this area is designed only to enforce basic standards of civilised behaviour.

This puts the spotlight on the quality of the requisite knowledge, and its extent. Issues as to the extent of the knowledge necessary to be established are important where, for example, primary fraudsters may have invited others to assist them in their dishonest designs on a strict 'need to know' basis as happened in *Bank of Tokyo-Mitsubishi UFJ Ltd, KBC Bank NV v Baskan Gida Sanayi Ve Pazarlama AS and Ors*.[96] How much of the principal fraudster's scheme must the defendant know before incurring liability for the whole, or part, of the consequences? There are dicta pointing both ways.

[5.31] Some indirect guidance may be obtained from the analysis of the Court of Appeal in *IS Innovative Software Ltd v Howes*.[97] The defendant was a typical 'bit-player' in a larger conspiracy in which he became involved on a need-to-know basis. Having resigned as managing director of the claimant company, he was approached by three of its other employees who, fearing redundancy, sought to improve the financial consequences of being dismissed by a dishonest scheme whereby they hoodwinked the company into thinking that they had been employed on terms requiring notice to be given expiring on particular dates. For that purpose they persuaded the defendant dishonestly to sign letters of employment and to backdate them to a time when he had been managing director of the claimant company, so as to make it appear that they had been employed upon the terms which they sought to assert. Quite separately, and without the defendant knowing about it, they fabricated and then backdated a statement of general terms and conditions of employment which provided the requisite termination provisions, and then used the combination of the letters and the general terms to achieve their dishonest ends. The defendant thought that the letters which he had dishonestly backdated stated no more nor less than the terms of employment which had actually been agreed, albeit otherwise than in writing, at the material time.

[5.32] Both the trial judge and the Court of Appeal rejected the company's claim that the defendant was party to that part of the other defendants' unlawful means

---

94. *Meretz Investments NV and Anor v ACP and Ors* [2007] EWCA 1303.

95. At para 174 (p 289).

96. *Bank of Tokyo-Mitsubishi UFJ Ltd, KBC Bank NV v Baskan Gida Sanayi Ve Pazarlama AS and Ors* [2009] EWHC 1276 (Ch).

97. *IS Innovative Software Ltd v Howes* [2004] EWCA Civ 275.

conspiracy which caused the company's loss. Giving the judgment of the court, Neuberger LJ said:[98]

> In this case, [the defendant] agreed to sign the backdated letters, thereby appearing to give each of the four employees written contractual rights backdated to 1st November 2000, whereas in fact they had no such written contractual rights. Accordingly, as the judge found, he was party to an unlawful means conspiracy. We would also accept that it could fairly be said that this conspiracy, and in particular the signing of the backdated letters was 'directed to' the company, in the sense that the purpose of executing the letters in a backdated form was to induce the company to believe that they had been signed by [the defendant] at a time when he had power to bind the company.

However, he held that the judge was entitled, indeed correct, to conclude that the defendant should not be liable for the damages suffered by the company as a result of the unlawful means conspiracy, because the nature of the damage suffered arose from a provision not contained in the backdated letter wrongly executed by the defendant, but from a document which he did not know was going to be brought into existence, whose terms he did not know, and the existence of whose particular term (which actually caused the damage to the company) he had no reason to know of or even suspect. Neuberger LJ's analysis suggests that where a bit-player in a multifaceted fraud knows only of one aspect of the fraud, and is ignorant of the others, he may not be liable for anything more than the loss properly attributable to that part of the fraud of which he is aware.

[5.33] According to Briggs J in *Bank of Tokyo*,[99] there is no simple doctrinaire answer to the conundrum presented by such a case. The answer lies in a painstaking analysis of the extent to which the particular defendant shared a common objective with the primary fraudsters, and the extent to which the achievement of that objective was to the particular defendant's knowledge to be achieved by unlawful means intended to injure the claimant. The judge felt his solution was reflected in the following passages in Nourse LJ's judgment in *Kuwait Oil*:[100]

> … It is sufficient if two or more persons combine with a common intention, or, in other words, that they deliberately combine, albeit tacitly, to achieve a common end.
>
> ...
>
> Thus it is not necessary for the conspirators all to join the conspiracy at the same time, but we agree with the judge that the parties to it must be sufficiently aware of the surrounding circumstances and share the same object for it properly to be said that they were acting in concert at the time of the acts complained of.

---

98.   At para 44.

99.   *Bank of Tokyo-Mitsubishi UFJ Ltd, KBC Bank NV v Baskan Gida Sanayi Ve Pazarlama AS and Ors* [2009] EWHC 1276 (Ch).

100.   *Kuwait Oil Tanker Co SAT v Al Bader* [2000] 2 All ER (Comm) 271 at para 111 (on pp 312–3).

He approached the analysis of the facts before him, for the purpose of deciding whether the plaintiffs had established a claim in unlawful means conspiracy against either of the defendants, by asking, separately in relation to each of them, the following questions:

(i)   What objective did the defendants share with each other?

(ii) Did the attainment of that objective, to their knowledge, involve the use of unlawful means?

(iii) Did the use of such unlawful means for the attainment of that objective necessarily (in the sense of being the obverse of the coin) involve the infliction of injury upon the plaintiffs?

(iv) To what extent if at all was the plaintiffs' loss attributable to an injury necessarily (in the same sense) caused by the attainment of that common objective by the use of those unlawful means?

Unlawful means

[5.34] The ordinary requirement in conspiracy to injure or 'simple' conspiracy claims of intent being predominant in the mind of the defendant is replaced in the second form of the tort by the requirement to show that unlawful conduct has been the means of the intentional infliction of harm to the plaintiff.

The concept of 'unlawful means' for the second form of the tort of conspiracy includes a wide range of wrongs. The label 'unlawful means' identifies unlawful means as an element in the cause of action. It can be unhelpful in drawing attention away from the requirement in all examples of the tort to demonstrate an intention by the defendant to injure the plaintiff.[101] A combination that does damage to the plaintiff by means of torts such as intimidation[102] or procurement of breach of contract,[103] crimes such as fraud, breaches of the Constitution, lies to the plaintiff[104] or breach of the rules of natural justice[105] may be actionable. In *McMullan v Mulhall and Farrell*[106] the Supreme Court held that the words 'McMullan is not a member of any union, and you must dismiss him' were not defamatory of the plaintiff: they did not touch the plaintiff in his vocation, nor were they spoken of him in the way of his calling, so as to be actionable

---

101. Observed by Briggs J in *Bank of Tokyo-Mitsubishi UFJ Ltd, KBC Bank NV v Baskan Gida Sanayi Ve Pazarlama AS and Ors* [2009] EWHC 1276 (Ch), para 825.

102. *Rookes v Barnard* [1946] AC 1129.

103. *Stratford v Lindley* [1965] AC 269; *Sherriff v McMullen* [1952] IR 236; *Cotter v Ahern* [1976–77] ILRM 248.

104. *Greenhalgh v Mallard* [1947] 1 All ER 255.

105. As alleged, though not sustained, in *McGowan v Murphy* (10 April 1967, unreported) SC; see, too, *Evaskow v International Brotherhood of Boilermakers* (1969) 9 DLR (3d) 715.

106. *McMullan v Mulhall and Farrell* [1929] IR 470.

without proof of special damage. Hence, the jury's finding of damages for slander and conspiracy was set aside.[107]

[5.35] *Lonrho Ltd v Shell Petroleum & BP Ltd (No 2) (Lonrho)*[108] provided a rare occasion for the English courts to consider whether unlawful means are limited to wrongs independently actionable. The appellants alleged that the respondents had committed a conspiracy to use unlawful means against them by supplying Rhodesia with oil contrary to a sanctions order which forbade such conduct. It was argued that by so doing they had helped to support the illegal regime in Rhodesia to the economic detriment of the appellants. The Houses of Lords rejected the claim. The first limb of the decision[109] held that, as the purpose of the sanctions order was to stop the supply and delivery of oil to Southern Rhodesia by withdrawing the previously existing right of British citizens and companies to trade in oil to that country, the order could not be said to have been imposed for the benefit or protection of the particular class of persons who were engaged in supplying or delivering oil to that country, or to create a public right to be enjoyed by all subjects of the Crown who wished to avail themselves of it. In those circumstances, contravention of the sanctions order by the respondents could not amount to a breach of statutory duty which would give the appellants a right to recover in tort any loss caused by such contravention. Lord Diplock appeared to be saying that no civil action in tort could lie unless the statutory contravention was independently actionable. At the time Elias and Ewing observed[110] that the House of Lords in *Lonrho* was not directed to certain authorities suggesting that the concept of unlawful means apparently extended beyond wrongs independently actionable. Elias and Ewing's view of the principle involved has been endorsed over time.

The Supreme Court (McCarthy, Finlay and Hederman JJ concurring) in *Taylor v Smyth and Ors*[111] rejected the modification in *Lonrho*, the unlawful means in the case being breach of constitutional rights.[112]

[5.36] In *OBG Ltd v Allan*[113] (para **7.43**) Lord Hoffmann and the majority of the House of lords endorsed a restrictive definition of 'unlawful means' for the purpose of the separate 'unlawful means' tort, which is detailed in **Ch 7**. He said that acts against a

---

107. The action was instituted by the plaintiff to recover damages for slander and for conspiracy. The defendants suggested the statement of claim did not rely upon defamation as a separate cause of action and that slander was only mentioned as an illegal means by which the object of the alleged conspiracy was to be attained or as an illegal object of the conspiracy itself. Yet Fitzgibbon J was of the opinion the statement of claim could 'fairly be regarded as containing an allegation of damage by slander and a claim to recover compensation therefor, in addition to the claim for damages for conspiracy' [1922] IR at 477. Contrast Lord Denning in *Ward v Lewis* (para **5.27**).

108. *Lonrho Ltd v Shell Petroleum Co Ltd* [1982] AC 173.

109. The second limb was mentioned at para **5.18**.

110. Elias and Ewing, 'Economic Torts and Labour Law: Old Principles and New Liabilities' (1982) Camb LJ 321 at 337.

111. *Taylor v Smyth and Ors* [1991] IR 142, 170, see *Dicta* (para **5.23**).

112. *McGowan v Murphy* (10 April 1967, unreported), SC.

113. *OBG Ltd v Allan* [2008] 1 AC 1.

third party count as unlawful means only if they are actionable by that third party or would have been actionable if the third party has suffered loss. The House did not mention the tort of conspiracy. The issue in *Total Network SL v Her Majesty's Revenue and Customs Commissioners*[114] was whether the 'unlawful means' tort has the same actionability restriction in conspiracy. The facts concerned a 'missing trader' fraud. The offence relied on was the common law offence of 'cheating the public revenue' under s 32(1)(a) of the Theft Act 1968, which is not civilly actionable. The Court of Appeal held it was prevented by binding authority from finding for the Commissioners. The House of Lords unanimously allowed the Commissioners' appeal, overruled the contrary precedent and held that for the tort of conspiracy, 'unlawful means' should not be confined to wrongdoing otherwise actionable by the claimant. Counsel for the respondents had argued that to do otherwise would be irreconcilable with the reasoning in *Mogul Steamship Co Ltd v McGregor Gow & Co*[115] and *Quinn v Leathem*,[116] implicit in passages in which[117] is that the very act carried out in pursuance of the conspiracy, and on which the claim is founded may, if carried out by an individual, not be actionable by a third party. Further, the unlawful means tort and conspiracy have basic differences that do not lend themselves to the transposition of principle from one to the other. Lord Walker:

> Criminal conduct engaged in by conspirators as a means of inflicting harm on the claimant is actionable as the tort of conspiracy, whether or not that conduct, on the part of a single individual, would be actionable as some other tort. To hold otherwise would, as has often been pointed out, deprive the tort of conspiracy of any real content, since the conspirators would be joint tortfeasors in any event.

[5.37] Thus, 'unlawful means' for conspiracy has a broader meaning than for the other 'unlawful means' torts.[118] Nonetheless, the unlawful conduct must, if it is to qualify as an element in the tort, be in fact the means whereby the relevant loss is inflicted upon the claimant. Lord Walker said in the *Total Network* case:[119]

> In my opinion your Lordships should clarify the law by holding that criminal conduct (at common law or by statute), can constitute unlawful means, provided that it is indeed the means (what Lord Nicholls of Birkenhead in the *OBG* case called ... 'instrumentality') of intentionally inflicting harm ... What is important, to my mind, is that in the phrase 'unlawful means' each word has an important

---

114. *Total Network SL v Her Majesty's Revenue and Customs Commissioners* [2008] UKHL 19, [2008]2 WLR 711. As O Sullivan notes, Case Comment (2008) Camb LJ 459, the panel of Law Lords in *Total Network* was almost entirely different from that in *OBG* so the views of Lord Hoffmann and Lord Nicholls about the relationship between the torts are not known. *Total Network* leaves uncertainty as to important questions not least why conspiracy should differ from the other 'unlawful means' torts.

115. *Mogul Steamship Co Ltd v McGregor Gow & Co* (1889) 23 QBD 598, [1892] AC 25.

116. *Quinn v Leathem* [1901] AC 495.

117. *Mogul* at 616 and 645; *Quinn* at 511 and 538.

118. A position which used to be the other way round: see Carty, *An Analysis of the Economic Torts* (OUP, 2001) at 21.

119. *Total Network SL v Her Majesty's Revenue and Customs Commissioners* [2008] UKHL 19, [2008] 2 WLR 711 at paras 95–96 of his speech (at p 450).

part to play. It is not enough that there is an element of unlawfulness somewhere in the story.

In *Colliers CRE Plc v Pandya and Ors*[120] Seymour J agreed with the broad approach in *OBG*:

> The proposition that a combination of two or more people to carry out a scheme that is criminal in its nature and is intended to cause economic harm to some person does not, when carried out with that result, constitute a tort actionable by that person is, in my opinion, unacceptable. Such a proposition is not only inconsistent with the jurisprudence of tortious conspiracy, as Lord Walker has demonstrated and explained, but is inconsistent also with the historic role of the action on the case.

The description of the unlawful means conspiracy given by the High Court in *Iarnród Éireann v Holbrooke and Ors*[121] (para **5.08**), is in line with the House of Lords in *Total Network*.

[5.38] Certain categories of unlawful means involving unconstitutional acts, breach of a penal statute and breach of contract are considered next.

Unconstitutional acts

[5.39] A threat to violate a constitutional right will amount to an unlawful act or, depending on the circumstances, to unlawful means. There are likely to be (at least) two constitutional wrongs involved where trade union officials threaten strike action in order to compel an employer to dismiss a non-unionist employee. Firstly, there is the threatened violation of the employee's right to continue to earn a livelihood. That is the end-product of the official's action. Secondly, the employee will be penalised on account of exercising a constitutional right of dissociation and he will be penalised if his employer yields to the unionists' coercion – whether he is dismissed lawfully or unlawfully at common law will not be relevant. Once dismissed, the employee becomes a victim of a violation.

[5.40] In *Meskell v CIE*[122] (para **2.23**), the plaintiff sought:

(i) A declaration that his dismissal was effected for the purpose of wrongfully coercing him to be at all times a member of one of the trade unions designated and an unlawful interference with his rights under the Constitution;

(ii) A declaration that his dismissal was in pursuance of a conspiracy and a combination between the defendants and the four trade unions for the purpose of wrongfully coercing him to undertake at all times to be a member of one of the designated trade unions and was a denial and violation of, and an unlawful interference with, his rights under the Constitution;

---

120. *Colliers CRE Plc v Pandya and Ors* [2009] EWHC 211 (QB).

121. *Iarnród Éireann v Holbrooke and Ors* [2000] ELR 109.

122. *Meskell v CIE* [1973] IR 121. See de Blaghd, 'Trade Union Law 1973 Style' (1974) 107 ILT & SJ 71.

(iii) Damages for his dismissal as having been effected in violation of his constitutional rights and freedoms.

Teevan J, the trial judge, dismissed the plaintiff's action on the grounds, *inter alia*, that the object or purpose of the agreement between CIE and the unions was not to injure the plaintiff. Although he treated the case as one for damages for conspiracy,[123] Teevan J never went beyond discovery of the object of the conspirers to the means, lawful or unlawful, which they used. In the Supreme Court, Walsh J, in a judgment with which O Dálaigh CJ and Budd J agreed, made the distinction the trial judge had not made. He agreed with the latter that the object of the agreement concluded between CIE and the four unions concerning trade union membership was the well-being of the company and the unions, and even of the members of the unions. However, the plaintiff's complaint was that the means adopted to achieve this end were unlawful. 'If that is so', said Walsh J, 'then there was a conspiracy.' He continued:

> To infringe another's constitutional rights or to coerce him into abandoning them or waiving them in so far as that may be possible is unlawful as constituting a violation of the fundamental law of the State and in so far as such conduct constitutes the means towards an end not in itself unlawful the means are unlawful and an agreement to employ such means constitutes a conspiracy. If damage results, it is an actionable conspiracy.

[5.41] The appellant based his claim on Art 40.6.1°iii and Art 40.6.2° of the Constitution[124] and also on *Educational Co of Ireland v Fitzpatrick (No 2)*[125] (where, it will be recalled, the Supreme Court held that the right of citizens to form associations and unions conferred the implicit right to abstain from joining them). In the circumstances, Walsh J held that Meskell was entitled to a declaration that this interference was a denial and violation of, and an unlawful interference with, his constitutional rights and that the agreement with CIE and the four unions to procure or cause that dismissal was an actionable conspiracy, because the means employed constituted a breach or infringement of the plaintiff's constitutional rights. The plaintiff was also held entitled to damages.

[5.42] *Meskell* was followed by the High Court in *Cotter v Ahern*[126] where an agreement by members of the INTO and the manager of a national school to prevent the appointment or promotion of a national teacher as part of a general campaign or

---

123. For he knew of 'no such right of action as that claimed for what is described as the positive duty of the defendants to abstain from interference with the plaintiff's constitutional rights and freedom.' On appeal, the case of *Byrne v Ireland* [1972] IR 241 was expressly referred to by the Supreme Court when declaring Teevan J incorrect on this point. The Supreme Court held in *Byrne* that a constitutional right can be protected or enforced by action even though such action may not fit into ordinary forms of action at common law or in equity. (In fairness one must point out that Teevan J gave judgment in *Meskell* three years or so before the Supreme Court accorded Miss Byrne the redress she sought against Ireland.) See de Blaghd, 'Trade Union Law 1973 Style' (1974) 107 ILT & SJ 71.

124. *Meskell v CIE* [1973] IR 121, at 134.

125. *Educational Co of Ireland v Fitzpatrick (No 2)* [1961] IR 345.

126. *Cotter v Ahern* [1976–77] ILRM 248.

objective to try and ensure that he, and all other national teachers in any particular area or in the whole country, would become and remain a member of a trade union, was held to amount to coercing or penalising that person into abandoning or waiving his constitutional right to dissociate and, as such, an actionable conspiracy. Finlay P held that:

> an agreement by two or more persons to prevent the appointment or promotion of a national teacher as a part of a general campaign or objective to try and ensure that they and all other national teachers in any particular area or in the whole country will become and remain a member of a trade union is to coerce or penalise that person into abandoning or waiving his constitutional right and as such is an actionable conspiracy.

Unlike in *Meskell,* there was no actual agreement here to promote trade union interests; such aspirations as the INTO had merely constituted a general campaign or objective. The defendants' prevention of the plaintiff's appointment constituted the object of their agreement. But did they seek to coerce or penalise the plaintiff into abandoning or waiving his constitutional right? The facts vary significantly from *Meskell* in this respect. Meskell received a letter of termination from his employer making his re-employment dependent on agreeing to join a particular union. In *Cotter* the defendant was informed by one of the unsuccessful candidates that the plaintiff (who had been successful) was not a member of the INTO. He thereupon sent for the latter and informed him of what had been said. He did not expressly request Cotter to withdraw from his acceptance of the position of principal teacher nor suggest he was in any way prepared or willing to cancel that appointment. The plaintiff had in fact made up his mind to join the INTO – to waive his right of dissociation, and was penalised irrespective of that. The INTO did not favour Cotter's appointment on personal grounds which related to his attitude towards the union. The case arguably involved a conspiracy to infringe Cotter's right to earn a livelihood, which from a constitutional viewpoint involved an unlawful right.[127]

[5.43] In **Ch 2**, the constitutional wrong involved in *Crowley v Ireland, INTO*[128] was discussed (para **2.44**). The difference was highlighted between the basis which appeared to have grounded the plaintiff's success, namely conspiracy, and the wrong

---

127. Coercing an employer to dismiss one or more of his employees because they are non-unionised is likely to amount of a constitutional wrong: breach of the employer's freedom of association (para **2.32**). An interesting possibility might be the invocation of the union's coercive behaviour vis-à-vis the employer as 'unlawful' means leading to the injurious act of which the plaintiff complains. If this argument were to find favour with the courts, an agreement between defendants to coerce an employer in such a way as to enable the coercion to be dubbed unlawful would be an actionable conspiracy (in the sense of being unconstitutional), irrespective of the object of that action. This could be applied to an unlimited range of coercive union activity.

128. *Crowley v Ireland, INTO* [1980] IR 102. In *Conway v INTO* [1991] ILRM 497 exemplary damages were awarded to one of the victims of actionable conspiracy in *Crowley* though the Supreme Court recognised that not every breach of constitutional right would attract such damages.

enunciated in *Hayes v INTO*,[129] the sequel to *Crowley*, where it was emphasised that 'this is not an action based on tort.'[130]

Acts contravening a penal statute

[5.44] Acts which are illegal because they contravene a penal statute comprise a difficult and controversial form of unlawful means. There are conflicting English judgments on the subject. The House of Lords recognised in *Lonrho v Shell Petroleum Co Ltd (No 2)*[131] that the proper approach is one of 'construction', ie that the approach which is taken for breach of statutory duty in ordinary civil cases should likewise be adopted to determine whether means are unlawful in tort. The question of whether a breach of statute gives rise to civil liability is difficult.[132] Where a criminal statute provides for a penalty only, the plaintiff can bring no action for damages suffered by reason of the breach unless he can bring himself within one of two exceptions to the general rule by proving either:

(a)   that the statutory duty was imposed for the benefit of a particular class of which he forms one member; or

(b)   that a public right as been infringed and he has suffered special damage from the interference.[133]

If a statute provides special remedies in respect of wrongs done in contravention of it, this will normally rule out the possibility that any such private right exists. In Ireland if the approach of the House of Lords in *Total Network* is adopted (para **5.36** *et seq*), the legal niceties in this area should be sidestepped.

Breach of contract

[5.45] A combination to effect a breach of contract, following *Cooper v Millea*[134] and *Riordan v Butler*,[135] would appear actionable. Where there is a threat to break a contract, this would be a combination to intimidate. Since Irish courts have dubbed a breach of contract 'illegal'[136] and put it in the same category as violence for purposes of the tort of intimidation, it is doubtful whether it could be excluded from the category of unlawful means for the purposes of civil conspiracy.[137] A threat to break a contract

129. *Hayes v INTO* (6 October 1986, unreported), HC.
130. Potentially relevant in relation to the immunities, in particular Industrial Relations Act 1990, s 13.
131. *Lonrho v Shell Petroleum Co Ltd (No 2)* [1981] 2 All ER 456.
132. *Clerk and Lindsell on Torts* (19th edn, Sweet and Maxwell, 2005) paras 25–125.
133. *Gouriet v Union of Post Office Workers* [1978] AC 435 at 497–500 *per* Lord Diplock; and *Lonrho* [1981] 2 All ER at 461–462 *per* Lord Diplock.
134. *Cooper v Millea* [1938] IR 749.
135. *Riordan v Butler* [1940] IR 347.
136. As the House of Lords later did in *Rookes v Barnard* [1964] AC 1129.
137. Note how in *Rookes v Barnard* [1964] AC 1129 Lord Devlin tried most emphatically to leave this point open.

must in fact be less meritorious than an action involving actual breach when it comes to determining unlawful means. This means a third party to the contract can be sued in tort: a conspirator can be liable even where it is not possible to establish that he has procured any breach of the contract concerned but where he has combined with a common design with others.

STATUTORY IMMUNITY: INDUSTRIAL RELATIONS ACT 1990, S 10

[5.46] Section 10 of the Industrial Relations Act 1990 reads:

> (1) An agreement or combination by two or more persons to do or procure to be done any act in contemplation or furtherance of a trade dispute shall not be indictable as a conspiracy if such act committed by one person would not be punishable as a crime.
>
> (2) An act done in pursuance of an agreement or combination by two or more persons, if done in contemplation or furtherance of a trade dispute, shall not be actionable unless the act, if done without any such agreement or combination, would be actionable.
>
> (3) Section 3 of the Conspiracy, and Protection of Property Act 1875 and subsections (1) and (2) of this section shall be construed together as one section.

Section 3 of the Conspiracy, and Protection of Property Act 1875 reads:

> Nothing in this section shall exempt from punishment any persons guilty of a conspiracy for which a punishment is awarded by any Act of Parliament.
>
> Nothing in this section shall affect the law relating to riot, unlawful assembly, breach of the peace, or sedition or any offence against the State [...]
>
> A crime for the purposes of this section means an offence punishable on indictment, or an offence which is punishable on summary conviction, and for the commission of which the offender is liable under the statute making the offence punishable to be imprisoned either absolutely or at the discretion of the court as an alternative for some other punishment.
>
> Where a person is convicted of any such agreement or combination as aforesaid to do or procure to be done an act which is punishable only on summary conviction, and is sentenced to imprisonment, the imprisonment shall not exceed three months, or such longer time, if any, as may have been prescribed by the statute for the punishment of the said act when committed by one person.

[5.47] It will be recalled that after the Trade Union Act 1871 a strike could no longer be treated as a criminal conspiracy as being in restraint of trade. But in *R v Bunn*[138] (para **5.03**), it was held that it might nevertheless amount to a criminal conspiracy at common law to coerce or molest an employer in the conduct of its trade or business, notwithstanding that no criminal acts were involved. Hence the rationale of the Conspiracy and Protection of Property Act 1875, which legalised strikes in so far as the action was taken 'in contemplation or furtherance of a trade dispute', subject to the exceptions concerning breach of contract, in ss 4 and 5 thereof, and considered in para

---

138. *R v Bunn* (1872) 12 Cox 316.

6.03. Section 7 deals with intimidation and 'watching and besetting' (see Chs 8 and 10 respectively). The potential importance of criminal conspiracy was illustrated in *R v Jones*.[139]

Potentially wide application more apparent than real

[5.48] Section 9 of the Industrial Relations Act 1990 limits the statutory protections in s 11 (picketing), s 12 (inducing breach of the contract of employment, and intimidation re same), and s 13 (trade union immunity in tort) to authorised trade unions, the holders of negotiation licences, and the members and officials of such trade unions, and not otherwise, para **9.55** *et seq*. This limitation does not apply to the protection for conspiracy in s 10 of the 1990 Act, making the immunity apparently wider in reach for those organising strike or industrial action.

But the scope of the protection in s 10 of the 1990 Act is more apparent than real, in light of the section's narrow application. Under s 10 (1) of the 1990 Act, for criminal conspiracy, the act involved must not constitute a crime if done by one person. Immunity is given to the wrongdoers' combination: conspiracy to commit a crime is not protected. Moreover, the protection against civil actions under s 10(2) of the 1990 Act is slight. The difference in wording between sub-ss (1) and (2) is significant. The former refers to an agreement or combination; the latter to 'an act' done pursuant to same. For immunity in relation to civil conspiracy, there must first of all be an 'act' to attract immunity (para **5.12**). As well as an 'act', the objective of the combination, sub-s (2) requires it be done in pursuance of the combination. Recall that there is no doctrine of merger whereby when the acts are tortious, the conspiracy merges in the tort (para **5.28**). If the act is not actionable when done without combination, there is no protection. This limits the protection to 'simple' conspiracy cases, the first form of the tort (para **5.14**) concerning which, in relation to tortious claims, the aspirations of trade unions are considered sufficient justification for liability not to arise. The time has long gone when simple conspiracy was developed by the courts as a weapon against trade unions. The interests of trade unions are regarded by the courts as equivalent to those of businesses and employers. Thus s 10 of the 1990 Act is of little importance except perhaps where there are mixed motives and the predominant motive of the industrial action is, say, a desire to punish an employee as in *Quinn v Leathem*.[140] In such cases, the action would almost certainly not be taken in 'furtherance of a trade dispute' and so it would not be protected. On the golden formula, 'in contemplation or furtherance of a trade dispute', see para **9.75** *et seq*.

'Actionable'

[5.49] The section does not qualify the word 'actionable', which appears twice in sub-s (2). It does not say by whom it should be actionable (on which, see further para **6.91** *et seq*), nor in relation to which wrongs. Thus, an act without combination could be actionable for the purposes of s 10 of the Industrial Relations Act 1990 in tort,

---

139. *R v Jones* [1974] ICR 310.
140. *Quinn v Leathem* [1901] AC 495.

contract, constitutional law, equity and so on. Where workers agree to break their contracts by engaging in industrial action, eg refusing to answer the telephone, s 10(2) will not protect. Only if the act is *not* actionable, and the conditions as to parties and the golden formula are met, does the immunity apply. Does 'not actionable' mean not actionable because of the act being rendered immune under the Act of 1990? If so, a combination to induce a breach of the contract of employment where breach follows (an 'act') would enjoy immunity. The answer to this question is almost certainly no, and is discussed at para **6.92**.

[5.50] The importance of the protection diminishes when it is considered that for strikes outside of the 'suspension' doctrine, and for probably all forms of industrial action, s 10(2) will not apply in any event. In Britain s 219 of the Trade Union and Labour Relations (Consolidation) Act 1992 provides that 'an agreement or combination by two or more persons to do or procure the doing of any act in contemplation or furtherance of a trade dispute shall not be actionable *in tort* if the act is one which, if done without any such agreement or combination, would not be actionable in *tort*' (emphasis added).[141]

Non-application to one-worker disputes

[5.51] Without prejudice to what is said about the narrow application of s 10, other limitations on the immunities are found in the Act of 1990. Section 9 provides that where, in relation to one-worker disputes regarding the employment or non-employment or terms or conditions of or affecting the employment of the worker, there are agreed procedures availed of by custom or in practice in the employment concerned, or provided for in a collective agreement, for the resolution of individual grievances, including dismissals, the immunities in ss 10, 11 (picketing) and 12 (inducing breach of the contract of employment, and intimidation in relation to same) shall apply only where those procedures have been resorted to and exhausted. See further para **9.26**.

Non-application to action contrary to outcome of secret ballot

[5.52] Section 17(1) of the Industrial Relations Act 1990 provides that the same sections, ss 10, 11 and 12, shall not apply in respect of proceedings arising out of or in relation to a strike or other industrial action by a trade union or a group of workers in disregard of or contrary to, the outcome of a secret ballot relating to the issue or issues involved in the dispute. In the case of ballots by more than one trade union, the outcome of a secret ballot means the outcome of the aggregated ballots (sub-s (2)) and where two or more secret ballots are held, the ballot means the last such ballot (sub-s (3)).

---

141. An attempt to insert the words 'in tort' after 'actionable' in s 10(2) of the Industrial Relations Act 1990 failed in the Dáil. See 398 *Dáil Debates* Cols 495–497.

[5.53] In *Nolan Transport (Oaklands) Ltd v Halligan*[142] the Supreme Court reiterated that where industrial action is taken contrary to the outcome of a secret ballot:

- the individual workers will not have the benefit of the immunities (s 17),

- the trade union, on the other hand, will not lose its immunity because of s 17 of the 1990 Act but may lose its negotiating licence, and

- the restrictions on the right to an injunction to restrain industrial action will not apply (see further **Ch 11**).

Murphy J, with whom the other members of the court agreed, said that the legislature can, and in the 1990 Act did, confer particular rights and duties on 'outsiders' in consequence of or by reference to the holding of, a secret ballot, eg s 17 of the 1990 Act. But unions were not penalised in that way. The statutory protection conferred upon a trade union, set out in s 13, means that if a union were to engage in industrial action in disregard of the wishes of its members expressed in a secret ballot, it would not forfeit the immunity conferred upon it by s 13. Instead it would risk the loss of its negotiating licence in accordance with the provisions of s 16 of the 1990 Act:

> Where employees engage in industrial action 'in disregard' of or contrary to 'the outcome of a secret ballot' their activities do not enjoy the statutory protections. ... From the point of view of the union the holding or not holding of the secret ballot or the manner in which it was held does not impinge in any way on the rights of the union, vis-à-vis the company employers. Their immunity under section 13 of the 1990 Act would remain unaffected.

[5.54] Section 10 of the 1990 Act repeats s 1 of the Trade Disputes Act 1906, whose importance was described by Citrine[143] as twofold:

> It makes it clear that the common law in relation to civil conspiracy is to have no application whatever to acts, otherwise lawful, which are done 'in contemplation or furtherance of a trade dispute'... Provided the act is done in contemplation or furtherance of a trade dispute, there is no longer any question as to whether there was a 'sufficient justification' or not.

Nowadays, however, s 10 is regarded as of little importance. The entire range of civil conspiracies which constitutes the second form of the tort are unprotected for trade unionists and those organising strikes or industrial action. As this chapter shows, the defendants must act with intent to injure the plaintiff in the second form of the tort but that does not have to be their predominant motive. Where intent to injure can be shown, the tort enables conspiracy to be alleged against an individual who cannot himself commit the tort in question, eg a trade unionist in a *Rookes v Barnard*[144] situation, who supports others who threaten to break their contracts of employment. Furthermore (para **5.45**), any two or more workers who agree to strike or take industrial action in breach of their contracts of employment could also be liable for

---

142. *Nolan Transport (Oaklands) Ltd v Halligan* [1998] ELR 177.

143. Citrine's, *Trade Union Law* (3rd edn, Stevens & Sons, 1967), 553–4.

144. *Rookes v Barnard* [1964] AC 1129. Para **8.04**.

conspiracy, on the assumption that a wrong rendered immune under s 12 of the Industrial Relations Act 1990 can nonetheless constitute unlawful means for tortious liability (para **6.92**).

[5.55] It is sometimes said that the tort of conspiracy is redundant as the unlawful means are themselves actionable. But as Rogers[145] and Eekelaar[146] say, the tort is useful against unlawful, intended economic harm. The fact of combination may make a court more ready to grant an injunction. Evidentially, as in a trade dispute, it may be useful to allege conspiracy where it is not easy to show which individual defendant did the unlawful acts alleged.[147]

---

145. Rogers, *Winfield and Jolowicz on Tort* (15th edn, Sweet & Maxwell, 1998) 648.
146. Eekelaar, 'The Conspiracy Tangle' 106 LQR (1990) 223.
147. Eekelaar, 224. *Rookes v Barnard* [1964] AC 1129.

Chapter 6

INDUCING BREACH OF CONTRACT

INTRODUCTION

[6.01] Irish law affords no recognition to a 'right to strike' as such. Strike and industrial action are almost invariably in breach of the contracts of employment of the participants. Those who organise strike or industrial action, trade union officials or other strike leaders, will usually be liable for one or more of the economic torts, most obviously that of inducing or procuring breach of contract – the participants' breaches of their employment contracts.[1] The limited liberty that exists to organise strikes and industrial action derives from the statutory immunities. As this chapter shows, the boundaries of this tort have been extended, frequently bringing obscurity.

[6.02] To the non-lawyer, the tort of procuring breach of contract highlights the law's inadequacy when dealing with a collective phenomenon such as industrial action. A court faced by industrial action looks for a breach of contract or some other breach that will give rise to civil sanctions on the level of the individual relationship of employment. Thus Lord Radcliffe in *Stratford v Lindley*:[2]

> What puts the defendants in the wrong in legal analysis is that they have used the procuring of breaches of contract to enforce their policy of attacking Stratford. I cannot say, when I look at the facts of the case, that this strikes me as a satisfactory, even realistic dividing line between what the law forbids and what the law permits ... one sees again how easily a slight difference in the framing of the embargo order might have avoided incitement to breach of contract, while still achieving a virtual cessation of the plaintiff's business ... In my opinion, the law should treat a resolution of this sort according to its substance, without the comparatively accidental issue whether breaches of contract are looked for and involved; and by its substance it should be either licensed, controlled or forbidden.

It is arguable whether liability based upon breach of the contract of employment provides a rational basis for distinguishing illegitimate industrial action. Even in systems in which strong emphasis is put on the employer-employee relationship it has become progressively more obvious that such action cannot be regarded only from the point of view of each individual engaged in it; it must rather be viewed as action of a specific type, with a predominantly collective character.

Breach of contract as criminal wrongs

[6.03] First something will be said of breach of contract comprising criminal wrongs under ss 4 and 5 of the Conspiracy and Protection of Property Act 1875. Section 4

---

1. For the purposes of the Unfair Dismissals Acts 1977–2007 civil servants are deemed to be 'employees' with 'contracts of employment' by the Civil Service (Amendment) Act 2005. See Redmond, *Dismissal Law in Ireland* (2nd edn, Bloomsbury Professional, 2007), 489.
2. *Stratford v Lindley* [1965] AC 269.

applies to a person employed in the supply of gas or water to the public who breaks his contract of employment in circumstances which make it probable that the public will be deprived of their supply. The text is as follows:

> Where a person employed by a municipal authority or by any company or contractor upon whom is imposed by Act of Parliament the duty, or who have otherwise assumed the duty of supplying any city, borough, town, or place, or any part thereof, with gas or water, wilfully and maliciously breaks a contract of service with that authority or company or contractor, knowing or having reasonable cause to believe that the probable consequences of his so doing, either alone or in combination with others, will be to deprive the inhabitants of that city, borough, town, place or part, wholly or to a great extent of their supply of gas or water, he shall on indictment as hereinafter mentioned, be liable either to pay a penalty not exceeding twenty pounds or to be imprisoned for a term not exceeding three months, with or without hard labour.

This was extended to electricity workers by the Electricity Supply Act 1927, s 110. Section 5 makes it a criminal offence to break a contract of service with the probable consequence of endangering human life, or causing serious bodily injury, or exposing valuable property to destruction or serious injury:

> Where any person wilfully and maliciously breaks a contract of service or of hiring, knowing or having reasonable cause to believe that the probable consequences of his so doing, either alone or in combination with others, will be to endanger human life, or cause serious bodily injury or to expose valuable property whether real or personal to destruction or serious injury, he shall on conviction thereof by a court of summary jurisdiction, or on indictment as hereinafter mentioned, be liable either to pay a penalty not exceeding twenty pounds, or to be imprisoned for a term not exceeding three months, with or without hard labour.

[6.04] According to Citrine, the *mens rea* is provided in the words 'knowing or having reasonable cause to believe',[3] hence the word 'maliciously' is redundant. It means no more than that the person must be acting intentionally. The act or omission must be deliberate and intentional. The consequences need only be 'probable', it would be immaterial that the particular consequences were avoided by prompt action by the employer or another person and no public deprivation in fact ensued.[4] Section 5 is of wider application than s 4. For instance, the words 'serious' and 'valuable' are capable of making the section applicable to hospital personnel, ambulance drivers, fire brigade staff, security guards and so on.[5] Dockers, lorry drivers and other transport workers could be liable for damaging valuable property, such as by leaving food rotting on a quayside. Any wilful breach of contract is covered, thereby going beyond strike action. There is no record of anyone ever being prosecuted under this section. But the law, however provocative it may be, remains on the statute book and the possibility of prosecution remains. Even if no prosecutions are brought, persons affected by illegal

---

3.   Citrine, *Trade Union Law* (3rd edn, Stevens & Sons, 1967), 525.

4.   Citrine, 527.

5.   Kerr and Whyte, *Irish Trade Union Law* (Professional Books, 1987), 218.

action might bring a civil action based upon the breach of a penal statute, see para **7.25** *et seq.*

THE TORT DESCRIBED

[6.05] The wrong consists in the act of knowingly inducing or procuring a third party to break his contract to the damage of the other contracting party where there is no reasonable justification or excuse therefor.[6] It springs from a long established legal principle, namely that a person who knowingly procures another to commit a wrong against a third person is liable in tort as against that third person where he, the procurer, acts without sufficient justification. The wrong can consist in the infringement of a legal right such as a right arising under contract. So, if A intentionally induces B to break a contract between B and C, C may sue in tort. Inducement may be direct or indirect. For the indirect form of the tort, the wrongdoer must use unlawful means, and breach of contract must be a necessary consequence as between B and C. The tort has been extended from 'breach' to cover 'interference with performance' of a contract. This extension is questionable, however, following the House of Lords decision in *OBG Ltd v Allan*,[7] which has left a serious doubt over the indirect form of the tort. Ch 4 considers the extended form of the tort in light of *OBG*.

[6.06] The tort of intentionally procuring a breach of contract by one party thereto, without legal justification, and resulting in damage to the other party, has its origin in *Lumley v Gye*.[8] The plaintiff, manager of the Queen's Theatre, had a contract with Miss Wagner whereby she agreed to sing at his theatre for three months and not to sing anywhere else during that time. The plaintiff sued the defendant alleging that he induced Miss Wagner to break the contract by getting her to sing at Her Majesty's Theatre instead. Crompton J[9] did not place much importance on the origin or foundation of the law the plaintiff wished him to turn to, namely the law as to enticing of servants for:

> it must now be considered clear law that a person who wrongfully and maliciously, or, which is the same thing, without notice, interrupts the relation subsisting between master and servant by procuring the servant to depart from

---

6. Irish cases which proffer a definition can be misleading. See, eg, the High Court (O'Neill J) in *Iarnród Éireann v Holbrooke and Ors* [2000] ELR 109 where Hamilton J's *dicta* are cited from *Reg Armstrong Motors Ltd v CIE and British Rail* (2 December 1975, unreported), HC, 'a correct statement of the law on the essential ingredients of the tort of actionable *interference with contractual relations* or otherwise known as the tort of procuring or inducing breach of contract' (emphasis added). The judge went on to describe the ingredients of the indirect form of the tort of inducing breach of contract (para **6.38** *et seq*).

7. *OBG Ltd v Allan* [2008] AC 1. Applied in *Colliers CRE Plc v Pandya and Ors* [2009] EWHC 211 (QB).

8. *Lumley v Gye* (1853) 2 E & B 216. That the tort is a wrong known to Russian law, see *Intermetal Group Ltd and Trans-World (Steel) Ltd v Worslade Trading Ltd* (6 March 1998, unreported), SC.

9. Erle and Wightman JJ concurring; Coleridge J dissenting.

the master's service, or by harbouring and keeping him as servant after he has quitted it and during the time stipulated for as the period of service, whereby the master is injured, commits a wrongful act for which he is responsible at law.

Before this case, recovery was allowed only in respect of persons who were servants within the meaning of the Statute of Labourers. As Erle J put it:[10]

> It is clear that the procurement of the violation of a right is a cause of action in all instances where the violation is an actionable wrong, as in violations of a right to property, whether real or personal, or to personal security: he who procures the wrong is a joint wrongdoer, and may be sued, either alone or jointly with the agent, in the appropriate action for the wrong complained of.

Moreover, 'he who procures the wrong is a joint wrong-doer'.

[6.07] The reasons given for extending the action in *Lumley v Gye*[11] were that to sue the contract-breaker alone might not be adequate as he might be incapable of meeting an award of damages; moreover, the measure of damages in tort may be greater than in contract.

The rationale for the tort follows the established doctrine of joint tortfeasance. Inducement leads the law to 'impute' the commission of the same wrongful act to two or more persons at once.[12]

Since *Lumley v Gye,* recovery can be had for inducing breach of any kind of contract, whether of employment or otherwise. Thus, for example, an action has been entertained in relation to supply contracts,[13] contracts for the sale of goodwill,[14] barge hiring contracts[15] and sales of goods.[16]

[6.08] In *OBG*[17] Lord Hoffmann described *Lumley v Gye* as based on the general principle that a person who procures another to commit a wrong incurs liability as an *accessory.* In this he was supported by the rest of their Lordships. The important point to bear in mind about *Lumley* is that liability depended upon the contracting party having committed an actionable wrong. Lord Hoffmann cited Wightman J who had made this clear:[18] 'It was undoubtedly *prima facie* an unlawful act on the part of Miss Wagner to break her contract, and therefore a tortious act of the defendant maliciously to procure her to do so ...'

---

10.   *Lumley v Gye* (1853) 2 E & B 216 at 232.

11.   See Heydon, *Economic Torts* (2nd edn, Sweet & Maxwell, 1978), 28–29.

12.   *Per* Scrutton LJ in *The Kourst* [1924] P 140 at 155.

13.   *Lumley v Gye* (1853) 2 E & B 216, 230–231, 234.

14.   *Temperton v Russell* (No 2) [1893] 1 QB 715.

15.   *Stratford v Lindley* [1965] AC 269.

16.   *Goldsoll v Goldman* [1914] 2 Ch 603.

17.   *OBG Ltd v Allan* [2008] 1 AC 1; [2007] UKHL 21 [2007] 2 WLR 90.

18.   *Lumley v Gye* (1853) 2 E & B 216, at 238.

Although most commonly described as the 'tort of procuring [or inducing] breaches of contract',[19] the tort is sometimes described as one of 'interfering' with contract.[20] The difference between these two descriptions is detailed in para **4.07** where it was seen that the question of whether the tort is restricted to breach of contract, or covers interference with or prevention of, contract, is of fundamental importance. The trend of conflating these led to the idea that there is a 'unified' tort of causing harm by unlawful means, under which procuring breach of contract is subsumed. This was given the *quietus* by the House of Lords in *OBG*.

[6.09] This chapter details the essential elements of the tort of inducing or procuring a breach of contract, namely, knowledge that a person was inducing a breach of contract; intention to cause a breach of contract; the relevant inducement, direct and indirect; and the requirement of breach. The chapter then considers the defence of justification. Breaches other than breaches of contract, such as breaches of equitable, statutory, or constitutional duties are considered. The chapter concludes with a consideration of the statutory immunities in s 12A of the 1990 Act.

KNOWLEDGE AND INTENTION

[6.10] The House of Lords in *OBG* described the ingredients of the accessory tort of inducing a breach of contract as comprising:

- an intention to cause a breach of contract which is a necessary and sufficient requirement for liability;

- a person has to know that he was inducing a breach of contract and to intend to do so with knowledge of the consequences;

- a conscious decision not to inquire into the existence of a fact can be treated as knowledge for the purposes of the tort;

- a person who knowingly induced a breach of contract as a means to an end has the necessary intent even if he was not motivated by malice but had acted with the motive of securing an economic advantage for himself;

- a breach of contract which is neither an end in itself nor a means to an end but merely a foreseeable consequence of a person's acts does not give rise to liability; and

- there can be no secondary liability without primary liability, and therefore a person cannot be liable for inducing a breach of contract unless there has in fact been a breach by the contracting party.

---

19.   *Per* Evershed MR in *Thomson (DC) & Co Ltd v Deakin* [1952] Ch 646, 676.

20.   See, eg, Roxburgh J in *British Motor Trade Association v Salvadori* [1949] Ch 556. The tort of interference with contract by unlawful means was unsuccessfully pleaded in *Malone and Another v McQuaid and Registrar of Titles* [1998] IEHC 86; and in a successful application for an interlocutory injunction Macken J found the defendant's barring of the plaintiff from driving a school bus 'may have interfered with or brought about or otherwise induced a breach of contract' between the parties: *Donohue v Bus Éireann* [1999] ELR 306.

[6.11] Inducement without more is not actionable, as Lord Devlin said in *Rookes v Barnard.*[21] The defendant-procurer must have possessed the requisite knowledge and intention. There must have been a deliberate and intentional invasion of the plaintiff's contractual rights.[22] If the breach that occurs was simply the natural consequence of the inducement, it must be established that the defendant knew about the contract that has been breached although he need not know the relevant terms thereof. Ignorance of the contract's precise terms may, however, assist a defendant who denies any intention to cause breach.[23] It is possible that where the defendant could show he was in 'honest doubt' about the existence or validity of a contract, he may escape liability.[24] Once, however, it is shown that a defendant knew that a contract existed, the test of his intention is objective. According to Budd J in *McMahon Ltd v Dunne and Dolan:*[25]

> a person is presumed to intend the ordinary and necessary consequences of his acts. If the ordinary and probable consequences of the action of the defendants would be such as to cause a breach of contract then the intent would ordinarily be presumed.

[6.12] In *OBD Ltd v Allan,*[26] Lord Hoffmann discussed the ingredient of knowledge:

> To be liable for inducing breach of contract, you must know that you are inducing a breach of contract. It is not enough that you know that you are procuring an act which, as a matter of law or construction of the contract, is a breach. You must actually realize that it will have this effect. Nor does it matter that you ought reasonably to have done so. This proposition is most strikingly illustrated by the decision of this House in *British Industrial Plastics Ltd v Ferguson* [1940] 1 All ER 479, in which the plaintiff's former employee offered the defendant information about one of the plaintiff's secret processes which he, as an employee, had invented. The defendant knew that the employee had a contractual obligation not to reveal trade secrets but held the eccentric opinion that if the process was patentable, it would be the exclusive property of the employee. He took the information in the honest belief that the employee would not be in breach of contract. In the Court of Appeal MacKinnon LJ observed tartly [1938] 4 All ER 504, 513 that in accepting this evidence the judge had 'vindicated his honesty ... at the expense of his intelligence' but he and the House of Lords agreed that he could not be held liable for inducing a breach of contract.

> The question of what counts as knowledge for the purposes of liability for inducing a breach of contract has also been the subject of a consistent line of decisions. In *Emerald Construction Co Ltd v Lowthian* [1966] 1 WLR 691 union officials threatened a building contractor with a strike unless he terminated a subcontract for the supply of labour. The defendants obviously knew that there

---

21.   *Rookes v Barnard* [1964] AC 1129, 1212.

22.   *OBG Ltd v Allan* [2008] AC 1 and, *Mainstream Properties v Young* [2005] IRLR 964.

23.   Eg, *Square Grip Reinforcement Ltd v Macdonald* (1968) SLT 65, *Stratford Ltd v Lindley* [1965] AC 269.

24.   *Grieg v Insole* [1978] 1 WLR 302 at 336 *per* Slade J; *Smith v Morrison* [1974] 1 WLR 659.

25.   *McMahon Ltd v Dunne and Dolan* (1965) 99 ILTR 45 at 56.

26.   *OBD Ltd v Allan* [2008] AC 1, para 39 *et seq.*

was a contract – they wanted it terminated – but the court found that they did not know its terms and, in particular, how soon it could be terminated. Lord Denning MR said, at pp 700–701:

> 'Even if they did not know the actual terms of the contract, but had the means of knowledge – which they deliberately disregarded – that would be enough. Like the man who turns a blind eye. So here, if the officers deliberately sought to get this contract terminated, heedless of its terms, regardless whether it was terminated by breach or not, they would do wrong. For it is unlawful for a third person to procure a breach of contract knowingly, or recklessly, indifferent whether it is a breach or not.'

Lord Denning's statement has been followed in many cases without giving rise to difficulty, as Morgan J acknowledged in *Brimex Ltd v Begum*.[27]

Reasonable inference of knowledge

[6.13] It is sufficient if there is a reasonable inference as to knowledge from the facts. In *JT Stratford & Son Ltd v Lindley*,[28] there was a refusal to recognise the trade union (of which the defendants were officials) by a particular company, BK Ltd. Stratford was chairman of both the plaintiff company and of BK Ltd, an associated company. The plaintiff company hired out barges generally and repaired barges belonging to the Port of London Authority. The union told their members not to handle barges belonging to or being repaired by the plaintiff company. This brought the plaintiff's trade to a standstill. The plaintiff did not employ any men belonging to the union. The defendants did not tell BK Ltd about the embargo although they gave notice of it to an employers' association of which the plaintiff was a member. The plaintiff sought an interlocutory injunction. The Court of Appeal refused, but the House of Lords granted,

---

27.   *Brimex Ltd v Begum* [2007] EWHC 34, para 41. Cases following *OBG* include: *Kallang Shipping v AXA* [2008] EWHC 2761 (QBD Comm), Hirst QC held Axa Senegal must have known of a particular London arbitration clause. It knew that it was inducing a breach of contract by the second defendant and intended to do so. Axa Senegal's conduct, knowledge and intent was such as to make it liable for the tort of procuring that defendant's breach of the contract to arbitrate all disputes in London. *Sotrade Denizcllik Sanayi VE Ticaret AS v Amadou LO and Ors* [2008] EWHC 2762 (QBD Comm), Hirst QC held Axa Senegal must have known of a particular London arbitration clause. It knew that it was inducing a breach of contract by the receivers and intended to do so. Axa Senegal's conduct, knowledge and intent was such as to make it liable for the tort of procuring the receivers' breach of the contract to arbitrate all disputes in London. *Meretz Investments NV and Anor v ACP Ltd and Ors* [2007] EWCA 1303, CA, held on the facts that the requisite intention for the tort had not been made out, first defendant's breach of contract had simply been the unavoidable consequence of the second defendant's exercise of its contractual right as mortgagee to sell the development lease. *Scotcher v Kirkless MBC* [2008] QBD Merc, 11 June 2008, allegation re inducing breach of implied term of trust and confidence in contract of employment. See too, *National Commercial Bank Jamaica Ltd v Olint Corpn Ltd* [2009] 1 WLR 1405; *Sotrade Denizcilik Sanayi VE Ticaret AS v Amadou LO (The Duden)* [2009] 1 Lloyds Rep 145; *Yeeles v Lewis* [2010] EWCA 326; *BGC Brokers LP v Tullett Prebon Ltd and Ors* [2010] EWCH 484.

28.   *JT Stratford & Son Ltd v Lindley* [1965] AC 269.

an injunction. They did so in respect of the embargo in so far as it interfered with the hiring contracts. Lord Reid:

> The respondents knew that barges were always returned promptly on the completion of the job for which they had been hired, and it must have been obvious to them that this was done under contracts between the appellants and the barge hirers.[29]

[6.14] It was argued there was no evidence that they were 'sufficiently aware' of these contracts to know that their interference would involve breaches of these contracts. But Lord Reid thought it reasonable to infer that they did know. The House was doubtful, however, whether the defendants had sufficient knowledge of the repair contracts.

[6.15] Sufficient knowledge therefore is the criterion. Knowledge of the facts suffices – ignorance of the law is no defence.[30] In comparison to earlier authorities judges seem more ready to extrapolate from the evidence knowledge sufficient to establish liability.[31]

'Sketchy' evidence of a contract, based on daily orders, may suffice.[32] Belief that the contracts are not enforceable does not excuse the defendant: *Pritchard v Briggs*.[33] Thus, if union officials instruct their members to take industrial action, believing the functions involved in such action are voluntary rather than contractual, the officials may nonetheless commit the tort of inducing breach of contract. In *Metropolitan Borough of Solihull v National Union of Teachers*,[34] the union was ordered to rescind instructions calling upon its members not to undertake various duties, such as lunchtime cover and attendance at meetings outside school hours, which the union had regarded as voluntary. The High Court (Warner J) found there was a serious issue to be tried as to whether the functions in question were discharged pursuant to contractual obligations. It was not a question of lack of knowledge or honest doubt as to the legal result of known facts but lack of knowledge or honest doubt as to the facts themselves.[35] There was no suggestion in the case before Warner J that the NUT were ignorant or in doubt as to any of the material facts.[36]

[6.16] In *McMahon Ltd v Dunne and Dolan*[37] (para **6.46**), Budd J (High Court) prefaced his remarks by emphasising that he was considering an interlocutory application on which no final determination was to be made as to the correct interpretation of the law. The plaintiffs contended it was unnecessary to support their

---

29. See *Smith v Morrison* [1974] 1 WLR 659, 677; *Pritchard v Briggs* [1980] Ch 338, 413–525.
30. *JT Stratford & Son Ltd v Lindley* [1965] AC 269 at 324.
31. *Pritchard v Briggs* [1980] CW 338, 413–425.
32. *Crazy Prices (Northern Ireland) Ltd v Hewitt* [1980] IRLR 396, 399–400.
33. *Pritchard v Briggs* [1980] Ch 338.
34. *Metropolitan Borough of Solihull v National Union of Teachers* [1985] IRLR 211.
35. The court distinguished *Smith v Morrison* [1974] 1 WLR 659.
36. See criticism of this decision: (1985) ILJ 255.
37. *McMahon Ltd v Dunne and Dolan* 99 ILTR 45 (1965).

action to show the defendants had actual knowledge of any of the particular contracts involved. It was sufficient if the defendants could be fixed with constructive, as distinct from actual, knowledge that a contract existed either between the actual contracting parties, or between the party injured and some other party. Budd J referred to various *dicta* of their Lordships in *Stratford v Lindley*, on a matter where the law of England and Ireland was in most respects similar. They entitled the plaintiffs in *McMahon Ltd* to say that, so far as the law was concerned, they had strong support for the proposition that constructive knowledge was sufficient knowledge in the context. Just what type of constructive knowledge sufficed was, the judge recognised, a new point. If it was accepted that constructive knowledge sufficed, he queried whether:

> there [is] any reason for confining the ingredients of knowledge to knowledge of a specific contract between specific parties or actual knowledge of any particular contract. In many instances in modern life it must be obvious to the ordinary onlooker that some transaction is taking place on foot of some contract, particularly, where matters of payment and delivery are concerned. This applies *a fortiori* where the intervener has special knowledge of the course of dealing, the customs prevailing and the surrounding circumstances.[38]

Where a contract is obvious, Budd J continued, there must also be many instances in which the terms, or at least some of the terms, of the contract are likewise obvious:

> If some term, such as one requiring delivery to someone, clearly a party to the contract, is itself clearly discernible in the particular circumstances to a person to whom the existence of the contract is obvious, and that person procures a breach of that particular term of the contract, to the detriment of one of the parties, is there any valid reason in principle for exempting him from liability for what he has done, merely because he did not know who the other party was or of the existence of any particular form of contract or its exact conditions. I would think that, *prima facie*, a reasonable argument could be made for fixing such a person with liability on the basis of his constructive knowledge.[39]

The fair question which merited decision at the trial of the action relied on the fact that the defendants were in a position, from the nature of their work and the everyday knowledge gained therein, to know in a well informed way what went on with regard to commercial contracts relating to the import of goods. They would know that a commercial dealing was involved. In expounding his views above, including his adoption of certain *dicta* in the *Stratford* case, Budd J went further than the earlier UK authority, of fundamental importance in relation to inducement of breach of contract, namely *Thomson (DC) & Co Ltd v Deakin*.[40] There,[41] Jenkins LJ had said the tort was 'strictly confined to cases where it is clearly shown', *inter alia*, 'that the person charged with actionable interference knew of the existence of the contract and intended to procure its breach.' This dictum was adopted unconditionally by Hamilton J in *Reg*

---

38. See *William Leitch & Co v Leydon* [1931] AC 90; *Port Line Ltd v Ben Line Steamers Ltd* [1958] 2 QB 146, 165, 168–169; *Bowles & Sons v Lindley* [1965] 1 Lloyd's Rep 207. See also Wedderurn, '*Stratford v Lindley*' (1965) 28 MLR 205–206.
39. *McMahon Ltd v Dunne and Dolan* 99 ILTR 45 at 54.
40. *Thomson (DC) & Co Ltd v Deakin* [1952] Ch 646.
41. At 697–698.

Armstrong Motors Ltd v CIE and Ors.[42] The status of this case differs from *McMahon* in that the hearing consisted of the hearing of the action by agreement, due to considerations of time. Hamilton J conceded that, having regard to the speed with which the case was necessarily brought to trial, it was possible the facts had not been fully investigated. The court said the plaintiff company would have to establish, *inter alia*, that the defendant knew of the existence of the contracts and intended to procure their breach. The court made no reference to *McMahon*.

[6.17] In *Talbot Ireland Ltd v Merrigan,*[43] like *McMahon v Dunne* an interlocutory hearing, Henchy J for the Supreme Court said that:

> It is well established that where a defendant, knowing of a contract between the plaintiff and a third party, intentionally induces a third party to break that contract and thereby causes loss to the plaintiff a tort is committed unless there is a justification for the defendant's action.

The court did not need to explore the issue of knowledge any further, however, for it had found that the defendants:

> knew that contracts were in existence, executory or otherwise, between the company and its parent company in England; between the company and its suppliers; between the company and the Post Office etc.

Arguably *McMahon* involved recklessness rather than constructive knowledge and there is no reason why the former term should not have been used. Recklessness, or indifference, is next considered.

Recklessness or indifference

[6.18] Lord Denning MR's words in *Emerald Construction Co Ltd v Lowthian*[44] were set out in para **6.13**. They are often referred to as describing 'blind-eye knowledge': another term for recklessness.

> Even if they did not know the actual terms of the contract, but had the means of knowledge – which they deliberately disregarded – that would be enough. Like the man who turns a blind eye. So here, if the officers deliberately sought to get this contract terminated, heedless of its terms, regardless whether it was terminated by breach or not, they would do wrong. For it is unlawful for a third person to procure a breach of contract knowingly, or recklessly, indifferent whether it is a breach or not.

The 'element of interest' was sufficiently established if the defendants intended the party procured to bring the contract to an end by breach of it if there were no way of bringing it to an end lawfully. As Lord Diplock said in the same case:

> A defendant who acts with such intent runs the risk that if the contract is broken as a result of the party acting in the manner in which he is procured to act by the

---

42. *Reg Armstrong Motors Ltd v CIE and Ors* (2 December 1975, unreported), HC.
43. *Talbot Ireland Ltd v Merrigan* (30 April 1981, unreported), SC.
44. *Emerald Construction Co Ltd v Lowthian* [1966] 1 WLR 691.

defendant, the defendant will be liable in damages to the other party to the contract.[45]

Where a defendant is not only reckless but indifferent as to breach, liability is more likely to ensue.

[6.19] Moreover, in *Cotter v Ahern*[46] (paras **5.42** and **6.36**) it was said that 'an over scrupulous avoidance of ascertaining the true facts lest they should be imputed to have knowledge which would be inconvenient to their purpose' will not enable defendants to escape liability. In *Cotter,* a deputation of members of the INTO brought pressure on a school manager not to appoint a person as principal who was not a member of their union. The manager had just made the appointment. The members sought to resist liability for inducing breach of contract by contending that they had not been aware that a binding agreement had been made, but this contention was rejected. The President of the High Court noted that the members had taken great care not to enquire as to whether the plaintiff had been short-listed. But their knowledge of the usual procedures must have meant the defendants 'were aware or ought to have known of the existence of a contractual arrangement' between the manager and the appointee. Under Rules 15(1) and 18(1)(b) for National Schools drawn up by the Department of Education in 1965, appointment of teachers was subject to the Minister for Education's approval. If a teacher was appointed without prior official approval, the Minister might refuse payment of salary for any service given by such teacher. Thus Finlay P:

> In all these circumstances I am driven to the conclusion that these defendants were well aware that a decision had been made by the first-named defendant [manager of the national school] to appoint the plaintiff and that according to the usual procedures adopted for the making of such appointments, he the first named defendant, must have taken upon himself the implied obligation of seeking in a genuine and *bona fide* way the approval of the Bishop if necessary and of the Minister for Education for that appointment.

[6.20] This then was 'the contractual arrangement' of which the defendants were aware or ought to have known about. The President was not satisfied that they could escape liability by relying on the technicality of the consent of the Minister for Education which had yet to be obtained. They were therefore held guilty of the tort of procuring a breach of contract by the manager with the plaintiff.

The object of the defendants' actions, namely, a contractual arrangement, is questionable in so far as agreement was dependent upon a condition subsequent for its validity. Until approval by the Minister, irrespective of how predictable that approval might be,[47] it was arguably not a contract.[48]

---

45.   *Emerald Construction Co Ltd v Lowthian* [1966] 1 WLR 691 at 703.

46.   *Cotter v Ahern* [1976–77] ILRM 248, *per* Finlay P. See too *Manifest Shipping Co Ltd v Uni-Polaris Insur Co* [2003] 1 AC 496.

47.   It would be impossible to quantify the predictability of approval.

48.   Although there is Commonwealth authority that a breach of contract retains its quality even if performance was subject to the approval of an outside body: *Fabbi v Jones* (1972) 28 DLR (39) 224.

[6.21] In *OBD Ltd v Allan*, Lord Hoffmann regarded[49] it as in accordance with the general principle of law that a conscious decision not to inquire into the existence of a fact is in many cases treated as equivalent to knowledge of that fact: see *Manifest Shipping Co Ltd v Uni-Polaris Insurance Co Ltd*.[50] It is not the same as neglience, or even gross negligence, as in *British Industrial Plastics Ltd v Ferguson*,[51] for example, where the defendant negligently made the wrong inquiry, that was an altogether different state of mind. Lord Nicholls[52] spoke to the same effect:

> The additional, necessary factor is the defendant's intent. He is liable if he intended to persuade the contracting party to breach the contract. Intentional interference presupposes knowledge of the contract. With that knowledge the defendant proceeded to induce the other contracting party to act in a way the defendant knew was a breach of that party's obligations under the contract. If the defendant deliberately turned a blind eye and proceeded regardless he may be treated as having intended the consequence he brought about. A desire to injure the claimant is not an essential ingredient of this tort.

[6.22] The courts sometimes refer to 'blind eye knowledge'. Lord Nicholls found it helpful to refer to two short passages in the speech of Lord Scott in the *Manifest Shipping* case. First of all:[53]

> 'Blind-eye' knowledge approximates to knowledge. Nelson at the battle of Copenhagen made a deliberate decision to place the telescope to his blind eye in order to avoid seeing what he knew he would see if he placed it to his good eye. It is, I think, common ground – and if it is not, it should be – that an imputation of blind-eye knowledge requires an amalgam of suspicion that certain facts may exist and a decision to refrain from taking any step to confirm their existence. Lord Blackburn in *Jones v Gordon* (1877) 2 App Cas 616, 629 distinguished a person who was 'honestly blundering and careless' from a person who 'refrained from asking questions, not because he was an honest blunderer or a stupid man, but because he thought in his own secret mind – I suspect there is something wrong, and if I ask questions and make farther inquiry, it will no longer be my suspecting it, but my knowing it, and then I shall not be able to recover.'

And:[54]

> In summary, blind-eye knowledge requires, in my opinion, a suspicion that the relevant facts do exist and a deliberate decision to avoid confirming that they exist. But a warning should be sounded. Suspicion is a word that can be used to describe a state-of-mind that may, at one extreme, be no more than a vague feeling of unease and, at the other extreme, reflect a firm belief in the existence of the relevant facts. In my opinion, in order for there to be blind-eye knowledge, the suspicion must be firmly grounded and targeted on specific facts. The

---

49. *OBG Ltd v Allan* [2008] AC 1, at 30; followed in *Global Resources Group Ltd v MacKay* (2009) SLT 104; *Calor Gas Ltd v Express Funds (Scotland) Ltd* (2008) SLT 123.

50. *Manifest Shipping Co Ltd v Uni-Polaris Insurance Co Ltd* [2003] 1 AC 469.

51. *British Industrial Plastics Ltd v Ferguson* [1940] 1 All ER 479.

52. *OBG Ltd v Allan* [2008] AC 1 at 192.

53. *Manifest Shipping Co Ltd v Uni-Polaris Insurance Co Ltd* [2003] 1 AC 469 at para 112.

54. *Manifest Shipping Co Ltd v Uni-Polaris Insurance Co Ltd* [2003] 1 AC 469 at para 116.

deliberate decision must be a decision to avoid obtaining confirmation of facts in whose existence the individual has good reason to believe. To allow blind-eye knowledge to be constituted by a decision not to enquire into an untargeted or speculative suspicion would be to allow negligence, albeit gross, to be the basis of a finding of privity.

In *Brimex Ltd v Begum*[55] it was alleged, unsuccessfully, that the sub-tenant, Brimex, knew, either because it fully knew or because it had blind eye knowledge, that a particular transaction was a breach of the terms of the headlease. It was not necessary, remarked Morgan J, to ask whether or not acting in that way with that knowledge amounted to dishonesty. 'It is not a relevant requirement of this tort.'

[6.23] Where there is an industrial dispute, it is advisable for prospective plaintiffs to provide prospective defendants with notice in the clearest terms of the contracts breach of which the latter are or will be procuring or have procured.

The statutory immunities do not depend on a union acting with the support of a ballot. But the immunities can be lost in other ways (for example, if the action is not 'in contemplation of furtherance of a trade dispute'), hence the British High Court decision in *Boxfoldia Ltd v National Graphical Association*[56] (para **3.37** *et seq*), contains important lessons for this jurisdiction. A letter conveying strike notice to an employer must be written with the utmost care. In *Boxfoldia* a letter written by a national officer of the defendant union to the plaintiff employer gave 14 days' notice of withdrawal of all NGA members' labour. Savill J held it could not be treated as having been written on behalf of the employees concerned giving contractual notice of the termination of their contracts of employment. Therefore the union had induced the employees wrongfully to repudiate their contracts of employment:

> ... the NGA were not intending to bring the contracts of employment to a lawful end, but instead were intent upon calling the members out knowing that this would be in breach of their contracts of employment or at least being reckless of whether or not that would result in a breach of those contracts.[57]

Inconsistent dealing

[6.24] It is actionable to have dealings with a contract breaker which the intervening party knows to be inconsistent with the contract: *Thomson (DC) & Co Ltd v Deakin*.[58] 'Inconsistent dealing' may sometimes be commenced by the third party without knowledge that the contract is being broken. If so, there will be no liability. If it is continued, however, after the third party has notice of the contract, an actionable wrong will have been committed. In *Reno Ergrais et Products Chemiques SA v Irish Agricultural Wholesale Society Ltd and Potash & Continental Ltd*[59] Hamilton J cited

---

55. *Brimex Ltd v Begum* [2007] EWHC 34.

56. *Boxfoldia Ltd v National Graphical Association* [1988] IRLR 383.

57. *Boxfoldia Ltd v National Graphical Association* [1988] IRLR 383 at 368.

58. *Thomson (DC) & Co Ltd v Deakin* [1952] Ch 646 at 694, *per* Jenkins LJ.

59. *Reno Ergrais et Products Chemiques SA v Irish Agricultural Wholesale Society Ltd and Potash & Continental Ltd* (8 September 1976, unreported), HC.

the above principle from *Thomson,* apparently with approval at least in so far as it enabled the applicant to make out a *prima facie* case in interlocutory proceedings.

[6.25] It has been suggested[60] that where there is inconsistent dealing, a risk of liability requires four things:

1.   A does not know that a breach of the contract between B and C will arise upon entering into a contract with B. However, continuing inconsistent dealings after being put on notice of the breach will constitute potential liability.

2.   A intends such a consequential breach to arise. This can be inferred from the facts.

3.   A induces such a breach by 'actively participating' in the negotiation of a contract with B which results in a breach of the existing contract between B and C.

4.   There is in fact a breach of the main contract between B and C as a result of the new contract being entered into.

In *OBG,*[61] Lord Nicholls referred to inconsistent dealing when considering the mental element necessary for the tort of inducing breach of contract:

> The defendant is made responsible for the third party's breach because of his intentional causative participation in that breach. Causative participation is not enough. A stranger to a contract may know nothing of the contract. Quite unknowingly and unintentionally he may procure a breach of the contract by offering an inconsistent deal to a contracting party which persuades the latter to default on his contractual obligations. The stranger is not liable in such a case.

Intention

[6.26] There must be an intentional invasion of the defendant's contractual rights. Asquith LJ described 'intention'[62] in *Cunliffe v Goodman:*[63]

> An 'intention' to my mind connotes a state of affairs which the party 'intending'... does more than merely contemplate: it connotes a state of affairs which, on the contrary, he decides, so far as in him lies, to bring about, and which, in point of possibility, he has a reasonable prospect of being able to bring about, by his own act of volition.

Lord Devlin said in *Rookes v Barnard*[64] there must be 'an intention to cause breach'. The focus is on the notion of intended breach rather than intended injury. The plaintiff

---

60.   Casey, 'Liability for "Innocently" or "Passively" Procuring a Breach of Contract' (2000) 7(10) CLP 235.

61.   *OBG Ltd v Allan* [2008] AC 1 at para [191].

62.   See Cane, 'Mens Rea in Tort Law' (2000) OJLS 533 in which he concludes that intention in tort law is a much less important ground of liability than negligence because emphasis is given to the interests of victims and to social values in constructing the concept of responsibility.

63.   *Cunliffe v Goodman* [1950] 2 KB 237 at 253.

64.   *Rookes v Barnard* [1964] AC 1129 at 1212.

must show he was targeted by the defendant and the target aimed at must be the plaintiff's contract. Lord Hoffmann in *OBG*[65] distinguished between ends, means and consequences. If someone knowingly causes a breach of contract, it does not normally matter that it is the means by which he intends to achieve some further end, or even that he would rather have been able to achieve that end without causing a breach. People seldom knowingly cause loss by unlawful means out of simply disinterested malice:

> On the other hand, if the breach of contract is neither an end in itself nor a means to an end, but merely a foreseeable consequence, then in my opinion it cannot for this purpose be said to have been intended. That, I think, is what judges and writers mean when they say that the claimant must have been 'targeted' or 'aimed at'.[66]

[6.27] Lord Nicholls in the same case regarded the defendant as responsible for the third party's breach because of his 'intentional causative participation' in that breach (para **6.25**). Causative participation alone is not enough. The additional necessary factor is the defendant's intent. He is liable if he intended to persuade the contracting party to break the contract. Intentional interference presupposes knowledge of the contract.[67]

Good motives are irrelevant. Equally, bad motives are irrelevant and do not need to be proved. Thus, if it is established that the defendants intended to procure a breach, it is no defence for them to show they were *bona fide* or that they lacked spite or ill-will.

In general it is very difficult to escape liability on the basis of absence of knowledge or intent.

[6.28] The House of Lords in *OBG* disapproved of the majority Court of Appeal's decision in *Millar v Bassey*.[68] Miss Bassey had broken her contract to perform for the recording company and it was a foreseeable consequence that the recording company would have to break its contracts with the accompanying musicians, but those breaches of contract were neither an end desired by Miss Bassey, nor a means of achieving that end.

THE INDUCEMENT

[6.29] Inducement may take the form of persuasion, procurement or inducement, direct intervention against the contract or the imposition of physical restraint. Mere facilitation is not sufficient.[69]

---

65.   *OBG Ltd v Allan* [2008] AC 1 at 30.
66.   *OBG Ltd v Allan* [2008] AC 1 at 30.
67.   'If the defendant deliberately turned a blind eye and proceeded regardless he may be treated as having intended the consequence he brought about. A desire to injure the claimant is not an essential ingredient of this tort.' *OBG Ltd v Allan* [2008] AC 1 at 63.
68.   *Millar v Bassey* [1994] EMLR 44.
69.   *Credit Lyonnais Nederland BV v ECGD* [1999] 2 WLR 540.

Where A persuades B to break his contract with C it will not provide an excuse if the person induced could have ignored the intervention and performed the contract.[70] Nor does it matter who initiated the talks which resulted in breach, nor whether B was resistant or otherwise. The persuasion may be smooth and peaceful, or it may involve a threat or ultimatum. Many cases in this jurisdiction have involved threats to withdraw labour. It will not affect liability where communication is made via an agent: *Daily Mirror Newspapers Ltd v Gardner.*[71]

[6.30] An employee is not liable for procuring a breach of a contract made between his employer and a third party where he acts *bona fide* and within the scope of his authority.[72] A person who approaches the employee of a company, someone who cannot be treated as its *alter ego*, cannot be said to be approaching the company directly and so will not be liable for any breach by the company[73] unlike the situation where a director or like officer empowered to act on behalf of the company is approached.[74] If directors of a company cause a breach of contract by the company in a board meeting, they are not liable in tort for procuring the breach.[75]

[6.31] In the direct form of the tort, unlawful means are not required. In many Irish cases, where a trade union delegation has succeeded in procuring a breach of the contract of employment between a worker and his employer (by the latter's summary dismissal, say, of the former), judges have got bogged down in a search for unlawful means (para **7.02** *et seq*).[76] It may be that in so doing they were influenced by the broader liability of what has been styled 'intentional interference with a person's employment by unlawful means'. Or it may be that their quest for unlawful means was an (ill-conceived) attempt to distinguish procurement from mere advice or the transmission of information.

[6.32] Courts are quite willing, it would appear, to find persuasion in trade disputes. In *Dublin Maritime Ltd v Ellis*[77] the High Court restrained the issuance of instructions to, or otherwise directing or encouraging in any manner whatsoever, all concerned with the loading, unloading and with the free passage of the vessel *MV Hermia,* to refuse to load or assist with the free passage of the said vessel. In *Union Traffic v TGWU,*[78] the

---

70. *JT Stratford & Son Ltd v Lindley* [1965] AC 269, 333.

71. *Daily Mirror Newspapers Ltd v Gardner* [1968] 2 QB 762.

72. *Said v Butt* 3 KB 497. *Sed contra* if he goes outside the scope of his authority: *Thomson (DC) & Co Ltd v Deakin* [1952] Ch 646, at 680–681 *per* Evershed MR.

73. *Thomson (DC) & Co Ltd v Deakin* [1952] Ch 646.

74. *Thomson (DC) & Co Ltd v Deakin* [1952] Ch 646.

75. *Scammell & Nephew Ltd v Hurley* [1929] 1 KB 419. But they could be held liable for conspiracy before the meeting to induce the board as a whole to break the contract: *De Jetley Marks v Greenwood* [1936] 1 All ER 863, 872–873.

76. See, eg, *Riordan v Butler* [1948] IR 347; *Hynes v Conlon* (1939) Ir Jur Rep 49.

77. *Dublin Maritime Ltd v Ellis* (1983, unreported), HC.

78. *Union Traffic v TGWU* [1989] IRLR 127.

Court of Appeal accepted that persuasion is enough to found the tort of inducing breach of contract. Bingham LJ gave it as his view that:

> the verb 'persuade' has a wide range of meanings as exemplified by the secondary meaning of the noun 'persuader.' Presence at the site would in my judgment be enough if it were clear, as I think it is, that that presence was intended and was successful in its object of inducing breaches of contract.

The case held that the mere fact of picketing can be regarded as an inducement to employees seeking to cross the picket line to break their contracts of employment and can also be regarded as an interference with business contracts by unlawful means if it is clear that the presence of the picket was intended and was successful in its object of inducing breaches of contract. In effect, any successful picket is potentially tortious and can be restrained unless rendered immune by statute.[79] This has important implications for picketing in s 11 of the Industrial Relations Act 1990.

[6.33] Generally, persuasion should be distinguished from the communication of mere information or advice, although one cannot help sympathising with Coleridge J (dissenting) in *Lumley v Gye*[80] who thought it practically impossible to draw such a line, it was 'a matter for the casuist rather than the jurist; still less is it for the juryman.' Nonetheless, authorities have laid down various guidelines. In *Thomson (DC) & Co Ltd v Deakin*[81] it was held that a 'mere statement of, or drawing of the attention of the party addressed to, the state of facts as they are' is not an inducement but only the transmission of information. What is required is some element of pressure, persuasion or procuration. Even if the defendant knows and indeed desires certain consequences, it will not render him liable if this element is lacking.

[6.34] Irish case law is far from clear. Not infrequently, the requirements of direct and indirect intervention with contract appear mixed up. The search for unlawful means was seen as necessary to establish inducement in *McCobb v Doyle*[82] where the defendants called to a particular place of employment to convey, not by way of any threat of violence or intimidation, but by pressure – in the knowledge that a strike would probably result – that the plaintiff's services should be dispensed with. The plaintiff was dismissed without notice. The concentration of the case is on whether or

---

79. *Pace Thomas v National Union of Mineworkers* [1985] IRLR 136, 148.

80. *Lumley v Gye* (1853) 2 E & B 216, 252. The High Court (O'Higgins J) held in *Meridian Communications Ltd v Eircell* (5 April 2001, unreported), HC that the process letters in connection with transfers of mobile phone services from defendant to plaintiff did not constitute an inducement or procurement of a breach of contract: they were true and accurate, reasonably expressed, and did not go beyond what could be considered advice, and the persons to whom they were addressed were told in them they were obliged to honour their contractual commitments. Similarly in *Iarnród Éireann v Holbrooke and Ors* [2000] ELR 109 where unplanned stoppages arose as a spontaneous reaction to an employee's grievance, the HC held, on the evidence, the employee's involvement was not of such a persuasive character as to enable it to conclude he 'did definitely and unequivocally persuade, induce or procure' the work stoppages.

81. *Thomson (DC) & Co Ltd v Deakin* [1952] 1 Ch 646, 686.

82. *McCobb v Doyle* [1936] IR 444.

not the defendants were immune from liability by virtue of the Trade Disputes Act 1906. The threat of a strike was not at the time regarded as illegal *per se*. There are no details in the report of the defendants' conversation, save that their visit was 'not characterised by any threat of violence or intimidation'. Their action was held to amount to interference with the right of some other person to dispose of his labour as he will (ie the plaintiff's right).[83] The headnote describes this tort as one of 'wrongfully inducing a breach of contract of employment.' Murnaghan J declined to find a trade dispute: hence the defendants were not protected.

[6.35] The case may be contrasted with *Hynes v Conlon*.[84] Here agreements were made between the representatives of a certain trade union and a firm of building contractors providing that the firm should not employ labourers who were not members of a trade union and if additional labour were required, preference should be given to labourers whose employment had recently been terminated, subject to there being suitable work available for them. Subsequently, the contractors agreed to employ the plaintiff, a labourer, who unknown to them was very much in arrears with his subscription to his trade union and was considered a 'lapsed member'. The representative of the trade union approached the contractors and asked them to dismiss the plaintiff, which they did without giving him proper notice or pay in lieu thereof. The High Court (Hanna J) held that no tort had been committed:

> There was nothing in the nature of a threat to the employer or in the nature of a severe warning that might be construed into [*sic*] a threat; and the view I take of what took place was no more than telling the employer the attitude which the union was taking up. If union officials could not do what was done in this case, they would be of little use ... So far as I can see, in this case there were no threats, no warning and no violence.

The absence of a request to the contractors to dismiss the plaintiff backed up by an express threat to strike saved the day for the defendants. There was arguably no less an actionable interference with the right of a man to 'dispose of his labour as he will' in *Hynes* than there had been in *McCobb*.

[6.36] There is a clear implication in *Cotter v Ahern*[85] that if one's intention is simply to convey information or advice it should be done by a single letter. A solemn deputation was seen as having the purpose of exerting maximum pressure and therefore amounting to a procuring event. The facts here (see para **6.19**) involved a meeting between the appointing school manager and members of the INTO. The former had offered an appointment as principal to the plaintiff who did not belong to the union. The defendants exerted pressure by informing the school manager who they were, and of the positions they held in the Cork City Branch of the INTO. They also informed him of their dissatisfaction with his decision to appoint the plaintiff and expressed the view that other teachers in the school might find it displeasing and difficult to work with him. They said that some or many of the parents who were

---

83. A right that Kingsmill Moore J later suggested may be a constitutional right under Art 40.3.2° (para **2.19**).
84. *Hynes v Conlon* (1939) Ir Jur R 49.
85. *Cotter v Ahern* [1976–77] ILRM 248.

members of trade unions might find it unsatisfactory to have what was described as an unassociated teacher as the principal of the school. The defendants mentioned that, as the plaintiff was not a member of the INTO, he would not derive the benefit of the union's group insurance and the school might therefore be inadequately or insufficiently insured. Finally, the chairman of the branch, who was among the deputation, asked whether the approval of the Bishop of Cork had been obtained (as was required) and when the answer was in the negative, he mentioned that those present would be prepared that evening to go to the Bishop of Cork to make representations against the plaintiff's appointment. The defendants' behaviour was held to amount to procurement of breach.[86]

Other direct intervention

[6.37] There are no Irish authorities directly on the point of inducement as 'other direct intervention'. This form of the tort comprises the doing of a wrongful act other than inducement which prevents the performance of a contract, although interference with a contract short of breach by unlawful means often concerns the same sort of liability. The act must be wrongful in itself, so that A commits no wrong where he prevents B from fulfilling his contract to C by buying every existing and available product B is obliged to supply to C. The usual examples given here involve kidnapping one of the contracting parties or stealing his tools or otherwise misappropriating them where these provide the only available means of performing the contract.[87] There is no reason why the person prevented from performing should not be able to sue as well as the other aggrieved contracting party, as the former did not intentionally break the contract.[88] Will the breach of a penal statute amount to a wrongful act? *Lonrho Ltd v Shell Petroleum Co Ltd*[89] suggests that the answer will depend on whether the breach, properly construed, would afford an action in tort for contravention.

Indirect inducement

[6.38] Sometimes a strike will not bring sufficient pressure on the employer to make him give in to the workers' demands. To make the industrial action more effective, the workers may take secondary action to isolate the employer from his commercial contracts. This involves persuading customers or suppliers of the employer with whom the workers are in dispute not to trade with the employer. The secondary boycott may be brought about directly, ie a direct approach is made to the customer or supplier to persuade him not to deal with the employer; or indirectly, where the workers employed by the supplier or customer are persuaded to take action. They may go on strike, but since this may leave them with no pay they are more likely to 'black' the employer who

---

86. See too *B&I Steampacket Co Ltd v Branigan* [1958] IR 128, telegram 'please give necessary notification to master' held not to mean giving requisite notice of termination.

87. *DC Thomson & Co Ltd v Deakin* [1952] Ch 646, at 702, *per* Morris LJ; at 696 *per* Jenkins LJ (see, similarly, *GWK Ltd v Dunlop Rubber Co Ltd* (1926) 42 TLR 376).

88. *Hersees of Woodstock Ltd v Goldstein* (1963) 39 DLR (2d) 449.

89. *Lonrho Ltd v Shell Petroleum Co Ltd (No 2)* [1981] 2 All ER 456.

is the object of the dispute, by refusing to send goods or materials to his premises or to collect goods from them. This is the indirect form of the tort.

[6.39] In *OBG Ltd v Allan*[90] Lord Hoffmann said he did not expect their Lordships to reject the unified theory of the tort adopted in *DC Thomson & Co Ltd v Deakin*[91] unless it had serious practical disadvantages (para **4.13** *et seq*). He thought it had been a source of confusion in more than one respect. The first problem he addressed was the notion of 'direct and indirect interference' (see para **6.54**). In the face of this surprising equivocation, the current status of *Thomson* is uncertain, certainly in England, and the paragraphs which follow must be read accordingly. *OBG* has yet to be considered by an Irish court. It is more difficult to prove knowledge and intention, the more indirect and remote the action of the defendants in interfering with the performance of the principal contract. Added to that, judges have not always applied the law with the same consistency.

[6.40] In *DC Thomson & Co Ltd v Deakin*[92] Jenkins LJ described the elements of the indirect form of the tort of inducing breach of contract:

> First, that the person charged with actionable interference knew of the existence of the contract and intended to procure its breach; secondly, that the person so charged did definitely and unequivocally persuade, induce or procure the employees concerned to break their contracts of employment with the intent I have mentioned; thirdly, that the employees so persuaded, induced or procured did in fact break their contracts of employment; and fourthly, that breach of the contract forming the alleged subject of interference ensued as a necessary consequence of the breaches by the employees concerned of their contracts of employment.

The judgment was approved by the House of Lords in *Merkur Island Shipping Corporation v Laughton*[93] (and was expressly not followed, it should be noted, by the House of Lords in *OBG*) and has been influential in later cases.[94]

[6.41] In *Thomson* the defendants were trade union officials. Thomson ran a non-union shop and dismissed a man who joined a union whereupon a boycott was organised and men employed at a supplier of the plaintiff's (the supplier), told their employer they might not be prepared to handle paper for the plaintiff. To play it safe, the supplier did not require their employees to load or deliver paper and informed the plaintiff they could not perform their contract. The plaintiff sought an interlocutory injunction against officials of the various unions concerned to restrain them from procuring any breach by the supplier of their contract with it. The Court of Appeal held in the circumstances there was no liability as the evidence did not establish any actual

---

90. *OBG Ltd v Allan* [2008] AC 1 at 28.
91. *DC Thomson & Co Ltd v Deakin* [1952] Ch 646.
92. *DC Thomson & Co Ltd v Deakin* [1952] Ch 646.
93. *Merkur Island Shipping Corporation v Laughton* [1983] IRLR 218.
94. Eg *Shipping Company Uniform Inc v International Transport Workers' Federation* [1985] IRLR 71.

knowledge of a contract between the plaintiff and the supplier, and, if the union officials thought there might be a contract, of its terms.

Breach must be a *necessary* consequence. Jenkins LJ[95] suggested that if A were to induce B, C's lorry driver, to refuse to carry goods to D, in order to cause a breach of contract with D, the breach of contract between the employer and D would not be a necessary consequence of the breach of contract of employment if C could engage another driver but did not do so. Only if it is impossible to find or impracticable to employ other workers to take the place of those who have left will the tort be established.[96]

[6.42] In *Stratford v Lindley*[97] (para **6.13**), the defendants were held liable for procuring breaches of the contracts to repair barges. The majority of their Lordships treated the case as one of indirect procurement since the trade union officials achieved their end by means of instructions issued to their members. The union officials knew barges were always returned promptly and this was obviously done under a contract of hiring. They were held to have sufficient knowledge of the contract to know an embargo would result in breach by the hirers.[98]

[6.43] Indirect interference, without unlawful means, will not do. Thus, a man who 'corners the market' in a commodity may well know it may prevent others from performing their contracts but he is not liable to an action for so doing. A trade union official who calls a strike on proper notice may well know it will prevent employees from performing their contracts to deliver goods, but he is not liable in damages for calling it. Indirect interference is only unlawful if unlawful means are used. In *Merkur Island Shipping Corporation v Laughton*[99] the Court of Appeal saw no difference, conceptually, between different expressions of indirect action designed to interfere with the performance of the principal contract, provided the conditions for the existence of a cause of action based on the tort were met. The House of Lords confirmed that there is an actionable common law tort of interference by unlawful means with the performance of a contract[100] (see on the extended tort, para **4.07**).

---

95.   *DC Thomson & Co Ltd v Deakin* [1952] Ch 646 at 699.

96.   That breach must be a necessary consequence of wrongful action was approved in *T Bradley Ltd v Duffy* (26 March 1979, unreported), HC.

97.   *Stratford v Lindley* [1965] AC 269.

98.   A minority differed, however, and looked upon the case as one of direct procurement by reason of a letter sent to the trade association to which the hirers of barges belonged. That letter made it clear to the Association of Master Lightermen, which in effect represented the hirers, that the hirers could not return the barges to the customers. It gave information about the embargo but 'the fact that an inducement to break a contract is couched as an irresistible embargo rather than in terms of seduction does not make it any the less an inducement', *per* Lord Pearce in [1965] AC 269 at 333. To view an embargo under the heading of direct procurement would involve an extension of liability, see Wedderurn, '*Stratford v Lindley*' (1965) 28 MLR 205, 207. Irish authority has so far looked upon the embargo as a form of indirect inducement.

99.   *Merkur Island Shipping Corporation v Laughton* [1983] IRLR 218.

100. *Merkur Island Shipping Corporation v Laughton* [1983] IRLR 218.

[6.44] *News Group Newspapers and Others v SOGAT*[101] involved picketing at the plaintiff's Wapping plant. Stuart-Smith J in the High Court held that there was actionable interference with the primary obligations of a contract between TNT Roadfreight Ltd (TNT) and the third plaintiff to distribute newspapers for the third plaintiff as and when the first or second plaintiff required. It had been the clear purpose and intent of those who committed these torts to obstruct by nuisance and intimidation the departure of TNT's lorries, to inflict delay and so interfere with what must obviously be a primary obligation of that contract. The unlawful means relied on were nuisance and intimidation, not interference with the drivers' contracts of employment. All the ingredients of the wider tort were established.

[6.45] The wider application of the tort could have startling implications for trade unionists as *Falconer v ASLEF and NUR*[102] illustrated, where a third-party member of the public succeeded in getting damages from a trade union for unlawful interference with his commercial contract arising out of an industrial dispute. The plaintiff had been prevented from travelling by train due to industrial action. He alleged wrongful interference with contract, the alleged contract (which was accepted by the Sheffield County Court but which may be doubted) being between British Rail (BR) and himself to provide him with rail travel. That the strike had a merely consequential effect upon passengers was rejected as 'both naïve and divorced from reality.' The intention in calling the strike was to create pressure on BR from passengers to accede to the unions' demands. Although the Conditions of Carriage contained an exclusion clause, that did not remove or exclude the primary obligations, it merely limited BR's liability so far as any specified train was concerned and empowered it to withdraw any service without breach.[103]

[6.46] *McMahon Ltd v Dunne and Dolan*[104] (para **6.16**) concerned sympathetic industrial action. A firm of timber merchants and builders' providers had entered into contracts with foreign firms for the purchase and sale of certain quantities of timber to be delivered to the plaintiff. Ten lots arrived at the relevant port over three successive months. They were discharged from ships, placed on the dock and paid for. The defendants had placed an embargo on the removal of all building materials from this port for the purpose of implementing a trade dispute alleged to exist between the workers employed by certain builders' providers in the surrounding area and their employers. The plaintiff, having sought unsuccessfully to obtain delivery of its goods, alleged it had been prevented from obtaining delivery and that the vendors of the goods had been prevented from effecting delivery because of the defendant's embargo. None

---

101. *News Group Newspapers and Others v SOGAT* [1986] IRLR 337.
102. *Falconer v ASLEF and NUR* [1986] IRLR 331.
103. Notwithstanding this decision, consumers affected by industrial action have been slow to follow *Falconer's* steps. Nor should it be viewed as a reliable precedent, not just because of the question mark surrounding the alleged contract in the case. The importance of intention to injure the plaintiff was given scant treatment. The influence of *Falconer* has been severely curtailed by *Barretts & Baird (Wholesale) Ltd v Institution of Professional Civil Servants* [1987] IRLR 3 (para **7.19**).
104. *McMahon Ltd v Dunne and Dolan* [1965] 99 ILTR 45.

of the plaintiff's employees belonged to the relevant union and no trade dispute existed between the plaintiff and the defendants or the relevant union. The plaintiff's action succeeded at an interlocutory stage (there is no record of a full trial), Budd J holding, *inter alia*, that the evidence adduced supported a *prima facie* case of unlawful procurement of a breach of contract by the defendants. The need for unlawful means for this form of the tort was stressed. The plaintiff alleged these lay in the procuring of the checkers at the port to commit a breach of their contracts with their respective employers in failing to carry out the normal duties of their employment. Budd J found it difficult to state precisely what the ingredients of the tort were. 'That is not fully and authoritatively decided here.'[105] The judge cited Jenkins LJ on breach as a necessary consequence in *Thomson's* case,[106] as indeed his Lordship's other observations on the tort. However, Budd J indicated that the latter's views as to the necessary ingredients of the tort might not be universally followed in England or here.

[6.47] The extreme form of the tort (as in *McMahon Ltd*) subsequently arose in a number of English cases, mostly concerning the blacking of ships at the instance of the International Transport Workers' Federation (ITF). In *Merkur Island Shipping Corp v Laughton*[107] the four essential preconditions for the existence of a cause of action based upon the tort of interference with the performance of a contract as stated by Jenkins LJ in the *Thomson* case were reaffirmed, and the defendant's argument that the case was only authority where there was indirect interference with the contracts of employment of those who were in fact intended to perform the principal contract was rejected.

[6.48] The inducement in indirect procurement cases is difficult to sketch. In *Sherriff v McMullen and Ors*,[108] the plaintiff, Sherriff, was the owner of a sawmill. The first-named defendant was president of the ITGWU. A dispute arose between Sherriff and his employees on the question of wages. At the start of the dispute, Sherriff had 12 employees engaged at the mill. They were members of the ITGWU. The matter was eventually referred to the Labour Court and strike action by the employees was deferred, by agreement, pending an investigation by that court. While the matter was pending before the court, all the employees of Sherriff wrote to the union announcing their resignation therefrom. At that date, some workmen who had been employed by Sherriff at a previous time, and who were temporarily unemployed owing to shortage of work, did not subscribe to this letter and remained members of the union. However, such workmen as were re-employed resigned from the union before recommencing work. The president of the ITGWU wrote to Sherriff informing him it was understood that he had persuaded his employees to resign from the union and warning him that, if such were the case, the members of the union throughout the country would refuse to

---

105. *McMahon Ltd v Dunne and Dolan* [1965] 99 ILTR 45 at 49.

106. It is doubtful whether intention should be presumed on the basis of 'the ordinary and probable consequences' of a defendant's acts in cases of indirect procurement *pace* Budd J at 56.

107. *Merkur Island Shipping Corp v Laughton* [1983] IRLR 218. The facts of the case were held to be indistinguishable from *Marina Shipping Co Ltd v Laughton and Shaw (The Antama)* [1982] QB 1127.

108. *Sherriff v McMullen and Ors* [1952] IR 236.

handle his products. He then wrote to another of the defendants, local secretary of the union, instructing him that members in the union 'should not handle goods for or from this particular firm.' Sherriff's workmen were also informed of this decision. On the same date, those of his workmen who had resigned from the union wrote informing it that their resignation from the union was voluntary, and not a result of pressure or promises made by the plaintiff. Later, one employee who had rejoined the union was re-employed by the plaintiff, and another employee rejoined the union as well. Then a company called Irish Shoe Supplies (1946) Ltd ordered a quantity of timber from the plaintiff who tried to make delivery on their instructions on three separate occasions. On each occasion, the company refused to take delivery of the timber because their workmen refused to handle it. Then workmen of another firm refused to repair machinery belonging to the plaintiff.

[6.49] The Supreme Court held that no trade dispute existed. Gavan Duffy P described the 'real purpose' of the defendants' action:[109]

> to teach Sherriff (and other employers who might be tempted to emulate him) the lesson that *nemo impune me lacessit* by giving him cogent, practical proof that a costly and disastrous *eric*[110] could and would be exacted by the Transport Union from an antagonist daring to use the seductive methods open to an employer to cast discredit upon the union.

He was of the opinion that the conduct of the defendants on the occasions when supplies could not be delivered went beyond the mere inducement of a breach of the contract of employment (a commercial contract could not be fulfilled) and beyond mere interference with trade or business. (Murnaghan J did not decide the point, nor did he express his agreement with it.)

[6.50] A similarly strict approach was taken in *Talbot (Ireland) Ltd v Merrigan*[111] where the divisional secretary of the defendant union issued a circular in which he sought the support of other unions for an embargo endorsed by the Executive Council of ICTU. The Supreme Court regarded the effect of the embargo as 'no mere empty request'. It went beyond any legitimate industrial action: it had in effect procured the breach of many contracts between the company and third parties.

Yet, as Kerr has pointed out,[112] it is doubtful if either direct or indirect procurement took place in either case. As to the former, the union's written instructions in *Sherriff* and the union circular and ICTU instruction in *Talbot* were directed at trade unions and their members, none of whom were parties to any commercial contracts they could break. They were not directed at companies or individuals who had commercial relations with Sherriff or Talbot.[113] As regards the indirect form of the tort – leaving

---

109. *Sherriff v McMullen and Ors* [1952] IR 236 at 255.

110. A 'fine' in ancient Irish law.

111. *Talbot (Ireland) Ltd v Merrigan* (30 April 1981, unreported), SC.

112. Kerr, 'Trade Disputes, Economic Torts and the Constitution: The Legacy of *Talbot*' (1981) 16 Ir Jur (ns) 241.

113. See on *Talbot* Von Prondzynski and McCarthy, 'Is the law above the trade unions?' (1981) *Irish Times*, 18 May.

unlawful means to one side – it ought not to have been presumed (if it was) that general exhortations such as 'refuse to handle goods for Sherriff' or 'Black Talbot' would be carried out unlawfully. Concerning the latter, for instance:

> Precisely the same effect, the blacking of Talbot (Ireland) Ltd, could have been achieved if employees gave due notice under their contracts of employment and went on strike when that notice expired …[114] Alternatively, the employees could have demanded the insertion of a 'hot cargo clause' into their contracts of employment.[115]

In other words, the trade union officials who wished to cause a breach of a commercial contract between the employer in dispute and one or more of his customers could have done so without risk of committing a tort.[116] The authority of *Talbot* is, or course, very weak since the judgment is not written down (para **2.62** *et seq*). But the same cannot be said of *Sherriff*.

[6.51] The law appears to have been more correctly dealt with by Hamilton J in *Reg Armstrong Motors Ltd v CIE*.[117] The plaintiff company was engaged in the assembly and distribution of motor vehicles in Ireland. A dispute arose between the company and ATGWU, which represented the car assemblers employed in the company, over the closure of the company's assembly plant. Following the ineffectiveness of talks to alleviate the redundancies, the four unions concerned in the organisation of motor assembly workers arranged a meeting at which it was decided to prevent the importation of fully built-up vehicles into the country. This decision was supported by the Trade Union Advisory Body to the Motor Industry, and by the executive council of ICTU. One of the unions concerned, ITGWU, informed the secretary of each of its docks branches of the ban, and asked for support in ensuring that fully built-up vehicles were not imported into Ireland. The plaintiff company had entered into contracts with CIE and British Rail (BR) for the importation of a number of such vehicles from Fishguard to Rosslare and their delivery to Dublin. The company sought

---

114. Yet it may be naïve to expect anything other than the same cynicism in these cases as the High Court displayed in a case involving direct inducement: *B & I Steampacket Co Ltd v Branigan* [1958] IR 128. There the court had to decide whether a direction in a telegram made by a union official to the union members to 'please give necessary notification to master' of a ship that the ship would not sail amounted to a direction to give due notice of termination. Regarding the telegram as a whole and taking the circumstances in which it was sent into account, Dixon J held that the official could not be permitted 'to maintain the impossible contradictory position' that, while the telegram meant that the crew were to refuse to sail the ship and break their contracts in this respect, at the same time they were to give the requisite notice of termination. Contrast *F Bowles Ltd v Lindley* [1965] 1 Lloyd's Rep 207.

115. Para **9.92**. Eg, where the employee agrees not to handle goods produced by an employer with whom the union is in dispute.

116. See *Report of the Royal Commission on Trade Unions and Employers' Associations* (mnd 3623, paras 878–93); the *Report of the Irish Commission on Industrial Relations* expressly adopted this view: para 720.

117. *Reg Armstrong Motors Ltd v CIE* (2 December 1975, unreported), HC.

an injunction restraining the defendants from procuring, or attempting to procure, any interference with the import and distribution of these cars.

[6.52] Had the defendants directly induced breach of these contracts? No, said Hamilton J, as the only direct contact between the ITGWU or its shop stewards and CIE or BR was the notification of the existence of the ICTU ban to the port manager at Rosslare. This was merely communicating information or advice and did not amount to persuasion or inducement. (See, similarly, *Thomson (DC) & Co Ltd v Deakin*[118] where an approach to suppliers informing them of the existence of a trade dispute and making it clear that their employees might refuse to carry supplies to the plaintiff company was held to be transmission of information, not an inducement.) The company alternatively alleged indirect inducement as the defendants had persuaded CIE and BR employees to refuse to handle the fully built-up vehicles that were the subject-matter of these contracts. Hamilton J held that the mere requesting of members' support by the ITGWU in ensuring that no such cars were imported could not amount to a persuasion, inducement or procurement of CIE employees (necessarily) to break their contracts of employment. The injunction sought was refused.[119]

[6.53] The mainstream of English authorities before *OBG Ltd v Allan*[120] seems to be in line with the stricter approach evident in *Talbot* and *Sherriff* so that there, as here, it has become extremely difficult to advise those who are taking part in industrial action as to when 'information' ends and 'persuasion' begins. The action of union officials in informing members in other sections of the union and at other places of work about a particular dispute with an employer may be held to amount to an inducement,[121] and it has been said that, since the statement made must always be construed in the context of the relative positions of the parties, even a 'suggestion' contained within such information can amount to inducement, if the defendant was desperately anxious to achieve the result of coercing the plaintiff.[122]

[6.54] In *OBG Ltd v Allan* the distinction between the original *Lumley v Gye* tort and its extension in *DC Thompson & Co Ltd,* a distinction between 'direct' and 'indirect' interference, and the very use of these terms, seemed to Lord Hoffmann 'to distract attention from the true questions which have to be asked in each case'. The latter requires the use of unlawful means while the former requires no more than inducement or persuasion. For example, in *Daily Mirror Newspapers Ltd v Gardner*[123] the Federation of Retail Newspapers (the federation) resolved to boycott the *Daily Mirror* for a week to put pressure on the publishers to allow its members higher margins. The

---

118. *Thomson (DC) & Co Ltd v Deakin* [1952] Ch 646.

119. The appeal to the Supreme Court resulted in the proceedings being sent back to the High Court so that, *inter alia*, proper pleadings could be exchanged and the issues accordingly defined between the parties (16 December 1975, unreported).

120. *OBG Ltd v Allan* [2008] AC 1.

121. *Torquay Hotel Co Ltd v Cousins* [1969] 2 Ch 106.

122. *Square Grip Reinforcement Ltd v Macdonald* [1968] SLT 65, 72–73 *per* Lord Milligan. See Wedderburn, 'The Labour Injunction in Scotland' (1968) 31 MLR 550.

123. *Daily Mirror Newspapers Ltd v Gardner* [1968] 2 QB 762.

federation advised their members to stop buying the papers from wholesalers. The publishers claimed an injunction on the ground that the federation was procuring a breach of the wholesalers' running contracts with the publishers to take a given number of copies each day. Counsel for the federation said it was a case of indirect procurement because the federation 'did not exert directly any pressure or inducement on the wholesalers: but at most they only did it indirectly by recommending the retailers to give stop orders'. Lord Denning said it did not matter whether one procured a breach of contract 'by direct approach to the one who breaks the contract or by indirect influence over others'. But in *Torquay Hotel Co Ltd v Cousins*[124] Lord Denning changed his mind. He said there was a distinction between 'direct persuasion' which was 'unlawful in itself', and bringing about a breach by indirect methods, which had to involve independently unlawful means. He treated the distinction as turning simply upon whether there was communication, directly or through an agent, between the defendant and the contract-breaker. Lord Hoffmann:[125]

> If this is what the distinction between 'direct' and 'indirect' means, it conceals the real question which has to be asked in relation to *Lumley v Gye* 2 E & B 216: did the defendant's acts of encouragement, threat, persuasion and so forth have a sufficient causal connection with the breach by the contracting party to attract accessory liability? The court in *Lumley v Gye* made it clear that the principle upon which a person is liable for the act of another in breaking his contract is the same as that on which he is liable for the act of another in committing a tort. It follows, as I have said, that the relevant principles are to be found in cases such as *CBS Songs Ltd v Amstrad Consumer Electronics plc* [1988] AC 1013 and *Unilever plc v Chefaro Proprietaries Ltd* [1994] FSR 135. By the test laid down in these cases, the federation could not have incurred any liability. They were not encouraging or assisting the wholesalers in breaking their contracts. They were simply advising their members to exercise their own freedom to buy whatever newspapers they liked. The wholesalers had no right to the co-operation of the retailers in enabling them to perform their contracts. Liability could not depend upon the accident of whether the federation had communicated (directly or through an intermediary) with the wholesalers. The distinction between direct and indirect interference was therefore irrelevant and misleading.

[6.55] A further disadvantage of the distinction between direct and indirect interference was its suggestion that the 'primary form' of the *Lumley v Gye* tort and the extension of the tort are mutually exclusive. Interference cannot be both direct and indirect. But, as Lord Hoffmann had said earlier, there was no reason why the same act should not create both accessory liability for procuring a breach of contract and primary liability for the separate tort of causing loss by unlawful means:

> In my opinion, therefore, the distinction between direct and indirect interference is unsatisfactory and it is time for the unnatural union between the *Lumley v Gye* tort and the tort of causing loss by unlawful means to be dissolved. They should be restored to the independence which they enjoyed at the time of *Allen v Flood*.[126]

---

124. *Torquay Hotel Co Ltd v Cousins* [1969] 2 Ch 106, 138–139.

125. *OBG Ltd v Allan* [2008] AC 1, at 28–9.

126. *OBG Ltd v Allan* [2008] AC 1 at 29.

Carty is emphatic that the process of extending the tort from its classic formulation should be reversed.[127]

BREACH

[6.56] The tort of inducing breach of contract requires breach of an existing and valid contractual obligation. In *OBG* the House of Lords regarded the breach of a contract as of the essence for this tort to exist.[128] What counts as a breach of contract? Lord Hoffmann saw no wriggle room: one cannot be liable for inducing a breach unless there has been a breach.[129] There is '[n]o secondary liability without primary liability'. Lord Denning's concept of an extended tort developed in *Torquay Hotel Co Ltd v Cousins*,[130] and approved by Lord Diplock in *Merkur Island Shipping Corpn v Laughton*,[131] had been made in the context of the unified theory (para **4.13** *et seq*). Similarly, said Lord Hoffmann, cases where interference with contractual relations were treated as coming within the *Lumley v Gye* tort[132] were really cases of causing loss by unlawful means.

[6.57] Clearly if the contract has not yet been formed, there is no breach.[133] It is possible to obtain a *quia timet* injunction even if no contract exists if the defendant has made it clear by his threats that he will, if it is concluded, procure its breach.[134] A plaintiff may rely on the likely inducement of breach of future contracts. This was accepted in *Union Traffic v TGWU*[135] wherein Bingham LJ cited an observation of Lord Upjohn in *Stratford v Lindley*:[136]

> I cannot accept that an injunction ought in some way to be limited so as to affect only existing contracts; such a limitation would fail to give the appellant company the protection, to which they have satisfied me they are entitled, of preserving the *status quo* until judgment so as to enable them to carry on

---

127. Carty, *An Analysis of the Economic Torts* (OUP, 2001) at 80.
128. A person who sets out to protect his own interests in the belief that he has a lawful right to do what he is doing does not have the intention required for the torts of inducing a breach of contract or conspiring to injure by unlawful means, even though the inevitable result of acting in that way will be to cause loss to another: *Meretz Investments NV and Anor v ACP and Ors* [2007] EWCA 1303 *per* Arden and Toulson LJJ, paras 124, 127, 174, 180.
129. *OBG Ltd v Allan* [2008] AC 1 at 31.
130. *Torquay Hotel Co Ltd v Cousins* [1969] 2 Ch 106, 138.
131. *Merkur Island Shipping Corpn v Laughton* [1983] 2 AC 570, 607–608, where he said there could be liability for preventing or hindering performance of the contract on the same principle as liability for procuring a breach.
132. Eg, *Dimbleday & Sons Ltd v NUJ* [1984] 1 WLR 67 and [1984] 1 WLR 427.
133. *Tru-Value Ltd v Switzer & Co* (10 March 1972, unreported), HC; *Reg Armstrong Motors Ltd v CIE* (2 December 1975, unreported), HC, 16; *McKernan v Fraser* (1931) 46 CLR 343.
134. *Torquay Hotel Co Ltd v Cousins* [1969] 2 Ch 106; *Brekkes v Cattel* [1972] Ch 105, 114.
135. *Union Traffic v TGWU* [1989] IRLR 127.
136. *Stratford v Lindley* [1965] AC 269, cited by Stamp J in *Torquay Hotel Co Ltd v Cousins* [1969] 2 Ch 106 at 118.

business in the usual way by entering into new contracts from time to time with their customers.

In *Irish Municipal Public and Civil Trade Union v Ryanair*[137] the defendant, in relation to a claim for inducing breach of contract, asserted that the relationship between the union and its members was not a contractual relationship but no authority was cited for the proposition and Laffoy J, correctly, declared herself not satisfied it was correct.

[6.58] It is not, of course, a tort to induce a person to perform his contractual obligations by means lawful in themselves. But it is not permitted for a defendant to say he was attempting to induce the contracting party to 'suspend' the contract when that party had no right to suspend the contract and the inducement in fact brought about a breach: *Emerald Construction Co Ltd v Lowthian*.[138]

This could be significant in the context of a *Becton Dickinson*[139] type argument. The effect of strike notice on the contract of employment is considered in **Ch 3**. Where strikers give notice lawfully to terminate their contracts, no tort is committed. If the notice is of inadequate length, it will be in breach of contract whatever its purpose. In England there is no rule of law that strike notices, even if of a length sufficient to terminate the contract, are notices of a forthcoming breach of contract; in Ireland a doctrine of suspension is espoused. Although it seems likely there will be no liability for breach of contract by virtue of the operation of an implied term that each contract permits suspension of its terms where lawful strike notice is served, some doubt is cast on this in para **3.37**, following the decision in *Boxfoldia*.

[6.59] No tort will be committed where the contract is void because unconstitutional, voidable[140] or void for reasons of incapacity or because it is contrary to public policy. Where a contract is illegal, the doctrine of severance may enable certain parts of it to remain valid and thus be capable of fulfilling the criteria necessary for liability. Where a contract is determinable, it is not a tort to induce one of the parties to determine it lawfully.[141] It will not avail a party to argue that the contract, breach of which he has induced, could have been terminated lawfully by the contracting party.[142]

Force majeure clause

[6.60] Is a breach which is not actionable in certain respects sufficient for the tort? Suppose there is a *force majeure* clause in the contract, as there often is, along the lines that:

> neither party shall be liable for any failure to fulfil any terms of this agreement if fulfilment is delayed, hindered or prevented by any circumstances whatever which is not within their immediate control including ... labour disputes.

137. *Irish Municipal Public and Civil Trade Union & Others v Ryanair* [2007] 1 ILRM 45, 57.
138. *Emerald Construction Co Ltd v Lowthian* [1966] 1 WLR 691.
139. *Becton Dickinson Ltd v Lee* [1973] IR 1.
140. *Greig v Insole* [1978] 3 All ER 449.
141. *McManus v Bowes* [1938] 1 KB 98.
142. *Emerald Construction Co Ltd v Lowthian* [1966] 1 WLR 691; *Square Grip Reinforcement Ltd v Macdonald (No 2)* (1968) SLT 65.

In *McMahon* (para **6.16**) the contracts in question contained well-known clauses exempting the seller from liability in case of *force majeure*. It was suggested by counsel for the defendants that where such a clause existed and delivery was prevented by reason of industrial action taken by persons outside the control of the seller resulting in the frustration of the contract, no breach of contract had been procured by the intervener. But Budd J did not follow this 'reasoning' because it seemed to him that 'such a clause predicates a right to delivery and merely exempts the seller from liability in the case of the intervention of *force majeure*.'[143] In any event he was quite satisfied there was a fair question to be tried on the matter. A helpful distinction was made by the Court of Appeal a few years later in *Torquay Hotel Co Ltd v Cousins*[144] where an injunction was granted against defendants who were taking action in a labour dispute calculated to cause a supplier to stop supplies under a standing contract, even though a clause, exactly that given above, exempted liability in the case of labour disputes. The clause was held to be 'an exception from liability for non-performance rather than an exception from obligation to perform.'[145] Had it been the latter, no liability for inducing any breach could have arisen.

[6.61] If there is a 'no-strike' or other clause in a collective agreement, that agreement itself, as between the collective parties thereto, will be regarded as legally binding. Depending on the circumstances, breach by one of the collective parties may be induced. Where the employment contract incorporates the terms of a collective agreement containing such a clause, it may be a difficult question of construction whether the obligation concerned is one which is capable of incorporation in an individual's employment contract.[146] Whether a 'no-strike' clause would be regarded as binding on an individual worker depends on whether an individual or collective approach is taken.[147]

[6.62] Where industrial action short of a strike is induced, there may be heads of liability which rest on considerations other than breach as to performance of the work itself. Thus a defendant may induce workers to act in breach of their obligation of mutual trust and confidence[148] or of fidelity to the employer (in the case of, for example, a go-slow or work to rule) or in breach of their obligation to carry out the work as agreed. Likewise, it would seem a refusal to cross a picket line in the performance of the contract of employment constitutes a breach of contract.[149]

---

143. *McMahon Ltd v Dunne and Dolan* 99 ILTR 45 (1965) at 55.

144. *Torquay Hotel Co Ltd v Cousins* [1969] 2 Ch 106.

145. *Per* Russell LJ *Torquay Hotel Co Ltd v Cousins* [1969] 2 Ch 106 at 143. For further on this see *Photo Productions Ltd v Securicor* [1980] AC 827 (HL) in general support.

146. See on this Rideout's *Principles of Labour Law* (4th edn, Sweet & Maxwell, 1983), 28–31.

147. Such a clause, if regarded as collective in nature, would be unlikely to be regarded as suitable for incorporation; in *Rookes v Barnard* [1964] AC 1129, counsel (foolishly) conceded that the no-strike clause was part of the employment contract.

148. See Redmond, 'The Implied Obligation of Mutual Trust and Confidence – A Common Law Action for "Unfair" Dismissal' (2009) IELJ Vol 6 No 2, 36.

149. But see the exceptional decision in *Johnson v Union Lighterage Co* (1924) 18 Lloyd's Rep 419.

Breach may relate to contractual rights but also to rights in equity or under statute or the Constitution.

Equity

[6.63] *Lumley v Gye* extends beyond the sphere of contractual relations. Breach of trust or fiduciary or equitable duties may be induced. It is wrongful knowingly and intentionally to induce a breach of an equitable obligation. In *Prudential Assurance Co Ltd v Lorenz*[150] insurance agents in dispute with their employer were persuaded to withhold payment to their employer of premiums which had been collected on his behalf. This was held to be a breach of their fiduciary duty to account,[151] which was treated as an obligation arising under the general law, independently of contract. It was recognised that the equitable wrong could also be a breach of contract. But the statutory immunity did not apply to it. The inducers had knowingly instigated a breach of trust and thereby interfered with the rights of the employer. Equity adopts a wide view of possible liabilities.

Not all judges are happy to 'tortify' these wrongs. In *Metall und Rohstoff AC v Donaldson Lufkin & Jenrette*[152] the Court of Appeal declined to find a tort of inducing breach of trust. Most cases have involved the indirect form of the tort and hence 'unlawful means', discussed in para **7.23**.

Statute

[6.64] A similar situation arises in connection with statutory duties. The possibility of a tort of inducing breach of statutory duty occurred in *Meade v Haringey BC*[153] and in *Associated Newspapers Group v Wade*.[154] Many employees are subject to statutory duties in Ireland. For example, the Merchant Shipping Act 1894 contains a number of restraints on the activities of seamen: eg, it is an offence for a seaman to neglect or refuse without reasonable cause to join his ship; it is also an offence for anyone to persuade a seaman to neglect his duty (ss 221 and 236). For liability, the breach itself must be actionable. If the statute either expressly or by implication permits the employer to base a civil action on the breach of statutory duty – if, in other words, he has a right to require compliance with the statute – then anyone instigating industrial action in breach of the statute will be liable as a joint wrongdoer for interfering with this right, and the immunities will be irrelevant since they do not extend to a breach of the duty. This is of great importance particularly since an interlocutory injunction may be obtained simply on the basis that there is an arguable case that the breach of statute gives rise to a civil right of action. In *Cunard SS Co Ltd v Stacey*[155] the Court of Appeal

---

150. *Prudential Assurance Co Ltd v Lorenz* (1971) 11 KIR 78.

151. See especially 84–85.

152. *Metall und Rohstoff AC v Donaldson, Lufkin & Jenrette* [1990] 1 QB 391. See the remarks of Hoffmann LJ in *Law Debenture Trust v Ural* [1993] 1 WLR 138 at 151 and the more sympathetic approach of the court in *Crawley BC v Ure* [1996] QB 13.

153. *Meade v London Borough of Haringey BC* [1979] 1 WLR 637.

154. *Associated Newspapers Group Ltd v Wade* [1979] ICR 664.

155. *Cunard SS Co Ltd v Stacey* [1955] 2 Lloyd's Rep 247.

granted an interlocutory injunction to restrain union officials from breaking the second provision set out above in the Merchant Shipping Act 1894 and inducing seamen to break the former. The court was prepared to hold, at least provisionally, that the measures were designed in part for the protection of shipowners and might therefore form the basis of a civil action. For employees whose employment is governed by statute, a starting point for advisors should include the relevant act.

It can be alleged that breaches of statutory duty are being brought about either by the workers taking part, as in the English 'Docks Dispute' case in 1989,[156] or by other parties as in *Barretts & Baird (Wholesalers) Ltd v IPCS*.[157]

[6.65] An interesting problem arises where the statutory right interfered with is one which has its own procedure for enforcement. Might it be argued that the statutory procedure is the only method of enforcing the right? Suppose the issue concerns procuring an employer to take action which infringes a worker's right not to be unfairly dismissed? The employee will have a remedy against the employer under the Unfair Dismissals Acts 1977–2007. But will he also be able to sue the employees who induced the employer to infringe his statutory right? Irish courts may yet be persuaded that they should permit the unfairly dismissed worker to take action against those who, by exerting pressure on the employer, brought about his dismissal. Even if this cause of action were denied him, he may nevertheless have a different cause of action if the defendants have secured his dismissal by using unlawful means.

[6.66] Public sector employees are affected by a little known section in the Offences Against the State Act 1939, s 9(2), which reads:

> 9—(2) Every person who shall incite or encourage any person employed in any capacity by the State to refuse, neglect, or omit (in a manner or to an extent calculated to dislocate the public service or a branch thereof) to perform his duty or shall incite or encourage any person so employed to be negligent or insubordinate (in such manner or to such extent as aforesaid) in the performance of his duty shall be guilty of a misdemeanour and shall be liable on conviction thereof to imprisonment for a term not exceeding two years.

Subsection (3) provides that every person who attempts to do anything prohibited by sub-s (2) or who aids or abets or conspires with another person to do any such thing or advocates or encourages the doing of any such thing, 'shall be guilty of a misdemeanour and shall be liable on conviction therefor to imprisonment for a term not exceeding twelve months'. This imposes criminal liability on the persons inducing or 'inciting' the public sector workers. The acts envisaged range from those calculated to dislocate 'the public service' to far lesser acts which may have that effect on a 'branch' thereof. The wrongdoings by the person employed are wide-reaching, stemming from refusal and neglect, to negligence or insubordination.

[6.67] It is also a misdemeanour to induce any member of An Garda Síochána to withhold his services or to commit a breach of discipline and to incite any person

---

156. *Associated British Ports v TGWU* [1989] IRLR 399.
157. *Barretts & Baird (Wholesalers) Ltd v IPCS* [1987] IRLR 3.

subject to military law[158] to refuse to obey lawful orders from a superior officer or to refuse to perform any of his duties or to commit any other act in dereliction of his duty. The former is contained in s 59 of the Garda Síochána Act 2005:

59.—(1) A person is guilty of an offence if he or she induces, or does any act calculated to induce, any member of the Garda Síochána to withhold his or her services or to commit a breach of discipline.

(2) A person guilty of an offence under subsection (1) is liable—

(a) on summary conviction, to a fine not exceeding €3,000 or imprisonment for a term not exceeding 12 months or both, or

(b) on conviction on indictment, to a fine not exceeding €50,000 or imprisonment for a term not exceeding 5 years or both.

[6.68] In the Defence (Amendment) Act 1990 there are a number of restrictions on the legal entitlement of members of the Defence Forces to join trade unions and/or engage in industrial action. They are as follows:

Section 2(4). A member shall not become or seek to be a member of a trade union, or of any other body (other than an association) which seeks to influence or otherwise be concerned with the remuneration or other conditions of service of members.

Section 6. A person who is subject to military law shall neither endeavour to persuade nor conspire with any other person to endeavour to persuade a member to join a trade union or other body (other than an association referred to in section 2(4) of this Act.

[6.69] Workers in An Post engaged in industrial action likewise may violate s 84 of the Postal and Telecommunications Services Act 1983, which provides that any person who 'delays or detains any … postal packet or does anything to prevent its due delivery' shall be guilty of an offence. The Telegraph Act 1863, s 45, provides that any

---

158. Defence Act 1954, ss 254–255. The issue of An Garda Síochána's right to take industrial action was debated in recent times following the announcement of the Garda Representative Association (GRA) on 7 December 2009 that it planned to ballot its members on industrial action. Gardaí who take industrial action are denied the protection of the Industrial Relations Act 1990 as they are excluded from the definition of 'worker' under the Act, nor are they protected under the Unfair Dismissals Act 1977–2007. Following the announcement by the GRA on 7 December 2009, the Garda Commissioner wrote to all Garda members to warn them that any industrial action would leave them open to prosecution and could ruin the Gardaí's relationship with the public. The Garda Commissioner also relayed the advice that he had received from the Attorney General outlining the provisions in the 2005 Act and stressing that members of the GRA who took industrial action could be targeted in civil actions by the State and other parties. Following internal negotiations, the GRA decided to survey its members on protesting about the reduction in their pay by way of a questionnaire rather than hold a trade union style ballot for industrial action. The questionnaire also reminded members of the legal implications of voting in favour of industrial action. The legislation imposes an express ban on gardaí joining or being members of a trade union, as distinct from representative bodies.

person in the employment of the company (Telecom Éireann) who 'by any wilful or negligent act or omission prevents or delays the transmission or delivery of any message' shall be guilty of an offence.

[6.70] *Cunard v Stacey*[159] illustrates that persons affected by illegal industrial action might bring a civil action based upon the breach of a penal statute. Could a member of the public whose business is likely to be adversely affected by threatened or actual industrial action under s 9(2) of the Offences Against the State Act 1939 seek an injunction to restrain the industrial action? The law is uncertain with, as ever, narrow and wide views. A statute imposing a criminal penalty is generally not read as providing a private right of action unless the statute indicates a contrary intention.[160] It is a matter of construction of the statute. Moreover, the statute must have been intended to benefit a certain 'class' of person instead of the public at large. As against this, there are cases which accept a more general proposition that there is a civil cause of action where a person suffers harm either through the inevitable, foreseeable or intended consequences of the unlawful acts of another. A great deal is likely to depend on who is the intended target of the industrial action.

The Constitution

[6.71] The principle of making the violation of a right an actionable wrong may create further unprotected liability, outside of equitable and statutory instances, where industrial action is taken which brings about an infringement of constitutional rights. The person who owes the constitutional duty could in the ordinary way be proceeded against by an aggrieved plaintiff but it may also be possible for the latter to take action against the procurer of the breach. The seeds of an action of this sort are to be found in *McCobb v Doyle*[161] where Murnaghan J looked upon the action of trade union officials who had secured the dismissal without notice of a workman as interfering with 'the plaintiff's right to dispose of his labour.' *Crowley v INTO*[162] involved facts which might have enabled such an approach to be developed but the relief sought ruled this out.

[6.72] The gamut of constitutional rights that could or might be involved is considerable, see **Ch 2**. It remains to be seen whether, if such an action were permitted, a distinction would be drawn between procuring a breach of, as opposed to mere interference with, a constitutional right. Constitutional rights are not the same as other rights at common law or in equity: at common law, for example, an apparently valid transaction may be devoid of effect if it constitutes, at the same time, an abuse of the Constitution. On this basis it is possible that, in the indirect form of the tort, the mere act of infringing or interfering with another's constitutional rights may render the procurer liable whether or not unlawful means have been used.

---

159. *Cunard SS Co Ltd v Stacey* [1955] 2 Lloyd's Rep 247.
160. Eg Data Protection Act 1988, s 7.
161. *McCobb v Doyle* [1938] IR 444.
162. *Crowley v INTO* [1980] IR 102.

JUSTIFICATION

[6.73] To procure a breach of contract intentionally is actionable independently of the motive or reason for so doing, since the action depends on breach of the plaintiff's right and is not based upon the spite or ill-will of the defendant. However, a defence of justification exists. Kingsmill Moore J said in *Sherriff v McMullen*[163] that the 'procurement of a breach of contract without legal justification has for long been a tort in its own right.' The judge found it unnecessary and, in the present state of the law probably impossible, to define exactly what was and what was not legal justification. That was also, as he acknowledged, the view of Russell J in *Brimelow v Casson*.[164] The most frequently approved test for justification is Romer LJ's in *Glamorgan Coal Co v South Wales Miners' Federation*:[165]

> regard must be had to the nature of the contract broken; the position of the parties to the contract; the grounds for the breach; the means employed to procure the breach; the relation of the person who breaks the contract; and ... to the object of the person in procuring the breach.

[6.74] According to Carty,[166] case law provides a framework for the defence, in line with the rationale of the tort. It reveals that the defence covers three areas: protecting private rights, protecting private interests and protecting the public interest. The first of these seems most likely to bring success to the defendant. Darling J said in *Read v Friendly Society of Operative Stone Masons*[167] that the justification for interference with the plaintiff's right 'must be an equal or superior right in themselves'. A collision of contracts would be a case in point.[168] As to private interests, it is likely that a defence of justification might be acceptable based, for example, on the protection of health and safety. An employment grievance would not justify a defendant in inducing breach of contract or procuring withdrawal of labour.[169] Justification based on public interest might relate to the use of public powers or privileges.

[6.75] In *Brimelow v Casson*[170] it was assumed a defendant can raise 'public morality' as a defence to the tort, and a defence of justification was held to exist on public policy grounds. Breaches of contract were procured with the object of compelling a theatrical

---

163. *Sherriff v McMullen* [1952] IR 236 at 247.

164. *Brimelow v Casson* [1924] 1 Ch 302, at 313.

165. *Glamorgan Coal Co v South Wales Miners' Federation* [1903] 2 KB 545 at 574.

166. Carty, *An Analysis of the Economic Torts* (OUP, 2001), 73.

167. *Read v Friendly Society of Operative Stone Masons* [1902] 2 KB 88 at 96.

168. See Lord Nicholls in *OBD* at 63. 'For completeness I mention but without elaboration, that a defence of justification may be available to a defendant in inducement tort cases. A defendant may, for instance, interfere with another's contract in order to protect an equal or superior right of his own as in *Edwin Hill & Partners v First National Finance Corpn plc* [1989] 1 WLR 225'.

169. 'Having regard to the fact that [the defendant] was bound by the well-established grievance procedures, a fact which was readily acknowledged ... in evidence', *per* O Neill in *Iarnród Éireann v Holbrooke and Ors* [2000] ELR 109 at 114.

170. *Brimelow v Casson* [1924] 1 Ch 302.

manager to pay a living wage to chorus girls in his employment. It was established that the women had been driven to supplement their income by immoral earnings and the defendants (members of a protection committee) were held justified in their action because of their duty both to their calling and to the public. The decision must be seen as exceptional, however, and ought not to be regarded as sanctioning breaches of contract where common interest or public duty seem to require it.[171] Public policy in Ireland would include the Constitution. Thus a defendant could plead justification where he induced, say, a strike by workers in opposition to a refusal by their employer to allow them to join a trade union.

[6.76] Public policy does not extend to a defence of justification protecting the interests of members of a trade union, for that is ultimately a form of self-interest, which is no defence.[172] Thus it is no justification to show that workmen were induced to break their contracts in order to keep up the price of coal by which their wages were regulated: *South Wales Miners' Federation v Glamorgan Coal Co*.[173] The point was reiterated by Lord Atkinson in *Larkin v Long*:[174]

> The fact that members of a trade union are merely acting in obedience to a rule of their union believed by them to be for their benefit is no defence to an action for the breach of any contracts they have entered into, *Read v Friendly Society of Operative Stone Masons* [1902] 2 KB 88, 732, and still less is it a defence to the wilful and malicious infringement in combination of that legal right of personal freedom of action which they claim for themselves, but which others are entitled to quite as fully and as absolutely as they are.[175]

[6.77] But compliance with trade union rules, *pace* Lord Atkinson, may constitute justification in some circumstances.[176] A defendant is justified in inducing a person to break his contract with the plaintiff if the defendant himself has a prior contract.[177] A collective agreement in Irish law is legally enforceable, it would appear.[178] Hence a union might be justified in inducing an employer to break a contract which is inconsistent with a prior contract (ie collective bargain) between the employer and the

---

171. Heydon, *Economic Torts* (2nd edn, Sweet & Maxwell, 1978), 42–43.
172. Heydon suggests that as a matter of public policy there may be something to be said for the advancement of labour as a public interest (*Economic Torts* (2nd edn, Sweet & Maxwell, 1978), 44). If employers can try to get labour as cheaply as possible, why should not labour struggle to sell itself expensively? There is American authority for the view that attempts to increase employment or improve working conditions advance a 'public interest' and should be justified. But the principles generally recognised in this jurisdiction are against that approach.
173. *South Wales Miners' Federation v Glamorgan Coal Co* [1905] AC 239.
174. *Larkin v Long* (1915) 69 ILTR 121, 124. In relation to conspiracy to injure, however, see paras **5.19–5.20**.
175. See too *Cooper v Millea* [1938] IR 749 at 757.
176. These cases can be explained on the ground of 'inconsistent transactions': *Clerk and Lindsell on Tort* (19th edn, Sweet and Maxwell, 2005), 25–49 *et seq*.
177. *Smithies v National Assoc of Operative Plasterers* [1909] 1 KB 310.
178. *Goulding Chemicals Ltd v Bolger* [1977] IR 211.

union. The *dictum* above (para **6.76**) may be somewhat misleading for *Read* does not bolt the door against recovery where there has been breach of a prior agreement between an employer and a collective body such as the defendants in that case. The facts in *Read* involved an apprentice who sued officers of the society for inducing his employer to break his apprenticeship agreement. The society alleged that the agreement had been made in breach of a prior agreement by the employer with the society to observe its apprenticeship rules. The defence of justification was raised by the defendants and, although unsuccessful, the defence might have been proved in more appropriate circumstances.[179] Equally, it would appear that a trade union and persons acting on its behalf would be justified, in proper circumstances, in procuring the breaking of a contract entered into by a member of the union in breach of a rule by which he was bound at the time on the basis that the rules of a trade union constitute a contract between the members which is valid (though not directly enforceable).

[6.78] *Hynes v Conlon*[180] was referred to earlier (para **6.35**) in relation to 'inducement.' It will be recalled that the defendants' action was held not to amount to an actionable procurement. It was not necessary for the defendants to raise the defence of justification, for the tort as such had not been proved.[181] To see the case, therefore, as a far-reaching one in relation to which it is 'by no means certain that courts in the United Kingdom would take the same attitude'[182] is to misread the judgment. The case cannot be viewed as authority for the proposition that trade union activities may be justified because they are recognised institutions in the law having certain powers which must be exercised for the good of workmen and for the good of the community they represent, and 'if union officials could not do as they did, they would not be of much use'.

[6.79] A person may be justified in interfering with the plaintiff's contract if he has some enforceable financial interest in the affairs of the person who is persuaded to break the contract. The promoter of a play, for instance, who induces the dismissal of an actress, is justified by the need to protect his investment in the success of the play.[183] Or it may be justified to induce an employee of the plaintiff to break his contract so as to help the defendant to save property from fire.[184] Or consumers may complain to those who provide services, particularly where they are in the nature of public utilities: a train passenger who secured the dismissal of a conductor by complaining of his behaviour to the company superintendent was able successfully to invoke 'privilege to protect the public interest.'[185]

---

179. See the judgments of Darling J in the Divisional Court, *Read v Friendly Society of Operative Stone Masons* [1902] 2 KB 88, at 96, and Stirling LJ in the Court of Appeal, *Read v Friendly Society of Operative Stone Masons* [1902] 2 KB 732, at 741.
180. *Hynes v Conlon* (1939) 5 Ir Jur Rep 49.
181. See *Allen v Flood* [1898] AC 1, 129 (Lord Hershell).
182. Citrine, *Trade Union Law* (3rd edn, Stevens & Sons, 1967), 76.
183. *Knapp v Penfield* 256 NVS 41 (1932).
184. *Prairie Oil & Gas Co v Kinney* 192 p 586 (1920).
185. *Lancaster v Ramburger* 71 NE 298 (1904).

[6.80] It cannot amount to a tort if a doctor or other professional person advises a client to give up his employment on health or other appropriate grounds. Equally if a passing person (doctor or otherwise) advised a sick man who collapsed in the street to go home, thus causing the latter to break a contract, he would be justified even though the advice was not given under a duty to do so. *Bona fide* parental advice that an engagement should be broken has been held lawful.[186]

[6.81] Malice is generally not relevant but may provide a clue at the defence stage. It has been suggested, for example, that action may not be justified where the plaintiff acts 'maliciously and with intent to injure' a union.[187] Likewise or perhaps conversely, malice may indicate that the justification put forward by the defendant is not the real reason for his action.[188]

[6.82] There is no need to prove justification if a defendant is entitled to immunity under s 12A of the Industrial Relations Act 1990 (para **6.87**). Justification arises as a defence also in relation to 'simple' conspiracy (para **5.18**) and perhaps intimidation (para **8.14**). There, it is easier to establish. In the tort of procuring breach of contract there are strong interests deserving of protection: those of the contracting parties in the performance of the agreement and of the public in the security of contracts. *Pacta sunt servanda.*

DAMAGE

[6.83] It is essential to prove damage, unless the breach is such as must 'in the ordinary course of business' inflict damage on the plaintiff.[189] In *Jones Brothers (Hunstanton) Ltd v Stevens*[190] no damage was suffered as the plaintiff's servant would not return to his employment. There is no clear statement in Irish law as to the rules governing remoteness of damage in this tort. Intended damage is recoverable. Is reasonably foreseeable damage likewise recoverable? Or may one recover for directly caused but unforeseen damage?

[6.84] Although the last mentioned is unlikely, it seems that reasonably foreseeable damage is recoverable. In *Riordan v Butler*[191] the plaintiff was employed to do a plastering job at £4 per week. But for the interference of the defendants, he would have continued to work for 15–16 months more. He was found entitled to 'substantial damages.' An award of £150 was therefore allowed to stand. It is clear that a plaintiff is bound to minimise his loss.[192] So where, as in that case, a person was 'idle' for eight weeks before getting another job and that was 'reasonable' he was compensated for

---

186. *Gunn v Ban* 1926 IDLR 855. Where there is no jurisdiction for breach of a promise to marry, this form of the tort no longer arises.
187. *Cory Lighterage Ltd v Transport and General Workers' Union* [1973] 1 WLR 792, at 815 and 817 *per* Lord Denning MR.
188. *Sidney Blumenthal & Co Inc v US* 30F 2d 247, 249 (1929).
189. *Goldsoll v Goldman* [1914] 2 Ch 603 at 615 *per* Neville J.
190. *Jones Brothers (Hunstanton) Ltd v Stevens* [1955] 1 QB 275.
191. *Riordan v Butler* [1940] IR 347.
192. *Per* O'Connor J in *O'Connor v Martin* [1949] Ir Jur Rep Ir Jur Rep 9, 11.

each workless week. In times of recession it would be a luxury to talk about a 'reasonable' period of idleness. Clearly, however, a plaintiff employer is not bound to recruit new staff where his employees walk off the job and this would only make matters worse: *B & I Steampacket Co Ltd v Branigan*.[193] The defendants were liable for the natural and probable consequences of their tort in *Cotter v Ahern*.[194] In *Boxfoldia Ltd v NGA*[195] the strike induced by the union led to the employer being forced to make some non-striking workers redundant. The redundancy payments were held to be losses that were reasonably foreseeable as a result of the tort.

It ought to be possible for the damages recoverable to be greater than the damages which would be if pursued in contract alone. Compensation for lost status is recoverable such as continuity of service for purposes of employment protection statutes. Damage must be foreseeable at the time of breach unlike straightforward contract cases where damage must be foreseeable at the time of contracting.[196]

[6.85] In addition to damages, an injunction or declaration may be obtained. The remedy most often sought is the labour injunction. This is fully discussed in Ch 11. The normal rules governing the granting of injunctions apply to this tort. The mere existence of a doubt as to the plaintiff's right (eg, under contract), breach of which he seeks to restrain, does not of itself constitute a sufficient ground for refusing an injunction, though it is always a circumstance which calls for the attention of the court.[197] Future conduct may also be enjoined.[198]

PROPER PLAINTIFF

[6.86] A difficulty associated with this tort can be the proper plaintiff. Upjohn LJ in *Boulting v Association of Cinematograph, Television and Allied Technicians*[199] said:

> If A procures B to break his contract with C, C can complain because A commits a well-established tort against C. But B has no right at law to restrain A from attempting to suborn him from his duty to C. He must resist A's efforts by strength of will. If B succumbs to A's blandishments and contracts with him in breach of his duty to C, B can have no right to complain of A's conduct if A performs his contract with B which the latter has so wrongly entered into.

See, too, Russell LJ in *Camden Exhibition Ltd v Lynott*.[200] On this basis the employer in dispute with a union would not usually be a competent plaintiff in an action for indirectly inducing breach of contract. In direct forms of the tort, as a general principle, only the target of the industrial pressure, normally the employer, can sue.

---

193.   *B & I Steampacket Co Ltd v Branigan* [1958] IR 128, 136.

194.   *Cotter v Ahern* [1976–77] ILRM 248.

195.   *Boxfoldia Ltd v NGA* [1988] IRLR 383.

196.   Heydon, *Economic Torts* (2nd edn, Sweet & Maxwell, 1978), 36.

197.   *McMahon Ltd v Dunne and Dolan* 99 ILTR 45 at 52 *per* Budd J.

198.   *McMahon Ltd v Dunne and Dolan* 99 ILTR 45 at 46.

199.   *Boulting v Association of Cinematograph, Television and Allied Technicians* [1963] 2 WLR 529, at 567.

200.   *Camden Exhibition Ltd v Lynott* [1963] 2 WLR 529, at 567.

STATUTORY IMMUNITY, INDUSTRIAL RELATIONS ACT 1990, S 12(a)

[6.87] The full text of s 12 of the Industrial Relations Act 1990 reads:

> An act done by a person in contemplation or furtherance of a trade dispute shall not be actionable on the ground only that–
>
> (a)   it induces some other person to break a contract of employment, or
>
> (b)   it consists of a threat by a person to induce some other person to break a contract of employment or a threat by a person to break his own contract of employment, or
>
> (c)   it is an interference with the trade, business, or employment of some other person, or with the right of some other person to dispose of his capital or his labour as he wills.

Only the first of these provides immunity for the liability discussed in this chapter. The second deals with the tort of intimidation and is considered in **Ch 8**. The third is analysed in **Ch 7**.

[6.88] The predecessor to s 12(a), s 3 of the Trade Disputes Act 1906, conflated the first two paragraphs above, and read:

> An act done by a person in contemplation or furtherance of a trade dispute shall not be actionable on the ground only that it induces some other person to break a contract of employment or that it is an interference with the trade, business or employment of some other person, or with the right of some other person to dispose of his capital or his labour as he wills.

In so far as it concerned inducement to break a contract, s 3 was in the same terms as s 12(a). The Commission of Inquiry on Industrial Relations[201] commented on s 3 of the Act of 1906:

> Trade union officials who induce their members to come out on strike without giving the requisite notice to end their contracts of employment commit a tort for which, but for this provision, they could be sued personally for damages.[202]

---

201.   The Commission's main recommendations in relation to matters coming within what was formerly the Trade Disputes Act, s 3 were:

   (1) the statutory definition of a trade dispute should exclude all forms of sympathetic industrial action rather than 'blacking' (para 726).

   (2) industrial action not complying with the amended definition of trade dispute proposed would forfeit existing legal immunities (para 737).

   The Commission cited the Donovan Report in Britain, which recognised in 1968 that the law on this subject was 'far from clear.' It reproduced the 1968 Report as to the position concerning inducement of breaches of commercial contracts in trade disputes. Some of the paragraphs culled from Donovan needed qualification in the light of Irish law (eg, para (3) required a reference to the effect of *Becton Dickinson Ltd v Lee* [1973] IR 1). The Commission did not recommend any change in the law on secondary action. Trade union officials had nothing to fear provided 'they are careful as to the means employed to this end' (para 722). It was unduly influenced, perhaps, by its stress on a mandatory disputes procedure (paras 239–263). Disputes procedures could not by definition be observed by those taking sympathetic action. It excluded blacking as it was 'not readily amenable to regulation by law'.

   This is true to the extent that union officials induce a strike in breach of contract where the primary target in the dispute is the employer. (contd .../)

The possibility of liability emerging in Ireland based on mere interference with contract short of breach was not mentioned. Nor was the issue of unlawful means as immune wrongs (para **6.92**), still less the 'proper plaintiff' dilemma (para **6.86**).

[6.89] As in the case of conspiracy, given immunity in s 10 of the 1990 Act, the protection afforded by s 12(a) is limited. It does not exempt actual breaches of contract by employees, albeit that employers are unlikely to sue in the circumstances. It does not extend to inducements which do not amount to a breach of contract because, for instance, of the presence in the contract of a *force majeure* clause (para **6.60**). It does not protect the use of independently actionable means otherwise tortious, or criminal, for there will then be some other ground of action. The extended form of the tort which encompasses action short of breach, such as interference with contract or with contractual performance, is likewise not protected (para **4.07**).

[6.90] Most fundamentally, s 12(a) relates only to contracts of *employment*. It is no defence to an action for inducing a breach of a contract of another kind. Interference with a person's business may result in many contracts being broken, as Murnaghan J observed in *Sherriff v McMullen*.[203] Most often these will be contracts with customers and suppliers as well as contracts of employment. For example, breach of a time charter in *Cattle Express Shipping Corporation of Liberia v Cheasty and the International Transport Workers Federation*[204] was obviously outside the statutory protection. Not only are other contracts not included in s 12A, but inducing other breaches such as breach of statutory duty, or breach of trust, are not covered. It certainly cannot extend to protect against the unlawful means tort (**Ch 7**) as the wording is that of the *Lumley v Gye*[205] tort. This can be asserted on the statutory language alone. It is supported by the House of Lords' decision *in OBG Ltd v Allan*.[206] 'Contract of employment' means *prima facie* a contract between an employer and workman.

If inducement of breach is not justifiable (para **6.73**), it is questionable whether the golden formula (para **9.75** *et seq*) is complied with. Action will most probably not be 'in furtherance' of a trade dispute.

---

202. (contd) The situation is different where a third party is deliberately and intentionally damaged by the officials' action which is designed to bring about a breach of (say) commercial contracts concerning the third party so that he will bring pressure to bear on the 'primary employer'. Later, the Commission adverted to this type of case. Where a person induces a breach of the contract of employment with knowledge of another contract, deliberately with a view to preventing one party from performing it, there is liability at common law. In Citrine's view, said the Commission, 'this type of action is not protected by the Act.' The Commission recognised that the section covered only contracts of employment and that many other contracts can be broken by strikes. Where breach is merely incidental, the Commission recognised that mere inducement of breach of the contract of employment would not give rise to liability at common law.

203. *Sherriff v McMullen* [1952] IR 236.

204. *Cattle Express Shipping Corporation of Liberia v Cheasty and the International Transport Workers Federation* (19 April 1983, unreported), HC.

205. *Lumley v Gye* (1853) 2 E & B 216.

206. *OBG Ltd v Allan* [2008] AC 1.

'Shall not be actionable'

[6.91] A number of issues arise. The first concerns the plaintiff. In *Stratford v Lindley*,[207] Lord Pearce suggested that in s 3 of the Trade Disputes Act 1906 the expression 'shall not be actionable' meant only that it should not be actionable at the suit of the employer and afforded no protection against liability in tort in respect of any third party who suffered damage as a result of the breach of contract of employment that had been so induced. This view has often been taken out of context: a full reading of the relevant passage shows Lord Pearce was concerned to establish that the immunity provided by s 3 did not extend to cases where detriment resulted to a third person based on the unlawfulness of a threat by workers to strike in breach of contract. His words, construed apart from this context, have received a chequered reception from the courts, summarised by Templeton J in *Camellia Tanker Ltd SA v International Transport Workers Federation*.[208] In *Morgan v Fry*[209] Lord Denning MR rejected Lord Pearce's dictum as a correct statement of the law. A narrow construction of s 3 was impliedly rejected in *McMahon Ltd v Dunne and Dolan*[210] where a 'fair question' was found on the facts. The plaintiff was not the employer in dispute but this did not rule out an assumption that the applicability of the Trade Disputes Act 1906, s 3, would be appropriately discussed at the full trial. In *Hadmor Productions Ltd v Hamilton*[211] the House of Lords re-established very emphatically that the words 'shall not be actionable in tort' *do not* mean 'shall not be actionable only by the employer' whose employees are parties to the trade dispute.

[6.92] More specifically the second issue concerns the extent to which wrongs for which a specific statutory immunity has been granted can constitute unlawful means. It is a matter of great significance in Ireland as well as in Britain as union tactics have changed. Take the case of *Talbot (Ire) Ltd v Merrigan*,[212] where the secondary boycott involved seeking to put pressure on Talbot (Ire) Ltd by disrupting its relationship with customers and suppliers. Or take any 'blacking' case which is almost certain as a preliminary to 'effective' action to involve breaches of contracts by workers. Under the Industrial Relations Act 1990 the immunity in s 12(a) means there is no liability for inducing breaches of contracts of employment where the action is in contemplation or furtherance of a trade dispute. But could such inducements constitute unlawful means for the purposes of procuring a breach of commercial or other contracts? If the answer is No, then the ingredients for such torts would not be made out. The point was never settled in Britain or in Ireland under the 1906 Act. It was contended that inducing breaches of employment contracts should not be treated as unlawful means by the employer party to those contracts, for otherwise primary strikes would be unprotected since they almost inevitably result in the primary employer breaking commercial

---

207. *Stratford v Lindley* [1964] 3 All ER 102 at 114.
208. *Camellia Tanker Ltd SA v International Transport Workers Federation* [1976] ICR 274 at 285–289.
209. *Morgan v Fry* [1968] 2 QB 710 at 729.
210. *McMahon Ltd v Dunne and Dolan* 99 ILTR 45.
211. *Hadmor Productions Ltd v Hamilton* [1983] 1 AC 191.
212. *Talbot (Ire) Ltd v Merrigan* (18 April 1981, unreported), SC.

contracts. Hence some judges implied this further immunity and denied any cause of action to the employer who was a party to the relevant employment contracts.

[6.93] Some judges, however, were not prepared to extend this implication to prevent the other party to the commercial contract from suing. This was irrelevant where industrial action was not aimed at secondary parties but where it was, on this view, the latter would have a claim. Other judges took a broader view that immune wrongs could not be unlawful means against anyone. In this way both primary and secondary action were protected. This view may explain why Walsh J in *Becton Dickinson Ltd v Lee*[213] doubted the correctness of *Cooper v Millea*.[214] In Britain the matter was clarified by s 13(3) of TULRA 1974, which attempted to return to the abstentionist policy of the early twentieth century in labour relations. Subsection (3) of s 13 provides as follows:

> For the avoidance of doubt it is hereby declared that – (a) an act which by reason of sub-section (1) or (2) above is not actionable; (b) a breach of contract in contemplation or furtherance of a trade dispute; shall not be regarded as the doing of an unlawful act or as the use of unlawful means for the purpose of establishing liability in tort.

This was repealed by the Employment Act 1980, s 17(8). In *Hadmor*, by a construction of the Employment Act 1980, s 17(8), which could not be justified on the basis of traditional canons, Lord Denning took the view that parliament must have intended not merely to restore the doubts about whether immune wrongs can constitute unlawful means but also to indicate positively that they should be so regarded. The House of Lords roundly rejected Lord Denning's construction. Lord Diplock said s 13(3) of TULRA could be repealed because it had 'become wholly otiose.' The result of this is that in that jurisdiction many potentially unlawful means have been rendered acceptable by parliament, at least in the context of trade disputes.

[6.94] In Ireland the issue has never been seriously debated either between the social partners or in the Oireachtas. Kingsmill Moore J (High Court) and Gavan Duffy P (Supreme Court, Murnaghan J and Maguire CJ *dubitante*) suggested that immune wrongs could be treated as unlawful means by a primary employer in *Sherriff v McMullen*.[215] *Talbot (Irl) Ltd v Merrigan*[216] seemed to hold that an act rendered 'not actionable' still amounted to 'unlawful means' where the plaintiff was the primary employer in the dispute. In a constitutional jurisdiction this is probably the correct construction of the statutory immunities in the 1990 Act. It cannot be a matter for implication where immunity from suit is concerned. Disabling what would otherwise be a plaintiff's constitutional right of access to the courts must be strictly limited to the statutory text. Politically, the Oireachtas did not grasp the opportunity to clarify this

---

213. *Becton Dickinson Ltd v Lee* [1973] IR 1.

214. *Cooper v Millea* [1938] IR 749 (see para **8.02**, fn 3).

215. *Sherriff v McMullen* [1952] IR 236 (noted in a case involving a secondary employer: *McMahon Ltd v Dunne and Dolan* 99 ILTR 45 at 57).

216. *Talbot (Irl) Ltd v Merrigan* (18 April 1981, unreported), SC.

important aspect of trade disputes law in the Industrial Relations Act 1990. Thus the ambit of the statutory immunities remains uncertain and probably limited.[217]

[6.95] The third issue which arises in relation to the words 'not actionable' concerns breach of contract. Whether or not inducement is actionable as a tort, the breach itself of the employment contract is actionable. It is arguable that a defendant may thus use 'unlawful means'. Section 13(3) of TULRA (para **6.91**) attempted to remove any doubt that a breach of contract in contemplation or furtherance of a trade dispute should not be regarded as an unlawful act or the use of unlawful means. The House of Lords in *Hadmor* (para **6.91**) provided no assistance on the interpretation of this particular provision when it was repealed by s 17(8) of the Employment Act 1980. The result appears to be, as *Clerk and Lindsell on Torts* summarises,[218] that a breach of contract is arguably 'unlawful means' and may be used by a claimant as part of an arguably good cause of action even in a trade dispute. 'If that is correct', they say, 'the law is in a surprising condition, and suffers from yet another illogicality that stems from the decision in 1964 to treat breach of contract as illegal means in tort' (referring to *Rookes v Barnard*).[219]

[6.96] The exceptions to the application of s 12(a) concern one-worker disputes (paras **5.51** and **9.26**) and action contrary to the outcome of a secret ballot (paras **5.52** and **9.68**), and it will be recalled that the immunities are restricted to members and officials of authorised trade unions (para **9.60**).

---

217. Kerr and Whyte submit that the view that immune wrongs should not constitute unlawful means should be approved in Ireland 'if not by judicial decision, then by a legislative amendment to the effect that an act rendered "not actionable" by section [12] shall not be regarded as the doing of an unlawful act or the use of unlawful means for the purpose of establishing liability in tort. For the law to be otherwise would mean that the ability of a trade union to order industrial action would be severely curtailed', *Irish Trade Union Law* (Professional Books, 1985), 261. The question should also be addressed whether s 12 alone is affected or the unlawful means torts in general.
218. (19th edn, Sweet & Maxwell, 2005), 25–169.
219. *Rookes v Barnard* [1964] AC 1129.

Chapter 7
CAUSING LOSS BY UNLAWFUL MEANS

NO CONSISTENT NOMENCLATURE

[7.01] Mapping the coastline of the economic torts has always been challenging. In other areas of the law of tort, there is widespread if not universal agreement as to the names attached to various liabilities. In the economic torts, however, and particularly in relation to the tort the subject matter of this chapter, one must look beyond the label given to a liability, by judges as well as by litigating counsel, to identify the liabilities in question as they may be described and substantiated by judicial authority and/or by tort texts. This is a daunting task but it is vital if the coastline is not to grow ever more unwieldy and the rationale for the various economic torts is to be preserved. In *OBG Ltd v Allan*[1] the label given to the tort considered in this chapter by each of Lord Hoffmann and Lord Nicholls differs. Lord Hoffmann, supported by the majority of their Lordships, called it the tort of 'causing loss by unlawful means'. To Lord Nicholls it is the tort of 'unlawful interference with business', which is perhaps more familiar and arguably less open-ended. As Simpson observes, 'interference with business' is a potentially broad concept but it is far from synonymous with the very open-ended label of 'causing loss' used by Lord Hoffmann.[2] It is doubtful whether the difference was merely semantic. The majority label probably arose from a deliberate attempt to frame the cause of action with a neutral title in order to assimilate cases of earlier courts, packaged together with, or as extensions of, the *Lumley v Gye*[3] tort. Under the broader formulation, the tort of causing loss by unlawful means includes, for example, the tort of unlawful interference with contractual performance and intimidation. The label could be said to assert the centrality to the tort of the 'unlawful means'. Lord Hoffmann's is the authors' preferred nomenclature and is adopted here.

The tort has always been a potential Achilles' heel for the right to take strike and industrial action within the statutory immunities. Read together with the provisions of the Industrial Relations Act 1990, a number of issues give rise to concern, as will be seen.

DIFFICULTIES WITH LABELS

[7.02] A good illustration of the difficulties with labelling can be found over 70 years ago when a head of liability emerged in Irish case law not once, twice but no less than four times in the space of two years. It was the tort of 'intentional interference with

---

1. *OBG Ltd v Allan* [2008] AC 1.
2. Simpson, 'Economic Tort Liability in Labour Disputes: The Potential Impact of the House of Lord's decision in *OBG Ltd v Allan*' (2007) 36 ILJ 468 at 471.
3. *Lumley v Gye* (1853) 2 E & B 216.

employment by unlawful [or, as it was frequently styled, illegal] means'. The first authority is *McCobb v Doyle*[4] wherein Murnaghan J[5] regarded it as 'well established law that any person who interferes with the right of some other person to dispose of his labour as he will, is liable to an action.' In *McCobb*, the defendants conveyed by 'pressure – by the knowledge that a strike would probably result – that the plaintiff's services should be dispensed with.' Yet the case cannot be regarded as authority for a '*Quinn v Leathem* without the conspiracy' type of liability for the precise nature of the wrongful interference lay in procurement of breach of the plaintiff's contract. In another authority that year, *Cooper v Millea*,[6] the plaintiff's dismissal had been procured by the defendants although not in breach of contract. In the High Court, Gavan Duffy J said:

> It is incontestable that the defendants interfered with the plaintiff's employment by illegal means; for a strike in breach of contract is unlawful and a threat or pre-intimation of unlawful action constitutes illegal means.

[7.03] The reasons prompting the judge's decision were finely balanced:

> In a case of this kind the apparent antinomy between the rights of organised labour and the rights of the private citizen may easily lead to confusion. It is the duty of the Courts firmly to uphold the legal rights of workingmen to combine; the right of combinations, recognised by statute in 1824 (when a repressive code, elaborated through three centuries in England, was repealed), has not been securely established, but only after a very severe struggle during the 19th century and through the indomitable courage and perseverance of workingmen against heavy odds; and the right to form unions, subject to control in the public interest, is expressly recognised by the Constitution. At the same time, as a matter of national social policy, every citizen is declared to have the right to adequate means of livelihood and, as a matter of law, every man is entitled to be protected against unlawful interference with his means of living, and that protection he is entitled to seek and obtain from the Courts. In the social conflict there will often be an apparent clash between these rights and, if there be any such clash in the present case, it must be resolved on principle; the rule of law in this country would be gravely impaired if sympathy (for I have been invited to shed tears) or other extraneous considerations were allowed to influence a decision. The interests of the individual and of organised labour must frequently collide; if the union wins, the victim may be crushed; yet his ruin may be as irrelevant in a court of law as the failure or success of a trade union's policy, for the injured man must prove that the law has been broken before the courts can give him any redress. It is regrettable that conflicting rights in this sphere of law are not more extensively regulated by statute; the inevitable result under the jurisprudence of this country and of England has often been that important questions as to how far organised labour may go have had to be decided by conceptions of individual judges as to what may or may not be lawful in the milky way of the common law, and some such judgments are by no means a certain guide. In the present case,

---

4.   *McCobb v Doyle* [1938] IR 444 (para **6.34**).

5.   At 449.

6.   *Cooper v Millea* [1938] IR 749.

however, I hope that it will be possible to find solid ground in the common law without resorting to juristic speculation and to confine my judgment to principles that are not seriously controverted. The governing principle is that trade unionists may lawfully combine for lawful common purposes, even though their action inflict irreparable harm upon an individual, so long, and so long only, as they confine their activities to lawful methods.

A threat to strike in breach of contract was not, the judge held, lawful. *Cooper v Millea* was expressly followed in *Riordan v Butler*[7] where O'Byrne J held that a threat to cease work immediately in breach of contract constituted unlawful means for a tort of 'intentional interference with the plaintiff's employment by illegal means'. The facts here, in common with *McCobb v Doyle,* involved a dismissal of the plaintiff in breach of contract. By 1940, when *Riordan* was decided, the sort of pressure applied in *McCobb* was regarded as unlawful. In *Riordan v Butler* counsel for the plaintiff alleged 'unlawful interference with the latter's employment by illegal means'[8] and that interference was particularised in the civil bill as: that the employer was 'induced to break his contract with the plaintiff.'[9]

[7.04] *Hynes v Conlon* came between *Cooper* and *Riordan.*[10] Among other things, Hynes alleged 'unlawful interference with his right to dispose of his labour.' The case on the facts dealt with inducing breach of contract. *Cooper v Millea* and *Riordan v Butler* concerned the tort of 'intimidation' but it took some time before the last-mentioned tort, in all its manifestations, was described as such. Intimidation is dealt with in **Ch 8**. It would nowadays be regarded as more correctly subsumed under the tort of causing loss by unlawful means. The principle behind this wrong is that it is tortious intentionally to damage another by means of an act which the actor is not at liberty to commit.

HISTORICAL EMERGENCE OF THE TORT

[7.05] Practitioners in the early years of the last century were familiar with Jenks' *A Digest of English Civil Law*[11] where the following head of liability appears:

> [A] person who, by the commission of an unlawful act, intentionally interferes with the trade, business, or employment of another person, whereby the latter suffers damage, is liable to an action for damages and an injunction by that other person.

---

7.   *Riordan v Butler* [1940] IR 347 at 353.

8.   *Riordan v Butler* [1940] IR 347 at 349.

9.   *Riordan v Butler* [1940] IR 347 at 347–8.

10.   *Hynes v Conlon* (1939) Ir Jur Rep 49.

11.   Jenks, *A Digest of English Civil Law* (Butterworths, 1921).

Five cases are cited in support: *Garret v Taylor*,[12] *Tarleton v McGawley*,[13] *Carrington v Taylor*,[14] *Ibbotson v Peate*[15] and *Pratt v British Medical Association*.[16] Jenks added an observation in parenthesis:

> *Semble*: the act must be 'unlawful' but need not be actionable *per se* (*Conway v Wade* [1909] AC 506; Pratt *op sup*). It is difficult to know what 'unlawful' means in this connection.[17]

These cases are still cited today, eg by the House of Lords in *OBG Ltd v Allan*.[18] Even in a precedent-based common law system, it has been questioned 'whether these limited reports of liabilities imposed in entirely different circumstances some 200 or 400 years ago should be treated as any part of an acceptable justification for redefining the scope of economic tort liability in the 21st century.'[19]

[7.06] Many years after they had been decided, two of the cases cited by Jenks – *Garrett* and *Tarleton* – were approved by the House of Lords in *Allen v Flood*[20] as instances of loss being caused by unlawful means. In the first and earliest of these, *Garret v Taylor*,[21] there were threats to malign and annoy by vexatious litigation

---

12. *Garret v Taylor* (1620) Cro Jac 567.

13. *Tarleton v McGawley* (1793) I Peake 270.

14. *Carrington, v Taylor* (1809) II East 571.

15. *Ibbotson v Peat* (1865) 54 LJ Exch 118.

16. *Pratt v British Medical Association* [1919] 1 KB 244.

17. In *Cooper v Millea*, Gavan Duffy J took the unusual step of underlining that the plaintiff's civil bill belonged to 'the elusive category of actions for intentional interference with a man's employment by illegal means' and he referred to Jenks' *Digest*, [1938] IR 749 at 758.

18. *OBG Ltd v Allan* [2008] AC 1.

19. Simpson, 'Economic Tort Liability in Labour Disputes: The Potential Impact of the House of Lords' Decision in *OBG Ltd v Allan*' (2007) ILJ 468 at 473.

20. *Allen v Flood* [1898] AC 1.

21. As to the other cases, *Carrington v Taylor* held that firing at wild fowl to kill and make a profit of them by one who was at the time in a boat on a public river of open creek so near to an ancient decoy on the shore as to make the birds there take flight was liable for willful disturbance of and damage to the decoy for which an action on the case was maintainable by the owner. The plaintiff possessed the decoy for wild ducks, mallards, teal and widgeon. The defendant sought his livelihood by shooting wild fowl from a boat on the water for which boats, with small arms, he had a licence from the Admiralty for fishing and coasting along the shores of Essex. Apart from firing his fowling-piece, the defendant had killed several widgeons. The Court of King's Bench relied on an earlier decision in *Keeble v Hickeringill* (1707) II East 574. There the declaration charged the defendant with firing a gun with design to damnify the plaintiff and frighten the wild fowl from his decoy. Holt CJ said, 'When a man useth his art to seduce [ducks] to sell and dispose of for his profit, this is his trade; and he that hinders another in his trade or livelihood is liable to an action for so hindering him … where a violent or malicious act is done to man's occupation, profession or way or getting a livelihood; there an action lies in all cases'. *Carrington v Taylor* gives little information as to the reasons for judgment. It does not allege that the plaintiff traded in wild fowl. (contd .../)

customers of a quarryman so as to induce them to discontinue business with him. The plaintiff suffered damages for loss of custom and was allowed to recover. In *Tarleton v McGawley* the master of a slave trading ship fired at a natives' canoe off the coast of Africa which was about to do business with another ship similarly engaged so that the natives, in panic, ceased to do business with that ship. The plaintiff recovered damages because he had been caused loss by what Lord Kenyon called the 'improper conduct' of the defendant.

[7.07] The first recognizable formulation of the tort can be said to be as early as 1898 in *Allen v Flood*, a demarcation case (para **5.04**). The plaintiff workers were dismissed after a trade union official had advised their employer of their colleagues' intention to walk out if they remained employed. The walk out would not have been in breach of contract and the plaintiffs were lawfully dismissed. The trial judge found no evidence of conspiracy, intimidation or breach of contract. The plaintiffs alleged a malicious interference with their livelihood. The Court of Appeal was prepared to hold the defendants liable for maliciously procuring the lawful dismissal of the plaintiffs. But the House of Lords, by a majority, held motive was not a permissible mechanism for imposing economic tort liability. Lord Herschell said that provided the defendants did not resort to unlawful acts, they would be entitled 'to further their interests in a manner which was to them best and most likely to be effectual'. The absence of unlawful means meant no liability. The majority members of the House reviewed earlier cases to underline the importance of unlawfulness.[22]

[7.08] In 1907 Sir John Salmond published the first edition of his textbook on torts[23]. *Garret v Taylor, Tarleton v M'Gawley* and *dicta* in *Allen v Flood* were placed in a

---

21. (contd) In *Allen v Flood* [1898] AC 1 at 136, Lord Herschell seemed to regard the authority as important only because it showed *Keeble v Hickeringill* was not founded on interference with trade (without more) or dependent on the presence of malice. *Ibbotson v Peat* (1865) 54 LJ Exch 118 held that a person whose game is enticed away from his land by a neighbour is liable to an action for exploding combustibles so as to be a nuisance to the latter. Lord Herschell was concerned to identify the general principle involved in these cases and above all to show they were not limited to interference with trade:

> No doubt in some of the cases referred to the wrong was of such a nature that it is difficult to imagine circumstances in which precisely the same wrong could have caused damage to a person not in trade; but the act was not wrongful merely because it affected the man in his trade, though it was this circumstance which occasioned him loss.

He did not doubt that everyone has a right to pursue his trade or employment without 'molestation' or 'obstruction' if those terms are used to imply some act in itself wrongful. But this 'is only a branch of a much wider proposition, namely, that everyone has a right to do any lawful act he pleases without molestation or obstruction [at 138]'.

22. Bagshaw, 'Can the Economic Torts be Unified' 18 OJLS (1998) 729 at 730, [The majority view] 'is the foundation of the general economic tort of causing economic harm by unlawful means.'

23. *Salmond on Torts* (Stevens and Haynes, 1907).

chapter headed 'Intimidation' and the principle which they were said to illustrate was stated as follows:

> The wrong of intimidation includes all those cases in which the harm is inflicted by the use of unlawful threats whereby the lawful liberty of others to do as they please is interfered with. The wrong is of two distinct kinds, for the liberty of action so interfered with may be either that of the plaintiff himself, or that of other persons with resulting damage to the plaintiff. In other words, the defendant may either intimidate the plaintiff himself, and so compel him to act to his own hurt ['two-party intimidation'] or he may intimidate other people and so compel them to act to the hurt of the plaintiff ['three-party intimidation'].

This passage greatly influenced the reasoning of some of the Law Lords in *Rookes v Barnard*,[24] the celebrated English case on intimidation, which emphasised the elements of threat and response.

[7.09] At the same time, judges never seemed in doubt that a broader tort existed. In *Pratt v BMA*[25] (also mentioned by Jenks) the court's reasoning embraced a wide form of liability, though its application to the facts was narrow. The defendants in *Pratt* had instituted and pursued a boycott against the plaintiffs by means of threats and coercive action. They sought to justify this on the ground that the plaintiffs' conduct in acting as the medical officers of a certain medical dispensary was detrimental to the honour and interests of the profession. The plaintiffs suffered pecuniary loss and succeeded in establishing, to the satisfaction of McCardle J, that they had a good cause of action. The judge declared that:

> A single person or a body of persons commits an actionable wrong if he or they inflict actual pecuniary damage upon another by the intentional employment of unlawful means, such as threats or coercive action, to injure that person's person, even though the unlawful means may not comprise any specific act which is *per se* actionable and actual malice is not proved.

The judge found he could draw no distinction between a threat to cause a strike and a threat to inflict upon a man the slur of professional dishonour: 'Each may produce intimidation.'

[7.10] *Quinn v Leathem*[26] (para **5.05**) involved facts similar to *Allen v Flood* but with the additional ingredients of combination and threats. By distinguishing the fact of combination in *Quinn v Leathem*, the House of Lords was able to impose liability for intended harm, even though no unlawful means were used. There are clear statements in *Quinn v Leathem* about the tort of 'unlawful interference with trade, business or employment' the rationale of which was described by Lord Lindley:[27]

> A person's liberty or right to deal with others is nugatory, unless they are at liberty to deal with him if they choose to do so. Any interference with their liberty to deal with him affects him. If such interference is justifiable in point of

---

24. *Rookes v Barnard* [1964] AC 1129 (para **8.03**).
25. *Pratt v BMA* [1919] 1 KB 444.
26. *Quinn v Leathem* [1901] AC 495.
27. *Quinn v Leathem* [1901] AC 495, 534–535.

law, he has no redress. Again, if such interference is wrongful, the only person who can sue in respect of it is, as a rule, the person immediately affected by it; another who suffers by it has usually no redress; the damage to him is too remote, and it would be obviously practically impossible and highly inconvenient to give legal redress to all who suffer from such wrongs. But if the interference is wrongful and is intended to damage a third person, and he is damaged in fact – in other words, if he is wrongfully and intentionally struck at through others, and is thereby damnified – the whole aspect of the case is changed: the wrong done to others reaches him, his rights are infringed although indirectly, and damage to him is not remote or unforeseen, but is the direct consequence of what has been done.

Elias and Ewing contend 'many statements in *Quinn v Leathem* are simply irreconcilable with *Allen v Flood* and so support the view that it is a tort deliberately to harm another without justification.'[28]

[7.11] In *Sorrell v Smith*[29] the House of Lords seemed in no doubt that liability could exist where economic loss was caused by unlawful means. Thus Lord Dunedin:[30]

> … even although the dominating motive in a certain course of action may be the furtherance of your own business or your own interests, as you conceive those interests to lie, you are not entitled to interfere with another man's method of gaining his living by illegal means.

But not all members of the House of Lords were always so convinced. Lord Devlin said in *Rookes v Barnard*:[31]

> I do not think it is necessary for the house to decide whether or not malicious interference by a single person with trade business, or employment is or is not a tort known to law … I mean *Quinn v Leathem* without the conspiracy.

[7.12] Further clarification of this tort in England coincided, not surprisingly, with the period of battledore and shuttlecock between courts and parliament in the matter of trade union immunities. In *Stratford v Lindley*[32] two of their Lordships referred to an alternative ground for granting an injunction, namely, that the respondents' action made it practically impossible for the appellants to do any new business with the barge hirers. It was not disputed that such interference was unlawful if unlawful means were employed.[33] It will be recalled, from the facts of *Stratford* (para **6.13**) that the case could not be one of intimidation. Lord Reid regarded it as undisputed that there is a tort of causing loss by unlawful means distinct from Salmond's tort of intimidation. Historically, therefore, this tort was lurking in the case law.

---

28. Elias and Ewing, 'Economic Torts and Labour Law: Old Principles and New Liabilities' 41 CLJ (1982) 321 at 324.

29. *Sorrell v Smith* [1925] AC 700.

30. *Sorrell v Smith* [1925] AC 700 at 719. It is significant that Gavan Duffy J cited with approval a dictum of Lord Dunedin in *Sorrell v Smith* in the course of his judgment in *Cooper v Millea* [1938] IR 749 at 757.

31. *Rookes v Barnard* [1964] AC 1129 at 1215–16.

32. *Stratford v Lindley* [1965] AC 269.

33. See *Stratford v Lindley* [1965] AC 269 at 324.

[7.13] It is generally agreed that the modern emergence of the tort of causing loss by unlawful means can be ascribed to Lord Denning in *Daily Mirror Newspapers Ltd v Gardner*[34] and by the time of *Torquay Hotel Co Ltd v Cousins*,[35] he was able to reiterate that the tort of 'interference with trade by unlawful means' existed in English law:

> I have always understood that if a person interferes with the trade or business of another, and does so by unlawful means ... then he is acting unlawfully, even though he does not procure or induce any actual breach of contract.

Subsequently the tort was relied on in important English decisions. In *Acrow (Automation) Ltd v Rex Chainbelt Inc*[36] an American corporation was made liable to the plaintiffs in circumstances where it had assisted an associated company in defying an injunction granted to the plaintiffs against that company to restrain a breach of contract. So to assist a party who disobeys an order of the court was itself a contempt of court and amounted to an interference by unlawful means with the plaintiffs' business, it was held by the Court of Appeal. In *Hadmor Productions Ltd v Hamilton*[37] the House of Lords assumed without argument that the tort existed. Here the plaintiffs operated a facility company which made films for other television companies to broadcast. They made 15 programmes about 'pop' musicians. Two were the subject of a licence to Thames Television and were shown by them. It was unclear at the hearing whether the remainder were the subject of a firm contract to license or not but, even if so, Thames Television were clearly under no contractual obligation to show them. The defendants were three members and officials of a trade union. They were concerned that the use of facility companies would further restrict the already limited employment opportunities available to their television members and lead to redundancies. They also alleged that Thames were in breach of an agreement which required them to consult with the union before transmitting programmes from facility companies. The union officials threatened to black any of Hadmor's programmes which Thames sought to transmit. In the event this proved unnecessary since there was evidence that Thames had decided not to show them even before they knew of the 'blacking' decision. Hadmor sued for interference with business by unlawful means and succeeded in the Court of Appeal, but failed before the House of Lords. Lord Diplock referred to the tort upon which the plaintiff relied, namely interference with trade or business by unlawful means, the means consisting of threats by the defendants that they would induce other persons, namely union members employed by Thames, to break their contracts of employment with Thames: 'It is important to recognise that we now have a separate and distinct tort of interference with the business of another by unlawful means.'[38]

[7.14] The strength of these authorities, culminating in *Hadmor*, led some commentators to express surprise that the tort's identity took so long to accept and

---

34.   *Daily Mirror Newspapers Ltd v Gardner* [1968] 2 QB 762, 783.
35.   *Torquay Hotel Co Ltd v Cousins* [1969] 2 Ch 106 at 139.
36.   *Acrow (Automation) Ltd v Rex Chainbelt Inc* [1971] 1 WLR 1676.
37.   *Hadmor Productions Ltd v Hamilton* [1982] ICR 114, [1982] 2 All ER 1042.
38.   *Hadmor Productions Ltd v Hamilton* [1983] 1 AC 191 at 202–3.

recognise. Elias and Ewing[39] regarded a 'clear recognition' of the tort as important, an unlawful threat is but one form or species of unlawful means and the 'new' tort rendered certain conduct unlawful which would not fall within the scope of the established torts of conspiracy, inducing breach of contract and intimidation. This occurred where the plaintiff's interests were affected not by an unlawful threat, as in intimidation, but by an unlawful act. According to Elias and Ewing:

> The tort comes into its own either if it applies where the unlawful means are not independently actionable ... or where the unlawful means are directed towards a third party in order to harm the plaintiff.

In relation to the latter, without the 'new' tort, the plaintiff would have no remedy arising directly out of the wrongful act since it is not committed against him[40] and, of course, as Elias and Ewing observed, as in all torts involving the use of unlawful means, an important feature is that this form of liability protects not merely the plaintiff's legal rights but also his wider interests, such as the business expectations of an employer, or the expectation of continued employment of a worker. (The last-mentioned would include interference with contract short of breach where unlawful means would be a prerequisite for liability.)

[7.15] *Cotter v Ahern*[41] and *Becton Dickinson Ltd v Lee*[42] involved more familiar categorisation of the economic torts. But the broader form is not altogether absent from Irish law reports, eg *McMahon Ltd v Dunne and Dolan* (para **6.16**).[43] However, there is still a tendency for this tort to be given diverse labels and to be tagged on to other economic torts, without its being a cause of action in its own right, it is treated as a type of safety net.[44] It is added on to an existing economic tort such as inducing breach of contract, or appears confused with the tort of interference with contractual performance. Imprecision regarding the tort is compounded by the fact that the majority of cases where it is pleaded are interlocutory, a stage at which judges do not resolve the law finally.

[7.16] The tort's role in the scheme of statutory immunities is often misunderstood, a hasty reading of s 12C of the 1990 Act being proffered as affording immunity (see further para **7.40** *et seq*).

---

39. Elias and Ewing, 'Economic Torts and Labour Law: Old Principles and New Liabilities' (1982) 41 CLJ 321 at 335.

40. Eg, where the defendants actually strike in breach of contract and as a result an employer terminates the plaintiff's contract with due notice; the plaintiff would not have a ground upon which to sue the defendants if a broader head of liability did not exist.

41. *Cotter v Ahern* [1976–77] ILRM 248.

42. *Becton Dickinson Ltd v Lee* [1973] IR 1.

43. *McMahon Ltd v Dunne and Dolan* 99 ILTR 45.

44. Eg, the plaintiffs claimed, *inter alia*, commission of the tort of 'intentional interference with the plaintiff's contractual and commercial relations or the plaintiffs' economic and commercial interests' in *Irish Municipal Public and Civil Trade Union & Others v Ryanair* [2007] 1 ILRM 45. Similarly, in *Irish Sugar Ltd v Parlon and Ors* (29 November 2001, unreported), HC the plaintiff claimed 'inducing breach of contract, unlawful conspiracy and intentional interference with the plaintiff's economic interests.'

Recognition of the tort's existence by lawyers is timely not least because of the mechanical fixation with contract law as providing the dividing line between the legality and illegality of industrial action.

The law could have said long ago that there must be 'fair play.'[45] Instead it chose a general and formalistic principle, namely that intentional damage need be repaired if it is inflicted by impermissible means, that is, by methods reprobated by the law of crime, tort and contract. The essence of the tort was described by Lord Hoffmann in *OBG Ltd v Allan*[46] as:

> (a)   a wrongful interference with the actions of a third party in which the claimant has an economic interest and
>
> (b)   an intention thereby to cause loss to the claimant.

These ingredients are now considered. First the requirement of intention to cause loss, then the unlawful means.

INTENTION

[7.17] Intention[47] in this tort is clearly distinguishable from that in inducing breach of contract. In the latter it is to effect breach of contract, in the former, damage to the plaintiff.

Wide and narrow views

[7.18] There are varying views on the subject of intention. Some support a wide definition of intentional harm, covering foresight of inevitable or probable[48] consequences. This was the view of Woolf LJ in *Lonrho v Fayed*.[49] But there is a majority of judicial opinion in support of a narrow definition requiring deliberate harm, with the wrongdoer 'targeting' the plaintiff. This is evident in *Allen v Flood*,[50] *Quinn v Leathem*,[51] *Rookes v Barnard*[52] and *Lonrho v Fayed*.[53] Action must be 'directed against' a plaintiff, or he must be 'struck at' or 'deliberately interfered with'.

---

45.   In the US see the tort of unjustifiable interference or '*prima facie* tort theory': *Tuttle v Buck* 19 NW 949 (1909).

46.   *OBG Ltd v Allan* [2008] AC 1 at 31.

47.   *Douglas v Hello! Ltd* [2005] EWCA Civ 595 contains an extensive consideration of the meaning of 'intention' in the economic torts.

48.   *National Phonographic Co v Edison-Bell* [1908] 1 Ch 335 *per* Lord Alverstone.

49.   *Lonrho Plc v Fayed (No 1)* [1990] 2 QB 479.

50.   *Allen v Flood* [1898] AC 1 at 96.

51.   *Quinn v Leathem* [1901] AC 495.

52.   *Rookes v Barnard* [1964] AC 1129 at 1208.

53.   *Lonrho v Fayed (No 1)* [1990] 2 QB 479.

The 'object and intention' of the defendant must be to injure. Academic commentators support this approach.[54]

[7.19] The narrow view resulted in Henry J deciding that people inevitably harmed by strike action would be unable to show the necessary intention to harm in *Barretts & Baird v IPCS*.[55] In *OBG* Lord Hoffmann said Henry J was right to decide that a strike by civil servants in the Ministry of Agriculture in support of a pay claim was not intended to cause damage to an abattoir which was unable to obtain the certificates necessary for exporting meat and claiming subsidies. The damage to the abattoir was neither the purpose of the strike nor the means of achieving that purpose, which was to put pressure on the government. But a loss may be intended even though it was the means of achieving the end of enrichment, as distinct from a loss that was merely a foreseeable consequence of the defendant's actions. In *Douglas v Hello! Ltd*[56] the Court of Appeal concluded that for liability in relation to the unlawful means tort it was necessary to prove the defendant acted with the intention of causing harm to the plaintiff either as an end in itself or as a necessary means to achieving an ulterior motive. Lord Hoffmann dismissed this as 'giving an artificially narrow meaning to the concept of intention' but did not expand further on what he meant.

[7.20] Lord Nicholls in *OBG* said a defendant may intend to harm the claimant's business either as an end in itself or as a means to an end.[57] He may intend to harm the claimant as an end in itself, eg where he has a grudge against the claimant. More usually, a defendant intentionally inflicts harm on a claimant's business as a means to an end, to protect or promote his own economic interests. Intentional harm inflicted against a claimant in either of these circumstances satisfies the mental ingredient of this tort. This is so even if the defendant does not wish to harm the claimant. 'Lesser states of mind do not suffice ... In particular a defendant's foresight that his unlawful conduct may or will probably damage the claimant cannot be equated with intention for this purpose.'[58] He must *intend* to injure *the claimant*. The intent must be a cause of the defendant's conduct in the words of Cooke J in *Van Camp Chocolates Ltd v Aulsebroks Ltd*.[59]

[7.21] The tort is strongly one of intention. If it were otherwise, it would prove a major problem for those taking industrial action, where the action would have an inevitable

---

54. Heydon, *Economic Torts* (2nd edition, Sweet & Maxwell, 1977), 65–66; Sales and Stilitz, 'Intentional Infliction of Harm by Unlawful Means' 115 LQR (1999) 411; Weir, 'Chaos or Cosmos: *Rookes*, *Stratford* and the Economic Torts' (1964) CLJ 230; Payne, 'Inducing Breach of Contract' 7 CLP (1954) 94; Elias and Ewing, 'Economic Torts and Labour Law: Old Principles and New Liabilities' (1982) 41 CLJ 321.

55. *Barretts & Baird v IPCS* [1987] IRLR 3. See *Falconer v ASLEF and NUR* [1986] IRLR 331(para **6.45**).

56. *Douglas v Hello! Ltd* [2005] EWCA 595 at [224]; generally on intention see [159]–[225].

57. *OBG Ltd v Allan* [2008] AC 1 at 57.

58. *OBG Ltd v Allan* [2008] AC 1 at 57.

59. *Van Camp Chocolates Ltd v Aulsebroks Ltd* [1984] 1 NZLR 354, 360.

impact on a wide range of third parties, customers and commercial clients of the employer in dispute.

Motive irrelevant

[7.22] It is not significant that the predominant motive of the defendant is to pursue his own interest as opposed to injuring the defendant.[60] Motive is not relevant. As Lord Hoffmann put it in *OBG*,[61] the ends which were intended may be different. *South Wales Miners' Federation v Glamorgan Coal Co Ltd*[62] shows one may intend to procure a breach of contract without intending to cause loss. Likewise one may intend to cause loss without intending to procure a breach of contract. In both cases it is necessary to distinguish between ends, means and consequences. One intends to cause loss even though it is the means by which one achieves the end of enriching oneself. On the other hand, one is not liable for loss which is neither a desired end nor a means of attaining it but merely a foreseeable consequence of one's action.

UNLAWFUL MEANS

Scope wide and uncertain

[7.23] Judges tended to decide whether particular means were unlawful without considering the underlying principles which should determine that question. Since the House of Lords' decision in *OBG Ltd v Allan*[63] a distinguishing principle has emerged in British law based on independent actionability of unlawful means. Before considering this development, and for a better appreciation of its signifance, the paragraphs which follow illustrate the uncertain scope of unlawful means in decisions before *OBG*. They also detail a comprehensive analysis by academic commentators, Elias and Ewing,[64] which contrasted two approaches later to be considered by the House of Lords in *OBG*.

McMahon and Binchy[65] recognise that doing 'an unlawful act' means leaving to judicial exegesis the task of defining what constitutes an unlawful act:

> inevitably courts will be driven to enquire whether the breach of a statutory duty or of a contract, or the commission of a particular tort, or the breach of trust or other equitable obligation is an 'unlawful act'. This may well not be the most appropriate type of question to ask.

The House of Lords in *OBG*, as will be seen, provided a clear answer to this question. As and when the opportunity arises in this jurisdiction to analyse the unlawful means tort, the decision will doubtless be highly persuasive.

---

60. *Lonrho Plc* [1992] 1 AC 448v *Fayed (No 1)* [1990] 2 QB 479 at 488.
61. *OBG Ltd v Allan* [2008] AC 1 at 35.
62. *South Wales Miners' Federation v Glamorgan Coal Co Ltd* [1905] AC 239.
63. *OBG Ltd v Allan* [2008] AC 1.
64. Elias and Ewing, 'Economic Torts and Labour Law: Old Principles and New Liabilities' (1982) 41 CLJ 321.
65. McMahon and Binchy, *Law of Torts* (3rd edn, LexisNexis, 2000), 32.86.

An act in criminal contempt of court in exercise of contractual rights was held not to constitute unlawful means but an act in civil contempt was: *Chapman v Honig*[66] and *Acrow (Automation) Ltd v Rex Chainbelt Inc*,[67] respectively. Perjury was not unlawful but the failure of a subpoenaed witness to appear was: *Cabassi v Fernando*,[68] or the use of improperly instituted litigation: *Roberts v JF Stone Ltd*.[69] Nor could it confidently be stated that unlawful means for purposes of one tort would be considered unlawful means for purposes of another. In *Rookes v Barnard* Lord Devlin held that a breach of contract was unlawful means for the purposes of intimidation but left open the question whether it would be so for the purposes of conspiracy.[70] The logic of this is questionable. It is clear, however, following the House of Lords in *Total Network SL v Her Majesty's Revenue and Customs Commissioners*,[71] that 'unlawful means' has a broader meaning for conspiracy than the other unlawful means torts (para **5.36**).

[7.24] In general, torts and breaches of contract[72] constituted unlawful means. In *Lonrho v Fayed*[73] Dillon LJ asserted that liability did not depend on 'a complete tort' as there was 'no valid reason why the tort should need, as against the third party, to have been complete to the extent that the third party had himself suffered damage'. Eekelaar observed that as the tort allows the transfer of the unlawfulness of acts to the benefit of the plaintiff, it is not necessary for the tort to be 'completed' by the infliction of harm on the third party, the damage being suffered by the claimant.[74] In the case of breach of contract, a claimant may decide to rely on the tort of indirect interference with contract. Should an Irish court follow *OBG*, this choice is unlikely to be available (para **6.38**).

[7.25] Unlawful means was also held to reside in breaches of fiduciary duties and equitable obligations (para **6.63**). This raised the debate on the continued division of civil wrongs.[75] Some cases accepted crimes[76] and breaches of statutory provisions,[77] not civilly actionable in themselves, as sufficient unlawful means. Others were more

---

66.   *Chapman v Honig* [1963] 2 QB 502.

67.   *Acrow (Automation) Ltd v Rex Chainbelt Inc* [1971] 1 WLR 1676.

68.   *Cabassi v Fernando* (1940) 64 CLR 130.

69.   *Roberts v JF Stone Ltd* (1945) 172 LT 240, 242.

70.   *Rookes v Barnard* [1964] AC 1129, 1210.

71.   *Total Network SL v Her Majesty's Revenue and Customs Commissioners* [2008] UKHL 19, [2008] 2 WLR 711.

72.   *Rookes v Barnard* [1964] AC 1129 at 1168.

73.   *Lonrho v Fayed (No 1)* [1990] QB 479 at 489.

74.   Eekelaar, 'The Conspiracy Tangle' (1990) 106 LQR 225, 226.

75.   Smith, 'Constructive Trust for Breach of Fiduciary Obligation' 114 LQR (1998) 14; Berg, 'Accessory Liability for Breach of Trust' 59 MLR (1996) 443.

76.   *Rookes v Barnard* [1964] AC 1129; *ex p Island Records* [1978] Ch 122; *Acrow (Automation) Ltd v Rex Chainbelt Inc* [1971] 1 WLR 1676.

77.   *Lonrho v Shell (No 2)* [1982] AC 173.

hesitant.[78] The Court of Appeal also exhibited a willingness to accept non-actionable wrongs as unlawful means.[79]

[7.26] There is English authority for the view that it may be unlawful to interfere with a private right (arising independently of statute) by using unlawful means even though the means are not independently actionable. The jurisdiction of the Court of Chancery is to protect property and it will interfere by injunction to stay any proceedings which go to the immediate, or tend to the ultimate, destruction of property: thus Malins VC in *Springhead Spinning Co v Riley.*[80] These words proved controversial in England. In *Gouriet v Union of Post Office Workers*[81] the House of Lords held that a private individual could not apply to the court for an injunction to restrain a breach of the criminal law without the consent of the Attorney General. But this principle was qualified to the extent that an injunction would lie where the criminal action interfered with some private right of the plaintiff or where he suffered some special damage as a consequence of the defendant's breach of duty. *Springhead Spinning* was treated as good law by two of their Lordships.

[7.27] A very wide construction of the rights falling within this principle regarding enforcement of private rights was given by the Court of Appeal in *Ex parte Island Records.*[82] Rights which the dissenting Shaw LJ described as 'too nebulous and amorphous to carry the aspect of a right susceptible of legal protection'[83] were held entitled to protection. The case involved an attempt to restrain 'bootleggers'. The statute prohibiting this was not found to be capable of conferring private rights on the plaintiffs who were performers and record producers. But Lord Denning MR and Waller LJ were willing to grant the injunction requested as the plaintiffs had in their view suffered an interference with their rights. The producers had lost their right to the exclusive service of the performers, the performers their right to royalties. Lord Denning said that 'a man who is carrying on a lawful trade or calling has a right to be protected from any unlawful interference with it.' To him it was a right in the nature of a property right. The House of Lords in *Lonrho Ltd v Shell Petroleum Ltd*[84] later disapproved of the broad statement of protection afforded by the Court of Appeal in *Ex parte Island Records*. The category of rights protected was too widely formulated. In *Warner Bros Record Inc v Parr*[85] Julian Jeffs QC held that an unlawful act causing special damage to property rights is actionable in tort if the damage is of a kind contemplated by the statute.

---

78. Re crimes, see *Hargreaves v Bretherton* [1959] 1 QB 45; *Chapman v Honig* [1963] 2 QB 502; *Harrow LBC v Johnstone* [1997] 1 WLR 459.

79. *Associated British Ports v TGWU* [1989] ICR 557 at 579 and 585; *Law Debenture Trust Corpn v Ural Caspian Oil Corpn* [1994] 3 WLR 1221, at 1235.

80. *Springhead Spinning Co v Riley* (1868) LR 6 Eq 551, 558–559.

81. *Gouriet v Union of Post Office Workers* [1978] AC 435.

82. *Ex parte Island Records* [1978] Ch 122.

83. *Ex parte Island Records* [1978] Ch 122 at 132.

84. *Lonrho Ltd v Shell Petroleum Ltd (No 2)* [1982] AC 173.

85. *Warner Bros Record Inc v Parr* [1982] 2 All ER 455.

[7.28] In *RCA Corp and Anor v Pollard*[86] Vinelott J expressed the view provisionally that 'an unlawful act which infringes a right of property is an actionable wrong founding a claim in damages and, in an appropriate case, a right to an injunction.' In his view there was nothing in *Lonrho* inconsistent with this principle. The case went on appeal to the Court of Appeal where Vinelott J was reversed. The facts involved another 'bootlegging' operation. Oliver LJ pointed out that no case cited before the court went so far as to confer a cause of action where the damage complained of was merely economic damage as an incidental result of the breach of a prohibition in a statute not designed to protect the interests of a class to which the plaintiff belonged:

> If the principle extends thus far, I can, I confess, see no logical reason why it does not extend to the full extent suggested by Lord Denning MR in the *Island Records* case. The possibilities are indeed startling. Does an action for an injunction lie at the suit of a householder in Chelsea to restrain a known burglar from robbing houses in the borough because the publicity attached to burglars in Chelsea depreciates the value of his property.

The courts therefore pared the roots of the tort of interference with private rights by unlawful means.

[7.29] Rogers noted[87] that the definition of unlawful means tended to be passed over with little analysis while Fleming[88] described the courts' approach as casuistic 'without any evident rationale related to policy ends and suffering from some inexplicable inconsistencies'.

[7.30] A comprehensive analysis was attempted by Elias and Ewing.[89] As earlier referred to (para **7.23**) they contrasted the two approaches later considered by the House of Lords in *OBG*. The first adopts the narrow view that only wrongs which are *independently actionable* can constitute unlawful means. This raises the further question of: actionable by whom – by the plaintiff or by a third party – and does 'actionable' refer to civil as well as criminal actionability? If the means must be independently actionable, it would follow that all torts and breaches of contract would create liability, as would most common law crimes as they usually also constitute torts, and a breach of statutory duty would if, on the traditional principles of construction, such breach would give rise to a civil action in respect thereof. Elias and Ewing went one step further, however, and said there was no reason in principle why the means should be independently actionable if it was accepted that:

> The essence of the tort of interfering with trade, business or employment by unlawful means is the use of unlawful means specifically directed to coerce the plaintiff or to benefit the defendant directly at the plaintiff's expense.

---

86. *RCA Corp and Anor v Pollard* [1982] 2 All ER 468.

87. Rogers, *Winfield and Jolowicz on Tort* (15th edn, Sweet & Maxwell, 1998), p 651.

88. Fleming, *Winfield and Jolowicz on Tort* (15th edn, Sweet & Maxwell, 1998), p 700.

89. Elias and Ewing, 'Economic Torts and Labour Law: Old Principles and New Liabilities' (1982) 41 CLJ 321 at 335.

[7.31] Thus, it was the deliberate use of unlawful tactics intended to damage the plaintiff which was crucial. The intention to harm the plaintiff did not by itself establish liability (*Allen v Flood*) and neither did the commission of an unlawful act (*Lonrho*). But, said the authors, the combination of these two elements created a sufficient nexus between plaintiff and defendant to certain authorities which suggest that the concept of unlawful means apparently extended beyond wrongs independently actionable. The first authority was *Daily Mirror Newspapers Ltd v Gardner*[90] where it was held that action in breach of the Restrictive Trade Practices Act 1956 constituted unlawful means even though it seemed unlikely that an action in damages for breach of that statute would lie.[91] The next decision was *Acrow (Automation) Ltd v Rex Chainbelt Inc*[92] (para **7. 13**) where the Court of Appeal held that an act in contempt of court could constitute unlawful means. And there was even some authority, they wrote, for the view that the use of improper means possibly not even unlawful may create liability. In *National Phonograph Co Ltd v Edison Bell Consolidation Phonograph Co Ltd*[93] the defendants persuaded a third party to sell them goods manufactured by the plaintiffs by deceiving the third party as to their identity. They would not have sold the goods had their identity been revealed. Since the third party suffered no loss, he would have had no cause of action. Nevertheless, telling lies was unlawful for the purposes of creating a cause of action in the plaintiffs. In *Associated Newspapers Group Ltd v Wade*[94] Lord Denning suggested that interference with the press could constitute unlawful means because it was contrary to a fundamental public interest.

OBG: a distinguishing principle, independent actionability

[7.32] *Pace* Elias and Ewing, to deny the quality of independent actionability to unlawful means comes perilously close to cutting across the ban imposed by *Allen v*

---

90.   *Daily Mirror Newspapers Ltd v Gardner* [1968] 2 QB 762 must be seen against the background of a general approach to penal statutes for purposes of economic torts, alongside decisions such as *Crofter Hand Woven Harris Tweed Co v Veitch* [1942] AC 345 where Lord Wright regarded it as clear that strikers who acted in a manner infringing s 7 of the Conspiracy and Protection of Property Act 1875 were committing a criminal act which was also an 'illegal' act for purposes of the law of tort without stopping to inquire into the 'construction of the statute.' Similarly in *Ex parte Island Records* [1978] Ch 122 CA (para **7.27**).

91.   See further Frinche, 'The Juridical Nature of the Action of Penal Legislation in the law of Tort' (1960) 23 MLR 233.

92.   *Acrow (Automation) Ltd v Rex Chainbelt Inc* [1971] 1 WLR 1676. In *Acrow Automation Ltd* the defendants' unlawful act consisted of a civil contempt of court. The defendants, said Lord Denning (at 1682): 'will themselves be guilty of contempt of court ... for they will be aiding and abetting the commission of a breach of the injunction. It has long been held that the court has jurisdiction to commit for contempt a person, not a party to the action, who, knowing of an injunction, aids and abets the defendant in breaking it. The reason is that in aiding and abetting the defendant, he is obstructing the course of justice.'

93.   *National Phonograph Co Ltd v Edison Bell Consolidation Phonograph Co Ltd* [1908] 1 Ch 335. Arguably a puzzling reference as on the facts the case is a straightforward application of the principle that unlawful means can reside in illegal or unlawful acts which 'are criminal or tortious in character.'

94.   *Associated Newspapers Group Ltd v Wade* [1979] ICR 664.

Flood on the development of a tort of intentionally and unjustifiably causing economic loss. It seems advisable to regard such inconsistent decisions as there are as being simply that – out of step with orthodox judicial policy. If the quality of non-actionability in unlawful means were accepted, it would greatly expand the role and scope of the defence of justification. This was the majority view of the House of Lords in *OBG Ltd v Allan*:[95] four members of the House did not favour the broader interpretation of unlawful means. Lord Hoffmann expressed two propositions. First, he was of the opinion that, subject to one qualification, acts against a third party count as unlawful means only if they are independently actionable by that third party.[96] The qualification concerned facts where the means were not actionable only because the third party suffered no loss. In the case of intimidation, for example, the threat will usually give rise to no cause of action by the third party because he will have suffered no loss. If he submits to the threat, as the defendant intended, the claimant will have suffered loss instead. It is nevertheless unlawful means, '[b]ut the threat must be to do something which *would* have been actionable if the third party had suffered loss.'[97] Given that the purpose of this economic tort is to provide a cause of action to the plaintiff, the intended target of the defendant's actions who has suffered economic injury, the fact that the third party has not suffered economic loss and hence has no actionable claim against the defendant should not preclude the imposition of liability under the tort. Procuring the actions of a third party by fraud[98] was very similar to procuring them by intimidation.

[7.33] Lord Hoffmann's second proposition was that:

> Unlawful means … consists of acts intended to cause loss to the claimant by interfering with the freedom of a third party in a way which is unlawful as against that third party and which is intended to cause loss to the claimant. It does not in my opinion include acts which are unlawful against a third party but which do not affect his freedom to deal with the claimant.[99]

A mere causal connection between the defendant's unlawful conduct towards the third party and the economic injury inflicted upon the plaintiff is not enough. The factual impact of the defendant's unlawful conduct must undermine, restrict or impede the third party's freedom to transact with the plaintiff. Some examples of unlawful conduct by the defendant, while wrongful towards, and actionable by, the third party, may be

---

95. *OBG Ltd v Allan* [2008] AC 1. Old cases of interference with potential customers by threats of unlawful acts clearly fell within this description. Recent cases had also concerned wrongful threats or actions against employers with the intention of causing loss to an employee (as *Rookes v Barnard* [1964] AC 1129) or another employer (as *JT Stratford & Son Ltd v Lindley* [1965] AC 269). 'In principle the cases establish that intentionally causing someone loss by interfering with the liberty of action of a third party in breach of a contract with him is unlawful' (at 32).

96. *OBG Ltd v Allan* [2008] AC 1 at 32.

97. *OBG Ltd v Allan* [2008] AC 1 at 32.

98. As in *National Phonograph Co Ltd v Edison-Bell Consolidated Phonograph Co Ltd* [1908] 1 Ch 335 and arguably too *Lonrho plc v Fayed* [1990] 2 QB 479.

99. *OBG Ltd v Allan* [2008] AC 1 at 32–3.

prohibited by law for reasons which have nothing to do with the plaintiff's economic interest.

[7.34] Taking these two propositions together, Lord Hoffmann rationalised, and perhaps recharacterised, some earlier decisions, including *RCA Corpn v Pollard*.[100] In his view, *Lonrho Ltd v Shell Petroleum Co Ltd (No 2)*[101] was an attempt to found a cause of action simply on the fact that the conduct alleged to have caused loss was contrary to law. The defendant's conduct was alleged to be a criminal offence but not actionable by anyone. Lonrho, it will be recalled from para **5.35**, owned and operated a refinery in Rhodesia supplied by a pipeline from the port of Beira. When Rhodesia declared independence in 1965, the UK imposed sanctions which made it unlawful for anyone to supply the country with oil. As a result, the refinery and pipeline stood idle until the independence régime came to an end. Lonrho alleged Shell had prolonged the régime by unlawfully supplying Rhodesia with oil through other routes and thereby caused it loss. The House of Lords decided the alleged illegality gave rise to no cause of action on which Lonrho could rely. '[T]here was no allegation that Shell had intended to cause loss to Lonrho, but I cannot see how that would have made any difference.'[102] Shell did not interfere with any third party's dealings with Lonrho and even if it had done so, its acts were not wrongful in the sense of being actionable by such third party.

[7.35] Lord Hoffman approved of the fact that the tort had not been extended beyond the descriptions given by Lord Watson and Lord Lindley in *Quinn v Leathem*:

> Nor do I think it should be. The common law has traditionally been reluctant to become involved in devising rules of fair competition, as is vividly illustrated by *Mogul Steamship Co Ltd v McGregor Gow & Co* [1892] AC 25. It has largely left such rules to be laid down by Parliament. In my opinion the courts should be similarly cautious in extending a tort which was designed only to enforce basic standards of civilised behaviour in economic competition, between traders or between employers and labour. Otherwise there is a danger that it will provide a cause of action based on acts which are wrongful only in the irrelevant sense that a third party has a right to complain if he chooses to do so ... it is not for the courts to create a cause of action out of a regulatory or criminal statute which Parliament did not intend to be actionable in private law.[103]

Nor, indeed, was it for the courts to invent that which Parliament did not create. Lord Hoffmann did not favour taking a very wide view of what can count as unlawful means such as any action which involves a civil wrong against another person or breach of a criminal statute. Some writers,[104] he noted, consider that a requirement of a specific

---

100. *RCA Corpn v Pollard* [1983] Ch 135 and *Isaac Oren v Red Box Toy Factory Ltd* [1999] FSR 785.

101. *Lonrho Ltd v Shell Petroleum Co Ltd (No 2)* [1982] AC 173.

102. *OBG Ltd v Allan* [2008] AC 1 at 34, *per* Lord Hoffman.

103. *OBG Ltd v Allan* [2008] AC 1 at 34.

104. Eg, Sales and Stilitz, 'Intentional Infliction of Harm by Unlawful Means' 115 LQR (1999) 411, and Weir, 'Chaos or Cosmos: *Rookes, Stratford* and the Economic Torts' (1964) CLJ 230.

intention to 'target' the claimant should keep the tort within reasonable bounds. Others[105] consider that it would be arbitrary and illogical to make liability depend upon whether the defendant has done something which is wrongful for reasons which have nothing to do with the damage inflicted on the claimant. Lord Hoffmann agreed with this latter view:[106]

> I do not think that the width of the concept of 'unlawful means' can be counteracted by insisting upon a highly specific intention, which 'targets' the plaintiff. That, as it seems to me, places too much of a strain on the concept of intention. In cases in which there is obviously no reason why a claimant should be entitled to rely on the infringement of a third party's rights, courts are driven to refusing relief on the basis of an artificially narrow meaning of intention which causes trouble in later cases in which the defendant really has used unlawful means.[107]

[7.36] Lord Nicholls, a voice of one, differed. He recited the broader and the narrower views. The principal criticism of the first is that it 'tortifies' criminal conduct. The principal criticism of the second, narrower view is that it would be surprising if criminal conduct were excluded from the category of 'unlawful' means in this context. His Lordship preferred the wider interpretation of 'unlawful means' and accepted the approaches of Lord Reid and Lord Devlin respectively in *Rookes v Barnard*[108] (distinction between 'doing what you have a legal right to do and doing what you have no legal right to do'[109] and, it was 'of course' accepted that a threat to commit a crime was an unlawful threat[110]). To him therefore, unlike Lord Hoffmann, 'unlawful means' embraced 'all acts a defendant is not permitted to do, whether by the civil law or the criminal law'.[111] Unlike Lord Hoffmann's second proposition (para **7.33**), which required the defendant's unlawful act to interfere with the freedom of the third party to deal with the claimant, Lord Nicholls took the view that the proper operating principle that determined if the defendant's wrongful acts ought to count as 'unlawful means' for the purposes of the economic tort could be ascertained by 'keeping firmly in mind that, in these three-party situations, the function of the tort is to provide a remedy where the claimant is harmed through the instrumentality of a third party.'[112] Under Lord Nicholls' approach, liability is imposed on a defendant only if he has, through the commission of an illegal act, used the third party as an instrument or weapon through whom his intention to cause economic harm to the plaintiff has been effected. The

---

105. Eg, Bagshaw's review of Weir in 'Can the Economic Torts be Unified' (1998) 18 OJLS 729–739 at 732.

106. At 35. Lord Hoffmann added a footnote. He did not intend to say anything about the question of whether a claimant who has been compelled by unlawful intimidation to act to his own detriment can sue for his loss. 'Such a case of "two party intimidation" raises altogether different issues'.

107. *OBG Ltd v Allan* [2008] AC 1 at 35.

108. *Rookes v Barnard* [1964] AC 1129.

109. *Rookes v Barnard* [1964] AC 1129 at 1168–69.

110. *Rookes v Barnard* [1964] AC 1129 at 1206–1207.

111. *OBG Ltd v Allan* [2008] AC 1 at 57.

112. *Douglas v Hello! Ltd* [2007] UKHL 21 at 266–270.

third party's subsequent actions, or inaction, must be an integral part of the immediate cause of the plaintiff's economic loss.

[7.37] In light of these two diverging approaches, another member of the House of Lords, Lord Walker, felt obliged to set out his views on the identification of the control mechanisation needed in order to stop the notion of unlawful means getting out of hand – eg a pizza delivery business which obtains more business, to the detriment of its competitors, because its drivers regularly exceed the speed limit and jump red lights. Referring to Lord Hoffmann's and Lord Nicholls' views respectively, Lord Walker proposed a wider test of unlawful means relying on the notion of instrumentality as the appropriate control mechanism. However:

> I would respectfully suggest that neither is likely to be the last word on this difficult and important area of the law. The test of instrumentality does not fit happily with cases like *RCA Corpn v Pollard*, since there is no doubt that the bootlegger's acts were the direct cause of the plaintiff's economic loss. The control mechanism must be found, it seems to me, in the nature of the disruption caused, as between the third party and the claimant, by the defendant's wrong (and not in the closeness of the causal connection between the defendant's wrong and the claimant's loss).

> I do not, for my part, see Lord Hoffmann's proposed test as a narrow or rigid one ... I would favour a fairly cautious incremental approach to its extension to a category not found in the existing authorities.[113]

Baroness Hale and Lord Brown agreed with the narrow approach of Lord Hoffmann. According to the former:

> The refinement proposed by my noble and learned friend, Lord Hoffmann, is entirely consistent with the underlying principles to be deduced from the decided cases. It is also consistent with legal policy to limit rather than to encourage the expansion of liability in this area.[114]

Violation of a Constitutional Right

[7.38] A threat to violate a constitutional right will amount to an unlawful act or, depending on the circumstances, to unlawful means. See further para **5.39**. Is such a wrong always independently actionable? In Ireland the concept of *locus standi* may be broader for constitutional actions. In contrast to the approach in *Gouriet*,[115] Budd J put the matter as follows in *Byrne v Ireland*:[116]

> The right of a citizen to have recourse to the courts for the determination of justiciable controversies between a citizen and the State itself was dealt with in *Buckley and Others (Sinn Féin) v The Attorney General* [1950] IR 67; at p 84 of the report O'Byrne J, having referred to the distribution of powers effected by Article 6 of the Constitution, goes on to say: 'The effect of that article and of Arts 34 and 37, inclusive, is to vest in the Courts the exclusive right to determine

---

113. *OBG Ltd v Allan* [2008] AC 1 at 75.
114. *OBG Ltd v Allan* [2008] AC 1 at 86.
115. *Gouriet v Union of Post Office Workers* [1978] AC 435.
116. *Byrne v Ireland* [1972] IR 241 at 293.

justiciable controversies between citizens or between a citizen or citizens, as the case may be, and the State. In trying these proceedings, the plaintiffs were exercising a constitutional right and they were, and are, entitled to have the matter in dispute determined by the judicial organ of the State'.

The judge was delivering the judgment of the Supreme Court. *Prima facie,* these words appear to recognise the right of a citizen, under the provisions of the Constitution, to have recourse to the courts for the purpose of having determined any justiciable controversy between a citizen and the State.

DAMAGE

[7.39] A final postscript may be added. The plaintiff in *Cooper v Millea*[117] claimed compensation for a willful invasion of his employment through illegal interference between himself and his employers, whereby he has been gravely injured. As Gavan Duffy J put it:

> Damage, the temporal loss actually sustained, is the gist of this action, where no contractual right has been infringed, and I have carefully considered the case law as to the damages which the plaintiff may recover; as, however, this aspect of the matter has not been discussed, I need only say that it is no new law that 'in all cases where a man has a temporal loss or damage by the wrong of another, he may have an action on the case, to be repaired in damages'.[118]

The High Court held that every reasonable presumption should be made as to the benefits likely to have accrued to the plaintiff but for his dismissal. It is difficult to avoid the conclusion that damages here were awarded as though *Cooper* had been wrongfully dismissed.

NO STATUTORY PROTECTION: INDUSTRIAL RELATIONS ACT 1990, S 12(c)

[7.40] Section 12(c) of the Industrial Relations Act 1990 provides that:

> An act done by a person in contemplation or furtherance of a trade dispute shall not be actionable[119] on the ground only that ... it is an interference with the trade, business, or employment of some other person, or with the right of some other person to dispose of his capital or his labour as he wills.

The predecessor to s 12 was s 3 of the Trade Disputes Act 1906, which read:

> An act done by a person in contemplation or furtherance of a trade dispute shall not be actionable on the ground only that it induces some other person to break a contract of employment or that it is an interference with the trade, business or employment of some other person, or with the right of some other person to dispose of his capital or his labour as he wills.

---

117. *Cooper v Millea* [1938] IR 749.
118. *Com Dig tit* 'Action on the Case'—A.
119. See para **6.91** *et seq.*

Neither protects against the liability described in this chapter unless the ordinary canons of statutory construction were to be abandoned and the need for unlawful means, absent from the statutory formulation, were to be implied. This could not stand alongside the words in s 12(c) 'on the ground only', nor could an immunity, which restrains constitutional rights such as the right of access to the courts, be so construed. This means the right to strike and to take industrial action are potentially limited in Ireland as much, arguably, as they were following decisions like *Taff Vale, Quinn v Leathem, Rookes v Barnard* and *Stratford v Lindley.*[120]

[7.41] When the second part of s 3 of the Trade Disputes Act, repeated without change in s 12(c) of the 1990 Act, was passed in 1906, Parliament intended to deal with the degree of uncertainty following *Allen v Flood.*[121] It had been suggested[122] both before and after the passing of the Act that, even in the absence of conspiracy, interference with business was actionable unless justified.[123] This 'leading heresy' was rejected by Lord Dunedin in 1925,[124] but it was not until then that *Quinn v Leathem*[125] was firmly based on conspiracy. Even then, some judges regarded the issue as unclear. Hence, as Citrine says:

> The second limb of [section 3], relating to interference with trade, business or employment … was intended not to alter the law but to clarify it and to remove doubts, and was explained as intended to give legislative effect to the decision in *Allen v Flood.*[126]

[7.42] In *Sherriff v McMullen,*[127] the appellants relied very strongly on the proposition that the second limb of s 3 of the 1906 Act protected any interference with trade in furtherance of a trade dispute, even if the interferer induced a breach, not merely of a contract of employment, but of any contract. They further submitted that all the defendants had really done was to induce breaches of contracts of employment. The president of the High Court, Gavan Duffy J, pronounced that:

> Section 3 is careful to say that the acts protected are not to be actionable on the ground only of inducing a breach of contract of employment or of interference with trade, business or employment. In other words, to be protected the act done must be one which, if it does induce a breach of contract of employment or interference with trade, does not otherwise constitute a tort …

---

120. *Taff Vale Railway Company v Amalgamated Society of Railway Servants* [1901] AC 426, *Quinn v Leathem* [1901] AC 495, *Rookes v Barnard* [1964] AC 1129 and *Stratford v Lindley* [1965] AC 269.

121. *Allen v Flood* [1898] AC 1.

122. Citrine, *Trade Union Law* (3rd edn, Stevens & Sons, 1967), 579–80.

123. *Giblan v National Amalgamated Labourers' Union* [1903] 2 KB 600; and see *Conway v Wade* [1909] AC 506.

124. *Sorrell v Smith* [1925] AC 700, 719.

125. *Quinn v Leathem* [1901] AC 495.

126. *Per* Sir J Walton, AG in (1906) 162 HC Deb (4th Ser) at col 1675 and *per* Sir E Carson at col 1676.

127. *Sherriff v McMullen* [1952] IR 236.

The President then referred to the recommendation, in the Majority Report of the Royal Commission on Trade Disputes and Combinations, issued a few months before the Act of 1906, in favour of protecting an act 'not in itself a tort' that interferes with a person's trade, business or employment (a reference to the more orthodox interpretation of the *Allen v Flood* clause in the Bill). In so far as s 3 protected *tortious* behaviour, it did this in the first limb, which protects inducements to break a contract of employment and the President concentrated on it. The defendants' actions were not protected by the section. They had (indirectly) induced breaches of service contracts, interfered with another person's trade and interfered with a commercial contract, knowingly and without justification. The Act could not therefore come to their aid as their conduct had gone beyond the intended scope of s 3.

[7.43] Section 12(c) of the 1990 Act is intended to protect acts which would at common law be lawful anyway. *Clerk and Lindsell on Torts* in reference to British law[128] say that by retaining the subsection on the statute book without amendment 'Parliament must have intended to allay some modern "doubt" about some liability.' Mere interference with trade, business or employment without the use of unlawful means is not in need of statutory immunity as no legal wrong is involved, and the provision was presumably re-enacted in 1990 for the same reason as in 1906, to remove all doubt or to allay some modern 'doubt' about some liability. Lord Pearce in *Rookes v Barnard*[129] described the provision as 'pointless.' Section 12(c) cannot protect where unlawful means have been used.

[7.44] For a brief period, erroneously, this was not the view in England. In *Hadmor Productions Ltd and Ors v Hamilton and Anor*,[130] Lord Diplock viewed the subsection with '1974 eyes' and took precisely the opposite view to that which had long been recognised and accepted. He asserted that the subsection did protect acts involving unlawful means. His interpretation was later relied on by the Inner House of the Court of Session in Scotland in *Plessey Co PLC v Wilson*[131] where action was protected, even though a trespass was thereby committed. Lord Emslie commented that the section protected unlawful acts at least: 'where the only consequences which give rise to a claim in reparation are interferences with the trade or business of the employer.'

[7.45] On this approach, which focused on the nature of the damage caused rather than the nature of the acts committed, a wide range of unlawful acts, including criminal acts, would be protected. For example, workers sitting in (eg, to protest against redundancies) who are liable to charges of forcible occupation or who smash up machinery or otherwise destroy property to cause it to perish, would attract the immunity. It is unlikely that such a result would ever be arrived at by an Irish court quite apart from the particular wording in the Act ('on the ground only') and constitutional considerations. Before Lord Diplock's novel assertion was allowed to bear any unwieldy fruit in Britain, Parliament stepped in and repealed s 13(2)

---

128. *Clerk and Lindsell on Tort* (19th edn, Sweet and Maxwell, 2005) at 786.
129. *Rookes v Barnard* [1964] AC 1129 at 1236.
130. *Hadmor Productions Ltd and Ors v Hamilton and Anor* [1982] IRLR 102.
131. *Plessey Co PLC v Wilson* [1982] IRLR 198.

altogether (Employment Act 1982, s 19). The second limb of s 3 of the 1906 Act is no longer given so-called 'immunity' in that jurisdiction.

[7.46] Thus the 'new' tort of causing loss by unlawful means, detailed in this chapter, enjoys no statutory immunity in Ireland, and is likely to provide the ground on which strike or industrial action may be fought in the courts. For public sector workers, subject to what has been said, inducing breach of or interfering with the performance of a statutory duty[132] could constitute unlawful means. This tort is likely to include the indirect form of the tort of inducing breach of contract. Causing loss by unlawful means is a tort of uncertain but flexible boundaries which awaits full examination by an Irish court. Until then, its very flexibility and uncertainty are more likely to help rather than hinder interlocutory applications. In England, where the statutory protections are considerably more far-reaching, it has been written:[133]

> It is not the case that the golden formula trade dispute defences provide a clear and complete boundary that separates industrial action that can be organised lawfully from that which is tortious. The interaction of shifts in the reach of the common law torts, the statutory defences and of course judicial practice in response to applications for ... [interlocutory] relief through labour injunctions is likely to continue to provide a degree of uncertainty over the extent to which English law recognises an effective 'right' – or rather 'freedom' – to strike.

---

132. See the *'Docks dispute' case* [1989] ICR 557, CA and HL.

133. Simpson, 'Economic Tort Liability in Labour Disputes: The Potential Impact of the House of Lords' Decision in *OBG Ltd v Allan*' (2007) ILJ 479.

Chapter 8

INTIMIDATION

EMERGENCE OF THE TORT

[8.01] In **Chs 4** and **7**, on the economic torts generally, and on unlawful interference with business, respectively, intimidation was described as one instance of wrongful behaviour under the banner of the wider tort of causing loss by unlawful means. Prior to 1964, the tort of intimidation was an 'obscure, unfamiliar and peculiar cause of action' having its roots in cases of physical violence and threats.[1] The modern form of the tort, as we will see, arose out of industrial relations circumstances. In general it does not appear to be insistence on too high a standard of conduct to require that people should not use threats to break their contracts as a means of causing loss to others. The difficulty is that in the field of labour disputes the rules that are reasonable and proper for the common law as a whole may not always be appropriate. It is generally assumed that wages and other terms and conditions of employment will be settled by voluntary negotiation between employers and unions. But a union representative is powerless in negotiation unless he has the ultimate weapon of being able to threaten a strike, just as the employer can ultimately refuse to employ the workers. The legal difficulty is that the right to threaten a strike or industrial action almost inevitably means to threaten breaches of contract. For a union representative to have the right to threaten industrial action therefore means he must have the right to threaten breaches of contract.

[8.02] In *Riordan v Butler*[2] the plaintiff had been wrongfully dismissed by his employer as a result of threats made by the defendants that they would cease work immediately if he was allowed to continue in employment. The High Court (O Byrne J) held that the threat to 'walk off the job' constituted sufficient unlawful means for purposes of the tort of intimidation. The defendants procured a breach of his contract by their threats or warnings. Had the Trade Disputes Act 1906 been applied to the procurement alone, the defendants would not have been protected – s 3 protected an act which is 'actionable on the ground only' of procurement, which meant that if there was additional liability, its efficacy was lost. Such liability here resided in the threat to break contracts. Before the judge ever reached the point of considering the Trade Disputes Act he decided, following an earlier decision in *Cooper v Millea*,[3] that

---

1.   Carty, *An Analysis of the Economic Torts* (OUP, 2001), 86.

2.   *Riordan v Butler* [1940] IR 347.

3   *Cooper v Millea* [1938] IR 749 in which a threat to induce breach of contract was held to constitute unlawful means. The judge was following a dictum of Gavan Duffy J in that case. Walsh J in *Becton Dickinson v Lee* [1973] IR 1, 30 regarded the decision as wrongly decided on its facts. He remarked that 'the case was apparently regarded by the learned trial judge as being a case where the defendants were threatening to break their own contract' but, it is submitted, this view of the trial judge cannot be supported on any reading of the latter's judgment. It is replete with references that indicate without a shadow of doubt that Gavan Duffy J understood what was going on. (contd .../)

185

unlawful means had been used and that the defendants were guilty of unlawful interference with the plaintiff's employment. On this reasoning, it was not material whether the plaintiff's employment was interfered with by way of breach of his contract of employment. What mattered was that unlawful means were used and that the defendants set out deliberately to harm the plaintiff.

[8.03] This judgment was later approved by the House of Lords in the seminal case on intimidation, *Rookes v Barnard*.[4] The plaintiff, Rookes, had been lawfully dismissed by his employer because of pressure brought to bear on him by the defendants. The pressure was in the form of threatened strike action by the defendants, a trade union official and the dismissed worker's colleagues, which constituted a threat to break their contracts of employment. The former employee sued for intimidation and conspiracy. He succeeded in persuading the court that the tort of intimidation extended beyond threatened physical harm to include threatened breach of contract. Both the Court of Appeal and the House of Lords agreed the tort existed but the former declined to accept that it extended to threats to break contracts. They were influenced by the fact that a tort so expressed would drive a coach and four[5] through the then statutory protections, encouraging lightning strikes. However, the House of Lords found for the plaintiff in a 'bold instance of judicial lawmaking'[6] and held that a threat to break a contract constituted sufficient unlawful means for liability. Lord Devlin regarded the

---

3.   (contd) A reason more germane for doubting *Cooper* might have been whether the plaintiff could appropriately rely on acts as unlawful means which were rendered immune from suit as between the employer and the officials concerned under s 3 for purposes of establishing liability (see further para **6.92**). If this issue, namely whether immune wrongs can constitute unlawful means, lay at the core of Judge Walsh's disapproval of *Cooper*, his reservations are critically important. If this is what he meant, he did not say so. But the means in each case were not the same. Hence when O'Byrne J says in *Riordan* that he is bound to regard the defendants' threat to walk off the job as unlawful means 'having regard to *Cooper v Millea*', he parts company from *Cooper*. It is incorrect to say *Cooper* concerned such a species of unlawful means. In *Kire Manufacturing Co Ltd v O'Leary* (29 April 1974, unreported), HC, O'Higgins J attempted to reconcile the two authorities on the basis that in *Cooper* the defendants were also fellow workers, although trade union officials as well. Hence, he said they were also threatening to break their own contracts.

4.   *Rookes v Barnard* [1964] AC 1129.

5.   See Lord Hoffmann for an interesting footnote on this expression in '*Rookes v Barnard*' (1965) 81 LQR 116 at 137, fn 69. The vehicle has lost two horses since the metaphor was originally coined by Sir Stephen Rice, James II's Chief Baron of the Exchequer in Ireland, who said before his appointment to the bench that he would 'drive a coach and horses through the [Irish] Act of Settlement', under which Protestants held a large part of the land. Rice was as good as his word; his court was 'crowded with suitors and a Protestant rarely succeeded there.' He was dismissed after the battle of the Boyne. In *Facchini v Bryson* [1952] 1 TLR 1386 at 1390 the coach lost all its horses and became 'an articulated vehicle.'

6.   Hoffmann, '*Rookes v Barnard*' (1965) 81 LQR 116 at 116. Wedderburn, 'Intimidation and the Right to Strike' (1964) 27 MLR 257 described the House of Lords as inventing a new extension of civil liability.

nature of the threat as immaterial. Thus the defendants were held liable and no immunity then existed under the Trade Disputes Act 1906.

[8.04] In *Becton Dickinson v Lee*[7] Walsh J described *Rookes v Barnard* as 'the case of a threat to strike in breach of contract and was treated as such by the Courts concerned', although, he pointed out, one of the three defendants was not under contract and was a trade union official acting as such and could not have threatened to break his own contract:

> His position does not appear to have been distinguished from the other two defendants who were under contract, although the case was fought on the question of whether or not protection was afforded by section 3 of the Act of 1906.

In fact, *Rookes v Barnard* threw the law relating to trade disputes into confusion in Britain. A threat to strike in breach of contract, irrespective of a no-strike clause, could amount to unlawful means. Equally, persons who threaten to strike without prior or with insufficient warning will be potentially liable. *Rookes* not only extended the common law liability of the strikers themselves but the finding against the trade union official showed that persons organising a strike in breach of contract or acting as a channel of communication between would-be strikers and their employer run the risk of being vulnerable to legal action. This threatened to undermine the statutory protection afforded under the Trade Disputes Act 1906, ss 1 and 3. According to Citrine,[8] it seemed to follow that an employer who was compelled to increase wages by a threat of a strike in breach of contract could sue those who had made the threat. The decision had ominous repercussions for trade unions in whose view the 'right to strike' was threatened. As its practical implications became clearer, the courts sought to confine it within reasonable grounds. At first it was thought the case turned on the presence of a 'no strike' clause in the contracts of employment. But a strike will often be in breach of contract, whether or not there is such a clause. *Morgan v Fry*[9] involved facts similar to *Rookes v Barnard* but without a 'no strike' clause. All the members of the Court of Appeal held, for different reasons, that the defendant had not committed the tort of intimidation. All distinguished *Rookes v Barnard* in that the notice of strike given by the defendant, Fry, was at least as long as that needed to be given by the employees to terminate their contracts of employment. In this case Lord Denning, concerned about the impact of *Rookes v Barnard* on the legality of primary industrial action, developed his notion of a strike upon due notice leading to the suspension rather than the breach of the contract of employment, a theme taken up by Walsh J in *Becton Dickinson v Lee*[10] (para **3.12** *et seq*). The significance of *Morgan v Fry* was overtaken by the Trade Disputes Act 1965 in Britain, a short Act declaring it not to be actionable for a person acting in contemplation or furtherance of a trade dispute to threaten 'that a contract of employment (whether one to which he is a party or not) will be broken.' The introduction of such a provision was not to happen in Ireland until the

---

7. *Becton Dickinson v Lee* [1973] IR 1.
8. Citrine, *Trade Union Law* (3rd edn, Stevens & Sons, 1967), 29.
9. *Morgan v Fry* [1968] 2 QB 710.
10. *Becton Dickinson v Lee* [1973] IR 1. See too *Bates v Model Bakery* [1993] 1 IR 359.

Industrial Relations Act 1990, hence the continuing importance of the doctrine of suspension to protect those involved in strikes. Of course, if put to the test, the doctrine of suspension may be found to be far less effective than one imagines (para **3. 27** *et seq*).

[8.05] This chapter analyses the salient features of intimidation. *Clerk and Lindsell on Torts* describe the tort thus:[11]

> A commits a tort if he delivers a threat to B that he will commit an act, or use means, unlawful as against B, as a result of which B does or refrains from doing some act which he is entitled to do, thereby causing damage either to himself or to C.

The plaintiff, whether it is B or C, must be a person whom A intended to injure. As Lord Evershed MR put it in *Rookes v Barnard* 'the intention ... of the threat was to injure.'[12] The injury must also be a direct response to the threat. The importance of the deliberate use of unlawful means to harm the plaintiff makes this tort one of *primary* liability. Thus it is part of the wider tort discussed in **Ch 7** and has the same rationale. In *Rookes v Barnard* the court had been invited to formulate a general principle of liability but the House of Lords opted to develop the tort of intimidation rather than embark on this exercise. It is fitting that Lord Hoffmann (as he became), who was critical of this in 1965,[13] should have led the House in *OBG* many decades later.

THE THREAT

[8.06] In *Hodges v Webb*[14] Peterson J described the tort as, 'An intimidation by one to another that unless the latter does not do something, the former will do something which the latter does not like.' A threat has been distinguished from a warning, although the distinction should not be allowed to detract from the primary ingredient of the tort, namely the intention to inflict harm unlawfully.[15] It is generally accompanied by coercion or molestation. Threats may be express or implied. Lord Devlin provided an example of the latter in *Rookes v Barnard*,[16] where a strike is engaged upon without previous negotiation with an employer, where the implication is clear that, unless the employer does certain things, the strike will be continued. A threat of 'union trouble' was held to be too vague in *Pete's Towing Services Ltd v NIUW*[17] as it could entail either lawful or unlawful conduct.

---

11. *Clerk and Lindsell on Torts* (19th edn, Sweet & Maxwell, 2006), 25–65.
12. *Rookes v Barnard* [1964] AC 1129 at 1183.
13. Hoffmann, '*Rookes v Barnard*' (1965) 81 LQR 116 at 121.
14. *Hodges v Webb* [1920] 2 Ch 70 at 89.
15. *Conway v Wade* [1909] AC 506 *per* Lord Loreburn, 510, *per* Lord James, 514; *Santen v Busnach* (1913) 29 TLR 214. Contrast *Rookes v Barnard* [1964] AC at 1199 *per* Lord Houlson whose view must be doubted.
16. *Rookes v Barnard* [1964] AC 1129 at 1208–1209.
17. *Pete's Towing Services Ltd v NIUW* [1970] NZLR 32.

[8.07] The suggested tort of harassment is to be distinguished from this tort.[18] There is no tort of coercion *per se*. The threat must relate to an unlawful act. Threatening to do what a person has a legal right to do does not create liability. A change of behaviour in the workplace may amount to unilateral variation of the contract of employment. For example, union officials may not wish to work with non-union workers. Instead of threatening to strike if the latter are not dismissed, they may inform the employer they will carry out their work duties in so far as possible by not associating with them.[19] Such 'advice' would go beyond mere information:[20] depending on the facts, it might constitute unlawful means. Earlier cases of intimidation mostly involved illegal acts which were criminal or tortious in character.[21] Lord Denning described 'violence, tort and breach of contract'[22] as included in unlawfulness but did not imply this list was exhaustive. Breaches of duty may also be relevant where they are imposed by law[23] or equity.[24] In general, unconstitutionality, acts of defamation, slander of goods or title, injurious falsehood, fraud or deceit, nuisance, trespass, breach of contract and possibly breaches of natural justice will render interference or threats tortious. In relation to breach of contract, there is no reason in principle why minor as well as major breaches should not suffice as unlawful means, but it may be more difficult in relation to the former to establish the illegality as a deliberate cause of the plaintiff's loss.

[8.08] Submission to the threat is essential to 'complete' the tort.[25] In *Whelan v Madigan*[26] a landlord resorted to 'outrageous behaviour' towards his tenants. Far from leaving the property, the tenants came together to take legal proceedings against the landlord. The landlord was held not guilty of intimidation (Kenny J).

TWO-PARTY INTIMIDATION

[8.09] Intimidation usually arises where there are three parties. However, it seems the tort may be committed not only when the person threatened is different from the

---

18.   Scott J in *Thomas v NUM* [1986] Ch 20. The concept of harassment and the tort of nuisance led to liability in *Khorasandjian v Bush* [1993] QB 727 CA, although the House of Lords restored nuisance to its role in *Hunter v Canary Wharf Ltd* [1997] 2 WLR 684. In the UK, see the Protection from Harassment Act 1997.

19.   *Morgan v Fry* [1968] 2 QB 710, 731–732.

20.   It was once thought that a threat could amount to intimidation even if the act threatened was itself lawful but Lord Dunedin in *Sorrell v Smith* [1925] AC 700, 719 condemned this notion as 'the leading heresy'.

21.   *Rookes v Barnard* [1964] AC 1129 at 1182; see, eg, *Garrett Taylor* (1620) Cro Jac 567; *Tarleton v M'*(1794) Peake 270*Gawley* (1793) 1 Peake 270.

22.   *Stratford v Lindley* [1965] AC 269, 283 *per* Lord Devlin. *Morgan v Fry* [1968] 2 QB 710.

23.   Eg, *Constantine v Imperial Hotels* [1944] KB 693 (breach of common innkeeper to receive guests).

24.   Eg, *Dixon v Dixon* [1904] 1 Ch 161.

25.   *Per* Stuart-Smith J in *News Group Newspapers Ltd v SOGAT (No 2)* [1987] ICR 181 at 204.

26.   *Whelan v Madigan* [1978] ILRM 136.

plaintiff but also when he is the same person – when, in other words, there are two parties, not three.[27]

[8.10] In Ireland, as has been seen in para **8.02**, a threat to break a contract was held unlawful in *Cooper v Millea*[28] by Gavan Duffy J who said:

> It is incontestable that the defendants interfered with the plaintiff's employment by illegal means: for a strike in breach of contract is unlawful and a threat or preintimation of unlawful action constitutes illegal means; the right of action is then established: see Lord Dunedin's speech in *Sorrell v Smith* [1925] AC 700 at 730.

In support of this, it is said the party threatened may have his remedies[29] but some illegalities do not themselves give remedies, and those which do may give inadequate redress and/or the range of recoverable loss may be greater in tort than in contract. On the other hand, there are policy difficulties, for example, privity of contract in accepting 'two-party' intimidation where the breach threatened is that of the defendant's own contract. Arguably two-party intimidation where the wrong threatened is breach of contract contravenes the logic of the law.

[8.11] Wedderburn[30] and Weir[31] argue for an all-or-nothing approach, albeit their solutions are different. Carty suggests a threatened breach of contract should be sufficient where there are three parties involved but not sufficient in two-party intimidation.[32] No privity problem arises in the former, because the plaintiff's cause of action is independent of the middleman's, it is irrelevant that the unlawful act is a breach of contract. However, in two-party intimidation, where the threat is of breach of contract, the form of the unlawful means is relevant. The threat to break a contract involves no separate tort. Burns[33] is of the view that there is 'no compelling reason' why the plaintiff should have the tort of intimidation available to him in a two-party

---

27. In *Rookes v Barnard* [1964] AC 1129, 1205 Lord Devlin accepted the two-party version of the tort set out in the then current edition of *Salmond on Torts* (13th edn, Sweet & Maxwell). See too *per* Lord Denning MR in *Stratford v Lindley* [1965] AC 269, 285; *per* Stuart-Smith J in *News Group Newspapers Ltd v SOGAT (No 2)* [1987] ICR 181, 204–5.
28. *Cooper v Millea* [1938] IR 749, followed in *Riordan v Butler* [1940] IR 347. See doubts expressed on its correctness in *Becton Dickinson v Lee* [1973] IR 1, fn 3.
29. Eg, for anticipatory breach. An action for intimidation may lie even if the threat does not amount to an anticipatory breach of contract: *Rookes v Barnard* [1964] AC 1129 at 1206–1207 *per* Lord Devlin.
30. Wedderburn, 'Intimidation and the Right to Strike' (1964) 27 MLR 257.
31. Weir, 'Chaos or Cosmos: *Rookes, Stratford* and the Economic Torts' (1964) CLJ 225 at 229.
32. Carty, *An Analysis of the Economic Torts* (OUP, 2001), 96. For general reluctance to accept two-party intimidation either *per se* or without qualifications, see *Winfield and Jolowicz on Torts* (11th edn, Sweet & Maxwell, 1979), 492; Hamson, 'A Further Note on *Rookes v Barnard*' (1964) CLJ 159, 168; Hoffman, '*Rookes v Barnard*' (1965) 81 LQR 116, 127–128.
33. Burns, 'Tory Injury to Economic Interests: Some Facets of Legal Response' (1980) 58 Can Bar Rev 134 at 135–6.

situation because his position is already protected. A threat to break one's contract gives rise to contractual and restitutionary remedies. Tort protection is not necessary.[34]

[8.12] This thinking resonated with the House of Lords in *OBG Ltd v Allan*.[35] When discussing unlawful means, Lord Hoffmann added a footnote. He did not intend to say anything about the question of whether a claimant who has been compelled by unlawful intimidation to act to his own detriment can sue for his loss. Such a case of 'two party intimidation', in his view, raised altogether different issues.

[8.13] All intimidation cases involve the same mould of liability: the tort of causing loss by unlawful means, whether the unlawful means constitutes a threat to strike or to procure a breach of contract. This was Lord Hoffmann's view, (para **4.16**), in *OBG Ltd v Allan*.[36] He described the tort as an inadequate label given by Salmond in the 1907 edition of his textbook on tort. Whether this becomes generally accepted remains to be seen. The statutory immunity for the broader tort is discussed at para **7.40** *et seq.*

JUSTIFICATION

[8.14] Justification may constitute a defence. In many ways it is surprising there should be a defence to unlawful threats. Lord Devlin mooted the possibility in *Rookes v Barnard*.[37] It has been suggested that trade union officials 'might well be justified' in intimidating an employer in order to remove persons who were troublemakers.[38] Where the defendants' motive was to further their trade union interests, this motive, however, will not avail them.[39] What has been said in **Ch 6** concerning justification in the context of the tort of inducing breach of contract applies to this tort, with perhaps even more efficacy, as the means here are *per se* unlawful, unlike in the direct form of the inducement tort.

STATUTORY PROTECTION: INDUSTRIAL RELATIONS ACT 1990, S 12(b)

[8.15] The full text of s 12 of the Industrial Relations Act 1990 reads:

> An act done by a person in contemplation or furtherance of a trade dispute shall not be actionable on the ground only that—
>
> (a)   it induces some other person to break a contract of employment, or
>
> (b)   it consists of a threat by a person to induce some other person to break a contract of employment or a threat by a person to break his own contract of employment, or

---

34.   Carty, *An Analysis of the Economic Torts* (OUP, 2001), 97.

35.   *OBG Ltd v Allan* [2008] AC 1 at 35.

36.   *OBG Ltd v Allan* [2008] AC 1.

37.   *Rookes v Barnard* [1964] AC 1129, 1206 and 1209. But see Kerr & Whyte, *Irish Trade Union Law* (Professional Books, 1985) at 242.

38.   Lord Denning in *Morgan v Fry* [1968] 2 QB 710, 729 and, in even stronger vein, in *Cory Lighterage Ltd v ITGWU* [1973] ICR 339, 356–357.

39.   See *Whelan v Madigan* [1978] ILRM 136, an illustration that outside of labour relations, the state of justification in this tort is no more certain.

(c)   it is an interference with the trade, business, or employment of some other person, or with the right of some other person to dispose of his capital or his labour as he wills.

A threat to induce was not explicitly covered in s 3 of the Trade Disputes Act 1906. Section 12(b) protects the tort of intimidation and was a significant addition to workers' immunities in the Industrial Relations Act 1990. The provision protects the threats of a trade union official to an employer to call a strike in breach of the contract of employment but it will be recalled that, as in *Cooper v Millea*,[40] where a third party is deliberately harmed by such a threat, different considerations apply. This will amount to causing loss by unlawful means and is not protected. Authorities so far in Ireland do not rule out the possibility of acts rendered immune under the statute being used as unlawful means for purposes of other torts (see para **6. 92**). Since breach of contract remains wholly unlawful, actions involving the use of such a breach or a combination to promote such breaches, will constitute unlawful means.

[8.16] In general s 12(b) does not protect the use of means otherwise tortious, or criminal and independently actionable, for there will then be some other ground of action. It does not protect against the extended form of the tort, where interference with contract or contractual performance is threatened. Contrast Britain, where the Trade Union and Labour Relations Act 1992, s 219(1)(b) refers to breach as well as to interference with performance of a contract. There, an action is not actionable in tort on the ground only 'that it consists in [the person's] threatening that a contract (whether one to which he is party or not) will be broken or its performance interfered with, or that he will induce another person to break a contract or interfere with its performance.' Section 12(b) relates only to contracts of *employment*. It is no defence to an action for threatening to induce breach of a contract of another kind. The Industrial Relations Act 1990 failed to grasp the real nettle of *Rookes v Barnard*.

[8.17] If *OBG Ltd v Allan*[41] is followed in this jurisdiction, as is hoped, it is uncertain whether s 12(b) will continue to have the effect it does. This is because the House of Lords regarded the tort of intimidation as part of the wider liability of causing loss by unlawful means. Changing the name or the label of the tort should not, it is suggested, deprive it of the protection in s 12(b). But whether the tort will continue with a separate, if discarded, identity is questionable.

[8.18] The exceptions to the application of s 12(b) concern one-worker disputes (paras **5. 51** and **9.26**) and action contrary to the outcome of a secret ballot (paras **5. 52** and **9.68**), and it will be recalled that the immunities are restricted to members and officials of authorised trade unions (para **9.60**). The 'golden formula' ('in contemplation or furtherance of a trade dispute') is considered at para **9.75** *et seq*.

---

40.   *Cooper v Millea* [1938] IR 749.

41.   *OBG Ltd v Allan* [2008] AC 1.

Chapter 9

SUBJECT MATTER OF A TRADE DISPUTE, PARTIES, AND ACTS 'IN CONTEMPLATION OR FURTHERANCE' OF A TRADE DISPUTE

INTRODUCTION

[9.01] The best way to analyse potential liability in relation to strike or industrial action is set out at para **4.27**. In this chapter, we consider the parties, context and subject matter of a trade dispute. Relevant questions are:

(i)   Is there a 'trade dispute' under s 8 of the Industrial Relations Act 1990?

(ii) Are 'the parties' – workers, employees and trade unions – eligible under that section for the Act's protection?

(iii) Is the action of the individuals whom it is sought to make personally liable in 'contemplation or furtherance' of a trade dispute?

Whether workers are picketing, or agreeing together to commit an unlawful act or inducing a breach of the contract of employment, they must satisfy the requirements as to the parties, context and subject matter of a trade dispute as defined in the Industrial Relations Act 1990. The Act is specific in its definition of 'workers,' 'employer' and 'trade dispute'. The phrase which occurs throughout the Act 'in contemplation or furtherance of a trade dispute' – the so-called 'golden formula' after Lord Wedderburn[1] – is a repetition from the Act of 1906 and has received a particular interpretation at the hands of the judiciary.

[9.02] Under this chapter's heading of 'trade dispute' attention is paid to terms and conditions of or affecting employment and recognition disputes, and to the nature of the rights and interests which may constitute a 'trade dispute' under the Act. Under 'parties', the Act's definition of 'workers' is considered, as is whether workers need share the same employer, whether workers out of employment are covered, the meaning of 'employer', whether a trade union can be party to a trade dispute, the definition of 'trade union', unofficial action and whether industrial action in violation of a peace obligation is covered. The golden formula 'in contemplation or furtherance of a trade dispute' is crucial to the Act's immunities. It bears directly on secondary, tertiary, and sympathetic action and the chapter ends with such action.

TRADE DISPUTE
Trade Dispute

[9.03] A 'trade dispute' in s 8 of the Industrial Relations Act 1990 means:

> any dispute between employers and workers which is connected with the employment or non-employment, or the terms or conditions of or affecting the employment of any person.

---

1.   *The Worker and the Law* (Penguin, 1965), 222.

Whether or not there is a trade dispute is an issue of fact. As ever, the onus on proving its existence falls upon the party alleging it: *Larkin v Long*.[2]

Connected with

[9.04] The dispute must be 'connected with' the matters set out in s 8. Whether a dispute about, say, an employer's ethical investment policies, carbon emissions or high-level corporate strategies could be said to be 'connected with' 'employment ... or terms or conditions ... affecting the employment, of any person' awaits future decisions. The House of Lords took the view in *NWL Ltd v Woods*[3] that *any* connection is sufficient. Likewise the Northern Ireland Court of Appeal in *Crazy Prices (Northern Ireland) Ltd v Hewitt*[4] said that, as long as there was a connection with the required subject matter, albeit tenuous, the statutory protection applied. Clearly, this will not be the case where the alleged connection is ostensible only.[5]

Personal quarrel

[9.05] To constitute a dispute, a mere personal quarrel or grumbling will not suffice. Lord Loreburn in *Conway v Wade*[6] said in reference to s 5(3) of the Trade Disputes Act 1906:

> I do not know that the definition is of much assistance. If this section is to apply there must be a dispute, however the subject matter of it will be defined. A mere personal quarrel or a grumbling or an agitation will not suffice. It must be something fairly definite and of real substance.

These words have been followed and applied in many Irish decisions. In *Barton v Harten*[7] the employer was carrying on his business in the ordinary way and had no dispute whatever with his employees. One of his assistants had been arrested by Government Forces and imprisoned for several months by the Executive Government. On his release, the relevant union demanded his reinstatement in spite of the fact that

---

2. *Larkin v Long* [1915] AC 814.
3. *NWL Ltd v Woods* [1979] ICR 867.
4. *Crazy Prices (Northern Ireland) Ltd v Hewitt* [1980] NI 150, 169; Kerr (1981) 32 NILQ 343.
5. *Huntley v Thornton* [1957] 1 WLR 321.
6. *Conway v Wade* [1909] AC 506. In order to compel Conway to pay a fine due to his trade union and to punish him for not paying it, Wade procured his employer's foreman to dismiss Conway by threats that unless the firm dismissed him, the union men in the firm's service would leave off work. This was not true. Conway had, in consequence, to quit his employment and so suffered damage. He brought an action against Wade for inducing his employers to dismiss him. The defendants pleaded the golden formula. The jury found there was not a trade dispute existing or contemplated by the men and that Wade's threats were uttered in order to compel Conway to pay a union fine and to punish him for not paying it. They awarded Conway damages. The House of Lords upheld this.
7. *Barton v Harten* [1925] 2 IR 37. See too *McCusker v Smith* [1918] 2 IR 432: an act done during an existing trade dispute may in reality be dictated by political or personal motives and so lose the protection of the Act *(per* Sir James Campbell CJ and Kenny J 439).

after an interval the man's job had been filled. The reason given by the union for their demand was that the assistant had been arrested and released without charge or trial. Molony CJ referred to Lord Loreburn in *Conway v Wade*[8] where he said:

> If, however, some meddler sought to use that trade dispute as a cloak beneath which to interfere with impunity in other people's work or business, a jury would be entirely justified in saying that what he did was in contemplation or in furtherance, not of the trade dispute, but of his own designs, sectarian, political, or purely mischievous, as the case might be.

These observations, said the Chief Justice, apply to a case where there is a genuine trade dispute but which is taken advantage of for an improper purpose, and they were still more strongly applicable to a case such as that before him where there was in reality no dispute at all but only an attempt on the part of an organisation to compel an employer to give employment to one who had been out of employment for a long time, and whose position had been filled in the ordinary course. The magistrate's finding that there was no trade dispute was accordingly upheld.[9]

[9.06] Where trade unionists do not act from spite or ill-will or a desire to injure the plaintiff, or as mischief makers, or instigators of strife, or where they do not manufacture, or threaten to manufacture, a trade dispute, *Conway v Wade* is obviously inapplicable. Hence in *Kenny v O'Reilly and Spain*[10] the Circuit Court held that the defendants were carrying out their duty of managing the business of the section of their union in ruling upon a question raised by a member of the section, and in determining a course of action accordingly.

Bona fide belief in dispute

[9.07] A union is not entitled to 'create' a dispute. The dispute must be fairly definite and of real substance. In *The Silver Tassie Co Ltd v Cleary*[11] a Mr Pinkerton was the managing director of the plaintiff company. He wished to take a more active part in the business and decided to become a working official of the company in the bar. He thereupon dismissed one of the employees. His reason for doing this was because, as he had entered the business himself, redundancy would result. The union objected to the dismissal and alleged that Pinkerton was victimising the dismissed worker because of previous demands which the union had made. They further contended that Pinkerton was attempting to turn his house into non-union premises. Pinkerton was warned by the unions that if he did not reinstate the worker, his premises would be picketed. He refused to accede to the union's request. Shortly afterwards, the Assistant Secretary of the union called the employees out. They left the premises under protest as each denied he had any dispute with Pinkerton. The company obtained an interlocutory injunction on the ground that the union had based its dispute on alleged intimidation. No

---

8.   *Conway v Wade* [1909] AC 506 at 512.

9.   Reference was made to *Barton v Harten* and to *Conway v Wade* by Johnston J in *Ryan v Cooke and Quinn* [1938] IR 512 at 524. The latter case was described by the judge as the one from which he 'got most assistance'.

10. *Kenny v O'Reilly and Spain* (1927) 61 ILTR 137.

11. *Silver Tassie Co Ltd v Cleary* [1958] 92 ILTR 27.

victimisation had been shown to exist, therefore there was no trade dispute. The following morning members of the union again called at the employer's premises and demanded the dismissed worker's reinstatement. This was rejected: they commenced to picket once more and the company obtained a further injunction. The Secretary of the union admitted in evidence that the union at all times was disputing the man's dismissal. Affirming the judgment of the High Court, the Supreme Court held that the genuineness of a trade dispute does not depend upon the true facts of the dispute, but rather on the *bona fides* of the parties to the dispute. To hold that there cannot be a dispute about the existence of a state of facts unless the court has first found such a state of facts exists 'would be to remove from the protection of the Act a large number of disputes and to impose on the definition of a trade dispute a limitation not found anywhere in the Act.' The judgment of the court was delivered by the Chief Justice who said:[12]

> The principal argument upon which the plaintiffs based their case in the Court was that the belief by the defendants in the existence of a state of facts which induced them to cause a dispute does not make such dispute a 'trade dispute' within the meaning of the 1906 Act, unless the Court finds the facts to be as the defendants believe them to be, or to put this in another way, the Act cannot give protection to this dispute unless the Court finds as a fact that the dismissal concerned was an act of victimisation by the plaintiff and that their purpose of so dismissing him was to turn the Silver Tassie into a non-Union house. No authority was cited for this proposition, but it was argued that unless the Court finds that the reasons put forward for the dispute are well founded, the defendants were being allowed to be the judges in their own cause.

[9.08] The Chief Justice also referred to *Conway v Wade* (para **9.05**), *per* Lord Loreburn. Further than this, he said, the cases had not gone. Clearly a dispute had to be genuine and not merely tolerable. So long as it was *bona fide* believed by the parties to be a dispute, the court would be satisfied. The court was of the opinion that the dispute raised by the union was the dismissal of the worker concerned and Pinkerton's refusal to reinstate him. The alleged victimisation and the alleged attempt to turn the place of employment into a non-union house may well have been the motives which led the defendants to raise the dispute but the trial judge looked upon those two issues for only one purpose, namely to ascertain whether the dispute was genuine or not. He found that the dispute was *bona fide*. The Supreme Court upheld this view.

[9.09] The *Silver Tassie* case was followed in *Ardmore Studios (Ir) Ltd v Lynch and Others*[13] where Budd J declared that the High Court did not have to determine on the facts whether there was in law (as the defendants alleged) a mutually agreed

---

12.   *Silver Tassie Co Ltd v Cleary* [1958] 92 ILTR 27 at 31.
13.   *Ardmore Studios (Ir) Ltd v Lynch and Ors* [1965] IR 1. Also in *Maher v Beirne* 63 ILTR 101 where Dixon J decided the question of the genuineness of the reasons for the dismissals in question although it was unnecessary for him to do so. All that needed to be proved (at 105), following his decision in the *Silver Tassie* case, was that there was a genuine belief that the two employees were dismissed because they had joined or intended to join the union and that there were grounds for that belief. See also *Educational Co of Ire Ltd v Fitzpatrick* [1961] IR 345.

arrangement of a binding nature for the supply of electricians to the company in accordance with a seniority panel (see para **9.11**) but rather 'whether there was on the part of the Union a genuine and *bona fide* belief that such an arrangement existed.'[14] This exercise will almost invariably involve considering whether the union was in reality inventing facts on which it could be stated that a dispute existed.

In the *Ardmore* case the plaintiff company carried on the business of managing film production studies. The company maintained a small permanent staff, and employed other staff, including electricians, on a non-permanent basis as required. An agreement was completed between the company and the Trade Union Studio Committee, consisting of representations of various unions whose members were employed at the studios. A list of names was compiled on which were placed the names of certain electricians who would be available for work when called upon by the company. These persons belonged to the Electrical Trades Union (Ireland) (ETU). This was known as the 'seniority list'. A dispute arose between the company and the electricians named on the seniority list and their union, and a picket was placed on the studio premises owned by the company. The dispute came before Budd J who refused to grant an injunction on the ground that the defendants at the date of the picketing had a *bona fide* belief that there was a binding agreement in existence whereby the company was bound to recruit from the seniority list.

[9.10] Subsequent to these proceedings, the business at the studios virtually closed down and the Industrial Credit Company, as holders of a debenture on the assets of the company, which was security for advances made to the company, appointed a receiver/manager who entered into possession of the studios and took over the management of the company. He agreed to let the studios to an English producer for production of a film and entered into an agreement with a group of unions for the supply of labour necessary for production of the film. The ETU was not a party to this agreement and labour was not recruited from its members or from the seniority list which had existed. The ETU and some members whose names were on the seniority list alleged that agreement existed between the ETU and the company by which the company was bound to recruit electricians from the seniority list. A picket was once more placed on the studios and the company sought to restrain it. McLoughlin J granted the relief sought because at the date of the second picket, the alleged agreement between the company and the union as to the seniority list had, he found, ceased to operate. Whatever about the binding nature of the agreement between the ETU and the company, even if in existence at the date of the appointment of the receiver/manager, it was not binding upon the receiver/manager.[15] The judge rejected the defendants' claim that even if the agreement was not binding on the receiver, the defendants *bona fide* believed it to be binding and had reasonable grounds for so believing. The union:

> tried to raise a dispute; ... the dispute the union sought to raise was based on a contention that the seniority list was binding on the receiver and that it was his

---

14.   *Ardmore Studios (Ir) Ltd v Lynch and Ors* [1965] IR 1 at 21.

15.   *In re Johnson & Co (Builders) Ltd* [1955] 1 CW 634 and *Robbie & Co v Witney Warehouse Co* [1963] 3 All ER 613 considered.

breach of that agreement which entitled the union to put a picket on the premises.[16]

McLoughlin J described the union as entirely misconceived in stating that the seniority list was endorsed in the High Court by Budd J. The defendants had invented a dispute in circumstances where they were either misconceived or mistaken, hence they could not be afforded the Act's protection.

[9.11] Very often inter-union disputes can create difficulties as to their genuineness. Recognition issues are particularly prone to accusations of inter-union rivalry. In *JT Stratford & Son Ltd v Lindley*[17] the appellants obtained an interlocutory injunction in the High Court, which was discharged in the Court of Appeal and was re-imposed in the House of Lords. The House held that the respondents who were officers of a trade union had not established a *prima facie* case that there was a trade dispute. On the facts it held that the respondents were acting only in the advancement of their union's prestige in rivalry with another union, and that they were not acting on behalf of any workman, or a refusal of such a claim. That case was distinguished by the Supreme Court in *Becton Dickinson Ltd v Lee*[18] (para **9.21** *et seq*), where Walsh J thought the facts before him fitted more neatly into the words used by Lord Pearce in *Lindley's* case:[19]

> when a union makes a genuine claim on the employers for bargaining status with a view to regulating or improving the conditions or pay of their workmen and the employers reject the claim, a trade dispute is in contemplation even though no active dispute has yet arisen.

The claim for recognition was genuine and *bona fide* and was therefore entitled to protection.

Acquiescence in, communication of, grievance

[9.12] A dispute remains a dispute when acquiescence by an employer is only apparent, due to the fact that he had no other choice: *B & I Steampacket Co Ltd v Branigan*.[20] Acquiescence will not necessarily be inferred in the case of workers who do not support a dispute: *Brennan v Glennon*.[21] But a dispute, as such, cannot go on forever. The onus of proving that a trade dispute continues to exist at the time of the trial is on the person asserting it. Counsel for the defendant's contention that 'once a trade dispute always a trade dispute' was roundly rejected by the Supreme Court in *Esso Teo v McGowan*.[22] If that were correct, said Griffin J, it could lead to strange and unjust results. For example, a workman who had a genuine trade dispute with his employer, and peacefully picketed the employer's premises in furtherance of it, could,

16.   *Ardmore Studios (Ir) Ltd v Lynch and Ors* [1965] IR 1 at 40–1.
17.   *JT Stratford & Son Ltd v Lindley* [1965] AC 269, 307.
18.   *Becton Dickinson Ltd v Lee* [1973] IR 1.
19.   *JT Stratford & Son Ltd v Lindley* [1965] AC 269 at 334.
20.   *B & I Steampacket Co Ltd v Branigan* [1958] IR 128, 102.
21.   *Brennan v Glennon* (26 November 1975, unreported), SC.
22.   *Esso Teo v McGowan* [1974] IR 148.

when the dispute was not resolved to his satisfaction, emigrate, work abroad for several years, retire from that employment, return home and resume picketing his former employer's premises. In the judge's opinion, 'although a trade dispute can be continued for very many years by appropriate action', it does in fact require such action to ensure its continuance. In the case before him, the defendant's behaviour was inconsistent with that of someone in a dispute. He gave no explanation of his delay with regard to various matters of pleading. Moreover, after his dismissal by the plaintiff (the alleged subject matter of the dispute), he had worked for nine months as a taxi driver and for over two years as a driver technician. In Budd J's opinion, the defendant had not taken all steps to keep the dispute alive. The Chief Justice put the matter more forcefully. On the evidence, the defendant had, long prior to commencing his action, abandoned his claim to be in dispute with his previous employer.

[9.13] An uncommunicated grievance cannot constitute a trade dispute. In some cases, a grievance may not need to be communicated expressly: the surrounding circumstances will make it apparent to the employer. In *Quigley v Beirne,*[23] the trial judge, Dixon J, found that neither of the employees had questioned the right of the plaintiff to dismiss him at any time prior to the commencement of the picketing. *Inter alia,* no request for reinstatement of either of the employees had been made nor had there been any request to submit the question to the union or to a conciliation board. The plaintiff was never informed of the reason for the picketing except in so far as he might infer it from prior letters from the union nor was he informed of what the union considered to be the trade dispute to which the placards of the pickets referred. The trial judge's findings were not upheld by the Supreme Court, however, which held on the facts that a trade dispute had arisen and 'that the employer was under no illusion as to the cause of the picketing.'[24] If the facts had been indicative of a grievance existing totally in the minds of the defendants, the outcome would have been otherwise.

Unconstitutional or illegal subject matter

[9.14] The subject matter of a trade dispute cannot offend against the spirit or letter of the Constitution. On fundamental rights that may be affected by industrial action, see **Ch 1**. Strikes or industrial action for purposes which violate constitutional rights will not be protected and nor, in all likelihood, will steps taken leading up to such action.

Likewise where the subject matter of a dispute is illegal, statutory immunities will not be extended to action taken in contemplation or furtherance thereof: *Doran v Lennon*[25] (it would have been illegal for the plaintiffs to pay increased wages without permission of the Minister by reason of an Emergency Powers Order, No 260 of 1943) and *Corry v NUVGATA*[26] (employment of a boy under 16 illegal). If a dispute has the object of making that which is unlawful lawful, it would be covered.

---

23.   *Quigley v Beirne* [1955] IR 62.
24.   *Quigley v Beirne* [1955] IR 62 at 74 *per* O'Byrne J.
25.   *Doran v Lennon* [1945] IR 315.
26.   *Corry v NUVGATA* [1950] IR 315.

The employment or non-employment of any person

[9.15] This phrase is considered under parties to the dispute, specifically in relation to 'workers' (para **9.32** *et seq*).

Terms or conditions of, or affecting the employment, of any person

[9.16] In order to obtain the protection of the 1990 Act, a trade dispute must be not only genuine but, as required by the definition of a trade dispute, it must be connected with 'the employment or non-employment or the terms or conditions of or affecting the employment, of any person'. Purely political disputes (eg, to bring down the government) are impliedly excluded.

Since the legislature made a distinction between the expressions 'terms' and 'conditions' of employment, it must mean it was intended that 'conditions of employment' should mean something different from, or additional to, 'terms of employment'. Some light may be cast on this from the era of the 1906 Act. In *Brendan Dunne Ltd v Fitzpatrick*[27] Budd J thought that in their ordinary meaning *prima facie* the words 'conditions of labour' of a workman appear to refer to the physical conditions under which a workman works such as appertain to matters of safety and physical comfort. The 'terms of employment' of a worker, on the other hand, either express or implied, appear to refer to matters such as hours of work, wages, holidays and overtime. The difficulty about this approach is that it conveys a false impression that matters of safety and physical comfort are not contractual matters. Frequently these will concern implied terms of the contract at common law.

Some conditions of labour may also be terms of employment. Likewise, indeed, terms of employment may include physical as well as psychological[28] conditions of work.

[9.17] An earlier decision that disputes as to training or business hours alone do not fall within the definition must be doubted. In *The Esplanade Pharmacy Ltd v Larkin*[29] the plaintiff company owned a chemist's shop, of which the directors were husband and wife. They employed a Miss M, a member of the Workers Union of Ireland (WUI). By an agreement between the Irish Drug Association of which the plaintiff company was a member and the WUI, the hours of duty of the union's members were limited to two hours on alternate Sundays and bank holidays. In the summer of 1953 the company stayed open all day on Sundays but outside those two permitted working hours, one or other or both of the directors attended the shop so that Miss M's conditions of labour were in no way affected. Following the representations of an employee of an adjacent chemist, the union requested the company to close the shop except for the permitted hours of duty. The union alleged that, by keeping open in the way it did, the hours and conditions of work of members of the union employed in the area might be worsened by reason of other chemists' shops resorting to the same course. Upon the company's refusal to accede to this request, the union instructed Miss M to leave her employment,

---

27. *Brendan Dunne Ltd v Fitzpatrick* [1958] IR 29 at 37.
28. *Scala Ballroom (Wolverhampton) Ltd v Ratcliffe* [1958] 3 All ER 220; *Elston v State Services Commission (No 5)* 1 NZLR 218, 234.
29. *The Esplanade Pharmacy Ltd v Larkin* (1954) 92 ILTR 149.

which she did. The union then picketed the premises. The Supreme Court held that the action of the WUI was an attempt to enforce an agreement as to trading hours for the particular premises involved, and that was a matter concerned with the employer's business rather than with the employee's conditions. There was therefore no trade dispute.[30] A trade dispute might arise in the future with other employers but what had happened so far was but a prelude to such a dispute. The dividing line is thin indeed. Business or trading hours are obviously interrelated with terms of employment.

[9.18] The *Esplanade* case was distinguished in *Brendan Dunne Ltd v Fitzpatrick*[31] where a union, acting for its members and at their request, asked the plaintiff company and its employees to cease the practice of opening and working late on one day in the week. The original complaint could not be regarded as a trade dispute having regard to the Supreme Court decision in the *Esplanade* case. Budd J could, however, distinguish the two cases by virtue of the fact that at a later stage in the dispute before him a letter had been addressed by the general secretary of the union to the staff of the plaintiff company, enclosing a resolution adopted by certain workers in the furniture trade in Dublin who were members of the union, calling upon the staff of the plaintiff company to refuse to observe hours of work outside those generally recognised by the trade. The staff failed to comply with that demand. As a result, the defendants were able to argue that the dispute arising between workmen and workmen related to the terms of employment or conditions of labour of those persons who were in the plaintiff company's employment, and that the dispute fell properly within the Act. Budd J held that the plaintiff company and the staff had entered into contractual relations with each other when they agreed to the opening of the premises, and working unusually late hours on one day a week. This agreement as to late hours was one which related to the terms of the employment of the company's employees.

[9.19] Therefore the dispute which arose between the defendants on the one hand, and the employees of the plaintiff company on the other, as to the hours of trading was a trade dispute within the Act of 1906 (a dispute could be between workmen and workmen under the 1906 Act). There is no reason why a court faced today with a dispute concerning trading or business hours under the 1990 Act should not regard these as involving terms of employment and, as such, of interest to other employees in the trade or business. The union would be taking up the cudgels on their behalf.

[9.20] The subject matter of a trade dispute might also concern fringe benefits and pensions (deferred pay),[32] allocation of work or work duties, disciplinary and grievance matters (though not in relation to one worker only, para **9.26**), trade union facilities, machinery for negotiation or consultation and procedures relating thereto.

The words 'of any person' in s 8 may be significant. Provided the dispute is between the proper parties, it would seem its subject matter may concern persons who are not

---

30. The case was followed in a similar dispute in *Bolger v O'Donoghue and Anor* (1957, unreported), HC Dixon J.

31. *Brendan Dunne Ltd v Fitzpatrick* [1958] IR 29.

32. *Universe Tankships Inc v International Transport Workers' Federation* [1983] 1 AC 366.

workers. Arguably they need not reside in Ireland.[33] Irish workers could therefore take industrial action to support colleagues in transnational enterprises.

The phrase terms or conditions 'affecting the employment' of any person enables a trade dispute to cover a broad spectrum of employment issues, eg workers' loss of overtime or similar work opportunities through sub-contracting or outsourcing.

Recognition disputes

[9.21] A recognition dispute comes within s 8 of the 1990 Act on the authority of *Becton Dickinson Ltd v Lee.*[34] 'Recognition' as defined by the Supreme Court in that case means that members of a union working in a particular firm desire their union to be accepted by the employer as their spokesperson and their negotiating agent in respect of their terms and conditions of employment.

Becton Dickinson broke new ground. In *EI Co Ltd v Kennedy*[35] Walsh J pointed out that there had been no decision of the courts in this country to the effect that a 'recognition dispute' is a trade dispute within the Act of 1906. But he did not suggest in any way that it could be so. He observed that there had been no decision on whether the Trade Disputes Act 1906, s 5, embraced either

(a)   a union's claims to be recognised as the sole representative of all the workers in a particular category of employment with an employer whether such workers are members or not, or

(b)   a claim by such employees as are members of a trade union to have that trade union accepted as the spokesman and representative of such member employees in any negotiations on questions of terms of employment or conditions of employment whether or not there is currently a dispute between the members and the employer under either of those headings.

[9.22] *Becton Dickinson* concerned a claim within the second paragraph. *Sherriff v McMullen*[36] was a precedent authority which *prima facie* did not augur well for the union in *Becton Dickinson*. In it Kingsmill Moore J had declared that the connection between a trade dispute and the terms of employment must be 'direct' and that, in the case of a recognition dispute, that connection did not exist.

The trade union did not have any members at the time of the dispute in the employment of the plaintiff; the employees who had been members had already resigned from the union undoubtedly influenced by their employer. The union claimed that the resignations were ineffective and sought to carry on a dispute on behalf of its alleged employee members. The resignations from the union were held to be effective. The union therefore was not acting for anybody. It did not claim to carry on the dispute on behalf of other members not in the employment of the plaintiff. It was held by Kingsmill Moore J that, as the union was not acting for any of its members, the union's

---

33.   See Wedderburn, 'Multi-National Enterprise and National Labour Law' (1972) 1 ILJ I2.

34.   *Becton Dickinson Ltd v Lee* [1973] IR 1.

35.   *EI Co Ltd v Kennedy* [1969] IR 69, 83.

36.   *Sherriff v McMullen* [1952] IR 236.

fight about the right of an employer to influence his workers to leave their union was not sufficient to create a trade dispute. In that context Kingsmill Moore J said:

> I think the connection with the terms of employment or conditions of labour, to which the definition section refers, must be something much more direct or immediate than any connection which is here suggested. The law is not disposed to attach legal consequences to such remote causes and I cannot hold that there was any trade dispute in existence ...

[9.23] In *Becton Dickinson*, however, Walsh J went to some lengths to establish that a recognition dispute was not a remote cause or issue. He declared that if workmen designate their trade union to be their spokesperson or representative in any negotiations on questions of terms or conditions of employment, whether or not there are currently negotiations or a dispute on these topics, they are doing something which is connected with their employment, and which they are endeavouring to make a term of their employment:

> if an employer refuses to treat with their designated representative or spokesman, then that refusal can constitute a dispute which is connected with the employment or the terms of the employment of the workmen and, therefore, can be a trade dispute.

The matter was no different when the workmen concerned had entered into a contract with their employer which, either expressly or by implication, stipulated that the workman's trade union should not be his spokesperson or representative. That was the factual position in *Becton Dickinson*. The workers' contracts of employment, which contained express undertakings on their part to join the National Engineering and Electrical Trade Union, excluded by implication any other trade union from representing them. The Commission of Inquiry on Industrial Relations in 1981 recommended that recognition disputes be removed from the Trade Disputes Act's protection[37] but the Oireachtas declined to take such a step in the 1990 Act.

Rights do not need to be strictly contractual

[9.24] The subject matter of a trade dispute is not confined to disagreement about contractual rights. In *Quigley v Beirne*[38] Lavery J said that the 1906 Act:

> is designed to permit within carefully designed limits certain actions to secure recognition of extra-legal claims of a particular nature and to bring pressure to bear on employers to observe certain principles and standards which the law does not impose.

Conflicts of interest as well as of rights are covered. Trade disputes may involve matters of legal right but ordinarily they are concerned with other matters. Lavery J further offered the view that, where contractual or other legal rights are concerned, the courts are the appropriate place for their enforcement. The absence of, for example, a legally binding agreement could not be cited by a plaintiff in his favour.[39]

---

37.   *Report*, para 685.

38.   *Quigley v Beirne* [1955] IR 62, 76.

39.   See *Ardmore Studios (Ir) Ltd v Lynch* [1965] IR 1.

[9.25] The Commission of Inquiry on Industrial Relations (1981) considered the distinction between disputes as to right and disputes as to interest.[40] It considered that where independent machinery had been established by statute to enable aggrieved persons to pursue their cases to finality, such persons should not be entitled to attempt to by-pass these procedures or to overturn decisions lawfully taken by having recourse to industrial action. The Commission recommended, therefore, that the statutory definition of a trade dispute should exclude disputes concerning dismissals and disputes arising under statutory anti-discrimination law. As will be seen in the next paragraph, the 1990 Act adopted a position heedful of this recommendation, while following a different course.

One-worker disputes

[9.26] Under s 9(2) of the 1990 Act, if the subject matter of a trade dispute concerns 'the employment or non-employment or the terms or conditions of employment of or affecting the employment of one individual worker' and 'the agreed procedures availed of by custom or in practice in the employment concerned, or provided for in a collective agreement, for the resolution of individual grievances, including dismissals … have not been resorted to and exhausted' the Act's protections under ss 10, 11 and 12 will not apply. This section exercises an important normative influence on the collective parties. It respects the distinction between disputes of right as against disputes of interest, and encourages the use of agreed procedures for disputes involving only one worker. Not infrequently, a dispute over, say, dismissal attracted a picket and brought a business to a standstill.

[9.27] The procedures envisaged by the Act may be internal or external and, if the latter, may involve resort to statutory officers or bodies such as a rights commissioner, the Labour Relations Commission, the Labour Court, the Director of the Equality Tribunal and the Employment Appeals Tribunal, but shall not include an appeal to any court: s 9(4). Generally, therefore, disputes about individual statutory rights do not obtain statutory immunity, something recommended by the Commission of Inquiry on Industrial Relations.[41]

[9.28] Depending on the circumstances, the procedures could be disciplinary or grievance procedures. The Act deems procedures to be exhausted if at any stage an employer fails or refuses to comply with them: s 9(3). A dispute as to whether procedures have been exhausted, or are deemed to be exhausted, could itself be a 'trade dispute' within the Act and fall to be dealt with in the normal way. Where there are procedures, but they are not 'normally' availed of, ie they have fallen by the wayside, the section will not have any relevance.

This subsection was successfully invoked in *Iarnród Éireann v Darby and O'Connor*.[42]

---

40.   *Report*, paras 686–710.
41.   Paras 701–704 of its *Report*.
42.   *Iarnród Éireann v Darby and O'Connor* (1991) *Irish Times*, 23 March, Morris J.

Political disputes

[9.29] The definition of the parties to a trade dispute excludes industrial action against the government unless the workers are employed by it. But, as Kahn-Freund wrote:

> Whatever the political colour of the Government, it is involved in industry, and the organisations of both sides of industry are involved in Government. Is not every major industrial problem a problem of governmental economic policy? Is it not true that, not only in publicly owned industries, governmental decisions on wages policies – whether statutory or not – on credits and on subsidies, on the distribution of industry and on housing and town planning, and on a thousand other things, affect the terms and conditions of employment at least as much as the decisions of individual firms. Where is the line between a strike to induce an employer to raise, or not to reduce, wages and a strike to press the government for measures which would enable the employer to do so?[43]

In *BBC v Hearn*[44] (para **9.79**), Roskill LJ observed that the phrase 'political dispute' is one which should be used in a court of law with considerable caution for it does not easily lend itself to precise or accurate definition. A dispute may appear superficially to be a political dispute and yet be *bona fide* because of its connection with terms and conditions of employment. If, for example, the effect of a wage freeze would affect claims already being processed, a dispute could be said to be connected with the statutory formula.

[9.30] In *Associated Newspapers Group Ltd v Flynn*[45] a one-day strike in protest against proposed industrial relations legislation, and in *Beaverbrook Newspapers Ltd v Keys*[46] a proposed 'Day of Action' against the UK government's economic policy, were respectively held not entitled to immunity. Little wonder that the President of the Services, Industrial, Professional and Technical Union (SIPTU) was quoted in October 2009[47] as saying that the industrial action and strikes forecast by Ireland's public sector trade unions for the weeks ahead (which included a national one-day strike) would not be against the pension levy or other government cutbacks but rather aimed at realising the terms of the national agreement reached a year before: '[To do the former] would take us into the realms of political strikes which are not provided for in the immunities that are set out in the [industrial relations] legislation'. The national agreement of September 2008 provided for increases of up to 6.5 per cent phased in over 21 months but the government froze such increases for more than 300,000 staff in the public sector. When the head of the Irish Bank Officials' Association apparently announced that the trade union movement needed to respond by taking action to oust the government[48], the general secretary of the Irish Congress of Trade Unions was quick to deny that the unions were planning anything of the sort or had any such policy.

---

43. Davies and Freedland, *Kahn-Freund's Labour and the Law* (3rd edn, Stevens & Sons, 1983), 317.

44. *BBC v Hearn* [1977] 1 WLR 1004, (1984) 3 JISLL 86.

45. *Associated Newspapers Group Ltd v Flynn* (1970) 10 KIR 17.

46. *Beaverbrook Newspapers Ltd v Keys* [1978] ICR 582.

47. (2009) *Irish Times*, 8 October.

48. (2009) *Irish Times*, 19 December.

The closer union activity comes to protesting about government policy, the greater the participants' potential exposure to liability, whether the policy affects them as workers or not.[49]

[9.31] Disputes on ideological grounds may or may not fall foul of the statutory protections. All will depend on the facts and their connection to the dispute's subject. For instance, if employees in a newspaper office threatened strike action should a particular article be published, that would probably not be protected, as the dispute would not be about terms and conditions of employment. Similarly, where employees pressurised an employer to dismiss someone who belonged, for example, to an extreme right-wing group, that would probably not be a trade dispute.

PARTIES

Workers

[9.32] The 1990 Act refers to the parties to a trade dispute in s 8; they are, quite simply, 'employers and workers'. In contrast, the Act of 1906 (s 5) stipulated that a trade dispute must be between 'employers and workmen or between workmen and workmen'. Until 1982 the expression 'workmen' in s 5 meant 'all persons employed in trade or industry, whether or not in the employment of the employer with whom a trade dispute arises.' It was a serious criticism of the Act of 1906 that, by virtue of judicial interpretation of s 5, the Act's protection was held to extend only to people working for commercial enterprises (although the government did not proceed against striking workers for damages or an injunction as they were entitled to do). Anyone employed in private industry or a commercial semi-state company was covered, but not public service employees, eg local authority, health and education workers. In earlier restrictive authorities such as *Smith v Beirne*,[50] it was held that a non-profit-making members' club was not 'employed in trade or industry' and hence could not be engaged in a trade dispute with the club. Similarly, in *British and Irish Steampacket Co v Branigan*,[51] it was held that a non-profit-making body could not be engaged in a trade dispute with it. These cases are now part of history.

[9.33] By virtue of the Trade Disputes (Amendment) Act 1982, the definition of 'workman' was amended to:

> all persons employed, whether or not in the employment of the employer with whom a trade dispute arises, but does not include a member of the Defence Forces or of the Garda Síochána.

---

49.   *National Union of Seamen and Firemen v Reed* [1926] 1Ch 536; *Duport Steels Ltd v Sirs* [1980] 1 WLR 142; *Westminster City Council v UNISON* [2001] IRLR 534 CA; *P v National Union of Schoolmasters/Union of Women Teachers* [2001] IRLR 532.

50.   *Smith v Beirne* [1954] 89 ILTR 24.

51.   *British and Irish Steampacket Co v Branigan* [1958] IR 128.

Under s 8 of the 1990 Act, a 'worker' for the purposes of trade disputes law in Pt II, means:

> any person who is or was employed whether or not in the employment of the employer with whom a trade dispute arises, but does not include a member of the Defence forces or of the Garda Síochána.

Today all workers are protected by the 1990 Act, with the exception of members of An Garda Síochána and the Defence Forces – 'worker and worker' disputes are no longer protected. Moreover, by not re-enacting the amendment of s 3 of the Conspiracy and Protection of Property Act 1875, contained in s 5(3) of the Act 1906, the protection from criminal conspiracy in relation to 'workmen and workmen' disputes is removed.

[9.34] Under the 1906 and 1990 Acts[52] the High Court has held that a 'fair issue' arises as to whether a self-employed person can be a proper party to a trade dispute. The term 'employed' is not defined as requiring a contract of employment. This could assume considerable importance in the context of s 11(1) of the 1990 Act, which concerns persons picketing at 'a place where *their* employer works or carries on business'. It is arguable that if they are not 'employees' (even if they are 'workers'), they are outside the subsection. The definition of 'employer' is wide enough to include a sub-contracting company,[53] someone working under a contract for services or indeed an individual sub-contractor.[54] The High Court has held that a 'fair issue' has arisen in a number of cases as to whether a person who is not employed under a contract of employment may claim statutory immunity.[55]

[9.35] Seasonal workers who are not re-engaged at the start of the new season[56] and temporary workers[57] are covered. Temporary agency workers are covered if employed under a contract of employment by an employer and, because of the width of the definition, temporary agency workers who are not 'employed' under a contract of employment by either the supplier or user of their labour[58] should likewise be covered.

Employment or non-employment

[9.36] The subject matter of a dispute can influence the 'parties' thereto. A 'trade dispute' under s 8 of the 1990 Act means a dispute, *inter alia*, which is connected with 'the employment or non-employment ... of any person.' A worker does not cease to be a worker because he has been dismissed and is out of employment, or has been forced

---

52. *Lamb Brothers (Dublin) Ltd v Davidson* [1978] ILRM 226; *Daru Blocklaying Ltd v Building and Allied Trades Union* [2002] 2 IR 619.

53. Contrast definitions for industrial relations generally in s 23 of the 1990 Act.

54. *Building and Allied Trade Union and Another v Labour Court* [2005] IEHC 109 at 125 per Murphy J.

55. Eg, *Lamb Brothers (Dublin) Ltd v Davidson* [1978] ILRM 226.

56. *McHenry Bros Ltd v Carey and Ors* (1984) 3 JISLL 80.

57. *Myerscough and Co Ltd v Kenny and Ors* (18 April 1975, unreported), HC.

58. They are expressly covered for unfair dismissal under the Unfair Dismissals (Amendment) Act 1993, s 13. See Kimber, 'Agency Workers and Employers' Responsibilities' (2005) 2 IELJ 79.

to take up other work, *per* Meredith J in *Ferguson v O'Gorman.*[59] The issue was not always free from confusion, however. In *Doran v Lennon*[60] Overend J (High Court) held that where employees on the instructions of their union had gone on strike after giving shorter notice than their contracts of employment required, their employer was entitled to regard this as a repudiation of their contracts of employment. Thereafter, there was no trade dispute in existence. Overend J declared that, if it were otherwise, every employee of a commercial firm who broke his contract and was dismissed for cause would be entitled to picket his late master's premises and yet claim the protection of the statute.[61] This view would now be regarded as wrong. It was rejected by the Supreme Court, which held the fact that the workers had had their employment lawfully terminated did *not* make them cease to be workers within the meaning of the Act: *Goulding Chemicals Ltd v Bolger.*[62]

[9.37] Is *every* person out of employment entitled to protection? In *Cunningham Bros Ltd v Kelly*[63] a dispute over a claim for higher redundancy payments than those in the Redundancy Payments Acts was held to be a 'trade dispute'. The 1990 Act does not use the expression 'dismissal' anywhere. 'Non-employment' in the 1906 Act was held to mean something different from, though not exclusive of, dismissal. It is difficult to ascertain the situations it was intended to include: *Bradbury Ltd v Duffy.*[64] In *Quigley v Beirne and Ors*[65] Dixon J said he thought the term meant something more like the attempt to compel the employment of a particular person but he was dealing with the case of a man who had been dismissed and it was not necessary for him to elaborate further. The judge referred, in this context, to *Barton v Harten*[66] (para **9.05**), in which an employee had been arrested and detained by the security forces for a year. After a reasonable interval, another person was employed in his place but, after his release, the union demanded the reinstatement of the man who had been detained although there was then no position available with his previous employer. It was held that there was no trade dispute:

> but only an attempt on the part of the organisation to compel an employer to give employment to one who had been out of his employment for a long time and whose position had been filled in the ordinary course.[67]

In *McHenry Bros Ltd v Carey,*[68] Hamilton J declared that the term 'non-employment' is much wider and must mean something more than mere 'dismissal'. It seemed to him

---

59. *Ferguson v O'Gorman* [1937] IR 620 at 634.
60. *Doran v Lennon* [1945] IR 315.
61. *Doran v Lennon* [1945] IR 315 at 326.
62. *Goulding Chemicals Ltd v Bolger* [1977] IR 211.
63. *Cunningham Bros Ltd v Kelly* (18 November 1974, unreported), HC.
64. *Bradbury Ltd v Duffy* (1984) 3 JISSL 86.
65. *Quigley v Beirne and Ors* [1955] IR 62 at 67.
66. *Barton v Harten* [1925] 2 IR 37.
67. *Barton v Harten* [1925] 2 IR 37 at 41.
68. *McHenry Bros Ltd v Carey* [1984] 3 JISLL 80.

there could be a valid trade dispute in respect of a person seeking initial employment as well as in respect of someone who is out of employment.

[9.38] McWilliam J was disturbed by the foregoing authorities in *Bradbury* (para **9.37**). While agreeing that the term 'non-employment' was much wider and must mean something more than 'dismissal,' it seemed to him there must be some restriction on the universality of the application of the term. To take an extreme case, he instanced a man starting a new business for which he requires 10 workmen. He may receive 50 applications but the judge did not accept the 40 unsuccessful applicants would be entitled to take any sort of industrial action solely because they had not been given jobs.[69] Again, in the case of a workman who has voluntarily left his job, a job which has since been filled, it could hardly be said that he is entitled to take industrial action because his former employer is unable to re-employ him at a job which is no longer available. In short the parameters of 'non-employment' are vague, a fact which could affect the issue of 'parties' to a trade dispute.

[9.39] As far as disputes regarding individual workers are concerned, the 1990 Act limits the immunities to cases where agreed procedures, if they exist, have been resorted to and exhausted: s 9 (para **9.26**).

Employer

[9.40] The 1990 Act, s 8, defines an 'employer' as 'a person for whom one or more workers work or have worked or normally work or seek to work having previously worked for that person.' This reflected then existing case law by clarifying that former workers, seasonal and casual workers, are within the scope of the Act. See too para **9.34**; the definition is wide enough to include a sub-contractor.

[9.41] Where a person with whom the workers or the union has a dispute is not an 'employer,' and does not employ labour, such a dispute is not a trade dispute within the Act. In *The Roundabout Ltd v Beirne*,[70] the owners of licensed premises closed them in circumstances giving rise to a trade dispute with the defendants. They then leased the premises with an option to purchase to the plaintiff company, the directors of which were the owners, their accountants and three barmen. When the licensed premises were subsequently reopened for business by the plaintiff company, the entire work of the premises was carried out by the directors themselves, no person being employed by them. The barman-directors were paid a fixed yearly sum by way of directors' remuneration at such irregular intervals and in such irregular proportions as was found convenient. The defendants had been picketing the premises throughout the period they were closed. They continued to picket them subsequent to their re-opening. Dixon J held that, as the plaintiff company was a legal entity distinct from the owners that had not taken over the licensed premises from the owners as a going concern, the trade

---

69. A view endorsed by O Higgins CJ in *Goulding Chemicals Ltd v Bolger* [1977] IR 211, 230 and by Costello J in *Michael McNamara & Co Ltd v Lacken* (1990 No 17675P) *ex tempore*.

70. *The Roundabout Ltd v Beirne* [1959] IR 423. See Ussher, *Company Law in Ireland* (Sweet & Maxwell, 1986), 26. See too para **10.99** re the injunction obtained in *Diageo*.

dispute with the owners did not attach to the premises as occupied by the plaintiff company.

[9.42] He further held the plaintiff company could not be 'employers' as it had thus far employed no staff. The judge conceded there was some basis for the suggestion that the new company was formed for the purpose of getting rid of the trade dispute, and also of enabling the employment of union staff to be dispensed with.[71] The formation of the new company might be a subterfuge, but the question he had to decide was not ruled by that:[72] 'the question I must decide is whether it is a successful subterfuge, capable of effectually achieving its purpose.' The case provides a rather startling example of the way in which, in appropriate circumstances, an employer might try to defeat the operation of the Act.

[9.43] *Roundabout* is not, however, a sound authority. There is no reason why the company could not have been regarded as an employer simply because it employed no staff. It had the competence and capacity to do so, and people would have been willing to seek work from it. The picketing of the premises in order to be reinstated turned the plaintiffs into an employer. A future court faced with the same issue is likely to look beneath any subterfuge, to the reality of the situation, as the Court of Appeal did in *Examite v Whittaker.*[73] There the Amalgamated Union of Engineering Workers had called a strike at a company called Baldwin's Industrial Services. Later a company called Examite Ltd was formed to trade under the name Cleveland Crane Hire. Only two shares were issued: one to the company's solicitor and one to the solicitor's secretary. This company soon took over the entire business of Baldwin's. As a result it argued it was not the employer with whom the defendants were in dispute. But Lord Denning was not convinced. He said, 'in these trade disputes I think we ought to pull aside any curtain over limited companies and see what the real truth is' and went on to say the plaintiffs were really the same employers as Baldwin's.

The definition of 'employer' in the 1990 Act refers, *inter alia*, to a person for whom workers 'seek to work having previously worked for that person'. This bolts the door of the *Roundabout* ruse.

[9.44] In the case of a transfer of undertaking, the transferee becomes the 'employer' of the transferred employees automatically. In *Westman Holdings Ltd v McCormack and Ors*[74] the defendants were employed by a company as bar and restaurant staff in a licensed premises. The lease of the premises expired whereupon the business was taken over by the immediate landlords who also took over the employment of the worker defendants. Soon afterwards the immediate landlords entered into a contract with the plaintiff to sell the premises together with fixtures and fittings with the benefit of the licence. Westman purported to terminate the employment of all employees in the premises, and business ceased a few weeks later. Prior to cessation of

---

71. *The Roundabout Ltd v Beirne* [1959] IR 423 at 427.
72. *The Roundabout Ltd v Beirne* [1959] IR 423 at 427.
73. *Examite v Whittaker* [1977] IRLR 312. Today transfer of undertakings law would apply to the facts.
74. *Westman Holdings Ltd v McCormack and Ors* [1991] ILRM 833.

the business, each worker defendant had received a sum of money and signed a discharge form acknowledging that this amount was in total discharge of all claims due to them and without admission of liability.

[9.45] An official of the Irish National Union of Grocers and Allied Trades Assistants, the eighth-named defendant and the trade union of which the worker defendants were members, claimed on their behalf that they were entitled to continue in the employment of the plaintiff under the European Communities (Safeguarding of Employees' Rights on Transfer of Undertaking) Regulations 1980.[75] The plaintiff rejected this claim and the worker defendants commenced to picket the premises by means of an official picket organised by their trade union. An interim order was granted restraining the picketing, and the picket was removed. An interlocutory order was then granted. The defendants appealed to the Supreme Court where two issues of law arose: first, whether the defendants' action in picketing the premises was protected by the provisions of s 11(1) of the 1990 Act on the basis that the plaintiff must be deemed to be their 'employer' within the meaning of the Act; and second, whether what had taken place between the plaintiff and the landlords constituted a transfer of undertaking and, if it did, whether the consequence was that the plaintiff must be deemed to be the employer of the defendants.

[9.46] The Supreme Court made an order continuing the interlocutory injunction on the basis that there were fair and *bona fide* questions to be tried on the legal issues raised. The plaintiff contended that none of the worker defendants was ever employed by it. The worker defendants submitted that 'their employer' in s 11 (1) of the 1990 Act must be construed as including an 'alleged employer', that is to say, a person claimed by a worker to have a contract of employment with him or an obligation to employ him, otherwise the subsection would lose its obvious purpose of protecting picketing in support of a dispute concerning non-employment. The court was satisfied this was a fair *bona fide* issue to be tried.

Employer-employer disputes

[9.47] Disputes between employers and employers are excluded from the definition of a 'trade dispute'. The Act does not apply, therefore, if there is a dispute between employers, or between an employer and his association, and a trade union decides to support one side or the other. *Larkin v Long*[76] concerned a refusal by a Master Stevedore to join the employers' association and, in an effort to force him to do so, the officials of his labourers' union called the labourers out on strike in breach of contract. The jury found that there was no dispute between an individual employer and his association. There was therefore no trade dispute. The House of Lords held that there was evidence on which the jury could reach this conclusion. On another view the case could be said to have affected terms and conditions of employment. Membership of the employers' association was promoted with the object of improving labour conditions

---

75.   Now the EC (Protection of Employees' Rights on Transfer of Undertakings) Regs 2003 (SI 131/2003).

76.   *Larkin v Long* [1915] AC 814. See, too, *Kantoher Co-op v Costello* (23 August 1984, unreported), HC.

in the docks, and the labour union had agreed that no union men would work for a non-member.

[9.48] Section 18 of the 1990 Act provides that ss 14–17 shall not apply to a trade union of employers. Ten employer associations are registered trade unions, including the Construction Industry Federation (CIF) and the Irish Business and Employers Confederation (IBEC).[77]

Trade unions

[9.49] A trade dispute is not limited to disputes between individuals, ie between an employer and his workers. It may be a dispute between a workers' trade union and an employer. A trade union never operates *in vacuo* but fulfils, or attempts to fulfil, its functions on behalf of its members. In so far as 'workers' under s 8 need not be in the employment of the employer with whom a trade dispute arises, a trade union that represents its worker-members should qualify as a proper party under the Act (provided the Act's other requirements are met).[78] This should certainly apply where trade unions are acting in a representative capacity.[79] It should also apply where none of the persons whose employment provides the subject matter of the dispute are members of the trade union as the Act, with the exception of s 11 on picketing, does not restrict its protection to circumstances where workers in a dispute are employed by the employer who is a party to the dispute. A trade union, it will be recalled, is an unincorporated association of workmen. The liability of a trade union *qua* trade union is not here in issue: s 13 of the Act of 1990 prohibits actions against trade unions, or against any members of the trade union, in respect of any tortious act alleged to have been committed in contemplation or furtherance of a trade dispute by or on behalf of the trade union. A trade union cannot be injuncted or proceeded against in tort (see further **Ch 6**).

[9.50] As has already been seen, past Irish courts have been over-fearful of trade unions stirring up trouble in a way injurious to individual rights and freedoms. Trade unions have been regarded as meddlers – see, for example, *Ryan v Cooke*[80] and *Doran*

---

77.   *Report of the Registrar of Friendly Societies 2006* at 16.

78.   Hence there must be a trade dispute as required and trade unions cannot 'with impunity intermeddle with relationships between employers and workers' initiating their own dispute with an employer as to the terms and conditions of employment even where 'perfect peace prevailed': *NWL Ltd v Woods* [1979] ICR 867, 877 *per* Lord Diplock. The Donovan Commission's Report (Cmnd 3623, para 822) recognised the fact that a trade union could qualify as a proper party: a dispute over the matters specified in the former s 5(3) of the Act of 1906 (now s 8 of the 1990 Act) between an employers' association representing employers and a trade union representing workmen was regarded by the Commission as a dispute between employers and workmen so as to qualify as a trade dispute.

79.   *Smith v Beirne* (1954) 89 ILTR 24 at 38 *per* Ó Dálaigh and *NALGO v Bolton Corporation* [1943] AC 166, *per* Lord Wright.

80.   *Ryan v Cooke* [1938] IR 512.

v Lennon[81] where no trade dispute was held to exist since none of the union members were employees of the employer with whom the union was in dispute.[82] In *Sherriff v McMullen*[83] Maguire CJ said there might be occasions on which members of a trade union might have a trade dispute with an employer, even though none of the employer's employees was a member of the trade union but went on to aver that 'it is not every dispute with a trade union which is a trade dispute'.[84] Where a dispute concerns the employment of persons who are not 'workers,' Dixon J took the view in a number of cases that a trade union cannot supply the missing element unless the union consists wholly of workers. This view was propounded in *Smith v Beirne*,[85] *Esplanade Pharmacy Ltd v Larkin*[86] and *B & I Steampacket Co Ltd v Branigan*.[87] In *Smith v Beirne* a majority of the Supreme Court accepted that the parties to a trade dispute could be an employer and a trade union which acted on behalf of its members in the trade of the employer, even where there was no actual dispute between the employer and his employees. In *Brendan Dunne Ltd v Fitzpatrick*[88] none of the employees of the plaintiffs were in dispute with their employer. It was the union of which the defendants were members that had raised such disputes as existed, acting on behalf of their members working in allied trades to that of the plaintiff. Budd J was satisfied that a section of the members of the union engaged in the trade had genuinely regarded themselves as aggrieved. The union merely voiced these objections and acted on their behalf so the dispute was one between workmen and an employer within the meaning of the definition. Budd J's decision, as he later said in *Ardmore Studios (Ire) Ltd v Lynch*,[89] amounted to a finding:

> that a union, acting on behalf of the workmen members, not employees of the particular employer with whom a dispute arises, can validly create a dispute with such an employer so that it falls within the definition of a trade dispute within the meaning of the Act.

[9.51] In *Ardmore Studios (Ir) Ltd v Lynch*[90] (para **9. 09**), it was submitted in the High Court before Budd J that a trade union can legitimately dispute on behalf of its members with an employer even though there is no dispute between that particular employer and any of its employees, whether trade union members or not, at the time. In that case the dispute was alleged to concern a seniority list notwithstanding the fact that none of the men affected were employed at the moment of the dispute. Budd J

---

81. *Doran v Lennon* [1945] IR 315.

82. McLoughlin J approved of this approach in *Crowley v Cleary* [1968] IR 261.

83. *Sherriff v McMullen* [1952] IR 236 at 252.

84. At 252. See *McCobb v Doyle* [1938] IR 444. Lord Parker in *Larkin v Long* [1915] AC 814 also conceded that there were situations where a dispute between an employer and officials of a trade union who had 'chosen to interfere' would be a trade dispute.

85. *Smith v Beirne* [1954] 89 ILTR 24.

86. *Esplanade Pharmacy Ltd v Larkin* 92 ILTR 149.

87. *B & I Steampacket Co Ltd v Branigan* [1958] IR 128.

88. *Brendan Dunne Ltd v Fitzpatrick* [1958] IR 29.

89. *Ardmore Studios (Ir) Ltd v Lynch* [1965] IR 1 at 16.

90. *Ardmore Studios (Ir) Ltd v Lynch* [1965] IR 1.

noted the reference to acting 'on behalf of a trade union' in s 2 of the Act of 1906. It was significant that picketing might be lawful if done on behalf of a trade union 'which carried at least some implication that the Legislature regarded trade unions as bodies with whom disputes may arise.'[91] However, he considered that, taken in conjunction with the definition of a trade dispute, it must be shown that the union 'is acting on behalf of its workmen members'. This means a trade union will not be protected it if initiates a dispute itself. Yet it would be wrong to assume that, in so doing, a trade union is necessarily acting on a frolic of its own.

[9.52] Later authority exhibits a similarly restrictive approach: *Reg Armstrong Motors Ltd v CIE*.[92] There Hamilton J seemed to exclude the possibility of a trade union being a proper party to a trade dispute involving lay-offs. He pointed out that all the employees of the plaintiff company who were members of the union concerned (ATGWU) had accepted the terms of an agreement proposed by the plaintiff's company. Consequently, there was no trade dispute between them and the plaintiff company. Such dispute as there was, was either between the plaintiff company and the ATGWU, or between the ATGWU and their members with a third party (General Motors Ireland Ltd). If, said Hamilton J, the dispute was between the ATGWU as such and the plaintiff company, that was not a valid trade dispute within the meaning of the Act of 1906. This must be wrong. The union continued to be concerned about the possible effect of future diversification on its members' conditions of employment. The ATGWU comprised 'workmen' within the meaning of the Act of 1906 and, it may be recalled, there was nothing in that Act which limited immunities to disputes between an employer and *his* employees.[93]

[9.53] Normally a union will have initiated a dispute on behalf of its members. The point was made by Lord Wright in *NALGO v Bolton Corporation*:[94]

> it would be strangely out of date to hold, as was argued, that a trade union cannot act on behalf of its members in a trade dispute, or that a difference between a trade union acting for its members and their employer cannot be a trade dispute.

Distinguish a situation where union members or officials act unconstitutionally, purporting to start a dispute on behalf of their members, which was not authorised by them. An official who acts 'on a frolic of his own' is not protected: *McCobb v Doyle*.[95]

[9.54] The 1990 Act maintains uncertainty regarding a trade union as party to a trade dispute where none of its members are in dispute with the employer party.

---

91. *Ardmore Studios (Ir) Ltd v Lynch* [1965] IR 1 at 14.

92. *Reg Armstrong Motors Ltd v CIE* (2 December 1975, unreported), HC.

93. See on this a case where a valid trade dispute had been found in such circumstances: *Beetham v Trinidad Cement Ltd* [1960] AC 132.

94. *NALGO v Bolton Corporation* [1943] AC 166 at 189.

95. *McCobb v Doyle* [1938] IR 144.

The meaning of 'trade union' for trade disputes law

[9.55] 'Trade unions' (see also para 1.07 *et seq*) are expressly referred to in the 1990 Act in reference to the restriction of immunities (s 9(1)), picketing (s 11) and to immunity from suit in tort (s 13). A trade union for purposes of Pt II of the 1990 Act means 'a trade union which is the holder of a negotiation licence under Pt II of the Trade Union Act 1941', ie an authorised trade union. There are at present some 55 such bodies, 45 of which are employee unions. Section 5 of the Trade Union Act 1941 enacts that a 'negotiation licence' means a licence issued by the Minister for Trade, Industry and Innovation authorising its holder to carry on negotiations for the fixing of wages or other conditions of employment. In Pt II of the Act of 1941 the word 'members', where it applies to a body not registered in the State under the Trade Union Acts 1871 to 1935, means 'members of such body resident within the State.'

[9.56] No body may be granted or hold a negotiation licence unless it is an authorised trade union fulfilling the conditions in s 7 of the Act of 1941. It is not lawful for any body of persons 'not being an excepted body' to carry on negotiations for the fixing of wages and conditions of employment unless it is the holder of a negotiation licence. 'Excepted bodies,' defined in s 6 of the 1941 Act[96] do not enjoy statutory immunities (hence Iarnród Éireann could claim damages in tort against the Irish Locomotive Drivers' Association and its officers in *Iarnród Éireann v Holbrooke and Ors*[97] although the claim was unsuccessful on the evidence).

Immunity in tort for trade unions

[9.57] Section 13 of the Industrial Relations Act 1990 protects trade unions from actions in tort where 'the golden formula' (para **9.76**) is satisfied. The section is sometimes thought of, incorrectly, as a catch-all section protecting trade unions where ss 11 and 12 of the 1990 Act do not apply. Section 13 reads:

> 13—(1) An action against a trade union, whether of workers or employers, or its trustees or against any members or officials thereof on behalf of themselves and

---

96. Defined as any of the following:

    a a body which carries on negotiations for the fixing of wages or other conditions of employment of its own (but no other) employees

    ...

    c a civil service staff association recognised by the Minister for Finance

    d an organisation of teachers recognised by the Minister for Education

    e the Agricultural Wages Board

    f a trade board established under the Trade Board Acts 1909 and 1918 and

    g a body in respect of which an order under sub-section (6) of this section is for the time being in force [ie where the Minister has by order declared that the section should not apply]

When the 1906 Act was extended to all employees save those in the Defence Forces and Garda Síochána in 1982, many public service unions, previously excepted bodies, became authorised bodies.

97. *Iarnród Éireann v Holbrooke and Ors* [2000] ELR 109 (HC), [2001] I IR 237 (SC).

all other members of the trade union in respect of any tortious act committed by or on behalf of the trade union in contemplation or furtherance of a trade dispute, shall not be entertained by any court.

(2) In an action against any trade union or person referred to in subsection (1) in respect of any tortious act alleged or found to have been committed by or on behalf of a trade union it shall be a defence that the act was done in the reasonable belief that it was done in contemplation or furtherance of a trade dispute.

The section repeats with the important modification of 'the golden formula', s 4(1) of the Trade Disputes Act 1906,[98] which read:

4—(1) An action against a trade union, whether of workmen or masters, or against any members or officials thereof on behalf of themselves and all other members of the trade union in respect of any tortious act alleged to have been committed by or on behalf of the trade union, shall not be entertained by any court.

[9.58] First of all, s 13 protects only trade unions, as such, from actions against them in their registered name or by means of a representative action and secondly, the tortious act alleged must be committed 'in contemplation or furtherance of a trade dispute' (para **9.76** *et seq*). Only in relation to actions against trade unions is there provision in the 1990 Act that a reasonable belief that an act complied with 'the golden formula' may be a defence. The belief must be subjectively held but must at the same time be reasonable, ie it is a hybrid 'objective-subjective' belief. This is a compromise between the subjective approach of Lord Diplock and the objective approach of Lord Wilberforce in *Express Newspapers Ltd v MacShane*[99] (para **9.81**). The third point to make about s 13 is that it does not affect the personal liability of individual trade union officials in relation to personal liability in tort even though in committing the tort they were acting on behalf of the union;[100] likewise if a person commits a tort jointly with a trade union.[101] The wording 'and all other members of the trade union' suggests that action in tort may be taken against a trade union on behalf of a section or part thereof. Lastly, the immunity applies only to actions in tort. Actions, for example, for breach of constitutional rights, public law rights, wrongful expulsion, to restrain the misapplication of funds, breach of equity, of contract or for restitution[102] are not affected. Under the 1906 Act it was the predominant judicial view that any form of

---

98. Section 4(2) read: '(2) In an action against any trade union or person referred to in subsection (1) in respect of any tortious act alleged or found to have been committed by or on behalf of a trade union it shall be a defence that the act was done in the reasonable belief that it was done in contemplation or furtherance of a trade dispute.'

99. *Express Newspapers Ltd v McShane* [1980] AC 672.

100. Cf Lord Moulton in *Vacher v London Soc of Compositors* [1913] AC 107 at 130, 131; *Bussy v Amal Soc of Railway Servants and Bell* (1908) 24 TLR 437. This point seems to have been overlooked in *Dublin City Council v TEEU and Ors* (9 June 2010, unreported), HC, Laffoy J.

101. *Eglantine Inn v Smith* [1948] NI 29.

102. *Universe Tankships Inc of Monrovia v International Transport Workers' Federation* [1980] IRLR 363.

action, including a *quia timet* injunction, could not be brought against a trade union on account of this section.[103] This was because of the phrase 'alleged to have been committed'. There are contrary views.[104]

[9.59] It is possible an attack on the constitutional validity of s 13 may be brought at some future point on the basis that it denies victims their constitutional right to litigate claims, fails to vindicate their rights to property (and bodily integrity in some instances) and violates the principle of equality.[105]

Immunities restricted to members and officials of authorised trade unions

[9.60] Section 11(1) of the Trade Union Act 1941 stated that ss 2, 3 and 4 of the Act of 1906 shall 'apply only' to trade unions holding a negotiation licence and 'members and officials of such trade unions and not otherwise'. Section 9(1) of the 1990 Act re-enacts s 11(1):

> Sections 11, 12 and 13 shall apply only to authorised trade unions which for the time being are the holders of negotiation licences and to the members and officials of such trade unions and not otherwise.

Section 10, which provides immunity in relation to conspiracy, is not included in sub-s (1). The words 'and not otherwise' unambiguously confine the Act's immunities to the unions and persons indicated. They continue the 1941 Act's abolition of the protection previously afforded *generally* by ss 2, 3 and 4 of the Act of 1906. Speaking of the 1941 Act, s 11(1), O'Higgins CJ said in *Goulding Chemicals Ltd v Bolger*[106] that one must regard s 11(1) as having the effect of re-enacting ss 2, 3 and 4 of the Act of 1906 as applying to the unions and persons mentioned by that subsection. What he had to say about s 11(1) is of interest when applied to the 1990 Act:

> It is well established that, if there is nothing to modify, nothing to alter, nothing to qualify the language which a statute contains, the words and sentences must be construed in their ordinary and natural meaning. It is to be presumed that words are not used in a statute without a meaning and, accordingly, a meaning must be given, if possible, to all the words used, for, as has been said, 'the legislation is deemed not to waste its words or to say anything in vain' *per* Lord Sumner in *Quebec Railway, Light, Heat and Power Co v Vanday* [1920] AC 662, 676.

---

103. Meredith J in *Irish Transport and General Workers' Union v Green* [1936] IR 471; *Corry v National Union of Vintners* [1950] IR 315; Winn LJ in *Torquay Hotel Ltd v Cousins* [1969] 2 Ch 106, 146–6.

104. *Boulting v Association of Cinematograph Television and Allied Technicians* [1963] 2 QB 606 at 643, 649; Upjohn and Diplock LJJ, *obiter* followed by Stirling J in *Camden Exhibition and Display Ltd v Lynott* [1966] 1 QB 555.

105. McMahon and Binchy raise and discuss the question in their *Law of Torts* (3rd edn, Butterworths, 2000), 855; see too Walsh J in foreword to Kerr and Whyte, *Irish Trade Union Law* (Professional Books, 1985), vi.

106. *Goulding Chemicals Ltd v Bolger* [1977] IR 211 at 226.

[9.61] Section 2 of the Act of 1906 protected 'one or more persons, acting on their own behalf or on behalf of a trade union.' How were these words to be construed in the light of s 11(1) of the Act of 1941? According to the Chief Justice:

> It seems to me that one is driven to the conclusion that the protection given by s 2 of the Act of 1906 is by s 11, sub-s 1, of the Act of 1941 to apply to authorised trade unions holding a negotiation licence and to the officers and members of these unions whether such officers and members act on behalf of the union or on their own behalf.[107]

In other words, a prerequisite in all cases is membership of an authorised trade union.

[9.62] The words 'trade union' did not appear in s 3 of the Act of 1906. Again, seeking a meaning and a sense in the application of that section under s 11(1) of the Act of 1941, the Chief Justice said it was:[108]

> not unreasonable to conclude that s 3 of the Act of 1906 appears to apply under s 11, sub-s 1, of the Act of 1941 to persons who are officers or members of a trade union holding a negotiation licence, whether such persons are acting on behalf of the union or on their own behalf.

[9.63] No problem arose with regard to the application of s 4 of the Act of 1906 in the limited field provided by s 11(1) of the Act of 1941. The section was clearly drafted to apply to trade unions.

[9.64] In *Goulding* all the defendants were members of an authorised trade union holding a negotiation licence, so the Chief Justice's exposition was *obiter*. The point has not been considered elsewhere, certainly not on any other occasion by the Supreme Court. If the court's analysis was correct, then the impact of s 11(1) of the 1941 Act has been insufficiently appreciated by judges and practitioners alike. It may well be that the seasonal workers in *McHenry Bros Ltd v Carey*[109] were members of a trade union holding a negotiation licence but, if they were, there is no reference to this in the judgment of Hamilton J nor was it thought necessary to make an explicit statement about it. Walsh J in *Darby v Leonard*[110] said it would be lawful for a dismissed employee to picket the premises of his ex-employer in furtherance of the dispute 'and for other persons acting on his behalf to do likewise'.[111]

---

107. *Goulding Chemicals Ltd v Bolger* [1977] IR 211 at 227.
108. *Goulding Chemicals Ltd v Bolger* [1977] IR 211 at 227.
109. *McHenry Bros Ltd v Carey* (1984) 3 JISLL 80.
110. *Darby v Leonard* (1973) 107 ILTR 82.
111. Must these other persons be members of an authorised trade union? If so, this provides one possible interpretation of McWilliam J's judgment in *Pennys Ltd v Kerrigan* (7 February 1977 unreported), HC, where a dismissed employee began to picket the plaintiff company's premises and was assisted by her father and sister-in-law, neither of whom were employed by the company. Injunctions were granted against the father and sister-in-law. The decision seems wrong unless explicable in this way.

[9.65] It is often contended that injustices follow from the restriction of immunities to authorised trade unions, their members and officials.[112] Take, for instance, a post-entry closed shop where a trade union is trying to enforce full union membership. Further suppose that there is a small group of workers who do not want to be coerced into joining. Pressure is put on the employer to get rid of the non-unionised workers under threat of a strike by the union. He succumbs. The non-unionised workers are dismissed. It seems extraordinary that their dismissal is probably *ultra vires* the employer's power as being unconstitutional while at the same time, because of s 11, the dismissed workers are precluded from taking any form of industrial action in order to obtain redress extra-judicially.

[9.66] On another view, the restriction constitutes an invasion of individual rights. The Oireachtas has placed the boot very much on the collective foot, in contrast to the general judicial attitude in the matter of labour relations. All persons who do not belong to authorised trade unions are at risk of legal proceedings, either civil or criminal, if they take industrial action. In so far as there may be an individual right to withdraw labour, the restriction may be suspect constitutionally (within the limited bounds of the right). Two members of the Supreme Court hinted about its possible unconstitutionality in the *Goulding* case. It is arguably vulnerable under various constitutional provisions, eg Arts 40.1,[113] 40.3.1° and 40.3.2°, 40.6. 1°(iii) and 45.

Unofficial action

[9.67] What about unofficial action? Industrial action may be unofficial because the initiative for it is taken at a lower level within the union structure. Unofficial strikes, from the outsider's point of view, are not any different from official ones. Many official strikes are unofficial because events have moved too fast. A large number of strikes which are initially unofficial are ratified within a short period of their commencement.

[9.68] The 1990 Act crucially requires trade unions to hold a secret ballot before strike or industrial action (see **Ch 11**). Under s 14(2)(a), every trade union is required to have in its rule book the requirement that it shall not organise, participate in, sanction or support a strike or other industrial action without a secret ballot. The rights referred to in sub-s (2) are 'conferred on the members of the trade union concerned and on no other person': s 14(3). Thus an employer cannot seek to enforce s 14 by injunction.[114] Failure to hold a ballot as required by s 14 constitutes a breach of contract between a member and his trade union and could provide 'unlawful means' for those torts requiring them as a prerequisite of liability. The 1990 Act in s 17 provides that the protection of ss 10, 11 and 12 (the immunities) shall not apply in respect of

---

112. The definition of trade union official in s 11(5) of the 1990 Act applies only for that section but the practical significance of this is uncertain.

113. Although the Irish courts' interpretation of the equality principle has been limited so far. See Forde, 'Equality and the Constitution' [1982] Vol XVII Ir Jur 295 at 310.

114. And see, before the 1990 Act, *Kenny v O'Reilly and Spain* (1927) 61 ILTR 137.

proceedings arising out of or relating to a strike or other industrial action 'by a group of workers in disregard of, or contrary to, the outcome of a secret ballot relating to the issue or issues involved in the dispute.'

[9.69] Where arrangements exist for the aggregation of ballot results, the outcome of a secret ballot refers to the outcome of the aggregated ballot vote: s 17(2). This provision is intended to deal with the circumstances which arose in *Gouldings Chemicals Ltd v Bolger*[115] (para **10.68**), and to overturn the Supreme Court to the extent provided. The provision on aggregation in s 17(2) is intended to allow the ICTU all-out picket arrangement to continue, but subject to a ballot. The Oireachtas clearly took the view that the all-out picket has brought a degree of order to picketing and that it would be unwise to undermine it. The secret ballot in s 17 is not necessarily one held in pursuance of s 14.

[9.70] The 1990 Act in principle protects unofficial action provided it is not in disregard of the outcome of a secret ballot and, as always, there is a trade dispute and that the parties are acting in contemplation or furtherance thereof. This means that, for example, disputes that are motivated by spite or ill-will (para **9.05** *et seq*) will be outside the saving power of the Act. *McCobb v Doyle*[116] concerned a situation where, acting on merely personal views, trade union officials procured the plaintiff's dismissal. Murnaghan J declared that:

> they cannot make a dispute in connection with their personal views a trade dispute because the dispute must be, not one that concerned them individually, but one that concerned the trade union of which they were members and officials.

Had the principles on which the defendants acted been accepted and 'formally adopted' by the local branch, there would have been 'no question' that a trade dispute would have arisen.[117]

[9.71] A spontaneous walkout of employees will not necessarily remove the workers concerned from the narrow path of the statutory protection. If the walkout constitutes a strike, it will be covered by the union rule book and, under the 1990 Act, that will require a secret ballot before any such action. Whether there has been a secret ballot is a matter of internal management of the union, its members might take action to restrain it, and there are potential implications under s 19 of the 1990 Act in relation to interim and interlocutory injunctions. Individual workers carrying out industrial action without a ballot may claim the statutory immunities. If there is a secret ballot before the

---

115. *Gouldings Chemicals Ltd v Bolger* [1977] IR 211.

116. *McCobb v Doyle* [1938] IR 44.

117. Many authorities in this area (eg, *O'Connor v Martin* [1949] Ir Jur Rep 9; *Brennan v Glennon* (26 November 1975, unreported), SC) are unhelpful. It is crucial when examining them to distinguish between the issue of the proper parties to a dispute and the further, separate, question of whether a dispute exists.

workers walk off the job, whether or not they attract the Act's protection will depend on whether they respect the outcome of the ballot.

[9.72] Nor need a shop steward or union official necessarily incur liability if they call employees out on strike without going through the procedures laid down in the union rule book[118] although once again a secret ballot will be required for any strike or industrial action under the rule book and if there has been a secret ballot the outcome will have to be respected. However, if the procedures in the rule book are given expression in a collective agreement and if, as frequently happens in Ireland, the dispute is about one individual worker, full liability would result for the officials concerned under s 9(2). Where union members participate in strike or industrial action without holding a ballot as required or where they hold a ballot and for one reason or another it is invalid, the restrictions in s 19 of the 1990 Act in relation to interim and interlocutory injunctions will not apply.[119]

Action in violation of a no-strike clause

[9.73] If a strike is called in violation of a no-strike or peace clause, the strikers could be vulnerable as Irish courts have declined at an interlocutory stage to apply the 1990 Act's protection where workers engage in strike or industrial action contrary to a collective agreement: see para **3.23** *et seq*. Moreover, such a strike would need the support of a secret ballot. 'No-strike' clauses generally provide for the postponement of industrial action until disputes have been processed through a grievance machinery of one sort or another, perhaps involving the LRC at the final stages. Sometimes arbitration is stipulated by the parties as the agreed method of redress. Of its very nature a no-strike clause binds the parties to the collective agreement, the employer and trade union or unions concerned.

[9.74] In *Kayfoam Woolfson Ltd v Woods*[120] Keane J held that industrial action which was in violation of a 'peace obligation' or 'no-strike clause' in a collective agreement was not entitled to the statutory immunity. The facts involved a shop steward of the Automotive, General Engineering and Mechanical Operatives' Union (AGEMOU) who had been dismissed by the plaintiff company. Pickets were mounted on the premises by an official of the union and 21 employees. It was not 'seriously in issue' that there was a trade dispute. The picketing was clearly in furtherance of the dispute

---

118. Although such action could lead to consequences even more serious under s 16(5) of the 1990 Act. Section 16(5) provides that where the Registrar of Friendly Societies is satisfied, after due investigation, that it is the policy or practice of a trade union persistently to disregard the secret ballot requirement in the rule book, the Registrar may issue an instruction to the trade union to comply with the requirement. Where the instruction is disregarded, the Registrar is obliged to inform the Minister for Trade, Enterprise and Innovation of failure to comply and the Minister may then revoke the union's negotiation licence. To avoid this, a union would need unequivocally to repudiate its official's actions.

119. *Nolan Transport (Oaklands) Ltd v Halligan* [1999] 1 IR 128 at 135 *per* O'Flaherty J and 156–157 *per* Murphy J.

120. *Kayfoam Woolfson Ltd v Woods* (4 June 1980, unreported), HC.

and all the other requirements of s 2 were satisfied. In spite of this, Keane J granted an injunction. The industrial action 'did not have the support of the relevant union'; moreover, the judge was prepared to accept that the picketing was unlawful as being in breach of a collective agreement which provided for the referral of disputes to the Labour Court conciliation machinery (no strikes until the Labour Court had issued a recommendation and two weeks' notice of any industrial action). The relevant agreement was a collective agreement between the union and the company, which provided that disputes between AGEMOU and the company were to be referred to the Labour Court. Yet the dispute before the court was not such a dispute, a consequence which flowed from the unofficial nature of the picketing. Nor were any of the defendants bound by the collective agreement (with the possible exception of the defendant union official who had signed the agreement). But to Keane J the various defendants had somehow 'acquiesced' in the agreement.

'IN CONTEMPLATION OR FURTHERANCE' OF A TRADE DISPUTE

[9.75] In **Ch 2** the interpretation of the Trade Disputes Act 1906 was discussed. The strict approach of judges manifested itself in relation to the 'golden formula' more than to any other term or clause within the Act of 1906. Lord Diplock in *Duport Steels Ltd v Sirs*[121] presented the ideal course for judges: if the meaning of a statute was plain and unambiguous, it was not for the judiciary to 'invent fancied ambiguities for failing to give effect to its plain meaning' because they believed that the consequences of so doing were 'inexpedient, unjust or even immoral'. He argued that it would endanger 'continued public confidence in the political impartiality of the judiciary if judges under the guise of interpretation provide their own preferred amendments to statutes.' Irish judges from time to time have echoed or foreshadowed such sentiments (eg Dixon J in *Connolly v Loughney*,[122] Maguire CJ in *Educational Co of Ireland Ltd v Fitzpatrick*[123] and Hamilton J in *Reg Armstrong Motors Ltd v CIE*).[124]

In Contemplation or Furtherance

[9.76] The defendants must have acted 'in contemplation or furtherance' of a trade dispute. The phrase, which is to be read disjunctively, occurs in ss 10, 11, 12, 13 and 19 of the 1990 Act. It means, as Lord Loreburn said, either a dispute must be imminent and the act done in expectation of, and with a view to, it or the dispute is already existing and the act is done in support of one side to it: *Conway v Wade*.[125] In either case, as has been seen (para **9.07**), the dispute must be genuine. When it used the words 'in furtherance', the legislature had in mind help, assistance or encouragement to such a dispute. On the other hand, to act 'in contemplation' of a dispute suggests that at the time of acting the dispute was 'thought of' by one of the parties. Once a decision in favour of a strike is taken, if, for example, a particular person's employment is

---

121. *Duport Steels Ltd v Sirs* [1980] 1 All ER 529 at 541.

122. *Connolly v Loughney* [1933] 87 ILTR 59.

123. *Educational Co of Ireland Ltd v Fitzpatrick* [1961] IR 345 at 378.

124. *Reg Armstrong Motors Ltd v CIE* (2 December 1975, unreported), HC.

125. *Conway v Wade* [1909] AC 506 at 512.

continued, a trade dispute is sufficiently imminent to protect the person or persons instrumental in communicating that decision to the employer: *Kenny v O'Reilly and Spain*.[126] But it is essential that the contemplation of such a dispute must be the contemplation of something impending or likely to occur. The words do not cover coercive interference where the intervener may have it in mind that, if he does not get his own way, he will devise some method of bringing a trade dispute into existence:

> To 'contemplate a trade dispute' is to have before the mind some objective event or situation. It does not mean a contemplative meditation or resolve in regard to something as yet wholly within the mind of a subjective character.[127]

These words were applied by the Supreme Court in *The Esplanade Pharmacy Ltd v Larkin*.[128] It would lead to strange and mischievous results, according to Lavery J, to accept a submission that, because someone else may do something which will create a dispute on account of the exercise by the plaintiffs of their ordinary rights, a trade dispute is imminent. Plaintiffs, for instance, might be required to close shop altogether or be picketed if they refused. The mere fact they carried on business might affect the prospects of the employment of others. But such a future dispute which may or may not arise could not as a contemplated event be said to justify the picketing of the plaintiff's premises.

[9.77] In *Norbrook Laboratories Ltd v King*[129] Lord Lowry LCJ noted that a person advocating or taking industrial action:

> could possibly have had two purposes, namely to bring the trade dispute to a successful conclusion and to injure the plaintiff, or, in creating and furthering the trade dispute, he could have been wholly or partly motivated by feelings of hostility toward the plaintiff. In either case he would have been acting 'in furtherance of a trade dispute', and action prompted by a bad or sinister motive or by a mixed motive does not fail by reason of the motive to be action in furtherance of a trade dispute. In other words the motive is not to be confused with the act itself or the purpose with which the action is done.

[9.78] It was sometimes averred in older cases involving secondary picketing[130] that action in contemplation or furtherance of a trade union dispute necessitated a clearly discernible 'connection' between the premises being picketed and the dispute in the sense that the employer (or the worker) affected by the action must be directly concerned with the dispute. Section 11 of the 1990 Act now obviates any such need (see further para **10.46** *et seq*).

[9.79] *Barton v Harten*[131] indicated that 'a clearly discernible connection' is not always sufficient to justify industrial action in the context of non-employment and that

---

126. *Kenny v O'Reilly and Spain* 61 ILTR 137 at 140.

127. *Conway v Wade* [1909] AC 506 *per* Lord Shaw at 552.

128. *The Esplanade Pharmacy Ltd v Larkin* 62 ILTR at 154.

129. *Norbrook Laboratories Ltd v King* [1983] NI 306 at 320.

130. Notably, *Ellis v Wright* [1976] IR 8. See, too, *Cleary v Coffey* (30 October 1979, unreported), HC.

131. *Barton v Harten* [1925] 2 IR 37.

something more is required. But there has been no exposition in later jurisprudence as to how this 'something more' should be ascertained, as McWilliam J remarked in *J Bradbury Ltd v Duffy and Whelan*.[132] It is up to the court in each case to determine on the facts whether the 'connection' is sufficient or otherwise (para **9.37** *et seq*). The meaning of this part of the golden formula was responsible for much of the exhausting legal point-counterpoint between the Court of Appeal and the House of Lords in Britain. The saga began with *BBC v Hearn*[133] (para **9.29**) where the Court of Appeal concentrated on the connection between the dispute and the subject matter thereof (as outlined in s 29 of the Trade Union and Labour Relations Act 1974). Officials of the Association of Broadcasting Staff threatened that their members would refuse to allow the BBC to televise the 1977 FA Cup Final in a way which would permit it to be viewed in South Africa. The Court of Appeal granted an injunction restraining the defendants from doing any act which would interfere with the broadcast. Although Pain J had held at first instance in *Hearn* that the dispute was over a demand for a new condition of employment, the Court of Appeal held that the matter had never reached this stage: 'it was coercive interference and nothing more'. Yet it is quite possible legally to turn such a 'dispute' into one which qualifies for the Act's protection. Lord Diplock pointed out in *NWL Ltd v Woods*[134] that:

> it [the dispute in *Hearn*] could readily have been turned into a dispute connected with terms and conditions of employment by a demand by the union that the contracts of employment of employees of the BBC should be amended to incorporate a term that they should not be obliged to take part in the transmission of sporting events to South Africa.

This approach could be adopted in secondary disputes (see para **9.92** below). The message from Lord Diplock is that unions might word their ultimatums more carefully.

[9.80] The Court of Appeal distinguished action 'in consequence' of a trade dispute in *Beaverbrook Newspapers Ltd v Keys*[135] from action 'in furtherance' of such a dispute. Lord Denning MR declared:

> You cannot chase consequence after consequence in a long chain and say anything that follows a trade dispute is in furtherance of it. It is far too remote to be protected by statute.

In the case in point, there was a pay dispute between the journalists and managers of the *Daily Mirror. Mirror* readers were changing to other newspapers as publication was suspended. The *Daily Express* decided to take advantage of this by increasing publication but the defendant, the General Secretary of the Society of Graphical and Allied Traders (SOGAT), issued instructions to his members to 'black' any extra

---

132. *J Bradbury Ltd v Duffy and Whelan* (1984) 3 JISLL 86.

133. *BBC v Hearn* [1977] 1 WLR 1004; (1984) 3 JISLL 86.

134. *NWL Ltd v Woods* [1979] 3 All ER 614 at 623, 624.

135. *Beaverbrook Newspapers Ltd v Keys* [1978] ICR 582.

copies of the *Express* that were printed. The Court of Appeal would not accept that there was a dispute between the employees and the *Express* over the existence of a contractual obligation either actual or in contemplation between the members of SOGAT and the *Express*. The only dispute was between the *Mirror* and its journalists and the defendant's action was not taken in furtherance of it. Lord Denning MR formulated the reason for his decision: in order for an act to be 'in furtherance' of a trade dispute, 'it must be directly in furtherance of it'.

[9.81] The majority of the House of Lords did not accept this objective interpretation in the later case of *Express Newspapers Ltd v McShane*.[136] Once more there was a pay dispute between journalists and the owners of several provincial newspapers. The journalists went on strike but the paper could continue to be published because newscopy was supplied by the Press Association. The National Union of Journalists (NUJ) therefore requested those of its members employed by the Press Association to come out on strike. But the continued supply of newscopy was not prevented as a result. The NUJ resorted to 'blacking' newscopy sent out by the Press Association. The Court of Appeal upheld the award of an injunction by Lawson J restraining the defendant from acting in furtherance of the primary dispute. Lawton LJ reiterated the belief that some limitation would have to be imposed upon the words 'in furtherance of' and that anyone seeking the protection of the Act had to establish not only that he had a genuine intention to achieve the objective of a trade dispute but also that acts done pursuant to that intention 'were reasonably capable of achieving that end'. Brandon LJ said that to be granted protection, a defendant had to show that the action taken 'was in fact reasonably capable of or had a reasonable prospect of achieving such furtherance'. The defendant argued that he honestly believed blacking would advance the journalists' cause, hence the action was 'in furtherance of' the journalists' dispute. In other words, the defendants urged a subjective approach. It may be useful to recall that such an approach is applied to the issue of establishing the *bona fides* of a trade dispute in this jurisdiction (para **9.07** *et seq*). Lord Denning MR said, however, that 'furtherance' was not a subjective concept. For the immunity to apply, action taken 'must help one side or the other in a practical way'. He was clearly trying to limit the construction of the golden formula in order to avoid a recipe for (as he saw it) anarchy.[137]

---

136. *Express Newspapers Ltd v McShane* [1980] AC 672. Contrast the objective approach of the Court of Appeal at *Beaverbrook Newspapers Ltd v Keys* [1978] ICR 582 and see the continuing objective approach of the Court of Appeal in *Associated Newspapers Group Ltd v Wade* [1979] IRLR 110; *Publishers Book Delivery Service v Filkins* [1979] IRLR 356; *Star Sea Corporation v Slater (The Camilla M)* [1978] IRLR 507; *NWL Ltd v Woods* [1979] 3 All 614; *NWL Ltd v Nelson* [1979] ICR 755; and the *Marabu Porr* case [1979] IRLR 331.

137. Ackner J in *United Biscuits (UK) Ltd v Fall* [1979] IRLR 110 followed the Court of Appeal and provided a further rider to its principle, namely that acts which were contrary to trade union policy or instructions of the union could not be in furtherance of a trade dispute.

[9.82] The House of Lords unanimously overruled the Court of Appeal in *Express Newspapers Ltd v McShane*.[138] There was some disagreement as to whether the test of furtherance was objective or subjective. Lord Diplock believed it was a subjective test:

> If the party who does the act honestly thinks at the time he does it that it may help one of the parties to the trade dispute to achieve their objectives and does it for that reason, he is protected ...[139]

The objective or remoteness test was criticised in that it enabled the courts to substitute their own opinion for that of trade union officials. Two other members of the House differed slightly *inter se*. Lords Keith and Scarman, whilst holding that the test was subjective, said the court would test the defendant's evidence by applying the usual tests of credibility. In other words, the court would be likely to reject the defendant's evidence '[i]f it should appear that no reasonable person versed in industrial relations could take the view that the act called in question was capable of furthering the dispute.'[140] This is the orthodox and respected way of approaching a subjective test. The courts will look to see if there are reasonable grounds for the defendant's belief. Lord Salmon seemed to combine a subjective test with one of credibility for he said the words meant that a person doing the act must 'honestly and reasonably believe that it may further the trade dispute'.[141] Lord Wilberforce, however, favoured an objective test. He said the immunity should not apply when the action was directed at secondary employees who had no means of influencing the primary employer. If the test was purely subjective, there would be no protection for anybody from the actions of extremists and fanatics when the action was accompanied by a statement that those taking it had the necessary belief. In the case before him he held the defendant's action was reasonably capable of furthering the primary dispute.

[9.83] The influence of *McShane* was considerable. For instance, the Court of Appeal in *Duport Steels Ltd v Sirs*[142] allowed the private steel companies' appeal against a refusal at first instance to grant an injunction to ensure that they did not get caught up in the escalating British Steel Corporation (BSC) strike. Lord Denning looked upon the dispute as a confrontation between the government and the trade unions and therefore not a trade dispute. The House of Lords overruled the Court of Appeal

---

138. The House at the same time upheld the decisions in *NWL Ltd v Woods* [1979] 3 All ER 614 and *NWL Ltd v Nelson* [1979] ICR 755 and expressly overruled *Star Sea Corporation v Slater (The Camilla M)* [1978] IRLR 507.

139. *Express Newspapers Ltd v McShane* [1980] AC 672 at 686.

140. *Express Newspapers Ltd v McShane* [1980] AC 672 at 692.

141. *Express Newspapers Ltd v McShane* [1980] AC 672 at 689.

142. *Duport Steels Ltd v Sirs* [1980] 1 All ER 529. See too the decision of Murray J in *Norbrook Laboratories Ltd v King* [1982] IRLR4 56 (noted by Simpson (1982) 4 DULJ 124), a case illustrating that the apparently wide construction of the trade dispute definition in *NWL* and *Hadmor*, and the qualifying words 'in contemplation or furtherance' in *MacShane* and *Sirs*, still leaves very real scope for a restrictive judicial approach to the availability of the golden formula defences. Murray J concluded that the Law Lords' decision in *MacShane* and *Sirs* that an honest intention was sufficient to satisfy the requirement of contemplation or furtherance was based on the premise that the defendant who was claiming the statutory protection gave evidence of his intentions.

holding there was no relevant difference between this case and *McShane*. Lord Diplock re-established a subjective test. His language and that of some of his brethren in effect constituted an invitation to Parliament to do something about the width and scope of the immunities:

> If the Executive Council honestly believed that a principal reason why BSC would not agree to raise wages to the level that the ISTC was demanding was because the Government was adhering to a policy of refusing to provide BSC with the money to do so out of public funds what could be better calculated to promote the success of the demands than to take steps to create a nationwide shortage of steel which would induce the victims of the shortage to put pressure on the government to change its policy.[143]

The UK Parliament was not unheedful of the irony in these words.[144]

[9.84] What is the position under the 1990 Act? To begin with, s 13(2) of the 1990 Act provides that it shall be a defence that the act was done 'in the reasonable belief that it was done in contemplation or furtherance of a trade dispute' where there are proceedings against any trade union or its trustees or against any members or officials thereof in respect of any tortious act alleged or found to have been committed by or on behalf of the trade union. This requires a subjective belief which must, however, satisfy the objective test of reasonableness. In this context, see also para **9.60** regarding s 9(1) of the 1990 Act and membership of an authorised trade union for application of the immunities. In the recent High Court case, *Dublin City Council v TEEU and Ors*,[145] Laffoy J took the view that s 13(2) of the 1990 Act cast some light on what the Oireachtas intended by the golden formula in enacting Pt II of the Act. She referred to the *via media* in s 13(2) between an objective and a subjective test and said:[146]

> it seems to me that in applying the provisions of Part II of the Act of 1990 to the defendants *including s 11(1)* and s 13, the question for the Court is whether, in maintaining the picket, the defendants are acting in the reasonable belief that their actions are in furtherance of the trade dispute between [their former employer] and the defendants [emphasis added].

This approach is questionable. First, because of the very different contexts involved. Section 13(2) concerns immunity of trade unions; s 11(1) that of individuals. Secondly, on the principles of statutory construction. The Oireachtas deliberately modified the golden formula in s 13(2) and excluded the modifier in the particularised immunities accorded to individual trade union members and officials. *Inclusio unius exclusio alterius*.

---

143. *Duport Steels Ltd v Sirs* [1980] 1 All ER 529 at 545.
144. In 1982 Parliament intervened to say that trade matters must be the predominant element: Employment Act 1982, s 18. It is enough if a person genuinely believes a trade matter to be his predominant motive but the remoteness test is not obliterated since objectives which would be too remote cannot be wholly or mainly connected with the dispute.
145. *Dublin City Council v TEEU and Ors* (9 June 2010, unreported), HC. See further para **10.83**.
146. Para 6.2.

[9.85] It would seem that under the 1906 Act Irish courts slowly evolved for individuals what amounted to an objective approach like that of the Court of Appeal. *Barton v Harden*[147] and *Ellis v Wright*[148] indicate the need for a clearly discernible connection between the action of the defendants and the dispute. This is reminiscent of a remoteness test. Indeed, the issue of remoteness arose in connection with recognition disputes.[149] It is extremely unlikely Irish judges will bypass what they perceive to be their duty to review the tactics of a party to a trade dispute and to determine whether the tactic employed is likely to further, or advance, that party's side of the dispute.

SECONDARY ACTION

[9.86] In some cases of secondary action an assessment of the particular head of tort liability will enable one to say straightaway that the industrial action concerned is outside the 1990 Act's protection. For example, if violence or intimidation accompany picketing, s 11 will not apply. Again, s 12 provides protection only in respect of the tort of inducing breaches of the contract of employment. Other contracts lie outside its scope.[150] If the particular tort committed amounts to procurement of a breach of commercial contract, then one need consider the impact of the statute no further.

[9.87] It may be helpful to provide some definitions.[151]

Primary Action consists of action taken by A, an employee of B, against B (eg, going on strike) in furtherance of a dispute with B.

Secondary action consists of action taken by A, in furtherance of the same dispute with B, against C, who has a direct commercial relationship with B (usually supplier or customer), designed to bring pressure to bear on B.

Tertiary action consists of action taken by A against D, who is not in any direct relationship with B, in order to put indirect pressure on B. D may have a commercial relationship with B at one remove, as in *McShane* (para **9.81**), or simply be a large concern, economic damage to which may influence the government to intervene in A's dispute with B – effectively the facts of the *Duport Steels* case (para **9.83**).

Sympathetic action consists of action taken by employees of C or D, or any other employer, either against their own employer (eg, by going on strike) or against B (eg, by blacking B's products) in support of A's dispute with B.

---

147. *Barton v Harten* [1925] 2 IR 37.

148. *Ellis v Wright* [1976] IR 8. See similarly *J Bradbury Ltd v Duffy and Whelan* (1984) 3 JISLL 86, 90; *Goulding Chemicals Ltd v Bolger* [1977] IR 211.

149. *Sheriff v McMullen* [1952] IR 236; *Becton Dickinson Ltd v Lee* [1973] IR 1.

150. See *Sherriff v McMullen Ltd* [1952] IR 236, *Talbot (Ireland) Ltd v Merrigan* (30 April 1981, unreported), SC.

151. Elias, Napier and Wallington, *Labour Law Cases and Materials* (Butterworths, 1980), 263.

[9.88] Much secondary or tertiary action consists of inducing and taking what is sympathetic action. The main areas of public and judicial concern have been the growth of tertiary action and the sympathetic action this may procure. Typically a union resorts to secondary action where it is in a strong position to bring pressure to bear on a party not in dispute who, in order to avoid that pressure, will use his position as a customer or supplier to pressurise the employer in dispute to reach a settlement. It may prevent the effects of primary pressure being undermined.

[9.89] The inclusion of various forms of sympathetic action, secondary or tertiary, in the term 'trade dispute' is important. The definition of 'worker' in s 8 of the 1990 Act includes a dispute between employers and workers 'whether or not in the employment of the employer with whom the dispute arises'. For example, workers who consider their own interests threatened may strike against their own employer to bring pressure to bear upon another employer and to force him to observe standard or recognised terms and conditions, or to employ only union labour. Such a strike will be in furtherance of a trade dispute even though there is no dispute between that employer and his own workers. Similarly, where there is a trade dispute between an employer and his own workers, the fact that other workers, who have no quarrel with the other employer, join in the dispute in sympathy does not alter its character. They, too, will be entitled to the protection of the Act. That sympathetic action by persons not originally parties to the dispute is entitled to statutory protection was clearly acknowledged by the Court of Appeal and the House of Lords in *Conway v Wade*.[152] Lord Loreburn[153] agreed with Cozens-Hardy MR[154] when he said of the 1906 Act that he was unable to limit the generality of s 3: 'An outsider, a mere busybody is equally exempt from liability'. Lord Loreburn added that:

> A dispute may have arisen, for example, in a single colliery, of which the subject is so important to the whole industry that either employers or workmen may think a general lockout or a general strike is necessary to gain their point. Few are parties to, but all are interested in, the dispute.[155]

[9.90] The fact that a section of the public, the government or the nation as a whole may be the third party to a greater or lesser degree does not affect the legality of industrial action. Once the original dispute is a trade dispute concerned with the matters specified in s 8 of the 1990 Act, the fact that third parties are involved is immaterial. Every strike brings pressure to bear upon some third party and every sympathetic strike sets out to do so. The public is often the third party through whom pressure is brought to bear upon an employer either deliberately or as a necessary

---

152. *Conway v Wade* [1909] AC 506.

153. *Conway v Wade* [1909] AC 506 at 512.

154. *Conway v Wade* [1908] AC 506 at 849.

155. Contrast Astbury J on the legality of the national strike in Britain in 1926 in *National Seamen's and Firemen's Union v Reed* [1926] Ch 536, which has created considerable confusion. See on this Goodhart, 'Legality of General Strike in England' Yale LJ (Feb 1927).

consequence of the strike or industrial action.[156] See para **6.45** as to whether a member of the public adversely affected may take legal proceedings.

[9.91] In sum, as far as 'parties' are concerned, all persons perpetrating secondary industrial action can in theory come within the Act. The test of 'directness' arises in relation to action which is allegedly 'in contemplation or furtherance' of a trade dispute. Most examples of secondary and tertiary action involving boycotting, blacking or inducement of breach of commercial contracts, most probably lie outside the golden formula or the immunities in the 1990 Act.[157]

'Hot-cargo' clauses

[9.92] Secondary action in theory may be turned into a trade dispute by resort to legal subterfuge. One could ensure that lawful secondary action affected a term in the individual worker's contract of employment. The essence of secondary action is industrial action against an employer who is not a party to the dispute. The easiest way to avoid this is to make the employer in question a party to the trade dispute by taking industrial action against him. For example, workers who black goods in support of a dispute elsewhere are taking secondary action against their employer, which may be unlawful if it interferes with his contracts with road haulage firms to carry the goods. But if the workers doing the blacking (or the union of their behalf) were to demand of the employer that they should not be required to handle the blacked goods, called in North America a 'hot-cargo' clause, there is authority to support the view that this would create a trade dispute between the workers and their employer – hence their blacking would be transformed from secondary to primary action against their employer in furtherance of that dispute.[158] Trade unionists have not resorted to legal casuistry, however, when crafting strike notices.

---

156. A general strike is not illegal *per se*. The early case of *R v O'Connor* [1943] 4 St Tr (NS) 935 established that so far as the common law is concerned a strike to bring pressure to bear upon the government by peaceful means is not unlawful. The case concerned advice given to the working classes to agree to desist from working, for the purpose of obtaining the People's Charter. The first count charged the defendants with unlawfully encouraging others not to work, but without violence. The Attorney General submitted that any combination to produce a cessation of labour among a large class of the community was an offence against the state if it was done to promote a change in the law.

157. The relevance of the connection inherent in a customer/supplier relationship accordingly diminishes.

158. See *BBC v Hearn* [1977] IRLR 269 (Pain J) at 272, 273, (Lord Denning) at 275; *NWL Ltd v Woods* [1979] IRLR 478 (Lord Diplock) at 483.

Chapter 10
PICKETING

INTRODUCTION

[10.01] The right to picket is a powerful weapon. There can be few who do not view the prospect of being picketed without grave disquiet. Just as trade unionists would claim that this hard-won 'right' ought not to be unreasonably curtailed, likewise the rights of the public and those who may be affected by the exercise of the right must be considered. The exercise of the picket must not be allowed to exceed what the law permits.[1]

The prestige and authority of the picket is a phenomenon with a long tradition in Ireland.[2] The plethora of Irish cases on picketing which find their way into English law texts is not surprising.

[10.02] The tradition and power of the strike weapon grew out of the great liberal landslide in England in 1906, which, as already noted, resulted in the Trade Disputes Act of that year. A few short months after the Act became law, there was an attempted enforcement of it in Belfast by the Labour leader, Jim Larkin, in a most dramatic way. In the summer of 1907, during a dock strike, he had thousands of united Protestant and Catholic workers face a cordon of police and military who were preventing strikers from entering the docks. Larkin halted at the cordon and produced a copy of the Trade Disputes Act and read out its very brief clauses to the military commander who then stood aside and allowed him and a picket of workers to enter the docks to wild cheers from his supporters.

The 'sympathetic' strike developed around the same time. In the summer of 1907 in Belfast almost all the unskilled workers, carters, dockers, coal-fillers, seamen and many others were at one time either on strike or locked out. Even the Royal Irish Constabulary threatened to strike at one stage: Larkin's speech deploring their bad working conditions encouraged them. From 1907 to 1913 the power of the strike picket grew. Irish unions were fighting for their existence and for recognition, as well as for better wages and conditions. During 1911 there were strikes throughout Ireland, from Belfast to Cork, from Dublin to Wexford, and pickets became a daily sight. The power of the picket further increased during the Dublin strike of 1913 when about 20,000 workers were locked out because they were determined to join Jim Larkin's union.

---

1. See *Goulding Chemicals Ltd v Bolger* [1977] IR 211 at 239; *Educational Co of Ireland Ltd v Fitzpatrick (No 2)* [1961] IR 345 at 390. A Canadian case of interest is *Industrial Hardwood Products (1996) Ltd v International Wood and Allied Workers of Canada, Local 2693* [2001] OJ No 28 §§ 14 and 37 ('Picketing is a vital and constitutionally sanctioned means of collective expression in modern labour relations').
2. See in general Boyd, *The Rise of the Irish Trade Unions 1729–1970* (Anvil, 1971); McCarthy, *Trade Unions in Ireland 1894–1960* (IPA, 1977).

[10.03] In Ireland, therefore, the prestige of the strike picket is over 100 years old. Its midwife was the 1906 Act. Picketing practice used to be directed at preventing the use of blackleg labour and persuading colleagues to join the strike. But attention has increasingly turned to secondary activity, ie picketing not one's own place of work but someone else's. As a result, commercial contracts may be broken. The Industrial Relations Act 1990 addressed this development.

Under the Act of 1906 the rules were stringently interpreted by judges[3] and those applicable were frequently misunderstood. These cases are still relevant where there is no inconsistency in statutory wording. An Garda Síochána also possess powers to control picketing. Subject to the protection afforded by s 11 of the Industrial Relations Act 1990, there are several heads of criminal and civil liability potentially applicable to pickets.

THE CONSTITUTION: IS THERE A RIGHT OR A FREEDOM TO PICKET?

[10.04] Picketing is primarily a means of communication, persuasive in intent. In Ireland there is no legal right to picket and picketing has attracted only scant attention under the constitutional guarantee of free assembly in Art 40.6.1°(iii). *In Brendan Dunne Ltd v Fitzpatrick*[4] the plaintiffs were granted an injunction to restrain the defendants from picketing their premises by way of protest against late opening hours on one evening a week. The method of late opening had been agreed between the plaintiffs and their employees. Among other things, the defendants invoked the protection of Article 40.6.1°(iii) (para **2.02**). On the constitutional point Budd J said:

> The right of the citizens to assemble peaceably and to express their opinions freely are guaranteed only subject to public order and morality. As I read Article 40 the rights guaranteed are subject to the overriding proviso that in the exercise of such rights public order is not to be disturbed ... To my mind, if citizens in the course of an assembly commit a breach of the peace, or some other breach of the law, they thereby disturb public order and their actions are not protected by the Constitution in respect of the breach of the law committed.

> Prior to the coming into operation of the Constitution the picketing or watching and besetting of premises was unlawful unless justified by the Trade Disputes Act, 1906, ... I am unable to find that the law as it stood is in any way inconsistent with the terms of the Constitution ...

Earlier, Budd J had said that the existence of a trade dispute involved 'the right to picket'[5] but could not have intended to imply that any such legal right exists.[6] In

3. Avowedly so. See, for example, O'Daly J (as he then was) in *The Esplanade Pharmacy Ltd v Larkin* (1954) 62 ILTR 149 at 156: 'picketing, otherwise watching and besetting, a premises is lawful only in the conditions defined in the Trade Disputes Act 1906; and the Act, being in derogation of common law rights, has no wider scope that is found clearly marked out in it.'
4. *Brendan Dunne Ltd v Fitzpatrick* [1958] IR 29. Note the concept of 'peaceful' picketing was repeated by Walsh J in *EI Company Ltd v Kennedy* [1968] IR 69 at 74.
5. See likewise Walsh J in *EI Co Ltd v Kennedy and Others* [1968] IR 69 at 90.
6. The *Report of the Commission of Inquiry on Industrial Relations* (1981) misleadingly referred to 'the right to picket'.

relation to picketing, as to any other action in contemplation or furtherance of a trade dispute, statute provides immunities and these in turn depend upon the precise terms of the relevant section being fulfilled. Any ultra-liberal interpretation of the Trade Disputes Act 1906 was condemned by Fitzgerald J in *Becton Dickinson Ltd v Lee.*[7] Such interpretation, coupled with the failure of the authorities to enforce the law, in his view[8] 'has led to a public misconception and belief that a right to protest carries with it a right to picket. That is not the law.'

[10.05] Is there a freedom to picket? The case of *Lyons v Wilkins*[9] has been regarded as authority for the view that the mere presence of pickets is illegal at common law. According to Lord Lindley MR:

> to watch or beset a man's house with a view to compel him to do or not what is lawful for him not to do or to do is wrongful and without lawful authority unless some reasonable justification for it is consistent with the evidence. Such conduct seriously interferes with the ordinary comfort of human existence and ordinary enjoyment of the house beset, and such conduct would support an action on the case for nuisance at common law.

Citrine regards this authority as extremely doubtful.[10] Lord Denning (dissenting) in *Hubbard v Pitt*[11] (para **10.13**) took the view that picketing which is not protected by trade disputes legislation is, nevertheless, lawful:

> Picketing is lawful so long as it is done merely to obtain or communicate information, or peacefully to persuade; and is not such as to submit any other person to any kind of restraint or restriction on his personal freedom.

In *Dublin City Council v TEEU & Ors,*[12] the defendants argued that the picketing was lawful at common law even if it was not lawful by virtue of s 11(1) of the Act of 1990. The Judge did not consider it necessary or appropriate to determine that issue but she did make what she referred to as 'some general observations'. She stated:[13]

> The interesting argument that, irrespective of s 2 of the Act of 1906, peaceful picketing confined to persuasion or communication of information is not unlawful at common law, the position advocated on behalf of the defendants, did not recive judicial approbation in this jurisdiction before the enactment of the

7. *Becton Dickinson Ltd v Lee* [1973] IR 1.
8. At 41.
9. *Lyons v Wilkins* [1899] 1 Ch 255.
10. Citrine, *Trade Union Law* (3rd edn, Stevens & Sons, 1967), 558–562. That peaceful picketing was never criminal – see *R v Selsby* (1947) 5 Cox 495; *R v Druitt* (1867) 10 Cox 592; *R v Shepherd* (1868) 11 Cox 325.
11. *Hubbard v Pitt* [1975] ICR 308, a view espoused by Kerr and Whyte, *Irish Trade Union Law* (Professional Books, 1985), 284–9 and 297–8.
12. *Dublin City Council v TEEU & Ors* (9 June 2010, unreported), HC, Laffoy J.
13. At p 43.

Act of 1990. For instance, in *Esplanade Pharmacy Ltd v Larking & Ors* [1957] IR 285, O'Daly J, as he then was, stated (at p 298):

> But picketing, otherwise watching and besetting a premises is lawful only in the conditions defined in the Trade Disptues Act 1906; and the Act, being in derogation of common law rights, has no wider scope than is found clearly marked out in it.

> The Oireachtas, in enacting the Act of 1990, which followed a period of economic downturn and industrial unrest in the 1980s, and in particular, in enacting ss 8 to 19 inclusive in Pt II, which deal with trade disputes, set out to reform and codify the law on trade disputes, strikes and other industrial action, picketing and the involvement of trade unions. In my view, it would require a very convincing argument to lead to a conclusion that, in the context of a trade dispute within the meaning of s 8 of the Act of 1990, peaceful picketing by a trade union and its members, which is not lawful under s 11(1) of the Act of 1990, does not give rise to civil liability at common law. However, whether a suitably convincing argment can be made is a matter for another day.

[10.06] Picketing involving any sort of molestation, intimidation, nuisance or threats would not be lawful. To the extent that picketing involves no wrongful act, it seems permissible to say a picket is doing nothing unlawful and has – if not a right, at least a freedom – to act that way. In *Educational Co of Ireland Ltd v Fitzpatrick (No 2)*,[14] Kingsmill Moore J conceded in the Supreme Court that it might be possible to picket a premises so discreetly and unobtrusively as not to cause any intimidation or interference with the proper and convenient use of the premises but it did not seem to him that picketing 'as ordinarily conducted' fell within this description.

[10.07] The Irish Constitution takes its tenor from the common law in relation to picketing. It adds nothing new to the fabric which existed at the date of its coming into effect. But peaceful picketing as an act of assembly is constitutionally protected and to that extent it enjoys an enhanced status. Notwithstanding that picketing is statutorily protected, it may be possible to plead the existence of a constitutional right inherent in the plaintiffs which is allegedly violated or infringed by pickets. This area is little explored. It will be reverted to when the statutory protection in s 11 of the 1990 Act is considered (para **10.73**).

[10.08] Articles 10 and 11 of the European Convention on Human Rights (ECHR) concern freedom of expression and peaceful assembly respectively.[15] The European Convention on Human Rights Act 2003 has as its primary objective 'to enable further effect to be given, subject to the Constitution, to certain provisions of the [ECHR].' It is unlikely these Articles will add anything to the protections already found in the Constitution.[16]

---

14. *Educational Co of Ireland Ltd v Fitzpatrick (No 2)* [1961] IR 345 at 391.
15. Similarly on freedom of assembly, see Art 12 of the Charter of Fundamental Rights of the EU.
16. Contrast Lord Irvine LC in *DPP v Jones* [1999] 2 All ER 457 who expressed the view *obiter* that if English law did not give a right of peaceful assembly on the highway, Art 11 of the ECHR might in future require the common law to develop such a right.

We now turn to consider the various criminal and civil wrongs that may be perpetrated by pickets.

COMMON LAW

Trespass

[10.09] The civil wrongs most likely to be committed by pickets are trespass to the highway and nuisance; nuisance, not because of the obstruction to the highway, but because of the inconvenience caused to the persons being picketed. The particular importance of civil liability lies in the possibility of obtaining an injunction to restrain the picketing.[17] See **Ch 11** for a full discussion on the labour injunction in Ireland.

[10.10] Trespass to the highway involves an improper use of a public right of way. The right of the public in this regard has been described as 'a right to use [the highway] reasonably for passage and re-passage and for any other purpose reasonably incidental thereto': *Hubbard v Pitt*[18] per Forbes J. Picketing is not an act which is reasonably incidental to the right of passage but if the pickets constitute 'a moving crowd', ie a procession, it would not amount to trespass provided always that such use of the highway in the circumstances would not be unreasonable: *Lowdens v Keaveney.*[19]

The owner of the soil is the only person who can sue for trespass. Often this is the local authority. In theory, a local authority could proceed against pickets although it is unlikely that anything other than nominal damage would be suffered by it. The alternative remedy of an injunction would be likely to be awarded. The owner of adjacent land has no right to an injunction unless the road is a private one and he owns the soil under the highway up to the median line.

[10.11] In *Thomas Cook UK Travel Ltd and Thomas Cook Retail Ltd v Transport Salaried Staffs' Association and Ors*[20] the plaintiffs (Thomas Cook) proposed closing two stores. It carried out consultation under the Protection of Employment Act 1977 with its employee representatives who included its trade union representatives, the Transport Salaried Staff's Association (TSSA). Thomas Cook's offer of redundancy terms was rejected, and agreement could not be reached. They then served formal notice of redundancy on the majority of the employees employed at the two stores.

---

17.   See Wallington, 'Injunctions and the Right to Demonstrate' (1976) 35 CLJ 82.

18.   *Hubbard v Pitt* [1975] ICR 308 at 314.

19.   *Lowdens v Keaveney* [1903] 2 IR 82 at 89. In an injunction application by Marine Terminals Ltd against SIPTU, Clarke J took the view there was a real possibility the pickets had 'stepped over the bounds' of what was permitted when they were 'walking slowly in circles in front of the gate': 2009 IRN 2. The injunction granted restrained the defendants and all persons acting in concert from picketing 'otherwise than in a peaceful manner for the purpose of peacefully obtaining or securing information, or for the purposes of peacefully persuading any person to work, or to abstain from working' (as provided for in the Industrial Relations Act 1990, s 11(1)).

20.   *Thomas Cook UK Travel Ltd and Thomas Cook Retail Ltd v Transport Salaried Staffs' Association and Ors* High Court Record No 2009/7181P, 3 August 2009 (Peart J).

Following the announcement of the closure of the stores, a number of employees and trade union officials of the TSSA took possession of the Grafton Street premises, and refused to leave. Members of the gardaí were called in. Thomas Cook conveyed a letter to the employees advising them that their occupation of the building was unlawful and requesting them to vacate it. When requests to vacate were refused, Thomas Cook sought the assistance of the gardaí. Thomas Cook applied for an injunction claiming that the activities of the defendants were unlawful and did not enjoy protection under the Industrial Relations Acts 1946 to 2004 as trespass and unlawful occupation could not be classified as peaceful picketing.

[10.12] At an *ex parte* hearing of the High Court on 1 August 2009, Peart J granted an interim injunction restraining the defendants from interfering with access to, and egress from, and from trespassing upon and/or occupying, the relevant premises. Two days later, the High Court granted a permanent injunction in similar terms. The court further ordered the defendants forthwith to vacate the premises, and that the TSSA and the solicitors acting for the defendants convey to the defendants the legal advice received by the TSSA and direct them to vacate the occupied premises, advising that if they did not vacate the premises by 7 pm on 3 August 2009, and undertake to the court not to re-enter the premises, the court would hear an application for attachment and committal. Later that day, as the occupation continued, the court ordered that the defendants (save the union and one of the named officials) be attached on the ground that they had not complied with the Orders of the court. The defendants were ordered to appear to answer for contempt of court. The General Secretary of the TSSA undertook to comply with the Order which had been made. The following morning, the gardaí entered the occupied premises and removed the employees. They were brought before the High Court where they agreed to purge their contempt and to abide by the court Order already made. Peart J ruled that, on an exceptional basis, he would regard the purging of the contempt and the undertaking given on behalf of the defendants as sufficient to bring the application to an end. All those in custody were released and the issue of costs was adjourned to a later date.[21]

Nuisance

[10.13] Even if a picket is doing something allowed by the legislation on trade disputes, eg peacefully communicating information, he will nevertheless be liable if the purpose is to do something else as well, such as to obstruct the highway in an unreasonable way. Public and private nuisance are frequently restrained in picketing. Public nuisance is a crime (para **10.29**), but also, if a private individual suffers damage over and above that suffered by members of the public in general, it can ground a civil action: *Lyons v Gulliver*.[22] Private nuisance involves unreasonable interference with the use and enjoyment of land belonging to another. In *Hubbard v Pitt*[23] members of the Islington Tenants Campaign (the defendants) objected to the activities of the plaintiff

---

21. Costs were awarded against the TSSA and its General Secretary up to the end of Monday, 3 August 2009 but not including the costs in respect of the court's own contempt motion.
22. *Lyons v Gulliver* [1914] 1 Ch 631.
23. *Hubbard v Pitt* [1975] ICR 308.

estate agents in relation to developers who had allegedly been intimidating and harassing tenants. Between four and eight people began to picket the plaintiff's offices. They were restrained by interlocutory order in spite of the fact that they behaved in an orderly and peaceful manner throughout. The only judge to deliver judgment on the substantive issues in the Court of Appeal was the dissenting Lord Denning (whose views have generally been preferred). He realised that the granting of an injunction without any reference to the substantive issues made the court seem to prefer the plaintiff's interest of uninterrupted access to his commercial property to the defendants' interest in freedom of speech. Lord Denning disagreed with Forbes J at first instance who had granted an injunction where there had been no obstruction and no breach of the peace. The view of Lindley MR in *Lyons v Wilkins*[24] that picketing may of itself amount to a nuisance simply because of the attempt to persuade was condemned by Lord Denning as it 'has not stood the test of time.'[25] Said Lord Denning:[26]

> Picketing a person's premises is not unlawful unless it is associated with other conduct such as to constitute the whole conduct a nuisance at common law. Picketing is not a nuisance in itself. Nor is it a nuisance for a group of people to attend at or near the plaintiff's premises in order to obtain or to communicate information or in order peacefully to persuade. It does not become a nuisance unless it is associated with obstruction, violence, intimidation, molestation or threats.

It could thus be argued that the protection afforded under s 11 of the Industrial Relations Act 1990 does not render persons acting in contemplation or in furtherance or a trade dispute more privileged than other pickets.

[10.14] The English High Court judgment in *The Mersey Dock & Harbour Co v Verrinder*[27] should not be seen as undermining *Hubbard v Pitt*. The plaintiffs were the Port Authority for the Port of Liverpool. Amongst the premises they operated were a container terminal and a timber terminal. Due to the recession, the amount of work for haulage contractors at the docks had been drastically reduced. In addition, some ship-owners were said to have employed cowboy operators who undercut the established haulage operators. Liverpool drivers, members of the Transport and General Workers Union (TGWU), devised a scheme under which so-called 'container stamps' were issued to established haulage operators. Only vehicles with 'container stamps' would be serviced by dockers and other TGWU members. A small number of pickets began picketing the entrances to the two container terminals, severely affecting business. The company brought proceedings against five men it believed belonged to an *ad hoc* committee organising the picketing. The High Court (Fitzhugh J) granted an interlocutory injunction restraining the pickets. It held that the picketing of entrances

---

24.   *Lyons v Wilkins* [1899] 1 Ch 255 at 267.

25.   At the time of *Lyons v Wilkins* there was little authority to support Lindley MR's view and considerable authority against it (Citrine, *Trade Union Law* (3rd edn, Stevens & Sons, 1967), 558–562). Moreover, it is inconsistent with a later case, *Ward, Lock v Operative Printers' Assistants Society* (1906) 22 TLR 327.

26.   *Hubbard v Pitt* [1975] ICR 308 at 318.

27.   *The Mersey Dock & Harbour Co v Verrinder* [1982] IRLR 152.

to the terminals was capable in law of constituting a private nuisance and that, in determining whether there was a nuisance, violence and intimidation were not the only factors to which the court must have regard. In *Hubbard v Pitt*[28] Orr J made it clear that the defendant's intentions and states of mind formed 'a crucial question.' On the evidence in the case before him, it seemed to Fitzhugh J that the intention of the pickets was not merely to obtain or communicate information, it was to compel the company to ensure that at the terminals only haulage contractors preferred by the defendants were employed, to the exclusion of others not acceptable to them. In other words, the intention was to force the company to take some action against ship owners who employed cowboy drivers. This was tantamount to an attempt on the part of the defendants to regulate and control the container traffic to and from the company's terminals. If that was correct, the conduct was capable of constituting a private nuisance. The defendant's intention here resulted in coercive or intimidatory behaviour. This interpretation is preferable to regarding the judgment as based on the nebulous concept of 'intention'.[29]

[10.15] In *Tynan v Balmer*[30] pickets were walking in a circular movement in the public highway. They were held guilty of public nuisance. Quite apart from the statutory immunity, the court held that walking in a circle was an improper use of the highway and therefore a nuisance. A procession that moves from A to B, ie a proper use of the highway, would not be illegal, according to an early Irish authority earlier mentioned: *Lowden v Keaveney.*[31] In *Wall v Morrissey*[32] the Supreme Court held that not every obstruction of the highway amounted to a public nuisance. Members of the public could create temporary obstructions in the course of their normal uses of the highway.

Mass picketing was considered a nuisance, as well as any picketing outside the homes of non-strikers in *Thomas and Ors v NUM (South Wales Area) and Ors.*[33] Scott J also held that unreasonable harassment of workers who wished to use the highway to go to work could constitute a tort, a species of private nuisance. The facts concerned 50 to 70 pickets who daily hurled abuse.

[10.16] To sue for public nuisance, a person must have suffered special damage which is substantial, and over and above the public at large. Pecuniary loss does not need to be established. The defendants must have used the highway unreasonably. In *News Group Newspapers Ltd and Ors v SOGAT 82*[34] the pickets and daily demonstrators at

---

28. *Hubbard v Pitt* [1976] 1 QB 142, 188–198.
29. Contrast *Goulding Chemicals Ltd v Bolger* [1977] IR 211, dealing with the Trade Disputes Act 1906, s 2 from this viewpoint, which reveals a more clear-headed approach.
30. *Tynan v Balmer* [1967] 1 QB 91.
31. *Lowdens v Keaveney* [1903] 2 IR 82.
32. *Wall v Morrissey* [1969] IR 10.
33. *Thomas and Ors v NUM (South Wales Area) and Ors* [1985] IRLR 136.
34. *News Group Newspapers Ltd and Ors v SOGAT 82* [1986] IRLR 337.

the plaintiff's Wapping plant were found to constitute unreasonable use and the plaintiffs had variously suffered special damage.[35]

[10.17] Unlawful picketing may be restrained while lawful picketing is allowed to continue. In the ordinary way, as Clarke J observed in *P Elliot & Co Ltd v BATU*,[36] a court should not restrain picketing where it is legally justified, simply because there have been instances of an abuse of the 'right to picket'. But if pickets so abuse the right 'by the manner in which picketing is conducted, it may be that it is open to the court to prohibit picketing completely ...' He accepted the plaintiff's submission that, in order for a court to come to such a view, it would have to be satisfied that there were reasonable grounds for fearing that significant breaches of the manner in which picketing property be conducted would be likely to occur into the future.

CRIMINAL LIABILITY

Non-Fatal Offences Against the Person Act 1997, s 9

[10.18] Picketing may involve unlawful conduct. To begin with, a large area of criminal liability may be applicable. The section which proscribed certain offences in the Conspiracy and Protection of Property Act 1875, s 7,[37] was repealed and re-enacted with certain modifications by the Non-Fatal Offences Against the Person Act 1997, s 9. It reads:

> (1) A person who, with a view to compel another to abstain from doing or to do any act which that other person has a lawful right to do or to abstain from doing, wrongfully and without lawful authority—
>
> >   (a)   uses violence to or intimidates that other person or a member of the family of the other, or

---

35.   As follows: *The Times* lost journalists; employees had to be 'bused-in'; one worker suffered by having to come to work through the picket line.

36.   *P Elliot & Co Ltd v BATU* [2006] IEHC 340.

37.   Every person who, with a view to compel any other person to abstain from doing or do any act which such other person has a legal right to do or abstain from doing, wrongfully and without legal authority;

>   (1) Uses violence to or intimidates such other person, his wife or children, or injures his property , or
>
>   (2) Persistently follows such other person about from place to place, or
>
>   (3) Hides any tools, clothes, or other property owned or used by such other person, or deprives him of or hinders him in the use thereof, or
>
>   (4) Watches or besets the house or other place where such other person resides, or works, or carries on business, or happens to be, or the approach to such house or place, or
>
>   (5) Follows such other person with two or more other persons in a disorderly manner in or through any street or road

shall, on conviction thereof by a court of summary jurisdiction, or an indictment as hereinafter mentioned be liable either to pay a penalty not exceeding twenty pounds, or to be imprisoned for a term not exceeding three months; with or without hard labour.

(b)   injures or damages the property of that other, or

(c)   persistently follows[38] that other person about from place to place, or

(d)   watches or besets the premises or other place where that other person resides, works or carries on business, or happens to be, or the approach to such premises or place,[39] or

(e)   follows that other with one or more other persons in a disorderly manner in or through any public place

shall be guilty of an offence.

(2) For the purpose of this section attending at or near the premises or place where a person resides, works, carries on business or happens to be, or the approach to such premises or place, in order merely to obtain or communicate information, shall not be deemed a watching or besetting within the meaning of subsection (1)(d).

(3) A person guilty of an offence under this section shall be liable—

(a)   on summary conviction to a fine not exceeding £1,500 [€1,904.55] or imprisonment for a term not exceeding 12 months or to both, or

(b)   on conviction on indictment to a fine or to imprisonment for a term not exceeding 5 years or to both.

Prosecutions under s 7 were exceedingly rare. In the past, when it was more widely used, the section gave rise to difficult points of interpretation.[40]

Relying on authorities under the 1875 Act, it can be said that the introduction to the section applies to all five sub-headings in sub-s (1), so it must be established that there was an intention to compel another person to do or not to do something in relation to any of the acts specified in the sub-headings.

[10.19] What is the meaning of 'wrongfully' in sub-s (1)? Does it refer to an act that is wrongful apart from the statute or to an act that is wrongful for the sole reason that it contravenes the section? *Lyons v Wilkins*[41] suggested the latter but the Court of Appeal rejected this construction in *Ward Lock v Operative Printers Assistants Society*.[42] Fletcher-Moulton LJ, in a passage familiar to labour lawyers, said about the predecessor to s 9:

> It legalises nothing and it renders nothing wrongful that was not so before. Its object is solely to visit certain selected classes of acts which were previously wrongful – ie were at least civil torts – with penal consequences.[43]

An act is wrongful, therefore, if it is wrongful apart from the statute. This means that if it is protected by the Act of 1990, it is not actionable. In Ireland wrongfulness also includes unconstitutionality.

---

38.   See *Smith v Thomasson* (1890) 16 Cox 470; *Elsey v Smith* [1983] IRLR 292.
39.   *R v Wall* (1907) 21 Cox 401 at 403.
40.   *Fowler v Kibble* [1922] 1 Ch 487.
41.   *Lyons v Wilkins* [1899] 1 Ch 255.
42.   *Ward Lock v Operative Printers Assistants Society* (1906) 22 TLR 327.
43.   *Ward Lock v Operative Printers Assistants Society* (1906) 22 TLR 327 at 329.

[10.20] There are more difficulties of interpretation in the subheadings in sub-s (1), rarely considered by the Irish courts. English experience is illuminating.[44] On the meaning of intimidation in sub-s (1), while not wishing to provide an exhaustive definition of the term, James LJ said in *R v Jones*[45] that:

> Intimidate in this section includes putting persons in fear by the exhibition of force or violence, and there is no limitation restricting the meaning to cases of violence or threats of violence to the person.

Thus displays of force or violence against buildings and equipment are sufficient for intimidation. Offensive language which does not threaten violence might likewise constitute the same offence. There may be a difference between language which causes the person threatened to fear and be afraid and an actual threat to use violence or, as was held in *Judge v Bennett*,[46] the former may be sufficient for conviction. Irish courts might well take this view if *The State v District Justice O'Flynn*[47] is to be relied on. There, a picket shouted to a woman customer: 'Don't you know there is a strike on here? You should be ashamed of yourself. You are not entitled to go in there while there is a strike on'. The picket was convicted for 'offensive' language.

[10.21] **Chapter 8** deals with the tort of 'intimidation'. If, as in *Cooper v Millea*,[48] trade union officials threaten a strike unless a particular worker is dismissed, would such a threat of economic damage suffice? The only authority is *Tynan v Balmer*[49] where Chapman J at first instance considered whether *Rookes v Barnard*[50] (the classic English intimidation case) might affect the area. He was of the view that it might be held in due course to involve some extension of the scope of the criminal offence of intimidation but, he said, 'I do not think that in the present case I ought to embark upon a discussion of such a complex and recondite topic.[51]'

Rookes v Barnard, Cooper v Millea and other cases dealing with intimidation, if extended into this area, would considerably broaden its scope. Cases of intimidation may involve either three- or two-party offences. The cases just mentioned, and *Riordan v Butler*,[52] involved A threatening B and B acting to the detriment of C, ie three-party intimidation. They are therefore not within the scope of s 9. In order to obtain a conviction under s 9, two-party intimidation would be necessary and the act would have to be tortious apart from the statute of 1997. In *Goulding Chemicals Ltd v Bolger*[53] the Supreme Court declared that picketing was not lawful if designed by its manner or the number of participants to intimidate but in the absence of greater

---

44. *Gibson v Lawson* [1891] 2 QB 545; *Agnew v Munro* (1891) 28 SLR 335.
45. *R v Jones* [1974] ICR 310 at 318.
46. *Judge v Bennett* [1883] 4 TLT 75.
47. *The State v District Justice O'Flynn* [1948] IR 343.
48. *Cooper v Millea* [1938] IR 749.
49. *Tynan v Balmer* [1967] 1 QB 91.
50. *Rookes v Barnard* [1964] AC 1129.
51. Footnote 43, at 99–100. On appeal no reference was made to intimidation.
52. *Riordan v Butler* [1940] IR 347.
53. *Goulding Chemicals Ltd v Bolger* [1977] IR 211.

specificity the court cannot be taken to have been referring to one or other form of intimidation.

[10.22] The law of criminal conspiracy applies to all the subheadings of s 9(1). Persons who conspired to commit an offence under s 9 and who were actually present at the act itself would be particularly vulnerable to prosecution.

An individual who suffers damage to a private right as a result of action contrary to s 9 may injunct the criminal activity, or the Gardaí may proceed on their own account. The charge under s 9 must specify the wrongful nature of the act as well as its purpose (according to the introduction to the section). Section 9 creates only one offence so that a count which charges a defendant under more than one head – or with two items in the same head – is not bad for duplicity: *The State v District Justice O'Flynn;*[54] *AG v O'Brien.*[55]

[10.23] *AG v O'Brien* involved the watching and besetting of two grocery and provision shops, with the object of trying to compel the owner to close early. There was no evidence of a trade dispute. The accused were found guilty and bound over to keep the peace. The Court of Criminal Appeal (Kennedy CJ, Fitzgibbon and Murnaghan JJ) upheld the conviction. Watching and besetting, they declared, sought to compel the doing or abstaining from doing of an act one is legally entitled to do or not to do, and only one offence is constituted. While the two shops were covered in the same indictment, they were close to one another, constituted one set of business premises and the acts complained of were a simultaneous watching and besetting of both. Kennedy CJ was called on to comment in regard to the duration necessary to constitute the offence. He referred to *Charnock v Court*[56] and *Walters v Breen.*[57] In the first of these, Sterling J said:[58]

> There is nothing in the statute which defines the duration of watching. It may be, it seems to me, for a short time, when it speaks of attending at or near a house or place where the person resides, or works, or happens to be. The word 'attending' does not necessarily imply any lengthened attendance upon the spot, nor is there anything in the statute to limit its operation to a place habitually frequented by the workman, such as the house where he resides or the place where he works. On the contrary, the words 'place where he happens to be' seem to me to embrace any place where the workman is found, however casually.

In the later case, Sterling J referred to this decision and expressed the same opinion. According to Kennedy CJ, that view:

> which has held ground since then, does not seem to me to be contrary to the dicta of Pallas CB in *R v Wall.*[59] The Chief Baron had said, *inter alia*, that 'Watching involves persistent watching'.

---

54.   *The State v District Justice O'Flynn* [1948] IR 343.

55.   *AG v O'Brien* (1936) 70 ILTR 101.

56.   *Charnock v Court* [1899] 2 Ch 35.

57.   *Walters v Breen* (1899) 2 Ch 696.

58.   *Charnock v Court* [1899] 2 Ch 35 at 38.

59.   *R v Wall* (1907) 21 Cox CC 401 at 403.

It is probable that in this earlier case the Chief Baron, in his charge to the jury, meant the word 'persistent' to be understood in the sense of 'insistent'. The opinion of this Court is that, as regards time in any particular case, it is a matter of degree in relation to the circumstances and facts proven in evidence. An instance in connection with the offence under consideration would be the watching of a railway station for the purpose of meeting a train which was carrying workers to replace those on strike. There, in the case of any one train, there would be a definite time of arrival and attending at that time would probably be sufficient and certainly fifteen minutes would be sufficient. I am of opinion that watching in the particular context does not necessarily connote or involve long duration or, in fact, any specific duration of time. It is a matter of degree and entirely a matter for the jury to determine.

This is no doubt the correct approach. It was adhered to in later Irish judgments in relation to the Trade Disputes Act. In *Ferguson v O'Gorman*,[60] for example, Sullivan CJ declared that there was nothing in the Act of 1906 to limit the meaning of the word 'attend' and to make it inapplicable to prolonged and continuous action.

Motor Vehicles

[10.24] The importance of the juridical basis of the legislation in this country regarding trade disputes (immunities rather than rights) can be appreciated when it comes to the obstruction of motor vehicles. If there were a right to picket, trade unionists would be able to claim an entitlement to stop motor vehicles in order to persuade their drivers to proceed no further. But as there is no claim-right in respect of communicating information, the stopping of motor vehicles is not permitted: *Hunt v Broome*;[61] *Tynan v Balmer*.[62] Lord Reid put the matter thus in *Broome*:

> I see no ground for implying any right to require the person whom it is sought to persuade to submit to any kind of constraint or restriction of his personal freedom. One is familiar with persons at the side of the road signalling to a driver requesting him to stop. It is then for the driver to decide whether he will stop or not. That, in my view, a picket is entitled to do. If the driver stops, the picket can talk to him but only for so long as the driver is willing to listen.

[10.25] It seems, however, that, at least in England, a picket is not legally entitled to signal to a driver to stop. In *Kavanagh v Hiscock*[63] the police used their powers to prevent pickets approaching vehicles. The Divisional Court upheld a conviction when someone tried to push through a police cordon on the ground that the police officer reasonably apprehended a breach of the peace and that the police had a duty to regulate the use of the highway. This principle was not detracted from by the fact that the police and pickets had unofficially agreed beforehand that four of the pickets should be allowed to remain within the police cordon while the remainder were kept back by the police as a coach of 'blacklegs'[64] was anticipated. The defendant had objected when he saw these four pickets being cleared from within the cordon.

---

60. *Ferguson v O'Gorman* [1937] IR 620.
61. *Hunt v Broome* [1974] AC 597.
62. *Tynan v Balmer* [1967] 1 QB 91.
63. *Kavanagh v Hiscock* [1974] ICR 282.
64. That is, persons who continue, or attempt to continue, to work during a strike.

[10.26] In the Northern Ireland case of *Norbrook Laboratories Ltd v King*[65] the vehicle of a customer entering the premises being picketed was obstructed and intimidating remarks were made to him, a lorry was stopped by standing in front of it, the body of a car leaving the premises was subjected to 'drumming' and cars were parked so as to prevent lorries from entering the gate of the premises. Murray J in the Northern Ireland High Court found liability in nuisance without specifying precisely why all these acts were 'unlawful' or 'illegal'. Clearly, some acts were, eg obstructing the highway (*Hunt v Broome*)[66] and intimidating remarks to the driver (Conspiracy and Protection of Property Act 1875, s 7(1)). But there is no indication why the other evidence accepted by the judge revealed unlawful or illegal action.

[10.27] The British Society of Labour Lawyers has argued that the statutory provisions as to picketing should be extended to include a limited right to stop vehicles to communicate with the drivers thereof, due regard being had to other users of the highway.[67] The Donovan Commission did not like the idea of a right in such circumstances with a correlative duty, backed up by sanctions, to stop. It believed it would be impossible to define such a right in terms which would avoid 'considerable obstruction to the highway' and serious risk of personal injury to the pickets themselves.[68] Ireland's *Report of the Commission of Inquiry on Industrial Relations* (1981) made no reference to this point other than descriptively to note the legal position. The 1990 Act by implication rejected the need for such a right.

[10.28] In *P Elliott & Company Ltd v BATU*[69] the High Court (Clarke J) found:

> the way the picket was organised was such that vehicles approaching the site did not really have any option but to stop and converse with union officials prior to entering the site … after the driver of a vehicle had indicated an intention to enter into the site I am satisfied that there was a slow retreat by those involved on the pickets so as to permit the vehicle concerned to enter the site.

The plaintiff company had been granted an order previously and brought an application for breach of that order. Refusing the application, the court found nothing had occurred which amounted to a significant impairment of the ability of persons to enter the site very soon after they had indicated a wish to do so.

Public Nuisance

[10.29] Public nuisance covers any acts, big or small, which interfere with the rights of the public at large.

It is a criminal offence at common law (it is also a tort) to obstruct the public in the exercise or enjoyment of rights of way common to all, including the freedom to pass and re-pass on the highway. Unreasonable behaviour of some kind is necessary: *R v*

---

65. *Norbrook Laboratories Ltd v King* [1984] IRLR 200, noted Simpson (1982) 4 DULJ (ns) 124 and (1984) 6 DULJ (ns) 192.

66. *Hunt v Broome* [1974] AC 597.

67. Donovan Commission, Minutes of Evidence 63. Question 10112.

68. Cmnd 3623, para 874.

69. *P Elliott & Company Ltd v BATU* [2006] IEHC 340.

Clark (No 2).[70] Peaceful picketing is not of itself unreasonable and, unless there is something more, it is unlikely to attract liability. In practice public nuisance is rarely charged in this context.

Breach of the Peace

[10.30] To obstruct a garda officer in the execution of his duty is an offence contrary to common law. If a garda officer issues instructions in pursuance of his duty to control the highway, or where he reasonably apprehends a breach of the peace, a picket must comply. And:

> It is too late, at least in Ireland, to question the power of a constable, as a reasonable exercise of his duty to preserve the peace, to put a person into a safe place, who is not himself a wrongdoer, but who, if not removed, will become the subject of a breach of the peace.[71]

[10.31] In *Piddington v Bates*[72] two pickets were posted at each entrance to a factory in which about eight members of staff were working. Piddington was anxious to join the pickets but was told by a police constable that the number of pickets already posted was sufficient. 'I know my rights' he said, whereupon he pushed gently past the policeman, 'and was gently arrested.'

On the facts there was no obstruction, no intimidation, no threats or intimations of violence. The charge against the appellant was one of obstructing a constable in the execution of his duty. Lord Parker CJ upheld the appellant's conviction, taking the view that the police were within their rights when they limited the number of pickets.

The mere statement by a constable that he anticipated there might be a breach of the peace was not enough. There must exist proven facts from which a constable could reasonably have anticipated such a breach. Nor indeed, said the Lord Chief Justice, was it enough that in the constable's contemplation there was a remote possibility of a breach of the peace. Every case would turn on its facts. Were there reasonable grounds on which a constable charged with the duty to uphold the peace reasonably anticipated that a breach of the peace might occur? The question was whether the police here had drawn an arbitrary line. Why two pickets – why not three? The Lord Chief Justice's response to this criticism was '[f]or my part, I think that a police officer charged with the duty of preserving the Queen's peace must be left to take such steps as, on the evidence before him, he thinks proper.'

[10.32] The degree of force which may be used in dispersing unlawful assemblies (where picketing exceeds what is 'peaceful') depends once again on the facts, for the force used must always be moderate and proportionate to the circumstances of the case and to the end to be attained: *Lynch v Fitzgerald and Ors (No 2)*[73] per Hanna J. Gardaí have considerable power to control pickets where they merely apprehend a breach of

---

70.   *R v Clark (No 2)* [1964] 2 QB 315.
71.   *Coyne v Tweedy* [1895] 2 IR 167 *per* Fitzgibbon LJ.
72.   *Piddington v Bates* [1960] 3 All ER 660.
73.   *Lynch v Fitzgerald and Ors (No 2)* [1938] IR 382; 71 ILTR 212.

the peace (the assembly need not necessarily be unlawful). In such cases the statutory immunity for picketing cannot legalise a breach of the peace.

[10.33] In *Wershop v Metropolitan Police Commissioner*,[74] May J made it clear that a constable might only arrest without warrant a person who wilfully obstructed him in the execution of his duty if the nature of the obstruction was such that it actually caused or was likely to cause a breach of the peace or was calculated to prevent the lawful arrest of another person. In *Moss v McLachlan*[75] Skinner J observed, *inter alia*, that in reaching their conclusion, the police were bound to take into account all they had heard and read and to exercise their judgement and common sense on it as well as on the events taking place before their eyes.

Unlawful assembly, rout and riot

[10.34] Other common law crimes touching on breach of the peace include unlawful assembly, affray and riot. In *Barrett v Tipperary (NR) Co Council*[76] McLoughlin J adopted the following definition of 'unlawful assembly':

> An unlawful assembly at common law is an assembly of three or more persons (a) for purposes forbidden by law, such as that of committing a crime by open force; or (b) with intent to carry out any common purpose, lawful or unlawful, in such a manner as to endanger the public peace, or to give firm and courageous persons in the neighbourhood of such assembly reasonable grounds to apprehend a breach of the peace in consequence of it.

McLoughlin J had never come across a case in which unlawful assembly was held to exist where there was not some evidence of force or violence in the commission of an offence or some show of force or violence or some breach of the peace or of some conduct tending to excite alarm in the mind of a person of 'firm and reasonable courage'.

[10.35] An unlawful assembly becomes a rout 'so soon as the assembled persons do any act towards carrying out the illegal purpose which has made their assembly unlawful' such as setting out for the place where the purpose is to be carried into effect. The rout becomes a riot 'so soon as this illegal purpose is put into effect forcibly' by persons mutually intending to resist any opposition: *R v McNaughten*.[77] The common law on these matters is rarely resorted to nowadays.

STATUTORY OFFENCES

[10.36] Statutory offences may be relevant. The paragraphs which follow deal with the Offences Against the State Act 1939, an amending Act of 1992 and the Prohibition of Forcible Entry and Occupation Act 1971.

---

74.   *Wershop v Metropolitan Police Commissioner* [1978] 3 All ER 340.
75.   *Moss v McLachlan* [1985] IRLR 76.
76.   *Barrett v Tipperary (NR) Co Council* [1964] IR 22 at 28.
77.   *R v McNaughten* (1881) 14 Cox CC 576.

Offences Against the State Act 1939, s 28

[10.37] Picketing cannot take place in the vicinity of either House of the Oireachtas without falling foul of the Offences against the State Act 1939, s 28:

(i)   It shall not be lawful for any public meeting to be held in, or any procession to pass along or through, any public street or unenclosed place which or any part of which is situate within one-half of a mile from any building in which both Houses or either House of the Oireachtas is sitting or about to sit if either:

(a)   an Officer of the Garda Síochána not below the rank of Chief Superintendent has by notice given to a person concerned in the holding or organisation of such meeting or procession or published in a manner reasonably calculated to come to the knowledge of the persons so concerned, prohibited the holding of such meeting in or the passing of such procession along or through any such public street or unenclosed place as aforesaid, or

(b)   a member of the Garda Síochána calls on the persons taking part in such meeting or procession to disperse.

Penalties for contravention are laid down in s 2: a stated maximum fine, or three months' imprisonment or both.

The Offences Against the State (Amendment) Act 1972, s 4(1)

[10.38] The Offences Against the State (Amendment) Act 1972, contains a provision on meetings or utterances tending to obstruct justice. Under s 4(1):

(a)   Any public statement made orally, in writing or otherwise, or any meeting, procession or demonstration in public, that constitutes an interference with the course of justice shall be unlawful.

(b)   A statement, meeting, procession or demonstration shall be deemed to constitute an interference with the course of justice if it is intended, or is of such a character as to be likely, directly or indirectly to influence any court, person or authority concerned with the institution, conduct or defence of any civil or criminal proceedings (including a party or witness) as to whether or how the proceedings should be instituted, conducted, continued or defended, or as to what should be their outcome.

Subsection (2) provides penalties for contravention. Subsection (3) provides that nothing in the section is to affect the law as to contempt of court. Section 7(1) of the 1939 Act proscribes a meeting or demonstration that amounts to an attempt to obstruct justice, or any other branch of government or the performance of their functions by 'any member of the legislature' or any State officials or employees.

Forcible Entry and Occupation Act 1971

[10.39] The 1906 Act (still less the 1990 Act) did not confer a licence to enter upon property: *BHS Ltd v Mitchell*[78] and *PW Woolworth Ltd v Haynes*.[79] The tort of trespass has already been discussed (para **10.09**). An employer may seek to restrain the occupation or, as in the *Ranks* dispute,[80] it may seek an order of possession directed to the Sheriff to deliver up possession of the premises[81]. In this latter instance the role of An Garda Síochána is protective: *Attorney General v Kissane*.[82] Not only an employer may have rights to redress; an injured third party whose property is being wrongfully detained may sue: *Roadstone Ltd v Bailie*.[83]

[10.40] An occupation may contravene the criminal law, in particular the Forcible Entry and Occupation Act 1971[84] (the 1971 Act). There is confusion surrounding the use of this Act in trade disputes. Section 1(4) of the Forcible Entry Act states that, 'Nothing in the Act shall affect the law relating to acts done in contemplation or furtherance of a trade dispute within the meaning of the Trade Disputes Act 1906.' The Industrial Relations Act 1990 provides in s 3(3):

> In any enactment other than this Act, a reference to the Trade disputes Act, 1906 (repealed by this Act) or to any provision thereof shall, without prejudice to section 20 (1) of the Interpretation Act, 1937, be construed as a reference to any relevant provision of Part II of this Act.

Section 1(4) of the 1971 Act must, therefore, be construed as though 'Part II of the Industrial Relations Act 1990' were substituted for the Trade Disputes Act 1906.

The Irish translation of s 1(4) includes the phrase 'Ní dheanfaidh sé difear don dlí'. That sums up the aim of the sub-section. The Act of 1971 shall not make any difference to the Act of 1990: it is not intended to make anything under the Act of 1990 unlawful that was not unlawful beforehand. Unfortunately, however, the vagueness of the phraseology in s 1(4) does not make the task of its interpretation easy.

[10.41] Upon analysis, the subsection's aspirational statement appears to coincide with what is, anyhow, a descriptive one. For the Forcible Entry Act concerns criminal law and the Industrial Relations Act 1990, civil law, with one exception. The only section to involve the criminal law in the Industrial Relations Act is s 11 on picketing. Section 11 begins with a positive and global statement 'It shall be *lawful*'. This means that, if a picketer adheres to the statutory formula, he cannot be challenged for any breaches of the law whether, for example, nuisance at civil law or watching and besetting in criminal law. But picketing must, in any event, be 'at or near' a house etc,

---

78. *BHS Ltd v Mitchell* (18 April 1984, unreported), HC.

79. *PW Woolworth Ltd v Haynes* (19 July 1984, unreported), HC.

80. See (1984) *The Irish Times*, 22 May.

81. Rules of the Superior Courts Ord 47, r 2.

82. *Attorney General v Kissane* (1893) 32 LR Ir 220.

83. *Roadstone Ltd v Bailie* (10 November 1982, unreported), HC.

84. The offence of forcible entry arose under a number of old statutes, now repealed, for example, the Forcible Entry Acts of 1381, 1391 1429 and the Forcible Entry (Ireland) Acts of 1634 and 1786.

so by very definition, the offence of forcible entry would not be applicable. In June 1982, the Supreme Court directed the Gardaí to operate the Act against six employees occupying the premises of British American Optical Co Ltd during a trade dispute.[85]

[10.42] The law at present would permit the Act of 1971 to be used against workers in a trade dispute who have forcibly entered or remained in occupation of land. It would make no difference if they had a legal right of entry.[86] It should be noted, however, that the definition of 'forcibly' in s 1(1) begins with 'using or threatening to use force in relation to person or property ...' This is similar to the former requirement at common law that entry must occur in circumstances amounting to a breach of the peace or unlawful assembly.[87] When strikers enter a building, they undoubtedly effect an entry in the sense in which the word is intended under the Act. On the other hand, it will usually be possible for the entry itself to be made without threatening or resorting to force. It is vital to recall that more than mere trespass is required. An old test at common law used to be whether the show of force was calculated to deter the owner from sending away the invaders: *Milner v Maclean*.[88] Perhaps the greatest risk resides in the fact that circumstances amounting to force may be found in damage done to a building in the course of entering. Common law holds it is not 'forcible' to go into a building through a window or to open a door with a key or to lift a latch or to withdraw a bolt.[89]

[10.43] The definition of 'forcibly' in s 1(1) goes on to say that:

> ... participation in action or conduct with others in numbers or circumstances calculated to prevent by intimidation the exercise by any person of his rights in relation to any property shall constitute a threat to use force ...

It was no doubt felt necessary to include the above as the determination of what constitutes a threat to property is far more difficult to agree than a threat to the person. According to an old common law authority, the former could reside in 'such speeches as plainly imply a purpose of using force against those who shall make any resistance, as if one says that he will keep his possession in spite of all men'.[90] For example, militant and highly publicised demands made by workers sitting-in against their employer might be regarded as constituting threats to property if they were likely to inhibit the employer from taking steps to protect his premises.

If workers enter premises peaceably in a dispute and sit-in and continue during occupation to behave peaceably, they will not come within the Act of 1971.

[10.44] A person who encourages or advocates the commission of forcible entry or occupation is guilty of 'an offence': s 4. Hence accessories (other workers, trade union officials etc) might be potentially liable to prosecution.

---

85. (1982) *Irish Times*, 24 June. See too *Ross and Co Ltd v Swan* [1981] ILRM 416.

86. *R v Smyth* 5 C & P 201.

87. *Storr* (1765) 3 Burr 1698: *Blake* (1976) 3 Burr 1731.

88. *Milner v Maclean* (1825) 2 C & P 17.

89. 1 Hawk C 64, s 26.

90. 1 Hawk c 64, s 27.

INDUSTRIAL RELATIONS ACT 1990, s 11

[10.45] Pickets frequently induce breaches of contract – employment or commercial. A picket line *per se* induces others to break their contract of employment by not crossing it. The Commission of Inquiry on Industrial Relations recommended[91] that picketing should:

> Enjoy the protection of the law where carried out at or near a place where a person works, carries on business or happens to be while so working or carrying on business.

The Commission did not consider it reasonable that a person (employer or worker) should be subject to picketing at his home except where an employer conducts his business from his home. The Commission took the same view of picketing carried out in other places not related to the business activities of an individual.

Section 11 of the Industrial Relations Act 1990 effected major changes in the law on picketing. It is perhaps the most important section in Pt II of that Act.[92]

PRIMARY PICKETING

Trade Disputes Act 1906, s 2 and Industrial Relations Act 1990, s 11 contrasted

[10.46] Section 11(1) of the 1990 Act provides:

> It shall be lawful for one or more persons, acting on their own behalf or on behalf of a trade union in contemplation or furtherance of a trade dispute, to attend at, or where that is not practicable, at the approaches to, a place where their employer works or carries on business, if they so attend merely for the purpose of peacefully persuading any person to work or abstain from working.

Section 2 of the Trade Disputes Act 1906 (see **Appendix**), the predecessor to s 11, began similarly with the words 'It shall be lawful ...' One of the attempted amendments,[93] initially approved by the Parliamentary Committee on what eventually became the Trade Disputes Act 1906 and by a joint meeting between all Labour MPs and others, was to add to the picketing clause the phrase 'and such attending shall not be held to be a nuisance'. However, this did not find its way into the Bill.[94] The Attorney General thought the clause unnecessary as:

> It followed that any picketing which was held to be peaceable and reasonable and was conducted with the view of exercising rights under this section would be held by a court to be lawful and would not be held to be a nuisance.

The amendment would have been significant as it would have clarified for judges that, as the Attorney General believed, the picketing section gave positive rights.[95] Section 2

---

91. *Report*, 1981, para 743.
92. See, eg, 398 *Dáil Debates* Cols 562–563.
93. Kidner, 'Lessons in Trade Union Law Reform: the origins and passage of the Trade Disputes Act 1906' (1982) 2 LS 34 at 50.
94. See Hansard, Parl Debs Vol 162 col 1655.
95. Kidner, 'Lessons in Trade Union Law Reform: the origins and passage of the Trade Disputes Act 1906' (1982) 2 LS 34.

was interpreted narrowly, particularly in Ireland, and the law of nuisance was often used against pickets. The section was regarded as amounting to a licence to beset a person's premises, in contradiction of his right to quiet enjoyment, and therefore when the statute came under the eye of the courts, it was seen not to legitimise what before was wrongful, but rather to make a limited rule for limited circumstances. The courts sought to limit the effect of the section as much as possible.

[10.47] 'Lawfulness' is not limited to civil or criminal categories. Once the purpose of the picketing is as set out in s 11(1) of the 1990 Act, the action is immune from any liability. The fact that the defendants are themselves in breach of contract will be immaterial: *Kire Manufacturing Ltd v O'Leary*.[96] Nor is the immunity ousted by incidents taking place between one member of the picket and another employee if very short-lived and not part of a continuous or planned course of action or pursuant to instruction from the trade union concerned: *Maher v Beirne and Ors*.[97] Likewise, there must be sufficient evidence of the continuance of an unlawful mode of picketing if such was the case at the start of a strike to justify an interlocutory injunction on that ground: *EI Company Ltd v Kennedy*.[98] But overall the protection given is limited. If a picket's purpose changes, he no longer attracts the immunity. The courts ask whether anything unlawful was done other than that which was reasonably necessary for the communication of information. As will be seen, the section legitimises trespass to the highway but not to private property; it excuses a technical nuisance at common law. Outside of that, pickets are likely to attract liability and are particularly vulnerable when it comes to breaches of constitutional rights.

Section 2 of the 1906 Act

[10.48] The forerunner of s 11, as noted, was s 2 of the Trade Disputes Act 1906. It was said of s 2 that it:

> authorises the use of the highway by persons and for the purposes described in that section, and ... it therefore justifies a user of the highway which would constitute a trespass at common law. Whether the user proved in any particular case is such user as can be justified under the section will depend on the particular circumstances, including the acts and the conduct of the alleged trespassers.

Sullivan CJ was 'driven' to this conclusion in *Ferguson v O'Gorman*[99] thereby settling any ambiguity that resulted from earlier cases that the section did not justify a trespass. *Ferguson* concerned a trade dispute between the proprietors of a hairdressing business in Cork and the local branch of a trade union of which several of the defendants were members. On the instructions of the secretary of the union the defendant employees began to picket the plaintiff's premises. The picket consisted generally of from four to six persons, and it was carried on continuously, but peacefully, so as not to amount to an abuse of the highway. The Supreme Court, affirming the High Court, held that,

---

96.   *Kire Manufacturing Ltd v O'Leary* (29 April 1974, unreported), HC.

97.   *Maher v Beirne and Ors* (1958) 68 ILTR 101.

98.   *EI Company Ltd v Kennedy* [1968] IR 69.

99.   *Ferguson v O'Gorman* [1937] IR 620.

having regard to the provisions of s 2, the picketing by the defendants was a reasonable and usual mode of using the highway and did not constitute a trespass.

[10.49] Sullivan CJ referred to *Larkin v Belfast Harbour Commissioners*[100] and *McCusker v Smith.*[101] In the former, Larkin addressed a crowd of workmen on a quay the property of Belfast Harbour Commissioners, without the permission of their secretary, in breach of a by-law made by them. Following prosecution by the Commissioners, he was convicted of an offence against the by-law. On a case stated the Court of King's Bench held that the conviction was right. It was argued on behalf of Larkin that he was entitled under s 2 of the Act of 1906 to enter upon the quay for the purposes mentioned therein but that argument was rejected by every member of the court. Thus O'Brien LCJ:[102]

> Do the words 'to attend at or near a house or place where a person resides or works' authorise a person of the specified class … to attend not only in the immediate proximity of a house or place where a person resides or works, but in – within – the house or place itself? Does, in fact, the Act of Parliament authorise an entry into a house or place, against the will of the owner, for the purpose mentioned in the clause of the section which I have read? If this be so, the Legislature has, indeed, conferred on the specified class a right which I think neither trade unions nor anyone connected with them has ever before claimed – a right to invade the privacy of a man's house, or the factory or place of business where a man's work is carried on.

[10.50] To O'Brien LCJ s 2 of the Act of 1906 attempted to define what should not be intimidation[103] but it was not intended to enlarge the physical areas of operation of representatives of trade unions or of others. Madden J in a concurring judgment saw the effect of the legislation as legalising a course of action which might otherwise amount to a nuisance but 'the idea of trespass in or upon private property is wholly absent from that of picketing, peaceful or otherwise.' Likewise, Wright J saw the Act as legalising picketing in the vicinity of a house or place, as close to it as pickets may wish, 'but remaining outside.' Dodd J was equally adamant.

[10.51] In *McCusker v Smith*[104] it was held by the Court of King's Bench on a case stated that s 2 of the Act of 1906 did not authorise the defendant's entry into the hall of the complainant's licensed premises for the purposes specified in the section. Sir James Campbell CJ[105] concluded his judgment (in which Kenny J concurred) as follows:

> 'At' does not mean 'in' or 'upon'. This being settled law, there was evidence that some acts of the defendant were committed in or upon the premises, and therefore he could not justify his conduct under the section.

---

100. *Larkin v Belfast Harbour Commissioners* [1908] 2 IR 214.
101. *McCusker v Smith* [1918] 2 IR 432.
102. *Larkin v Belfast Harbour Commissioners* [1908] 2 IR 214 at 219–20.
103. The English High Court accepted these words in *British Airports Authority v Ashton* [1983] IRLR 287.
104. *McCusker v Smith* [1918] IR 432.
105. *McCusker v Smith* [1918] IR 432 at 440.

[10.52] In *Ferguson*[106] (para **10.48**), counsel for the appellants relied on these cases as establishing that s 2 of the Trade Disputes Act 1906 did not justify a trespass. In each of the cases concerned the section was held not to justify the particular trespass that was committed. Sullivan CJ referred to Madden J who said that the idea of trespass upon private property was wholly absent from that of picketing and to Dodd J who stated 'in the most general terms that the section did not justify a trespass':[107]

> But I do not think that either of these learned Judges had present to his mind a trespass on the soil of a highway as such, and accordingly, I do not think that their judgments can be relied on as indicating their opinion that such a trespass could not be justified under the section in question.

If the section could not be so construed, it would be difficult to give any reasonable interpretation to it. When the legislature had provided an immunity, said the Chief Justice:[108]

> it cannot reasonably have contemplated that such a house or place would be situated in a waste or no man's land. The usual approach to a residence or place of business is by a public highway and unless a right to attend at or near a residence or place of business is a right to attend on a public highway, I do not see how the right can be exercised at all, consistently with the decisions in *Larkin's Case* and *McCusker's Case* that private property may not be invaded.

To the extent that there is a trespass on the highway as opposed to trespass (not lawful entry, see below) on the premises of another, picketing was protected by the Trade Disputes Act 1906. *Larkin* and *Ferguson* were cited and approved by the Queen's Bench Division Court in *British Airports Authority v Ashton*.[109]

[10.53] Does the law of trespass apply to workers who are normally entitled to use premises as employees? Employees are 'invitees' at common law but their freedom to enter their employer's premises is not unfettered. It is limited to entry for the purposes of their work or for such purpose as may be permitted by their employer, eg attendance at union meetings. So where workers engage in industrial action which amounts to a repudiatory breach of their contracts of employment, their implied authority to remain on their employer's premises comes to an end. If they continue to remain on the premises after a reasonable period while refusing to work, they will be liable for trespass. Therefore, apart from the possible crime of forcible occupation (para **10.39**), every 'sit-in', 'sit-down' or 'stay-down' strike involves the tort of trespass.

Section s 11 of the 1990 Act

[10.54] The Industrial Relations Act 1990, s 11 made three important changes. It:

(a) replaced 'at or near' with 'at, or where that is not practicable, at the approaches to';

---

106. *Ferguson v O'Gorman* [1937] IR 620.
107. *Ferguson v O'Gorman* [1937] IR 620 at 648.
108. *Ferguson v O'Gorman* [1937] IR 620 at 648.
109. *British Airports Authority v Ashton* [1983] IRLR 287.

(b)   confined picketing to a person's own employer[110] (except as provided in sub-s (2)); and

(c)   confined picketing to a place where a person's own employer works or carries on business (except as provided in sub-s (2)).

The phrase 'at or near' allowed pickets to be placed at the entrances to shopping centres, port complexes and industrial estates where the dispute involved only one employer in these locations. Many of these locations were private property, a complicating factor. Section 11 goes a long way to meet the problems experienced in multi-site locations. The *Dáil Debates* on s 11 were much concerned with multi-employment sites such as ports, airports, shopping centres and industrial estates. The Minister emphasised the significance of the words 'at, or where this is not practicable' preceding 'at the approaches to' and predicted the courts would apply the test whether it was practicable to picket at the employer's place of business inside the location. If the owner of the location objected, the proviso would operate and the picket could then be placed outside.[111] A number of directions were approved in respect of picketing at ports and industrial estates by ICTU at its Annual Conference in 1984: the union engaged should seek permission from the Port Authority or the owners of the industrial estate to picket outside the premises. If refused, the picket will have to be maintained at the entrance to the port or industrial estate. The picket should then clearly indicate the employment being picketed and should make every effort to advise workers and their representatives at the port or industrial estate[112] of the limit of the picket.

[10.55] In *Malincross Ltd v Building and Allied Trade Union and Ors*[113] the defendants submitted that under s 11(a) of the 1990 Act they were entitled to picket at any place they worked or carried on work *in the past*.[114] Counsel referred the High Court (McCracken J) to the *Dáil Debates*, which disclosed that an amendment was moved to add the words 'or, at the commencement of the dispute, had normally worked or had normally carried on business'. This amendment had been withdrawn following a statement by the Minister for Labour that the situation was already covered by the words used, which the Minister called 'the historic present tense'. The judge did not think the views of the Minister in a Dáil debate should determine the construction of

---

110. Thereby excluding self-employed workers. On 'employer' within the European Communities (Safeguarding of Employees' Rights on Transfer of Undertakings) Regulations 1980, see *Westman Holdings Ltd v McCormack and Ors* [1991] 1 IR 151 (para **9.65**), similarly *Malincross Ltd v Building and Allied Trades Union and Ors* [2002] 13 ELR 78. In *G&T Crampton Ltd v Building and Allied Trades Union* [1998] ELR 4 the plaintiff successfully raised a fair issue to be tried between the parties that it was not the employer of the union members who were picketing its site. Before the 1990 Act the courts looked for a 'connection' between the plaintiff and the employer in dispute: *Bayzana Ltd v Galligan* [1987] IR 238.

111. 398 *Dáil Debates* Cols 497–512, 545–54.

112. Picketing an industrial estate was considered by the English Court of Appeal in *Rayware Ltd v Transport and General Workers' Union* [1989] ICR 457.

113. *Malincross Ltd v Building and Allied Trade Union and Ors* [2002] 13 LR 78.

114. Cf Trade Union and Labour Relations (Consolidation) Act 1992, s 220(3).

the section; nevertheless he thought he could have regard to them in determining whether, at the hearing of the action, there was a fair question to be tried as to the construction of the section. The hearing of an interlocutory injunction was not the time to enter into a detailed discussion on grammar, and the court was satisfied a fair case arose.

The phrase 'where their employer works or carries on business' was considered in *Dublin City Council v TEEU, Gannon and Cummins.*[115] Laffoy J refused the plaintiff's application for an interlocutory injunction on 27 April 2010. Following that refusal steps were taken by the parties to bring the matter on for trial expeditiously and the hearing took place towards the end of May 2010. The defendant union and its members were in dispute with the members' employers, Pickerings, who in the past had a contract from the plaintiff to service lifts at the local authority housing complex at Ballymun. The contract between the plaintiff and Pickerings was definitively terminated with effect from 25 March 2010. It was noted in the Judgment that the effect of the industrial action between the union and Pickerings, as regards the Ballymun premises, was that no servicing, maintenance or repairs were carried out to the lifts in the ten apartment blocks after 4 February 2010. The Court[116] noted that the application of s 11(1) to the facts raised two sub issues, namely:

(i) whether the defendants were acting 'in contemplation of furtherance of a trade dispute';

(ii) whether they were picketing at 'a place where their employer works or carries on business'.

In determining the answer to the first sub issue the court accepted the evidence of the union witnesess and held as follows:[117]

> In my view there is no doubt on the facts that the only objective behind the picketing by the defendants of the Ballymun premises from the outset has been, and is, to achieve a resolution of the trade dispute with Pickerings which is favourable to the Union and its members. While it is an unfortunate consequence of the implementation of that objective that extreme hardship has been, and is being inflicted on the tenants of the apartments in the Ballymun tower blocks, that outcome is not the defendants' objective and it is a matter of regret to them. On the basis of [the] evidence, I am satisfied that, in initiating the picketing, the defendants acted in the reasonable belief that picketing at the Ballymun premises would have the effect they aim for. I am satisfied that they continue to act in that belief, notwithstanding that the contractual relationship between Pickerings and the plaintiff had ceased.
>
> I reach that conclusion notwithstanding that, because of the changed circumstances, it may be reasonable to infer that the plaintiff may have even less clout against Pickerings since the 25 March, 2010, when the contractual relationship ceased, than it had between the commencement of the picketing and that date in relation to bringing about a settlement of the defendants' trade

---

115. *Dublin City Council v TEEU & Ors* (9 June 2010, unreported), HC, Laffoy J.

116. At 22.

117. At 32.

dispute with Pickerings which is favourable to the defendants. However, the officers of the Union are in a position to assess whether picketing the Ballymun premises, where their members as employees of Pickerings provided services in relation to the lifts for over twenty years, and which services are required on an ongoing basis, has the effect, to use the terminology used in one of the earliest cases in which the meaning of 'furtherance' of a trade dispute in the Act of 1906 was considered, *Conway v Wade* [1909] AC 506, of promoting the interest of either party, that is to say, Pickerings or the defendants, to the trade dispute. I am satisfied on the evidence ... that notwithstanding the defendants have continued picketing at the Ballymun premises, the termination of the plaintiff's contract with Pickerings, in the reasonable belief that their actions will have the effect of promoting the interests of the Union and its members in the dispute with Pickerings.

Therefore, I conclude that the picketing at the Ballymun premises is in furtherance of the trade dispute between Pickerings and the defendants within the meaning of s 11(1) of the Act of 1990.

It seems that the Court did not regard it as necessary to examine whether in reality the picketing of the Ballymun premises might result in a favourable resolution of the dispute from the union's point of view. The Court's decision was based on an acceptance of the evidence of the union official as to the purpose of the picketing and accordingly the Court accepted that the purpose was not to 'black' the premises so as to avoid any other lift contractor carrying out the work.

As to the test that should be applied for purposes of the golden formula, the Court looked to s 13(2) of the Act of 1990 and concluded that in applying the provisions of Pt II of the Act to the defendants, including s 11(1) and s 13, the question was whether, in maintaining the picket, the defendants were acting 'in the reasonable belief' that their actions were in furtherance of the trade dispute between Pickerings and the defendants. It is questionable, however, whether s 13(2), which concerns the immunity of trade unions against actions in tort (para **9.57**), can be viewed as casting any light on the interpretation of the golden formula in s 11(1) of the Act where the context, limited immunity for 'one or more persons ...', is markedly different, On the applicable test, see further para **9.79** *et seq.*

In examining the meaning of the phrase 'works or carries on business' Laffoy J referred, *inter alia* to *Malincross Limited v Building and Allied Trade Union*[118] and also at length to the meaning of the 'historic present' (a phrase used by the Minister during the passage of the Act through the Houses of the Oireachtas) and also to the meaning and effect of s 11(2). The Court then went on to hold:[119]

Having regard to the manner in which the Oireachtas has treated that additional requirement to render secondary picketing lawful, if it was the intention of the Oireachtas that the requirement as to the targeted employer working or carrying on business at the location of the picketing should apply not only at the commencement of the picketing but also throughout the continuance of the picketing it is strange that this was not spelt out in both subs (1) and subs (2).

118.   *Malincross Ltd v Building and Allied Trade Union* [2002] 4 IR 607.
119.   At 40.

The fact that it was not suggested that such was not the intention of the Oireachtas. It suggests that it is to be implied that the use of the present tense in both subsections, in imposing the requirement as to targeted employer working or carrying on business at the location of the picketing, indicates that the requirement is to be complied with when the picketing commences. In other words, although the present tense is used, it is open to the construction implicit that the point in time at which the state of affairs which is required to exist in order to render the picketing lawful – that the targeted employer 'works or carries on business' at the location of the picketing – is to be assessed when the picketing commences.

This interpretation of s 11(1) is somewhat strained and amounts to a finding 'once a lawful picket, always a lawful picket'.[120] The purposes of the picketing, a *sine qua non* for its legality, are linked to the venue being attended by the words 'so attend' in the subsection, ie, the picketers must so attend 'at a place where the employer works or carries on business'. The lawfulness of the attending must be judged on the facts presented to the Court. The Court, it is respectfully suggested, cannot apply the law to the facts before it on the basis of prior facts, in this case predating the proceedings by some ten weeks, which did not concern the plaintiff and which had been 'spent' before the proceedings were ever initiated. If in fact a new contractor had been engaged and if the Pickering employees had become employees of the second contractor, by virtue of the Transfer Regulations,[121] the pickeing would not have been lawful as there would have been no trade dispute as between the picketers and their 'new' employer. Laffoy J did state[122] that it was not practicable to consider the implications of each and every of the very many different circumstances in which the picketers' employers cease to work or carry on business at the location of the picketing after it commenced. She did however say that whatever the implications were they should not give rise to a situation which would be at variance or inconsistent with the purpose of the Oireachtas in confining lawful picketing to the location where the relevant employer works or carries on business when replacing s 2 of the Act of 1906. She suggested that the location of the picketing was only one of the strictures imposed on trade unions and workers who wished to engage in lawful picketing and she thought that the necessity to comply with the additional strictures must, even as a matter of common sense, narrow the circumstances in which lawful picketing may continue once the picketer's employer has departed the scene and must reduce, if not entirely eliminate, the possibility of picketing for a useless or illegitimate purpose. However, once Pickerings 'definitively' left Ballymun that picketing of those premises thereafter must have been in reality 'useless' notwithstanding the evidence as to the purpose of the pickets.

[10.56] The right to picket a person's home was removed under the 1990 Act, unless the person works or carries on business there. Whereas there is no right to invade the

---

120. The notion once a trade dispute, always a trade dispute was rejected by the Supreme Court in *ESSO Teo v McGowan* [1974] IR 148.

121. European Communities (Protection of Employees' Rights on Transfer of Undertakings) Regulations 2003 (SI 131/2003).

122. At 41.

privacy of a person's home, the entry of a picket onto private premises is not necessarily a trespass. Any person may call on another at his home for a lawful purpose: there is implied authority to do this in a reasonable manner. Equally, a person may enter an employer's business premises in the manner ordinarily permitted to see him or his representatives in connection with his business. This licence would not extend, needless to say, to picketing the employer's premises against his interests. The section does not cover cases where the occupier of private premises refuses to see the picket or requests him to depart. If the picket declines to oblige, he is invading the occupier's privacy and such force may be used as is reasonably necessary to evict him onto the public highway.

[10.57] Section 11 does not impose any numerical limit on pickets. Mass picketing is not unlawful[123] but excessive numbers may go beyond what is reasonably permissible and amount to obstruction or nuisance or a reasonable apprehension of a breach of the peace.[124] The court may restrain aspects of the picketing considered excessive.[125]

Finally, the changes regarding the labour injunction introduced by the Act of 1990 (**Ch 11**) do not apply:

> in respect of proceedings arising out of or relating to unlawfully entering into or remaining upon any property belonging to another, or unlawfully causing damage or permitting damage to be caused to the property of another: s 19(4).

SECONDARY PICKETING

[10.58] The Commission of Inquiry on Industrial Relations (1981) looked into the question of whether immunities should be limited in respect of secondary picketing. The subject is closely related to secondary industrial action.[126] The Irish Commission's recommendation failed to follow the logical approach of treating secondary picketing and secondary action in the same way. It recommended that secondary picketing should, in general, enjoy the protection of the law only where an employer has made special arrangements to circumvent the effects of legitimate industrial action.[127] The Commission's recommendations in regard to secondary action involved singling out

---

123. But see *Thomas v National Union of Mineworkers (South Wales Area)* [1985] IRLR 136.

124. *EI Co Ltd v Kennedy* [1968] IR 69 at 91 *per* Walsh J.

125. *PP O'Sullivan (Leinster) Ltd v Building and Allied Trades Union* (2001 No 17675P); *P Elliott & Co Ltd v Building and Allied Trades Union (No 1)* [2006] IEHC 340.

126. Around the same time, the UK Green Paper on Trade Union Immunities (1981) recognised the direct link: 'If all secondary action were made unlawful there would of course be a strong case for specifically withdrawing the immunity in respect of picketing in all circumstances except primary action.' It put forward the view that picketing at one's own place of work in the course of secondary action should be subject only to whatever limitations the law places on the secondary action itself (para 171).

127. *Report of Commission of Inquiry on Industrial Relations* (1981), para 731.

sympathetic action for exclusion from the statutory immunities (with the exception of 'blacking').[128]

[10.59] The 1990 Act deals with secondary picketing in s 11(2) and (3) as follows:

> (2) It shall be lawful for one or more persons acting on their own behalf or on behalf of a trade union in contemplation or furtherance of a trade dispute, to attend at, or where that is not practicable, at the approaches to, a place where an employer who is not a party to the trade dispute, works or carries on business if, but only if, it is reasonable for those who are so attending to believe at the commencement of their attendance and throughout the continuance of their attendance that the employer has directly assisted their employer who is a party to the trade dispute for the purpose of frustrating the strike or other industrial action, provided that such attendance is merely for the purpose of peacefully obtaining or communicating information or of peacefully persuading any person to work or abstain from working.
>
> (3) For the avoidance of doubt any action taken by an employer in the health services to maintain life-preserving services during a strike or other industrial action shall not constitute assistance for the purposes of sub-section (2).

This makes specific provision for the rare and exceptional circumstances in which picketing of an employer who is not a party to the trade dispute would have legal protection. It also has regard to the limited circumstances where serious injury or death might occur as a result of industrial action. The test of reasonableness introduces an objective criterion. Mere belief on the part of pickets will not suffice. Moreover, the belief must be held at the commencement of, and throughout the picket. The Act does not specify the form of any assistance. Any form of assistance will suffice, the most obvious being the supply of labour to the employer party.[129]

[10.60] In *Nolan Transport v Halligan & Ors*[130] the defendants visited other workplaces where their employer conducted business, purportedly to fundraise. The High Court (Barrington J) found the purpose of the visits went beyond seeking financial support and led directly to the difficulties the plaintiff had in unloading their lorries at customers' premises.

[10.61] During 2009, injunctions were granted in a number of secondary picketing cases. The Dublin Port Company was granted an injunction in August against two named defendants preventing them from blockading the River Liffey in support of striking workers employed by a company based in the Port. Diageo was also successful in obtaining an injunction against Technical Engineering and Electrical Union (TEEU)

---

128. The Commission also proposed that in a dispute where the dispute procedure recommended in paragraphs 239–263 had been complied with by a union, secondary picketing could be commenced by that union subject to the issue of appropriate notice. Following the receipt of such notice, the employer would be entitled to appeal to the proposed Labour Relations Court for a ruling that the proposed picketing did not comply with the provisions of the law.

129. See 398 *Dáil Debates* Col 564: Minister suggested the second employer must actively seek to frustrate the strike such as by filling orders on behalf of the first employer or by providing services to the first employer's customers on behalf of the first employer.

130. *Nolan Transport v Halligan & Ors* [1995] ELR 1.

members from placing pickets at St James's Gate Brewery. Diageo argued that as TEEU members were employed by contractors, not by it, there was no trade dispute with Diageo as the contractors were no longer working on the site when a picket was placed on the brewery, and therefore the picket constituted unlawful secondary picketing: Diageo had done nothing to assist the contractors in frustrating the strike action.[131] Pickets were set to be placed, in a separate dispute, at Coca-Cola's main Irish distribution centres in a dispute over plans to outsource jobs at the company's manufacturing and distribution centres in Dublin, Tuam, Waterford, Tipperary and Cork. The company successfully gained a High Court injunction against the pickets, not to prevent picketing taking place, but to ensure that pickets were conducted in an orderly manner. *Inter alia*, the injunction restrained the pickets from obstructing access to and egress from the premises of Cola Cola, HBC in Dublin, and that of a named new third party provider.[132]

THE PROPER PURPOSES

[10.62] Section 11, sub-ss (1) and (2) protect only when pickets have the purposes enumerated therein, namely:

    (a)   peacefully obtaining or communicating information; or

    (b)   peacefully persuading any person to work or abstain from working.

These purposes were also designated in the same terms under s 2 of the Act of 1906. Case law on that section is therefore highly persuasive. The Constitution may also be relevant.

Peacefully Obtaining or Communicating Information

[10.63] It cannot be described as a 'peaceful' way of 'communicating information' where pickets carry banners bearing inscriptions which are in fact untrue. In *Ryan v Cooke*[133] the defendants, on behalf of a trade union, obtained permission from the plaintiff to canvass her assistants to become members of their trade union. The plaintiff was then asked in writing for an assurance that she would only employ trade union labour and observe trade union conditions and was told that failure to give the required assurance would lead to the placing of a picket at the premises. Members of the picket carried banners or posters inscribed as follows:

> 'This firm refuses to employ trade union labour
>
> Support fair traders
>
> Trade Dispute. Monument Creamery [the plaintiff's creamery] refuses to employ trade union staff.'

The plaintiff had never refused to employ trade union labour. She succeeded in an action to restrain the defendants from attending at her premises for the purpose of

---

131. O'Neill, 'Navigating the Minefield – an Overview of the Law of Industrial Action' ELRI (AP-JU 2009), 91 at 100. See *BATU v Labour Court* [2005] IEHC 109 at 125 (para **4.53**).

132. Fitzgerald, 'Electrical dispute raises legal issues around picketing' IRN 26.

133. *Ryan v Cooke* [1938] IR 512.

watching or besetting or picketing the premises and from disturbing her in the conduct of the business or from interfering with her employees or customers. Holding that no trade dispute existed, Johnston J declared that not only was it unlawful to disseminate such a falsehood 'of a most dangerous type'[134] but the trade union had no right in the course of carrying out a picketing of a business firm to recommend to the public to go to a rival shop (on which, see para **10.65**). The defendants' conduct was held wrongful 'whether it is viewed from the point of view of conspiracy or of nuisance'.

[10.64] Nothing could have been more damaging than the picketing of premises in a congested thoroughfare like Henry Street, with the display of placards upon which a false announcement to the public was made, coupled with the presence of the police, who would give a sort of official sanction to the picketing in the eyes of some people and a sort of suggestion of a row in the eyes of others. The judge's next utterance is far from flattering to those who fall within the category to which he refers:

> The mental intelligence and the moral stamina of the people who frequent Henry Street in such crowds are of very varying quality, and probably the majority of the passers-by would not be in a very discriminating mood.[135]

[10.65] In *Quigley v Beirne*[136] a statement 'strike on' was held to amount to a false inscription on a placard and, although in the circumstances it did not make any practical difference to the outcome, O'Byrne J said[137] that 'care should be taken in future to avoid such mis-statements.'[138] Whether a picket may suggest to the public that they should do business with another arose for consideration in *Brendan Dunne Ltd v Fitzpatrick*.[139] In this case, it will be recalled, the plaintiffs successfully sought an injunction to restrain the defendants from picketing their premises by way of protest against late opening hours on one evening a week. Some of the placards were objected to on the grounds that they suggested to the public they should do business with other, presumably rival, firms. Placards containing the words:

> 'Support shops which close at 5.30
>
> You can buy contemporary furniture in Trade Union shops'

fell within that category.

---

134. At 522.
135. At 524–5.
136. *Quigley v Beirne* [1955] IR 62.
137. At 73.
138. Which suggests that a stringent approach is that preferred, *pace* Dixon J in the High Court in *Quigley* who did not regard the difference between 'strike on here' and 'trade dispute on here' as a practical one likely to be made by the general public. See too *The Esplanade Pharmacy Ltd v Larkin* 62 ILTR 149, 151. The High Court (Feeney J) in a case involving cargo handling company Marine Terminals Ltd against SIPTU, ICTU and 10 named workers and trade union officials, said he would not grant an injunction restraining workers from using strong language including the terms 'scab' and 'crime against Irish workers' during protests. However, he granted an injunction restraining the distribution of personal details of staff who were working through the dispute ((2009) *Irish Times*, 16 September).
139. *Brendan Dunne Ltd v Fitzpatrick* [1958] IR 29.

[10.66] Budd J referred to *Lyons v Wilkins*[140] where Vaughan Williams LJ dealing with s 7 of the Conspiracy and Protection of Property Act 1875, said:[141]

> I think that the fact that the communication invites the men to discontinue working for the master as soon as they lawfully may does not thereby cause the communication to cease to be a communication within the meaning of the proviso.

Such an invitation would seem, said Budd J, to be somewhat outside the mere communication of information 'but its legality has this high authority to support it'. But there was another view of the meaning of the section, namely that the legislature intended, when permitting picketing, to confine the activities of those taking part in pickets to the specified activities and it seemed to 'be supported by the wording of the section'.[142] The plaintiff company argued that the matter was concluded by the decision of Johnston J in *Ryan v Cooke* (para **10.63**). Counsel for the defence in *Brendan Dunne Ltd v Fitzpatrick* contended that these words were merely *obiter.* Budd J declared:[143]

> I cannot regard them as such. It is true that Johnston J had already decided that no trade dispute existed ... but he also decided that the picketing was unlawful in other respects, which might equally well have formed the sole basis of his decision. When a judge states two reasons for his decision the fact that one precedes the other does not alter the fact that both reasons are part of his *ratio decidendi.*

Accordingly, Budd J took the view that he should follow the decision. He held that the pickets were not entitled to recommend to the public to support other firms in the course of their picketing operations.

[10.67] If picketing is to be protected, it must be 'merely' for the purposes set out in the section. This was emphasised in *Newbridge Industries Ltd v Bateson and Cardiff*[144] where a lay-off was involved. The plaintiff company was in severe financial difficulties and negotiations with the Workers Union of Ireland (WUI) about reducing staff took place. The defendants started to picket the premises and at the time there was a trade dispute in existence. The terms on which the employees were to be laid off had not been agreed and the issue about whether a proposed bonus was to be conditional on a certain level of productivity had not been resolved. On the day picketing began, a lorry arrived at the company's premises for the purpose of taking delivery of fibre for carriage to a third party under an agreement for sale which the plaintiffs had with it. The driver of the lorry was stopped by the first-named defendant and there was a conversation between them after which the driver drove away without taking delivery of the fibre. The evidence established, according to Kenny J, that the picket was not put on for the purpose of obtaining or communicating information or of peacefully persuading any worker to work or abstain from working. It was put on to prevent the material in the factory being taken out of Newbridge. One of the defendants, a trade

---

140. *Lyons v Wilkins* [1899] 1 Ch 255.

141. At 274.

142. *Brendan Dunne Ltd v Fitzpatrick* [1958] IR 29 at 45.

143. *Brendan Dunne Ltd v Fitzpatrick* [1958] IR 29 at 45.

144. *Newbridge Industries Ltd v Bateson and Cardiff* (15 July 1975, unreported), HC.

union official, had candidly admitted as much. The first-named defendant, however, claimed he was picketing because he had been dismissed. Kenny J concluded that:

> If ... one of the reasons for the picketing was that [an employee] had been dismissed when he claimed that on grounds of seniority he should not, there might have been a mixed motive for the picketing but in the event I have no doubt that the main reason was to prevent removal of material from the factory.

[10.68] The introduction of the concept of motive and worse, of mixed motive, into picketing law is inconsistent with earlier authority in Ireland which made it clear that the protection of the section applies where the picketing is for one or more of the purposes mentioned in the section. It is also inconsistent with the later authority of, and indeed later dicta of, Kenny J in *Goulding Chemicals Ltd v Bolger*,[145] a case involving lay-offs, where the Chief Justice stressed that in relation to peaceful picketing what was relevant, and indeed crucial, was that those who attend to picket do so only for one or more of the purposes permitted by s 2 of the Trade Disputes Act. O'Higgins CJ recognised[146] that there was some confusion between the motive or reason for the action concerned and the purpose or object to be attained from the action, if taken. The motive behind the act of picketing, he stressed, was irrelevant. Kenny J seemed to have had some sort of metanoia in *Goulding*. He had no doubt that the defendants' prominent motive in deciding to picket was to compel the plaintiffs to re-open their factory at the East Wall. But if one were to adopt a 'predominant motive' test, he said, the power of the picket would be very thin. The judge held that s 2 dealt not with the predominant motive of trade picketing but with the aim of the attending at or near the premises:[147] 'In this case the purpose of attending as a picket at the East Wall was and is to persuade peacefully persons not to work.'

The word 'merely' does not mean the picketing must be confined to one or more of the purposes mentioned in the section, and that there must be no other purpose, however lawful in itself.[148] But in *R v Wall*[149] it was made clear that the section does not apply where neither of the statutory purposes is found.[150]

[10.69] Irish courts look for standards of reasonableness in relation to picketing.[151] In other words, quite apart from intimidation or nuisance and so on, reasonable methods

---

145. *Goulding Chemicals Ltd v Bolger* [1977] IR 211.
146. At 232.
147. At 249.
148. See *Ward, Lock and Co v Operative Printers' Assistants Society* (1906) 22 TLR 327.
149. *R v Wall* (1907) 21 Cox 401.
150. *Newbridge Industries Ltd v Bateson* (1988) 7 JISLL 191, *Becton Dickinson Ltd v Lee* [1973] IR 1 at 44, *per* Henchy J.
151. The original Trade Disputes Bill contained the phrase 'peaceably and in a reasonable manner', a phrase which was dropped as unnecessary: See (1906) 163 HC Deb (4th Ser) at cols 1415, 1459, 1569; (1906) 167 HC Deb (4th Ser) at col 282; and Hickling 'Restoring the protection of the Trade Disputes Act: some forgotten aspects' (1965) 28 MLR 708; Kidner, 'Lessons in Trade Union Law Reform: the origins and passage of the Trade Disputes Act 1906' (1982) 2 LS 34, 49.

are required for executing the proper purposes of the picketing. Budd J described the court's decision in *Brendan Dunne Ltd v Fitzpatrick*:[152]

> It seems to me that picketing is not lawful also if the methods adopted are such as to overawe those who happen to be on the premises being picketed or members of the public who might be minded to have business dealings with them, to the extent that people of ordinary nerve and courage may be prevented from doing what they have a lawful right to do. *The method of picketing must be reasonable having regard to all the circumstances.* [Emphasis added]

The judge went on to give some examples of unjustifiable picketing, for example, to place a picket consisting of a hundred or so persons on a small suburban premises with one or two staff. On the other hand it might be reasonable to place several quite large pickets on a large factory with several entrances.[153] The number of persons picketing should bear a reasonable relationship to the nature of the premises and the number of persons with whom the dispute arises. In the case before him Budd J held that the pickets attending at the plaintiff's premises (sometimes exceeding 60) were on occasions unduly large and by reason of their numbers would be calculated to frighten and overawe those picketed and members of the general public wishing to do business with them. Picketing on such occasions could not be said to have been merely for the purpose of peacefully obtaining or communicating information.

A similar view was endorsed in *EI Co v Kennedy*[154] wherein Walsh J said:

> The use of words such as 'scab' or 'blackleg' are historically so associated with social ostracism and physical violence as to be far beyond anything which might be described as mere rudeness or impoliteness and go beyond what is permitted by law. In the present context the reference made to the race or nationality of the employers could produce the same disorderly response and also go beyond what is permitted by law. Excessive numbers in pickets may also go beyond what is reasonably permissible for the communication of information or for the obtaining of information and may amount to obstruction or nuisance or give rise to a reasonable apprehension of a breach of the peace.

Persuading a person to work or abstain from working

[10.70] The one Irish authority touching on this purpose under the old Act is *Toppin v Feron*.[155] Here the defendants had failed in their efforts to obtain reinstatement of two dismissed employees (carters) and a trade dispute arose between them and the employer. The latter was also the proprietor of a theatre and to exert maximum pressure on him the defendants decided to picket the theatre to endeavour to dissuade people from going in. Large numbers were involved in the picketing, between 200 and 300, and it was not always peaceful. At times there were acts of violence and obstruction. The defendants were prosecuted for watching and besetting and in their defence pleaded s 2 of the Trade Disputes Act 1906 on the basis that 'working' therein

---

152. *Brendan Dunne Ltd v Fitzpatrick* [1958] IR 29 at 44.
153. See the Code of Practice on Picketing 1980 in England, which recommends six as a reasonable number of pickets: para 31.
154. *EI Co v Kennedy* [1968] IR 69 at 91. And in *Talbot (Ireland) Ltd v Merrigan* (30 April 1981, unreported), SC unruly picketing was restrained.
155. *Toppin v Feron* (1909) 43 ILTR 190.

meant carrying on any business transaction and that their act of picketing was to dissuade people from dealing with the employer. Baron Pallas LC in the King's Bench Division remitted the case to the justices on a point of law. He queried whether preventing people going into the theatre was within the saving clause of the Act (he thought that it was not) but the matter did not have to be finally decided one way or the other.

[10.71] Thus in Ireland, if pickets were to 'invite' as opposed to 'persuade' customers not to deal with a particular establishment, such a form of boycott is unlikely to be protected. Citrine takes the contrary view that picketing for such a purpose may be lawful quite apart from the section.[156] He cites a Canadian authority which held that it is not unlawful for pickets peacefully to picket the premises of a retailer and to exhibit signs truthfully stating that the latter refuses to deal with the persons whom they represent. There was no evidence that the picketing was likely to cause a crowd to gather and obstruct the entrance to the premises, nor that the pickets had any other desire than to promote their own business interests by persuading, inducing or compelling the retailer to do business with them.[157]

[10.72] In *Chieftain Construction Ltd v Building and Allied Trades Union*[158] the plaintiff building contractors employed the defendant building operatives until they were purportedly made redundant at the end of 2007. Some months later the defendants commenced picketing at the entrance to one of the plaintiff's building sites and continued picketing there on subsequent days. Various allegations were made by the plaintiffs. For instance, two of the defendants allegedly trespassed on to another construction site being operated by the plaintiffs and, while there, exerted pressure on two of the plaintiffs' tradesmen to cease working. Six of the defendants later entered the same site and again two plasterers were confronted. It was accepted by the plaintiffs, however, that as of the date of the hearing of the motion for an interlocutory injunction to restrain the picketing, the defendants' ongoing activities were confined to peaceful picketing of the entrances to the plaintiffs' two sites. The plaintiffs failed in the circumstances to characterise the defendants' ongoing actions as watching and besetting, trespass and the creation and maintenance of a nuisance. The High Court (Edwards J) refused to grant the relief sought.

Purpose must be consistent with the Constitution

[10.73] Freedom of association is discussed in **Ch 2**. Judicial interpretation of this constitutionally guaranteed freedom has cut back the protection afforded to pickets. In *Educational Co of Ireland Ltd v Fitzpatrick (No 2)*[159] the Supreme Court held that picketing could not be protected when its purpose was to induce employers to force

---

156. Citrine, *Trade Union Law* (3rd edn, Stevens & Sons, 1967) at 578.
157. *Wasserman v Sopman* [1942] 3 DLR 696.
158. *Chieftain Construction Ltd v Building and Allied Trades Union* [2008] IEHC 147.
159. *Educational Co of Ireland Ltd v Fitzpatrick (No 2)* [1961] IR 345.

other employees to join the union to which the pickets belonged. Kingsmill Moore J
(with O Dálaigh J, as he then was) said:[160]

> The Trade Disputes Act 1906, can no longer be relied upon to justify picketing
> in aid of a trade dispute, where that dispute is concerned with an attempt to
> deprive persons of the right of free association or free disassociation guaranteed
> by the Constitution. The definition of trade dispute must be read as if there were
> attached thereto the words, 'Provided that a dispute between employers and
> workmen or between workmen and workmen as to whether a person shall or
> shall not become or remain a member of a trade union or having as its object a
> frustration of the right of any person to choose with whom he will not be
> associated in any form of union or association shall not be deemed to be a trade
> dispute for the purposes of the Act.'

[10.74] The *Educational Co* case was applied in *Crowley v Cleary*[161] where the
defendant was the general secretary of a trade union which adopted a policy of
requiring all assistants employed in licensed premises to be members of the trade
union. The plaintiff was a publican who employed two assistants in his licensed
premises, of whom only one was a member of a trade union. The plaintiff's union
employee was not involved in any dispute either with the plaintiff or with the non-
union employee. The trade union had agreed with an association of employers of which
the plaintiff was not a member that all assistants employed in licensed premises should
be members of the trade union. The trade union endeavoured unsuccessfully to induce
the plaintiff to comply with the terms of this agreement and the defendant general
secretary threatened that he would place a picket at the plaintiff's licensed premises if
the plaintiff did not comply with such terms. The demands of the trade union could be
satisfied only by the plaintiff dismissing his non-union employee from his service or
by that employee becoming a member of the trade union. The plaintiff brought an
action in the High Court in which he sought an injunction restraining the defendant
from carrying out his threat. In granting the injunction McLoughlin J held that, even if
a trade dispute existed within the meaning of the Act of 1906, the threatened picketing
would not be lawful or protected by the statute even though the trade union had not
expressly required the plaintiff to dismiss his non-union employee and had not
expressly instructed the latter to apply for membership of the trade union. McLoughlin
J cited the extract above. The circumstances in *Crowley* he said, were distinguishable
from the circumstances in the *Educational Co* case in one feature only, namely that the
trade union in the case before him had taken no direct steps against the employee. It did
not say to him 'You must join the Union if you wish to retain your employment.' It did
not say to the plaintiff 'You must dismiss [the employee] from his employment unless
he joins the Union.' But 'its actions and intentions' said the judge, 'constituted a
subterfuge to bring about the same result'.[162] The union insisted on its policy of
requiring that every employee in the licensed trade should be a member of the union
and insisted that the plaintiff should enforce the agreement for carrying out its policy
although he was not a party to it. The union's general secretary acknowledged that the
only way the plaintiff could comply with its requirements was by dismissing the non-

---

160. At 398.
161. *Crowley v Cleary* [1968] IR 261.
162. At 268.

union employee from his employment because he was not a member of the union and the union threatened that if the plaintiff did not do so, his premises would be picketed in furtherance of the alleged trade dispute. In the circumstances the High Court followed the Supreme Court in the *Educational Co* case and held that the threatened picketing would be unlawful. The plaintiff was therefore entitled to the injunction sought in his statement of claim.

[10.75] If the inevitable consequences of acceding to a trade union's demands will be that a constitutional violation occurs, this would appear to be outside the saving power of the 1990 Act. Both cases just mentioned concerned an express constitutional right: Art 40.6.1°(iii). An implied constitutional right was invoked, successfully, in *Murtagh Properties Ltd v Cleary*[163] where a picket was mounted to compel employers to dismiss bar waitresses because they were women and for no other reason. This was held to be a breach of the women's personal right under Art 40.3.1° to earn a livelihood equally with men.

[10.76] Might pickets interfere with the right to work? The latter is an implied right under Art 40.3.1°. Section 11 permits peaceful persuasion of someone to work or to abstain from working. Suppose as a result of picketing work is forced to cease at a particular site (a common occurrence in Ireland because of the prestige of the picket) so that persons who might resist peaceful persuasion not to work (there may be good reasons for this) are prevented from continuing to earn their livelihood. Could they argue that the pickets had abandoned their statutory protection by perpetrating an unconstitutionality? If they could, the power of the picket would be significantly reduced. Hence, perhaps, the negative approach to this possibility in *Gannon v Duffy*.[164] In this case the plaintiffs were bricklayers and the defendants were officers of the Ancient Guild of Incorporated Brick and Stonelayers and Allied Trade Unions ('the Guild'). The plaintiffs obtained employment with a firm on terms alleged by the Guild to be unacceptable to it and which the Guild alleged contravened the terms of a Registered Employment Agreement made pursuant to the Industrial Relations Act 1946. The firm was a member of the Construction Industry Federation which, on behalf of its members, entered into the Employment Agreement with a number of trade unions including the Guild.

[10.77] The Guild, having formed the opinion that the employers were in breach of the Employment Agreement, commenced to picket the employer's building so that work on the site was stopped. The plaintiffs, appreciating that this activity was directed at their employment on the site, instituted proceedings claiming an injunction restraining the defendants and others from picketing, a declaration that they had a constitutional right to work and damages for the alleged wrongful acts of the defendants. By notice subsequent to that, the employers terminated the plaintiffs' employment, thereby justifying the latter's fears that the defendants' action was directed at their employment by the employers although there was nothing unlawful in the manner of the termination of their employment.

---

163. *Murtagh Properties Ltd v Cleary* [1972] IR 330.

164. *Gannon v Duffy* (4 March 1983, unreported), HC. Noted by Kerr and Whyte in 'Labour Law, Trade Disputes and the Constitution' (1984) 6 DULJ (ns) 187. See also para **2.53**.

[10.78] The plaintiffs' case rested on two grounds: first, that there was no trade dispute within the meaning of the Act of 1906; and second, that in so far as there was such a dispute, it did not avail the defendants because the action taken infringed the plaintiffs' constitutional right to work and not to be compelled to lose their employment because they did not belong to the Guild or did not comply with rules imposed by a union of which they were not members. On the first submission McWilliam J was of the opinion that there was a trade dispute within the meaning of the statute. On the second he referred to the *Educational Co Ltd* case, *Meskell v CIE*[165] and *Murtagh Properties Ltd v Cleary*[166] (see **Ch 2**). The judge then proceeded to confuse the requirement that there should be a trade dispute with the requirement that, that being so, the defendants' purpose should be lawful under s 2.

[10.79] Counsel on the plaintiffs' behalf argued that the action taken by the Guild was for the purpose of having the plaintiffs dismissed because they did not belong thereto and had tried to form a new trade union in opposition to the Guild but, according to McWilliam J:

> once I have formed the opinion that there is a genuine trade dispute with the employers I am also of opinion that it is not material that action in furtherance of this dispute bring additional advantages to the Guild or disadvantages or hardship to the Plaintiffs, even though the pursuit of these advantages alone might come within the *ratio decidendi* of the cases cited.

If the defendants' purpose had been adduced to show that the inevitable consequence of their action was that the plaintiffs' freedom of disassociation would be infringed, then it is difficult to see how, consistently with *Crowley v Cleary*[167] (a case apparently not relied on by counsel), the plaintiffs' argument would not have succeeded. McWilliam J dismissed the right to work argument, saying:

> I have very considerable doubts as to whether such a right can be held to be infringed so as to give a cause of action against a person who is lawfully trying to enforce his own rights.

This view can only be described as wrong. X may realise that by acting as he does, Y's constitutional right will be violated. If this violation follows as a foreseen and desired consequence of X's 'primary' intended act, then this consequence is intentional and should not be outside the net of protection. Moreover, enforcement of a civil legal right cannot be given precedence over protection of a constitutional one. See also para **2.53** *et seq*.

UNOFFICIAL PICKETS

[10.80] Not every 'unofficial picket' is protected. Pickets must belong to an authorised trade union: Industrial Relations Act 1990, s 9. This section is discussed in **Ch 9**, para **9.55** *et seq*.

---

165. *Educational Co Ltd case* [1961] IR 345; *Meskell v CIE* [1973] IR 121.
166. *Murtagh Properties Ltd v Cleary* [1972] IR 330.
167. *Crowley v Cleary* [1968] IR 261.

ICTU ALL-OUT PICKETING POLICY

[10.81] ICTU adopted its all-out picketing policy in 1970.[168] In general it sees the object of its picketing policy as being to identify pickets which have been placed as a result of democratic decisions of the trade union movement, and to secure that these pickets, and only these, have the support of trade union members.[169] The principle behind the 1970 policy is that a strike should be confined to the unions or workers immediately involved unless Congress authorises 'all-out' pickets which all members affiliated to it should not pass.

The constitutionality of an all-out picket is uncertain following *Talbot (Ireland) Ltd v Merrigan*[170] although, as pointed out (para **2.49**), the reliability of this judgment is open to doubt.

TRADE UNION OFFICIALS

[10.82] The position with regard to trade union officials is clarified in s 11(4):

> It shall be lawful for a trade union official[171] to accompany any member of his union whom he represents provided that the member is acting in accordance with the provisions of subsection (1) or (2) and provided that such official is attending merely for the purposes of peacefully obtaining and of communicating information or of peacefully persuading any person to work or abstain from working.

This was necessary as sub-ss (1) and (2) give protection for picketing only to workers. As with workers, trade union officials must be picketing lawfully and the question to be asked is whether the member picket is acting lawfully or not, ie has the 'proper purposes' analysed above. The trade union official must also represent the member or members picketing. The term 'represent' must be given its ordinary meaning. A 'trade union official' for purposes of s 11 is defined in sub-s (5) as 'any paid official of a trade union or any officer of a union or branch of a union elected or appointed in accordance with the rules of a union'.

---

168. See www.ictu.ie for 'A Guide to the Picketing Policy of the ICTU'.

169. An object made somewhat diffuse as a result of *Reynolds v Kavanagh* (11 November 1985, unreported), HC.

170. *Talbot (Ireland) Ltd v Merrigan* (30 April 1981, unreported), SC.

171. The singular imports the plural unless a contrary intention appears: Interpretation Act 2005, s 18(a).

Chapter 11

INJUNCTIONS TO RESTRAIN PICKETING AND OTHER INDUSTRIAL ACTION

INTRODUCTION

[11.01] The purpose of this chapter is to consider the circumstances in which the courts will grant injunctions restraining any of the wrongs outlined in the previous chapters where those organising or participating in the strike or industrial action, or picketing, are arguably outside the statutory protections. It also considers the statutory limitations imposed on the courts by the provisions of the Industrial Relations Act 1990 and deals with the practice and procedures relating to applications for such injunctions. For the benefit of non-legal readers, the chapter commences with an overview of the law relating to injunctions generally.

Injunctions

[11.02] An injunction is an order by a court restraining a person from performing some specified act (a prohibitory injunction) or compelling or requiring him to perform a specified act (a mandatory injunction).[1] Injunctions may be applied for and granted at various stages of legal proceedings. An interim injunction may be granted by the court, usually following an application on an *ex-parte* basis, restraining some act for a very short period of time. An *ex parte* application, that is without the other party being present, will only be entertained by the court in cases of considerable urgency. If the court grants an injunction on an interim basis, it will usually direct that the defendant have liberty to apply to the court, on notice, to have the injunction varied or discharged. An interim injunction will be rarely granted for longer than three of four days as the court will undoubtedly want to give to the other side an early opportunity to reply and be heard. An interlocutory injunction, either mandatory or prohibitory in nature, may be granted until the trial of the issue. The granting or refusal of an interlocutory injunction does not in any way bind the judge at the trial.[2] A permanent injunction may be granted following the trial of the matter.[3]

[11.03] A person who disobeys an order of a court, if he has knowledge of its terms, will be regarded as being in contempt of court and will, depending on the circumstances, be punished for that contempt and/or required to purge his contempt.

---

1. See generally Kirwan, *Injunctions Law and Practice* (Thompson Round Hall, 2008); Spray, *The Principles of Equitable Remedies* (7th edn, Sweet & Maxwell, 2007) and Bean, *Injunctions* (8th edn, Thompson Sweet & Maxwell, 2004).

2. See for example the discussion by Clarke J relating to injunctions to restrain dismissals in *Carroll v Bus Átha Cliath* [2005] 4 IR 184.

3. Exceptionally, a permanent injunction was granted by Peart J in *Thomas Cook v TSSA* High Court Record No 2009/7181P, 3 August 2009 at the interlocutory stage.

The imposition of a punishment, such as imprisonment, for civil contempt is intended to be coercive rather than punitive.[4] An injunction, particularly relating to picketing, is usually worded so that the order is addressed not only to the parties to the proceedings but also to all persons having notice of the making of the order. Accordingly, a person can be in contempt of court by being in breach of an order which was not specifically directed to him and which arose in proceedings in which he was not named as a party, provided he has notice of the making of the order and the contents of it.

The Discretionary Nature of Injunctive Relief

[11.04] Injunctions are equitable remedies and, accordingly, a court will not only consider the facts before it but will also give consideration to the principles of equity in determining whether to grant or refuse an injunction application. Kirwan[5] states that fourteen fundamental equitable principles can be identified; however, he states that five of them play a more prominent role in the granting or otherwise of injunctions. The five he lists are as follows:

(1)   equity acts *in personam*;

(2)   he who seeks equity must do equity;

(3)   he who comes to equity must come with clean hands;

(4)   delay defeats equity; and

(5)   equity, like nature, does nothing in vain.

American Cyanamid/Campus Oil Principles

[11.05] The leading cases in this jurisdiction[6] and in England[7] set out the principles which the court will consider, together with the principles of equity, in determining whether or not to grant an injunction at an interlocutory stage. The evidence before the court on an interlocutory injunction application will typically be limited to affidavits. Only in rare cases will the court have the benefit of oral evidence which can be challenged by cross-examination. In those circumstances the court does not decide to grant or refuse an injunction on any final determination of facts but rather by applying certain tests that have been developed by the courts and which are, in particular, set out in *Campus Oil* and *American Cyanamid*. Typically, a judge will warn, when granting or refusing an injunction, that he has not made any final determination on the facts and that that remains a matter for the trial. Prior to *American Cyanamid* there was certain confusion as to how strong a case needed to be before a court would grant an injunction. In the course of his judgment in *American Cyanamid*, Diplock LJ stated:[8]

> It is no part of the court's function at this stage of the litigation to try to resolve conflicts of evidence on affidavit as to facts on which the claims of either party

---

4.   See *Shell E & P Ireland v McGrath* [2007] 1 IR 671.

5.   Kirwan, *Injunctions Law and Practice* (Thompson Round Hall, 2008), p 100 *et seq.*

6.   *Campus Oil Ltd v Minister for Energy (No 2)* [1983] IR 88, [1984] ILRM 45.

7.   *American Cyanamid Co v Ethicon Ltd* [1975] AC 396, [1975] 2 WLR 316, [1975] 1 All ER 504.

8.   *American Cyanamid Co v Ethicon Ltd* [1975] AC 396 at pp 407–408.

may ultimately depend nor to decide difficult questions of law which call for detailed argument and mature considerations. These are matters to be dealt with at the trial. One of the reasons for the introduction of the practice of requiring an undertaking as to damages upon the grant of an interlocutory injunction was that 'it aided the court in doing that which was its great object, viz. abstaining from expressing any opinion upon the merits of the case until the hearing': *Wakefield v Duke of Buccleugh* (1865) 12 LT 628, 629. So unless the material available to the court at the hearing of the application for an interlocutory injunction fails to disclose that the plaintiff has any real prospect of succeeding in his claim for a permanent injunction at the trial, the court should go on to consider whether the balance of convenience lies in favour of granting or refusing the interlocutory relief that is sought.

As to that, the governing principle is that the court should first consider whether, if the plaintiff were to succeed at the trial in establishing his right to a permanent injunction, he would be adequately compensated by an award of damages for the loss he would have sustained as a result of the defendant's continuing to do what was sought to be enjoined between the time of the application and the time of the trial. If damages in the measure recoverable at common law would be adequate remedy and the defendant would be in a financial position to pay them, no interlocutory injunction should normally be granted, however strong the plaintiff's claim appeared to be at that stage. If, on the other hand, damages would not provide an adequate remedy for the plaintiff in the event of his succeeding at the trial, the court should then consider whether, on the contrary hypothesis that the defendant were to succeed at the trial in establishing his right to do that which was sought to be enjoined, he would be adequately compensated under the plaintiff's undertaking as to damages for the loss he would have sustained by being prevented from doing so between the time of the application and the time of the trial. If damages in the measure recoverable under such an undertaking would be an adequate remedy and the plaintiff would be in a financial position to pay them, there would be no reason upon this ground to refuse an interlocutory injunction.

It is where there is doubt as to the adequacy of the respective remedies in damages available to either party or to both, that the question of balance of convenience arises. It would be unwise to attempt even to list all the various matters which may need to be taken into consideration in deciding where the balance lies, let alone to suggest the relative weight to be attached to them. These will vary from case to case.

Where other factors appear to be evenly balanced it is a counsel of prudence to take such measures as are calculated to preserve the status quo.

It was clear from the foregoing that what the court required, in deciding to grant or refuse an injunction, was a claim with some merit, inadequacy of damages and if necessary an examination of the balance of convenience as between the parties.

[11.06] In *Campus Oil*, O'Higgins CJ expressed agreement with what was said by Lord Diplock in *American Cyanamid*. In the judgment he stated as follows:

Interlocutory relief is granted to an applicant where what he complains of is continuing and is causing him harm or injury which may be irreparable in the sense that it may not be possible to compensate him fairly or properly by an award of damages. Such relief is given because a period must necessarily elapse before the action can come for trial and for the purpose of keeping matters in *status quo* until the hearing.

Griffin J in *Campus Oil* also specifically adopted the views expressed by Lord Diplock in *American Cyanamid* and accordingly it is now well established that the test which will be adopted by a court in determining whether or not to grant an interlocutory prohibitory injunction is whether or not the plaintiff has made out a fair issue to be tried. If the plaintiff successfully meets that first test, then the court will examine the adequacy or inadequacy of damages and in examining that aspect of the case the court will look at not only the inadequacy of damages from the plaintiff's point of view but the inadequacy of any undertaking as to damages which might be given by the plaintiff in respect of the period whilst the injunction is in place. Finally, the court will examine where the balance of convenience lies.

Undertaking as to Damages

[11.07] It is normally a prerequisite to the grant of either an interim or an interlocutory injunction that the plaintiff give to the court an undertaking as to damages, that is that the plaintiff will compensate the defendant for any loss suffered by the defendant in the event that it is ultimately held that the injunction was wrongly granted. In *Pasture Properties Ltd v Evans*[9] Laffoy J put the principle in the following terms:

> The Plaintiff cannot get an injunction unless it can give an undertaking as to damages. If an injunction is wrongly granted at this stage and it so transpires at the hearing of the action, the Plaintiff must undertake to adequately indemnify the Defendant against any loss incurred by the Defendant by reason of the injunction being wrongly granted.

A court will also need to be satisfied that the plaintiff in fact has an ability to pay on foot of the undertaking although there are cases where an impecunious plaintiff may well obtain an injunction because of the special circumstances of the case.

[11.08] The court will also have regard to the adequacy of any such undertaking. In *Fitzpatrick v Commissioner of An Garda Síochána*,[10] Kelly J considered not only the adequacy of damages from the plaintiff's point of view but also the adequacy of the undertaking as to damages from the defendant's point of view. The applicant in that case sought, as part of judicial review proceedings, an injunction restraining his repatriation from United Nations service in Cyprus. The trial judge set out his views on the matter:

> In these circumstances, I am quite satisfied that the repatriation of the Applicant at this juncture, even if unlawful, will not give rise to any irreparable loss or damage being sustained by him. All of the losses and damage which have been averred to are, in my view, perfectly capable of being compensated for by an award of damages.

---

9.   *Pasture Properties Ltd v Evans* [1999] IEHC 214.
10.   *Fitzpatrick v Commissioner of An Garda Síochána* [1996] 7 ELR 244.

Furthermore, I am of the view that the calculation of those damages would not create a difficulty for the Court in excess of any other such claim which it frequently has to deal with asserting damage to reputation, good name or career prospects. Even if I am wrong in this view and the computing of such damages would be difficult, I must bear in mind what was said by Finlay CJ in *Curust Financial Services Ltd v Loewe Lack Werk* [1994] 1 IR 450 on this topic. He said (at p 469):

> 'Difficulty, as distinct from complete impossibility, in the assessment of such damages should not, in my view, be a ground for characterising the award of damages as an inadequate remedy.'

Turning then to the other side of the equation, I pose the question 'Would damages provide an adequate remedy for the Respondent if he is enjoined from repatriating the Applicant pending trial but succeeds in his defence?' I pose this question on the assumption that the Applicant is prepared to give an undertaking as to damages. In my view, it would be impossible to assess such damages. The Respondent is under a statutory obligation to direct and control the Garda force. If he is wrongfully prevented from so doing by the grant of an injunction in the circumstances of the present case, it is difficult to see how any Court could make an assessment in money terms of the damage caused to him by being forced to keep on United Nations duties, an officer whom he considers to be unsuitable. It is the Commissioner and not the Court that is charged with responsibility by statute for the direction and control of the Garda force. In the circumstances of this case, it appears to me that damages would be a wholly inadequate way of compensating for the damage which might be caused by the grant of this injunction.

PRACTICE AND PROCEDURE

[11.09] The jurisdiction to grant injunctions lies in the High Court. The Circuit Court has a limited jurisdiction in such matters; however, the power of the Circuit Court to grant an injunction is limited in essence to cases involving property or by way of ancillary relief to the main cause of action.[11] The District Court has no power to grant injunctive relief save that it has certain statutory powers to make orders, for example in family law matters, which have a similar effect to injunctions.

Commencement of Proceedings

[11.10] Proceedings in which an injunction might be sought to restrain picketing or the effects of other industrial action are typically commenced by way of plenary summons. The matter will first come to court, usually, on foot of a notice of motion and indeed such an application can be brought before the court even before the plenary summons is issued or served – although, of course, the plaintiff will be required to give an appropriate undertaking in relation to issuance and service of the proceedings. A plenary summons is an originating summons for the commencement of proceedings

---

11.   See *Rodgers v Mangan* (July 1996, unreported), HC (Geoghegan J).

with pleadings which is to be heard on oral evidence (except in respect of personal injury actions).[12] The plenary or originating summons sets out in relatively brief form the reliefs which are sought by the plaintiff in the proceedings.[13]

Applications for Injunctive Relief

[11.11] An application for injunctive relief will typically be grounded on a notice of motion, which will set out the interim and interlocutory reliefs sought by the moving party and will be grounded on an affidavit. In circumstances where urgent injunctive relief is sought, then a party may apply, *ex parte*, to the appropriate judge of the High Court. In circumstances where interim relief is being sought the application should be limited as much as possible to what is essential and indeed in many cases all that is sought, at that stage, is an application for 'short service'. Such an order typically does no more than truncate the period of notice which must be given to a party to compel their appearance before the court. The court's jurisdiction in this matter is to be found in Ord 52, r 3 of the Rules of the Superior Court, which provides that:

> In any case the Court, if satisfied that the delay caused by proceeding by motion on notice under this Order would or might entail irreparable or serious mischief, may make any order ex parte upon such terms as to costs or otherwise and subject to such undertaking, if any, as the Court may think just; and any party affected by such order may move to set it aside.

[11.12] As a general principle, mandatory injunctions will not be granted at the interim stage on the basis of an *ex parte* application except in the rarest of cases. An order that somebody is compelled by court to do something may be difficult to undo; also it would seem to be an extraordinary exercise by the court of its inherent jurisdiction to compel a person to do something in circumstances where that person has had no opportunity to address the court on the issues. It is possible to envisage extreme circumstances where a mandatory injunction might be granted in industrial relations disputes in circumstances, for example, where picketers had erected some barrier restraining entrance to or egress from a premises, although even in such cases it is likely that the order would be worded in prohibitory rather than mandatory terms. The test to be applied in applications for injunctions of a prohibitory nature are those set out in the *Campus Oil* and *American Cyanamid* cases and the first test is that the party applying for the injunction must show that there is a fair/serious issue to be tried. The test for a mandatory injunction is stronger. In *Maha Lingham v Health Service*

---

12. See Rules of the Superior Court, Ord 1, r 2 (SI 248/2005).

13. The **Appendix** contains sample pleadings consisting of draft plenary summons, draft notice of motion and draft grounding affidavits. The draft proceedings in the Appendix are for guidance only and the Authors take no responsibility whatsoever for the use by any party of these drafts as precedents for pleadings before the court. Readers are urged to ensure that pleadings are properly drafted by counsel in every case. The drafts attached herein are for illustrative purposes only.

Executive[14] Fennelly J, dealing with an application for an injunction to restrain a dismissal, expressed the following views:[15]

> ... the implication of an application of the present sort is that in substance what the plaintiff/appellant is seeking is a mandatory interlocutory injunction and it is well established that the ordinary test of a fair case to be tried is not sufficient to meet the first leg of the test for the grant of an interlocutory injunction where the injunction sought is in effect mandatory. In such a case it is necessary for the applicant to show at least that he has a strong case that he is likely to succeed at the hearing of the action. So it is not sufficient for him simply to show a prima facie case ...

Application for Injunctions

[11.13] It is normal practice that, prior to the commencement of legal proceedings, the parties will engage in correspondence. Typically, the plaintiff will set out the nature of his proposed case and, equally typically, the defendant will respond. The purpose of such pre-litigation correspondence is obviously to, if possible, reach agreement at the earliest stage of a dispute and also to give the parties an opportunity to explain their respective positions so as to avoid litigation at all. Whilst the nature of an application for interim injunction is by definition an urgent matter it remains preferable, if at all possible, that the plaintiff should communicate with the defendant pointing out the alleged wrongdoing and calling on the proposed defendant to cease the unlawful activity. Having regard to the obligation on the part of trade unions to give notice of impending industrial action, it is usual that either the employer or solicitors acting on behalf of the employer will write to the trade union in advance pointing out any defects and calling for non-implementation of the proposed action. The conduct which actually gives rise to the justification for the application for an injunction, however, often only arises after the industrial action has commenced such as picketers engaging in unlawful action such as trespass or blockading an entrance to a premises. It remains always preferable, however, that the offender be given an opportunity, no matter how short in time, to correct his conduct.

There is an absolute obligation on a party applying to court for an interim, or indeed an interlocutory injunction, to make full disclosure to the court of all relevant material. Any pre-action correspondence, including any reply, of course would have to be brought to the attention of the court.

Ex parte Application

[11.14] The following is the procedure adopted in practice in the High Court in respect of *ex parte* applications for interim injunctions. In the first instance, the plaintiff's lawyers will prepare a plenary summons, notice of motion and grounding affidavit(s). The affidavit will set out fully all relevant factors, including matters which may be adverse to the plaintiff's own case and typically will refer to and exhibit all relevant correspondence and other materials. During the legal terms, when courts are sitting, an

---

14.   *Maha Lingham v Health Service Executive* [2006] 17 ELR 137.

15.   At p 140.

initial application will be made to the judge in charge of the Chancery List, to the President of the High Court or to another appropriate judge of the High Court. The Judge should be advised at the call over of that day's list, or at some other suitable time during the court day, that it is intended to make an application. The Judge will usually indicate when an appropriate time will arise and the papers should be handed into court, particularly if there is a possibility that the Judge may have an opportunity to read the papers in advance of the application. If an application is to be made at a time when the court is not sitting, then the practice is that counsel acting for the moving party contacts the High Court duty Registrar and arrangements are made to make the application before the duty judge at a specified location and time.

[11.15] It is recognised that in matters of extreme urgency the proceedings might not in fact be issued out of the Central Office before the application is made to the judge. In those circumstances, the application will be made in 'intended proceedings' and the normal practice is that the plaintiff will give an undertaking to issue and stamp the appropriate court documents.

The affidavit

[11.16] The only evidence, normally, before the court in the course of an interim and/ or interlocutory injunction application will be on affidavit. The court may direct, on the application of either party, the cross-examination of deponents; however, that is unusual in injunction applications. Having regard to the fact that the only evidence before the court is that contained in the affidavit, it is critical that there be full and complete disclosure in the grounding affidavits. The deponent of the affidavit swears to the truth of his averments and any failure in this regard is just as serious as misleading a court in the course of oral evidence. The affidavit will typically set out the means of knowledge of the deponent and will describe the background to the application and the need for urgency. The body of the affidavit will set forth, in a full and frank manner, all of the relevant facts. It is important that the deponent of the affidavit act with utmost good faith. In this regard it is to be emphasised that the duty of the members of the legal profession is to assist the courts in the administration of justice and to ensure that all relevant matters are brought to the attention of the court including facts and submissions on the law which may be regarded as adverse to the interests of their own clients. The rule in relation to full disclosure, described as the 'golden rule' by Browne Wilkinson VC in *Tate Access Floors Inc v Boswell*,[16] is as follows:

> No rule is better established, and few more important, than the rule, 'the golden rule,' that a plaintiff applying for ex parte relief must disclose to the court all matters relevant to the exercise of the court's discretion whether or not to grant relief before giving the defendant an opportunity to be heard. If that duty is not observed by the plaintiffs, the court will discharge the ex parte order and may, to mark its displeasure, refuse the plaintiff further *inter partes* relief even though the circumstances would otherwise justify the grant of such relief.

---

16.   *Tate Access Floors Inc v Boswell* [1990] 3 All ER 303.

[11.17] In *F McK v DC, ST Ltd and BH Ltd*,[17] a case dealing with an allegation of material non-disclosure in an application under the Proceeds of Crime Act 1996, Clarke J referred to the obligation to make a full and frank disclosure in the following terms:

> The obligation of full disclosure is seen as a quid pro quo for the entitlement of the applicant to obtain what are, frequently, very onerous orders, without affording the person affected by those orders an opportunity to be heard.

Later in the judgment the judge made the following observations:

> As indicated above the underlying rationale behind that principle stems from a recognition that the making of an onerous restrictive order on an ex parte basis is a departure from the fundamental rule of fair procedures which entitles a party to be heard before an onerous order is made against it. That departure is justified in the limited circumstances which have been identified in the jurisprudence relevant to the making of orders such as Mareva and Anton Pillar Orders. It is, indeed, for that very reason that the circumstances in which such orders can be made are limited. In evolving the rules by reference to which such orders are given, the courts have been mindful of the need to balance the entitlement of plaintiffs to protection against wrongful actions with the legitimate entitlement of parties to be heard prior to the making of onerous orders against their interest. For that reason the jurisdiction is carefully defined and controlled.

It has been suggested that the obligation to make full and frank disclosure is somewhat diminished at the interlocutory stage having regard to the fact that the defendant is then in a position to present his own case.[18]

Undertaking as to Damages

[11.18] As pointed out earlier, the applicant for injunctive relief must give an undertaking as to damages in respect of any damage that may be suffered by the respondent in circumstances where it is ultimately determined that the injunction ought not to have been granted. Typically that undertaking is set out in the grounding affidavit.

Short Service

[11.19] It is normal practice in the course of an interim application to seek 'short service'. The applicant will often limit the interim relief sought to such an order and, indeed, in other cases the court may decide to grant only that relief. The effect of short service is to truncate the period of notice which must be given to a person directing them to attend before the court to deal with the matter and, typically, the court will couple any other interim order with an order for short service returnable at the earliest practical opportunity.

---

17. *F McK v DC, ST Ltd and BH Ltd* [2006] IEHC 185.

18. See Kirwan, *Injunctions Law and Practice* (Thompson Round Hall, 2008) at p 263.

Refusal to Grant Interim Injunction

[11.20] If a judge refuses to grant an application for an injunction made on an *ex parte* basis, it is not open to the applicant to bring the same application before another judge unless there has been a material change in circumstances such that, in effect, the second judge is being asked to rule on a different application. The obligation to make full and frank disclosure would obviously include an obligation to bring to the court's attention, in the course of the second application, full details of the first application, including the refusal. In the alternative, a party of course may appeal against the refusal.

Service

[11.21] The court will typically make orders as to the mode of service of any interim or interlocutory order that it may make and also provide for the service of the court documents, including affidavits. Typically, following an urgent interim application, the court will order that notification of the making of the order be advised by telephone and/or email and/or facsimile to appropriate parties. Such notification would be typically ordered in respect of any trade union involved in the matter and also on any solicitors who were known to be involved, whether by way of their involvement in correspondence or otherwise. The court will also direct personal service on the defendants and will in picketing cases usually direct that a copy of the order and/or notification of the making of the order be affixed in prominent locations at the premises being picketed or subject to other industrial action. The applicant will have to be in a position to satisfy the court ultimately as to the effectiveness of service and, in particular, proof of service will be critical in any application that a person is in contempt of court by reason of breach of such an order.

The Interlocutory Hearing

[11.22] The hearing of an application for interlocutory injunctive relief will arise either following the granting or refusal of an interim order, the granting of short service or the matter coming before the court in the normal course by way of motion on notice. An application for interlocutory injunction will usually come before the Chancery judge and, unless otherwise directed by the court, will normally be listed in the Chancery Motion lists in the High Court on Monday morning. It is practice, at the call over of such lists, to advise the court of the expected duration of the motion and, arising out of same, the matter will be managed by the court. The application may be adjourned from time to time to permit the filing of replying affidavits; however, depending on the urgency of the matter, relatively strict time limits might be imposed by the court or agreed by the parties. When all of the affidavits have been filed the matter will be dealt with by the court. The procedure which is adopted is that counsel for the moving party 'opens' the relevant papers. This typically involves referring the court to the plenary summons and the notice of motion and advising the court of the nature of the reliefs sought. Counsel might set out briefly an outline of the facts of the case or may proceed directly to 'open' the affidavits. Counsel for the applicant reads to the court the affidavits, usually in the order in which they have been filed, and, during the course of that opening, will draw the court's attention to relevant exhibits. At the conclusion of the reading of the affidavits Counsel for the applicant will make appropriate submissions and will refer the court to appropriate case law. counsel for the applicant will often have prepared, in advance, a written legal submission and he will be required to have available for the court, and for the other side, copies of the cases and other materials which he refers to either in his oral or written submissions. Counsel for the defendant will then reply. The defendant's affidavits will have been opened by counsel for the applicant and, accordingly, there is no need for that exercise to be undertaken a second time but counsel for the defendant will very often, for the sake of emphasis, refer back to the affidavits and in particular may refer the court to some of the exhibits or part thereof. Counsel for the defendant then replies on the law and again will have prepared an oral or written submission accompanied by case law and other legal materials. Finally, counsel for the applicant will have an opportunity to reply briefly. The judge will, of course, seek clarification on any factual or legal points that arise during the course of both sides submissions.

[11.23] Following consideration of the matter, the court will deliver its judgment on the interlocutory application. Such a judgment may be delivered immediately following the argument and this is known as an '*ex tempore*' judgment. Alternatively, the court may reserve, usually for a relatively short period, its judgment and same will be delivered at a later date. Either party may appeal the refusal or the grant of the injunctive relief to the Supreme Court.

[11.24] It is usual, particularly in circumstances where an injunction has been granted, for the court to give directions as to pleadings so as to ensure an early trial. In those circumstances the court may set out, or request the parties to agree, a timeframe for the delivery of the formal pleadings, that is a statement of claim and a defence. The court may also deal with other ancillary matters such as providing for the timeframe in which applications for discovery or other interlocutory applications may be made. The case may be subjected to a formal case management procedure and, having regard to the urgency of the matter, the case will either be listed in the normal list to fix dates or alternatively assigned a special date by the judge who is managing the proceedings.

INDUSTRIAL RELATIONS ACT 1990

[11.25] The Industrial Relations Act 1990 introduced significant changes in relation to picketing, particularly by limiting in certain respects the power of the court to grant injunctions. **Chapter 10** considers these changes and the jurisprudence developed under the Trade Disputes Act 1906 by reason of the fact that the core provisions of that Act are repeated in the 1990 legislation. It contrasts s 11 of the 1990 Act with s 2 of the Trade Disputes Act 1906. A comparison of the two sections shows that the permitting of peaceful picketing is based on the same fundamental principle, that is that such picketing shall be 'in contemplation or furtherance of a trade dispute', the '*golden formula*' (para **9.76** *et seq*). **Chapter 9** also considers the proper parties and the subject matter of a 'trade dispute', which are required under the 1990 Act for its protections to apply, As **Ch 10** describes, the changes evident in the 1990 Act clarify, and to a certain extent limit, the places where picketing may take place, including removing from the permissible locations the residence of an employer and clarifying in a most important way the limitation on what is known as secondary picketing.

STATUTORY RESTRAINT ON INJUNCTIONS

[11.26] The Industrial Relations Act 1990 imposed restrictions on the ability of employers to apply and obtain injunctions on an *ex parte* basis. The courts have a jurisdiction to grant an interim injunction following an application on an *ex parte* basis; in deciding whether or not to grant such an injunction, the court will apply the same tests as arise on an interlocutory application, that is the test set out in *Campus Oil*.[19]

[11.27] The bringing of an *ex parte* application arises because of the real or perceived urgency on the part of the applicant. In circumstances where such an application is made, without the presence of the other party, then there is an onus on the plaintiff applicant to ensure that the affidavit upon which the application is based sets out fully all relevant facts including matters which might be perceived as adverse to the case being advanced by the applicant.

The obligation to make disclosure during the course of an *ex parte* application is very wide and in particular applicants must not seek to obtain an order by withholding any relevant material, whether intentional or not. The courts do recognise that by reason of the urgency and the speed with which papers have to be prepared, errors may occur and relevant matters may be accidentally omitted. There is, however, a heavy duty of candour and care.[20]

The duty on the applicant is to make full and frank disclosure of all material facts. Material facts are those which it is material for the judge to know and materiality is to be determined by the court rather than by a party to the action. The applicant is under an obligation to make appropriate inquiries to ascertain material facts. Non-disclosure of facts of significant materiality may well justify the immediate discharge of the order; however, the court at all times retains onto itself a discretion.

[11.28] It was very common, prior to the enactment of the Industrial Relations Act 1990, for employers to make *ex parte* applications to restrain picketing of their premises. It was almost invariably the case that the employer could show that the balance of convenience lay with the granting of the order (typically based on some argument that there would be a failure to meet an urgent order or that products or goods would be damaged or spoiled) and also that damages were an inadequate remedy in circumstances where typically the picketers were not marks for damages. In those circumstances the employer merely had to satisfy the court that there was to be a fair issue to be tried. Much criticism was levelled, particularly by trade unionists, at what was perceived as an employer using, or perhaps abusing, the legal system to obtain an interim injunction, which often had the immediate effect of rendering the picketing wholly ineffective. If the picketers complied with the interim order, then the

---

19. *Campus Oil Ltd v Minister for Industry and Energy (No 2)* [1983] IR 88.
20. *Bambrick v Cobley* [2006] 1 ILRM 81.

immediate disruption of their employer's business would be resolved and typically the employer would be in a position, over the period of time until the matter came back before the court, to put in place alternative arrangements and had the time to get goods in or out of the premises as necessary. The rendering of the picketing ineffective was perceived by trade unionists as rendering the very strike weapon as being ineffective.

[11.29] Section 19(1) of the 1990 Act imposes a statutory restraint on an employer and provides that where a secret ballot has been held in accordance with the rules of a trade union, the outcome of which favours a strike or other industrial action, and the trade union, before engaging in that action, has given notice of not less than one week of its intention to engage in that action, then the employer is not entitled to apply to any court for an injunction restraining the strike or any other industrial action unless notice of the application has been given to the trade union and the members of the trade union who are a party to the trade dispute (see too para **9.68**). Whilst the statutory provision does not set out the period of notice which the employer must give to the trade union, the reality is that that period of notice will in effect be determined by the rules of court.[21] The courts regularly entertain applications for leave to serve short notice of a motion and nothing in s 19(1) prohibits such an application.

[11.30] Section 19(2) of the Act in effect shifts the onus of proof in injunction applications in favour of the defendants. That section provides that where a secret ballot has been held, and notice has been given of the strike or other industrial action, then a court 'shall not grant an injunction restraining the strike or other industrial action where the Respondent establishes a fair case that he was acting in contemplation or furtherance of a trade dispute'. The position is now that it is not for the employer to establish a fair case that the picketing is unlawful; rather, it is on the defendants to establish the assertion that the conduct was in contemplation or furtherance of a trade dispute.

[11.31] It is important to note that s 19(4) expressly provides that sub-ss (1) and (2) do not apply in respect of unlawful occupation of property or the unlawful causing of damage to property or in respect of any proceedings arising out of or relating to any action resulting or likely to result in death or personal injury.[22]

[11.32] Whilst the application for an interlocutory injunction can be defeated by the defendants, establishing a fair case that the action was in contemplation of furtherance of a trade dispute – the standard of proof required – is less clear. It is, however, suggested that the proof should be no different than in any civil proceedings, that is on the balance of probabilities. In *Nolan Transport (Oaklands) Ltd v Halligan*[23] this matter was considered. Murphy J spoke of the defendants having to 'comfortably demonstrate' compliance with the balloting and notice requirements. In *Malincross*

---

21.   See Rules of the Superior Court, Ord 52, r 6.

22.   A good example of the granting of an *ex parte* interim order in this regard is to be found in *Thomas Cook v TSSA* High Court Record No 2009/7181P, 3 August 2009 (Peart J).

23.   *Nolan Transport (Oaklands) Ltd v Halligan* [1999] 1 IR 128.

Ltd v Building and Allied Trade Union[24] McCracken J stated that he was satisfied that the plaintiff had raised a serious issue as to whether the picketing was authorised by the ballot. The condition precedent referred to in sub-s (2) had not been established and consequently did not apply. It was respectfully suggested that it would be preferable and more in accordance with the intention of the legislature if the test applied was to call on the picketers to show, on the balance of probabilities, that they have complied with the balloting and notice provisions and that the mere raising of a 'serious issue' by the employer to the contrary is insufficient.

SECRET BALLOTS

[11.33] Section 14 of the Act of 1991 imposed a new and important obligation on trade unions relating to secret ballots. The section provides that the rules of every trade union shall contain provisions for the holding of secret ballots and limits a union's ability to support industrial action in the absence of such ballots.[25] The section requires that the rules of a trade union will contain a provision that the union will not organise, participate in, sanction or support a strike or other industrial action without a secret ballot. The entitlement to vote in such a secret ballot must be accorded equally to all members whom it is reasonable, at the time of the ballot, for the union to believe will be called upon to engage in the strike or other industrial action. A union is obliged to take reasonable steps to ensure that every member entitled to vote in the ballot votes without interference from or constraint imposed by the union or any of its members, officials or employees and, so far as is reasonably possible, that such members be given a fair opportunity of voting.

[11.34] Subparagraph (c) of sub-s 14(2) provides that the management committee of the union is not obliged to sanction or support a strike even where the majority of those voting are in favour of the action, but the management committee is prohibited from organising, participating in, sanctioning or supporting against the wishes of the majority. The section provides for an exception to this rule where the ballot is undertaken by a number of unions and the aggregate majority of all of the votes cast favours the industrial action.

[11.35] The section further provides that where a secret ballot is conducted by a trade union which is affiliated to the Irish Congress of Trade Unions (ICTU) and is in favour of supporting a strike organised by another trade union, a decision to take such supportive action shall not be implemented unless the action is sanctioned by ICTU. The section also requires a union, as soon as practicable after the conduct of a secret ballot, to take reasonable steps to make known to its members entitled to vote in the ballot the number of ballot papers issued, the number of votes cast and the number of votes in favour and against the proposal.

It is important to note that the rights conferred by s 14(2) are conferred on the members of the trade union and 'on no other person'.[26]

---

24.   *Malincross Ltd v Building and Allied Trade Union* [2002] 13 ELR 78.
25.   The section became operative on 18 July 1992.
26.   See Industrial Relations (Amendment) Act 1991, s 14(3).

[11.36] Ballots for industrial action are often in respect of authorising the union to engage in a 'strike or other industrial action' or 'industrial action up to and including withdrawal of labour'. In *P Elliot & Co v Building and Allied Trade Union*,[27] Clarke J held that there was nothing legally infirm in a ballot seeking authorisation of 'industrial action up to and including the placing of pickets'. He expressed the view that it was consistent with the policy of the section that a trade union could seek authority, from its members, to engage in a range of industrial action leaving it up to the union's management committee to determine precisely what action should be carried out. He did, however, say that the industrial action actually engaged in must be 'fairly within the parameters of that authorised'.

[11.37] Some criticism can be made of the section in that it fails to set out any limit as to how long the mandate conferred by a ballot is to last, and there is some evidence of unions, particularly in employments with fraught industrial relations issues, seeking well in advance of any negotiations on disputed issues to put in place the authorisation for industrial action and to use that authorisation as a bargaining tool.

[11.38] The effect of taking part in a strike without a valid ballot is that the restrictions contained in s 19 as to the availability of interim and interlocutory relief will not apply. It will be recalled, para **11.29**, that any strike or industrial action taken by a trade union or a group of workers in disregard of or contrary to the outcome of the secret ballot will result in the provisions of ss 10, 11 and 12 (the immunity provisions) not applying.

---

27.   *P Elliot & Co v Building and Allied Trade Union* [2006] IEHC 340 (Clarke J).

APPENDIX

CONSPIRACY AND PROTECTION OF PROPERTY ACT 1875

[38 & 39 Vim]

An Act for amending the Law relating to Conspiracy, and the Protection of Property, and for other purposes.

[13th August 1875.]

Be it enacted by the Queen's most Excellent Majesty, by and with the advice and consent of the Lords Spiritual and Temporal, and Commons, in this present Parliament assembled, and by the authority of the same, as follows

1 Short title

This Act may be cited as the Conspiracy, and Protection of Property Act, 1875.

2 Commencement of Act

This Act shall come into operation on the first day of September one thousand eight hundred and seventy-five.

Conspiracy, and Protection of Property

3 Amendment of law as to conspiracy in trade disputes

An agreement or combination by two or more persons to do or procure to be done any act in contemplation or furtherance of a trade dispute between employers and workmen shall not be indictable as a conspiracy if such act committed by one person would not be punishable as a crime.

Nothing in this section shall exempt from punishment any persons guilty, of a conspiracy for which a punishment is awarded by any Act of Parliament.

Nothing in this section shall affect the law relating to riot, unlawful assembly, breach of the peace, or sedition, or any offence against the State or the Sovereign.

A crime for the purposes of this section means an offence punishable on indictment, or an offence which is punishable on summary conviction, and for the commission of which the offender is liable under the statute making the offence punishable to be imprisoned either absolutely or at the discretion of the court as an alternative for some other punishment.

Where a person is convicted of any such agreement or combination as aforesaid to do or procure to be done an act which is punishable only on summary conviction, and is sentenced to imprisonment, the imprisonment shall not exceed three months, or such longer time, if any, as may hdve been prescribed by the statute for the punishment of the said act when committed by one person.

4 Breach of contract by persons employed in supply of gas or water

Where a person employed by a municipal authority or by any company or contractor upon whom is imposed by Act of Parliament the duty, or who have otherwise assumed the duty of supplying any city, borough, town, or place, or any part thereof, with gas or water, wilfully and maliciously breaks a contract of service with that authority or

289

company or contractor, knowing or having reasonable cause to believe that the probable consequences of his so doing, either alone or in combination with others, will be to deprive the inhabitants of that city, borough, town, place, or part, wholly or to a great extent of their supply of gas or water, he shall on conviction thereof by a court of summary jurisdiction or on indictment as herein-after mentioned, be liable either to pay a penalty not exceeding twenty pounds or to be imprisoned for a term not exceeding three months, with or without hard labour.

Every such municipal authority, company, or contractor as is mentioned in this section shall cause to be posted up, at the gasworks or waterworks, as the case may be, belonging to such authority or company or contractor, a printed copy of this section in some conspicuous place where the same may be conveniently read by the persons employed, and as often as such copy becomes defaced, obliterated, or destroyed, shall cause it to be renewed with all reasonable despatch.

If any municipal authority or company or contractor make default in complying with the provisions of this section in relation to such notice as aforesaid, they or he shall incur on summary conviction a penalty not exceeding fife pounds for every day during which such default continues, and every person who unlawfully injures, defaces, or covers up any notice so posted up as aforesaid in pursuance of this Act, shall be liable on summary conviction to a penalty not exceeding forty shillings.

5 Breach of contract involving injury to persons or property

Where any person wilfully and maliciously breaks a contract of service or of hiring, knowing or having reasonable cause to believe that the probable consequences of his so doing, either alone or in combination with others, will be to endanger human life, or cause serious bodily injury, or to expose valuable property whether real or personal to destruction or serious injury, he shall on conviction thereof by a court of summary jurisdiction, or on indictment as herein-after mentioned, be liable either to pay a penalty not exceeding twenty pounds, or to be imprisoned for a term not exceeding three months, with or without hard labour.

TRADE DISPUTES ACT 1906

Chapter 47

An Act to provide for the regulation of Trades Unions and Trade Disputes.
[21st December 1906]

BE it enacted by the King's most Excellent Majesty, by and with the advice and consent of the Lords Spiritual and Temporal, and Commons, in this present Parliament assembled, and by the authority of the same, as follows:

1 Amendment of the law of conspiracy in the case of trade disputes 38 & 39 Vict c 86

The following paragraph shall be added as a new paragraph after the first paragraph of section three of the Conspiracy and Protection of Property Act, 1875: "An act done in pursuance of an agreement or combination by two or more persons shall, if done in contemplation or furtherance of a trade dispute, not be actionable unless the act, if done without any such agreement or combination, would be actionable."

2 Peaceful picketing

(1) It shall be lawful for one or more persons, acting on their own behalf or on behalf of a trade union or of an individual employer or firm in contemplation or furtherance of a trade dispute, to attend at or near a house or place where a person resides or works or carries on business or happens to be, if they so attend merely for the purpose of peacefully obtaining or communicating information, or of peacefully persuading any person to work or abstain from working.

(2) Section seven of the Conspiracy and Protection of Property Act, 1875, is hereby repealed from "attending at or near" to the end of the section.

3 Removal of liability for interfering with another person's business, &c

An act done by a person in contemplation or furtherance of a trade dispute shall not he actionable on the ground only that it iudllces some other person to break a contract of employment or that it is an interference with the trade, business, or employment of some other person, or with the right of some other person to dispose of his capital or his labour as he wills.

4 Prohitition of actions of tort against trade unions

(1) An action against a trade union, whether of workmen or masters, or against any members or officials thereof on behalf of themselves and all other members of the trade· union in respect of :my tortious act alleged to have been committed by or on behalf of the trade union, shall not be entertained by any court.

(2) Nothing in this section shall affect the liability of the trustees of a trade union to be sued in the events provided for by the Trades Union Act, 1871, section nine, except in respect or any tortious act committed by or on behalf of the union in contemplation or in furtherance of a trade dispute.

5 Short title and construction

(1) This Act may be cited as the Trade Disputes Act, 1906, and the Trade Union Acts, 1871 and 1876, and this Act may he cited together as the Trade Union Acts, 1871 to 1906.

(2) In this Act the expression "trade union" has the same meaning as in the Trade Union Acts, 1871 and 1876, and shall include any comhination as therein defmed, notwithstanding that such combination mav be the branch of a trade union.

(3) In this Act and in the Oonspiracy and Protection of Property Act, 1875, the expression "trade dispute" means any dispute between employers and workmen, or between workmen and workmen, which is connected with the employment or non-employment, or the terms of the employment, or with the conditions of labour, of any person, and the expression "workmen" means all persons employed in trade or industry, whether or not in the employment of the employer with whom a trade dispute arises; and, in section three of the last-mentioned Act, the words "between employers and workmen" shall he repealed.

INDUSTRIAL RELATIONS ACT 1990

No 19 of 1990

ARRANGEMENT OF SECTIONS
PART I
PRELIMINARY

PART II
TRADE UNION LAW

Trade Disputes

AN ACT TO MAKE FURTHER AND BETTER PROVISION FOR PROMOTING HARMONIOUS RELATIONS BETWEEN WORKERS AND EMPLOYERS, AND TO AMEND THE LAW RELATING TO TRADE UNIONS AND FOR THESE AND OTHER PURPOSES TO AMEND THE INDUSTRIAL RELATIONS ACTS, 1946 TO 1976, AND THE TRADE UNION ACTS, 1871 TO 1982.

[18th July, 1990]

BE IT ENACTED BY THE OIREACHTAS AS FOLLOWS:

PART I
PRELIMINARY

1 Short title

This Act may be cited as the Industrial Relations Act, 1990

2 Collective citations and construction

(1) This Act (other than Part II) and the Industrial Relations Acts, 1946 to 1976, may be cited together as the Industrial Relations Acts, 1946 to 1990, and shall be construed together as one Act.

293

(2) Part II of this Act and the Trade Union Acts, 1871 to 1982, may be cited together as the Trade Union Acts, 1871 to 1990, and shall be construed together as one Act.

3 Interpretation

(1) In this Act—

"the Minister" means the Minister for Labour;

"the Court" means the Labour Court;

"the Commission" means the Labour Relations Commission established by section 24.

(2) In this Act—

(a) a reference to a Part or section is to a Part or section of this Act unless it is indicated that a reference to some other enactment is intended;

(b) a reference to a subsection or paragraph is to the subsection or paragraph of the provision in which the reference occurs, unless it is indicated that a reference to some other provision is intended; and

(c) a reference to any other enactment shall, unless the context otherwise requires, be construed as a reference to that enactment as amended by or under any other enactment, including this Act.

(3) In any enactment other than this Act, a reference to the Trade disputes Act, 1906 (repealed by this Act) or to any provision thereof shall, without prejudice to section 20 (1) of the Interpretation Act, 1937 , be construed as a reference to any relevant provision of Part II of this Act.

PART II
TRADE UNION LAW 4

Trade Disputes

8 Definitions for Part II

In this Part, save where the context otherwise requires—

"employer" means a person for whom one or more workers work or have worked or normally work or seek to work having previously worked for that person;

"trade dispute" means any dispute between employers and workers which is connected with the employment or non-employment, or the terms or conditions of or affecting the employment, of any person;

"trade union" means a trade union which is the holder of a negotiation licence under Part II of the Trade Union Act, 1941 ;

"worker" means any person who is or was employed whether or not in the employment of the employer with whom a trade dispute arises, but does not include a member of the Defence Forces or of the Garda Síochána;

"industrial action" means any action which affects, or is likely to affect, the terms or conditions, whether express or implied, of a contract and which is taken by any number or body of workers acting in combination or under a common understanding as a means of compelling their employer, or to aid other workers in compelling their employer, to accept or not to accept terms or conditions of or affecting employment;

"strike" means a cessation of work by any number or body of workers acting in combination or a concerted refusal or a refusal under a common understanding of any number of workers to continue to work for their employer done as a means of compelling their employer, or to aid other workers in compelling their employer, to accept or not to accept terms or conditions of or affecting employment.

9 Application of provisions of Part II

(1) Sections 11, 12 and 13 shall apply only in relation to authorised trade unions which for the time being are holders of negotiation licences under the Trade Union Act, 1941 , and the members and officials of such trade unions, and not otherwise

(2) Where in relation to the employment or non-employment or the terms or conditions of or affecting the employment of one individual worker, there are agreed procedures availed of by custom or in practice in the employment concerned, or provided for in a collective agreement, for the resolution of individual grievances, including dismissals, sections 10, 11 and 12 shall apply only where those procedures have been resorted to and exhausted.

(3) Procedures shall be deemed to be exhausted if at any stage an employer fails or refuses to comply with them.

(4) The procedures referred to in subsection (2) may include resort to such persons or bodies as a rights commissioner, the Labour Relations Commission, the Labour Court, an equality officer and the Employment Appeals Tribunal but shall not include an appeal to a court.

10 Acts in contemplation or furtherance of a trade dispute

(1) An agreement or combination by two or more persons to do or procure to be done any act in contemplation or furtherance of a trade dispute shall not be indictable as a conspiracy if such act committed by one person would not be punishable as a crime.

(2) An act done in pursuance of an agreement or combination by two or more persons, if done in contemplation or furtherance of a trade despute, shall not be actionable unless the act, if done without any such agreement or combination, would be actionable.

(3) Section 3 of the Conspiracy, and Protection of Property Act, 1875, and subsections (1) and (2) of this section shall be construed together as one section.

11 Peaceful picketing

(1) It shall be lawful for one or more persons, acting on their own behalf or on behalf of a trade union in contemplation or furtherance of a trade dispute, to attend at, or where that is not practicable, at the approaches to, a place where their employer works or carries on business, if they so attend merely for the purpose of peacefully obtaining or communicating information or of peacefully persuading any person to work or abstain from working.

(2) It shall be lawful for one or more persons acting on their own behalf or on behalf of a trade union in contemplation or furtherance of a trade dispute, to attend at, or where that is not practicable, at the approaches to, a place where an employer who is not a party to the trade dispute works or carries on business if, but only if, it is reasonable for those who are so attending to believe at the commencement of their attendance and throughout the continuance of their attendance that that employer has directly assisted their employer who is a party to the trade dispute for the purpose of frustrating the strike or other industrial action, provided that such attendance is merely for the purpose of peacefully obtaining or communicating information or of peacefully persuading any person to work or abstain from working.

(3) For the avoidance of doubt any action taken by an employer in the health services to maintain life-preserving services during a strike or other industrial action shall not constitute assistance for the purposes of subsection (2).

(4) It shall be lawful for a trade union official to accompany any member of his union whom he represents provided that the member is acting in accordance with the provisions of subsection (1) or (2) and provided that such official is attending merely for the purpose of peacefully obtaining or communicating information or of peacefully persuading any person to work or abstain from working.

(5) For the purposes of this section "trade union official" means any paid official of a trade union or any officer of a union or branch of a union elected or appointed in accordance with the rules of a union.

12 Removal of liability for certain acts

An act done by a person in contemplation or furtherance of a trade dispute shall not be actionable on the ground only that—

(a) it induces some other person to break a contract of employment, or

(b) it consists of a threat by a person to induce some other person to break a contract of employment or a threat by a person to break his own contract of employment, or

(c) it is an interference with the trade, business, or employment of some other person, or with the right of some other person to dispose of his capital or his labour as he wills.

13 Restriction of actions of tort against trade unions

(1) An action against a trade union, whether of workers or employers, or its trustees or against any members or officials thereof on behalf of themselves and all other members of the trade union in respect of any tortious act committed by or on behalf of the trade union in contemplation or furtherance of a trade dispute, shall not be entertained by any court.

(2) In an action against any trade union or person referred to in subsection (1) in respect of any tortious act alleged or found to have been committed by or on behalf of a trade union it shall be a defence that the act was done in the reasonable belief that it was done in contemplation or furtherance of a trade dispute.

14 Secret ballots

(1) This section shall come into operation two years after the passing of this Act ("the operative date").

(2) The rules of every trade union shall contain a provision that

(a) the union shall not organise, participate in, sanction or support a strike or other industrial action without a secret ballot, entitlement to vote in which shall be accorded equally to all members whom it is reasonable at the time of the ballot for the union concerned to believe will be called upon to engage in the strike or other industrial action;

(b) the union shall take reasonable steps to ensure that every member entitled to vote in the ballot votes without interference from, or constraint imposed by, the union or any of its members, officials or employees and, so far as is reasonably possible, that such members shall be given a fair opportunity of voting;

(c) the committee of management or other controlling authority of a trade union shall have full discretion in relation to organising, participating in, sanctioning or supporting a strike or other industrial action notwithstanding that the majority of those voting in the ballot, including an aggregate ballot referred to in paragraph (d), favour such strike or other industrial action;

(d) the committee of management or other controlling authority of a trade union shall not organise, participate in, sanction or support a strike or other industrial action against the wishes of a majority of its members voting in a secret ballot, except where, in the case of ballots by more than one trade union, an aggregate majority of all the votes cast, favours such strike or other industrial action;

(e) where the outcome of a secret ballot conducted by a trade union which is affiliated to the Irish Congress of Trade Unions or, in the case of ballots by more than one such trade union, an aggregate majority of all the votes cast, is in favour of supporting a strike organised by another trade union, a decision to take such supportive action shall not be implemented unless the action has been sanctioned by the Irish Congress of Trade Unions;

(f) as soon as practicable after the conduct of a secret ballot the trade union shall take reasonable steps to make known to its members entitled to vote in the ballot:

(i) the number of ballot papers issued,

(ii) the number of votes cast,

(iii) the number of votes in favour of the proposal,

(iv) the number of votes against the proposal, and

(v) the number of spoilt votes.

(3) The rights conferred by a provision referred to in subsection(2) are conferred on the members of the trade union concerned and on no other person.

(4) Nothing in this section shall constitute an obstacle to negotiations for the settlement of a trade dispute nor the return to work by workers party to the trade dispute.

(5) The First Schedule to the Trade Union Act, 1871, is hereby extended to include the requirement provided for in subsection (2).

15 Power to alter rules of trade unions

(1) The committee of management or other controlling authority of a trade union shall, notwithstanding anything in the rules of the union, have power by memorandum in writing to alter the rules of the union so far as may be necessary to give effect to section 14.

(2) In the case of a trade union which is a trade union under the law of another country having its headquarters control situated in that country, the committee of management or other controlling authority referred to in this Part shall have the same meaning as in section 17(2) of the Trade Union Act, 1975.

16 Enforcement of rule for secret ballot

(1) Every trade union registered under the Trade Union Acts, 1871 to 1975, or a trade union under the law of another country shall, not later than the operative date, forward to the Registrar of Friendly Societies a copy of its rules incorporating the provisions referred to in subsection (2) of section 14.

(2) A trade union failing to comply with subsection (2) of section 14 or subsection (1) of this section shall cease to be entitled to hold a negotiation licence under Part II of the Trade Union Act, 1941 , and its existing licence shall stand revoked on the operative date.

(3) A body of persons shall not be granted a negotiation licence unless, in addition to fulfilling the relevant conditions specified in section 7 of the Trade Union Act, 1941 , and section 2 of the Trade Union Act, 1971 , as amended by section 21 of this Act, it complies with subsection (2) of section 14 and for this purpose that subsection shall have effect from the passing of this Act.

(4) A body of persons which is a trade union under the law of another country shall not be granted a negotiation licence unless, in addition to fulfilling the conditions referred to in subsection (3) and section 17 of the Trade Union Act, 1975 , it forwards, at the time of application for a negotiation licence, a copy of its rules incorporating the provisions referred to in subsection (2) of section 14 to the Registrar of Friendly Societies.

(5) Where the Registrar of Friendly Societies is satisfied, after due investigation, that it is the policy or practice of a trade union registered under the Trade Union Acts, 1871 to 1975, or a trade union under the law of another country persistently to disregard any requirement of the provisions referred to in subsection (2) of section 14 he may issue an instruction to the trade union to comply with the requirement. Where such an instruction is disregarded, the Registrar of Friendly Societies shall inform the Minister and the Minister may revoke the negotiation licence of the trade union concerned.

17 Actions contrary to outcome of secret ballot

(1) Sections 10, 11 and 12 shall not apply in respect of proceedings arising out of or relating to a strike or other industrial action by a trade union or a group of workers in disregard of or contrary to, the outcome of a secret ballot relating to the issue or issues involved in the dispute.

(2) In the case of ballots by more than one trade union, the outcome of a secret ballot referred to in subsection (1) shall mean the outcome of the aggregated ballots.

(3) Where two or more secret ballots have been held in relation to a dispute, the ballot referred to in subsection (1) shall mean the last such ballot.

18 Non-application of sections 14 to 17 to employers' unions

Sections 14 to 17 shall not apply to a trade union of employers.

19 Restriction of right to injunction

(1) Where a secret ballot has been held in accordance with the rules of a trade union as provided for in section 14, the outcome of which or, in the case of an aggregation of ballots, the outcome of the aggregated ballots, favours a strike or other industrial action and the trade union before engaging in the strike or other industrial action gives notice of not less than one week to the employer concerned of its intention to do so, that employer shall not be entitled to apply to any court for an injunction restraining the strike or other industrial action unless notice of the application has been given to the trade union and its members who are party to the trade dispute.

(2) Where a secret ballot has been held in accordance with the rules of a trade union as provided for in section 14, the outcome of which or, in the case of an aggregation of ballots, the outcome of the aggregated ballots, favours a strike or other industrial action and the trade union before engaging in the strike or other industrial action gives notice of not less than one week to the employer concerned of its intention to do so, a court shall not grant an injunction restraining the strike or other industrial action where the respondent establishes a fair case that he was acting in contemplation or furtherance of a trade dispute.

(3) Notice as provided for in subsection (1) may be given to the members of a trade union by referring such members to a document containing the notice which the members have reasonable opportunity of reading during the course of their employment or which is reasonably accessible to them in some other way.

(4) Subsections (1) and (2) do not apply—

    (a)   in respect of proceedings arising out of or relating to unlawfully entering into or remaining upon any property belonging to another, or unlawfully causing damage or causing or permitting damage to be caused to the property of another, or

    (b)   in respect of proceedings arising out of or relating to any action resulting or likely to result in death or personal injury.

(5) Where two or more secret ballots have been held in relation to a dispute, the ballot referred to in subsections (1) and (2) shall be the last such ballot.

NON-FATAL OFFENCES AGAINST THE PERSON ACT 1997

(No 26 of 1997)

9 Coercion

(1) A person who, with a view to compel another to abstain from doing or to do any act which that other has a lawful right to do or to abstain from doing, wrongfully and without lawful authority—

(a) uses violence to or intimidates that other person or a member of the family of the other, or

(b) injures or damages the property of that other, or

(c) persistently follows that other about from place to place, or

(d) watches or besets the premises or other place where that other resides, works or carries on business, or happens to be, or the approach to such premises or place, or

(e) follows that other with one or more other persons in a disorderly manner in or through any public place,

shall be guilty of an offence.

(2) For the purpose of this section attending at or near the premises or place where a person resides, works, carries on business or happens to be, or the approach to such premises or place, in order merely to obtain or communicate information, shall not be deemed a watching or besetting within the meaning of subsection (1)(d).

(3) A person guilty of an offence under this section shall be liable—

(a) on summary conviction to a fine not exceeding £1,500 or to imprisonment for a term not exceeding 12 months or to both, or

(b) on conviction on indictment to a fine or to imprisonment for a term not exceeding 5 years or to both.

INDUSTRIAL RELATIONS ACT, 1990, CODE OF PRACTICE ON DISPUTE PROCEDURES (DECLARATION) ORDER 1992

SI No 1 of 1992

WHEREAS the Labour Relations Commission has prepared a draft code of practice on dispute procedures, including procedure in essential services;

AND WHEREAS the Labour Relations Commission has complied with subsection (2) of section 42 of the Industrial Relations Act, 1990 (No 19 of 1990), and has submitted the draft code of practice to the Minister for Labour;

NOW THEREFORE, I, MICHAEL O'KENNEDY, Minister for Labour, in exercise of the powers conferred on me by subsection (3) of that section, hereby order as follows:

1. This Order may be cited as the Industrial Relations Act, 1990, Code of Practice on Dispute Procedures (Declaration) Order, 1992.

2. It is hereby declared that the draft code of practice set out in the Schedule to this Order shall be a code of practice for the purposes of the Industrial Relations Act, 1990 (No 19 of 1990).

GIVEN under my Official Seal, this 6th day of January, 1992.

MICHAEL O'KENNEDY,

Minister for Labour.

SCHEDULE
DRAFT CODE OF PRACTICE ON DISPUTE PROCEDURES, INCLUDING PROCEDURES IN ESSENTIAL SERVICES

SECTION I – INTRODUCTION

1. Section 42 of the Industrial Relations Act 1990 makes provision for the preparation of draft Codes of Practice by the Labour Relations Commission for submission to the Minister for Labour. (CF Appendix I).

2. In February, 1991 the Minister for Labour, Mr. Bertie Ahern, TD, requested the Commission to prepare codes of practice on dispute procedures and the levels of cover which should be provided in the event of disputes arising in essential services. When preparing this Code of Practice the Commission held meetings and consultations with the Irish Congress of Trade Unions, the Federation of Irish Employers, the Department of Finance, the Department of Labour, the Local Government Staff Negotiations Board, the Labour Court and representatives of the International Labour Organisation. The Commission has taken account of the views expressed by these organisations to the maximum extent possible in preparing this Code.

3. The Code recognises that the primary responsibility for dealing with industrial relations issues and the resolution of disputes rests with employers, employer organisations and trade unions. It is the intention of the Code to ensure that in line with this responsibility employers and trade unions:

(i) agree appropriate and practical arrangements for resolving disputes on collective and individual issues;

(ii) observe the terms of these agreements;

and

(iii) refrain from any actions which would be in contravention of them.

4. The Code is designed to assist employers* and trade unions in making agreements which recognise the rights and interests of the parties concerned and which contain procedures which will resolve issues in a peaceful manner and avoid the need for any of the parties to resort to actions which will lead to a disruption of supplies and services and a loss of income to employees and of revenue to employers.

5. The major objective of agreed procedures is to establish arrangements to deal with issues which could give rise to disputes. Such procedures provide for discussion and negotiation with a view to the parties reaching agreement at the earliest possible stage of the procedure and without resort to any form of industrial action.

6. The Code provides practical guidance on procedures for the resolution of disputes between employers and trade unions and how to operate them effectively. The principles contained in the Code are appropriate for employments in the public and private sectors of the economy irrespective of their function, nature or size.

7. The procedures in the Code provide a framework for the peaceful resolution of disputes, including disputes in essential services. The Code also provides general guidance to employers and trade unions on the arrangements which are necessary to ensure minimum cover or service where disputes which give rise to stoppages of work could have serious and adverse consequences for the community or the undertaking concerned and its employees.

* (The use of the word "employers" in the Code includes employer organisations where relevant and appropriate).

8. Although the Code has been prepared primarily for employments where terms of employment are established through employer/trade union agreements its general principles should be regarded as being applicable to other undertakings and enterprises and to their employees.

SECTION II – GENERAL PROVISIONS

9. Agreements between employers and trade unions on dispute settlement procedures can make a significant contribution to the maintenance of industrial peace. The dispute procedures contained in this Code should be seen as providing an underpinning for the conduct of industrial relations in an enterprise and in relationships between the parties.

10. Agreements on dispute procedures should be seen to be fair and equitable as between the interests of the parties and should include provision for the resolution of disputes on collective and individual issues and such procedures should be introduced where they currently do not exist.

11. Employers and trade unions should examine existing procedures at the level of the enterprise and take whatever steps may be necessary to ensure that the principles outlined in the Code are incorporated within them.

12. Dispute procedures should be as comprehensive as possible covering all foreseeable circumstances and setting out the consecutive stages involved in the resolution of disputes on collective and/or individual issues. Such procedures should include agreement on the appropriate level of management and trade union representation which will be involved at each stage of the procedure. The actions required of the parties at each stage of the procedure should be clearly indicated.

13. Agreements between employers and the trade unions should be in writing so as to eliminate the possibility of misunderstandings arising from lack of awareness of procedures or misinterpretation of informal arrangements which may have come to be regarded as "custom and practice".

14. Employees and management at all levels should be aware of the agreed procedures. Accordingly, arrangements should be made for these procedures to be communicated and explained through whatever means may be appropriate.

15. Dispute procedures should afford early access to disputes resolution machinery and to arrangements for the settlement of collective and individual issues within a reasonable timescale. The introduction of any specific time-limits for the operation of different stages of a disputes procedure is a matter for consideration by employers and unions at local level.

16. The procedures for building disputes on collective and individual issues should take account, where appropriate, of the functions of the relevant State agencies (The Labour Relations Commission, The Labour Court, The Rights Commissioner Service, The Equality Service and The Employment Appeals Tribunal) so as to facilitate the potential use of these services in the development and maintenance of good industrial relations.

17. Nothing in the Code precludes an employer and trade union in an enterprise, industry or service from adding other stages to their dispute procedures should this be considered appropriate.

18. The operation of dispute procedures should be reviewed from time to time with the object of improving the practical working of the procedures.

19. The Labour Relations Commission will provide assistance to employers and trade unions in formulating agreed dispute procedures in accordance with the Code.

SECTION III – EMERGENCY/MINIMUM SERVICE

20. While the primary responsibility for the provision of minimum levels of services rests with managements this Code recognises that there is a joint obligation on employers and trade unions to have in place agreed contingency plans and other arrangements to deal with any emergency which may arise during an industrial dispute. Employers and trade unions should co-operate with the introduction of such plans and contingency arrangements. In particular, employers and trade unions in each employment providing an essential service should co-operate with each other in making arrangements concerning:

(a) the maintenance of plant and equipment;

(b) all matters concerning health, safety and security;

(c) special operational problems which exist in continuous process industries—

(d) the provision of urgent medical services and suppliers;

(e) the provision of emergency services required on humanitarian grounds.

21. In the event of the parties encountering problems in making such arrangements they should seek the assistance of the Labour Relations Commission.

SECTION IV – DISPUTES PROCEDURES-GENERAL

22. The dispute procedures set out below should be incorporated in employer/trade union agreements for the purpose of peacefully resolving disputes arising between employers and trade unions. Such agreements should provide:

(a) that the parties will refrain from any action which might impede the effective functioning of these procedures;

(b) for co-operation between trade union and employers on appropriate arrangements and facilities for trade union representatives to take part in agreed disputes procedures;

(c) for appropriate arrangements to facilitate employees to consider any proposals emanating from the operation of the procedures.

23. Trade union claims on collective and individual matters and other issues which could give rise to disputes should be the subject of discussion and negotiation at the appropriate level by the parties concerned with a view to securing a mutually acceptable resolution of them within a reasonable period of time. Every effort should be made by the parties to secure a settlement without recourse to outside agencies.

24. In the event of direct discussions between the parties not resolving the issue(s), they should be referred to the appropriate service of the Labour Relations Commission. The parties should co-operate with the appropriate service in arranging a meeting as soon as practicable to consider the dispute.

25. Agreements should provide that, where disputes are not resolved through the intervention of these services and where the Labour Relations Commission is satisfied that further efforts to resolve a dispute are unlikely to be successful, the parties should refer the issues in dispute to the Labour Court for investigation and recommendation or to such other dispute resolution body as may be prescribed in their agreements.

26. During the period in which the above procedures are being followed no strikes, lock-outs or other action designed to bring pressure to bear on either party should take place.

27. Strikes and any other form of industrial action should only take place after all dispute procedures have been fully utilised.

28. Where notice of a strike or any other form of industrial action is being served on an employer a minimum of 7 days notice should apply except where agreements provide for a longer period of notice.

29. The procedure outlined in paragraphs 24 and 25 above refer to employees who have statutory access to the Labour Relations Commission and the Labour Court under the Industrial Relations Acts, 1946 to 1990. In the case of employees who do not have access to these bodies, for example, certain employees in the public services, discussions should take place between the parties concerned with a view to developing procedures which would be in accordance with the principles included in this Code to the extent that such procedures do not already exist. In developing such procedures the parties should have regard to such considerations as the size and complexity of the employments concerned, the nature of the services provided, and the terms of employment of the employees involved.

SECTION V – ESSENTIAL SERVICES – AGREEMENTS ON SPECIAL PRO-CEDURES:

30. In the case of essential services, additional procedures and safeguards are necessary for the peaceful resolution of disputes and these should be included in the appropriate agreements between employers and trade unions. These services include those whose cessation or interruption could endanger life, or cause major damage to the national economy, or widespread hardship to the Community and particularly: health services, energy supplies, including gas and electricity, water and sewage services, fire, ambulance and rescue services and certain elements of public transport. This list is indicative rather than comprehensive. The provisions of this section of the Code could be introduced by agreement in other enterprises or undertakings where strikes, lock-outs or other forms of industrial action could have far reaching consequences.

31. These additional procedures and safeguards should be introduced through consultation and agreement in all services and employments coming within the scope of paragraph 30 above. The parties should recognise their joint responsibility to resolve disputes in such services and employments without resorting to strikes or other forms of industrial action.

32. The introduction of these additional procedures and safeguards should be accompanied by arrangements for the dissemination and exchange of information relating to various aspects of the life of the undertaking concerned including its relationship with the community which it serves. Employees should make appropriate arrangements for consultation with the unions through the use of agreed procedures especially where major changes affecting employees' interests are concerned.

33. Except where other procedures and safeguards have been introduced which ensure the continuity of essential supplies and services, agreements negotiated on a voluntary basis should include one of the following provisions in order to eliminate or reduce any risk to essential supplies and services arising from industrial disputes:

(a) acceptance by the parties of awards, decisions and recommendations which result from the final stage of the dispute settlement procedure where these include investigation by an independent expert body such as the Labour Court, an agreed arbitration board or tribunal or an independent person appointed by the parties;

or

(b) a specific undertaking in agreements that, in the event of any one of the parties deciding that an award, decision or recommendation emerging from the final stage of the dispute settlement procedure is unsatisfactory they will agree on the means of resolving the issue without resort to strike or to other forms of industrial action, such agreements to include a provision for a review of the case by an agreed recognised body after twelve months, such review to represent a final determination of the issue;

or

(c) provision that the parties to an agreement would accept awards, decisions or recommendations resulting from the operation of the final stage of the dispute procedure on the basis that an independent review would take place at five yearly intervals to examine whether the employees covered by the agreement had been placed at any disadvantage as a result of entering into such agreement and if so to advise, having regard to all aspects of the situation, including economic and financial considerations, on the changes necessary to redress the position.

SECTION VI – ESSENTIAL SERVICES –
MAINTENANCE OF INDUSTRIAL PEACE

34. Where the parties have not concluded an agreement incorporating the procedures referred to in paragraph 33(a) (b) or (c) and otherwise where for any reason a serious threat to the continuity of essential supplies and services exists, or is perceived to exist, as a result of the failure of the parties to resolve an industrial dispute and where the Labour Relations Commission is satisfied that all available dispute procedures have been used to try to effect a settlement, the Labour Relations Commission should consult with the Irish Congress of Trade Unions and the Federation of Irish Employers about the situation. The objective of such consultation should be to secure their assistance and co-operation with whatever measures may be necessary to resolve the dispute, including, where appropriate, arrangements which would provide a basis for a continuation of normal working for a period not exceeding six months while further efforts by the parties themselves or the dispute settlement agencies were being made to secure a full and final settlement of the issues in dispute.

SECTION VII – REVIEW OF CODE

35. The Commission will review the draft Code and its operation at regular intervals and advise the Minister for Labour of any changes which may be necessary or desirable.

APPENDIX I

Codes of Practice:

Section 42 Industrial Relations Act 1990

(1) The Commission shall prepare draft codes of practice concerning industrial relations for submission to the Minister, either on its own initiative or at the request of the Minister.

(2) Before submitting a draft code of practice to the Minister, the Commission shall seek and consider the views of organisations representative of employers and organisations representative of workers, and such other bodies as the Commission considers appropriate.

(3) Where the Minister receives a draft code of practice from the Commission he may by order declare that the code, scheduled to the order, shall be a code of practice for the purposes of this Act.

(4) In any proceedings before a court, the Labour Court, the Commission, the Employment Appeals Tribunal, a Rights Commissioner or an Equality Officer, a code of practice shall be admissible in evidence and any provision of the code which appeals to the court, body or officer concerned to be relevant to any question arising in the proceedings shall be taken into account in determining that question.

(5) A failure on the part of any person to observe any provision of a code of practice shall not of itself render him liable to any proceedings.

(6) The Minister may at the request of or after consultation with the Commission by order revoke or amend a code of practice.

(7) Every order made under this section shall be laid before each House of the Oireachtas as soon as may be after it is made and, if a resolution annulling the order is passed by either House within the next twenty-one days on which that House has sat after the order has been laid before it, the order shall be annulled accordingly, but without prejudice to the validity of anything previously done thereunder.

INDUSTRIAL RELATIONS ACT 1990 (ENHANCED CODE OF PRACTICE ON VOLUNTARY DISPUTE RESOLUTION) (DECLARATION) ORDER 2004

SI No 76 of 2004

WHEREAS the Labour Relations Commission has prepared under subsection (1) of section 42 of the Industrial Relations Act 1990 (No 19 of 1990), a draft enhanced code of practice on voluntary dispute resolution where negotiation arrangements are not in place and where collective bargaining does not take place;

AND WHEREAS the Labour Relations Commission has complied with subsection (2) of that section and has submitted the draft enhanced code of practice to the Minister for Enterprise, Trade and Employment;

NOW THEREFORE, I, Frank Fahey, Minister of State at the Department of Enterprise, Trade and Employment, in exercise of the powers conferred on me by subsection (3) of that section, the Labour (Transfer of Departmental Administration and Ministerial Functions) Order 1993 (SI No 18 of 1993) (as adapted by the Enterprise and Employment (Alteration of Name of Department and Title of Minister) Order 1997 (SI No 305 of 1997)), and the Enterprise, Trade and Employment (Delegation of Ministerial Functions) Order 2003 (SI No 156 of 2003), hereby order as follows:

1. This Order may be cited as the Industrial Relations Act 1990 (Enhanced Code of Practice on Voluntary Dispute Resolution) (Declaration) Order 2004.

2. It is declared that the enhanced code of practice set out in the Schedule to this Order shall be a code of practice for the purposes of the Industrial Relations Act 1990 (No 19 of 1990).

3. The Industrial Relations Act 1990 (Code of Practice on Voluntary Dispute Resolution) (Declaration) Order 2000 (SI No 145 of 2000) is revoked.

SCHEDULE

1 – INTRODUCTION

1. Section 42 of the Industrial Relations Act 1990 provides for the preparation of draft Codes of Practice by the Labour Relations Commission for submission to the Minister, and for the making by him or her of an order declaring that a draft Code of Practice received by him or her under Section 42 and scheduled to the order shall be a Code of Practice for the purpose of the said Act.

2. Paragraph 9.22 of Partnership 2000 for Inclusion, Employment and Competitiveness established a High Level Group on Trade Union Recognition. The High Level Group, involving the Departments of the Taoiseach, Finance and Enterprise, Trade and Employment, the Irish Congress of Trade Unions (ICTU), the Irish Business and Employers Confederation (IBEC) and IDA – Ireland, considered proposals submitted by the ICTU on the Recognition of Unions and the Right to Bargain and took account

311

of European developments and the detailed position of IBEC on the impact of the ICTU proposals. As a result of these deliberations a set of procedures were put in place in the Code of Practice on Voluntary Dispute Resolution (S.I. No. 145 of 2000) and the Industrial Relations (Amendment) Act 2001.

3. Article 8.9 of Sustaining Progress Social Partnership Agreement 2003 – 2005 provides for the further development of employee representation. It was agreed by the trade union and employer organisations that there was a need to enhance the effectiveness of the existing procedures put in place in the Code of Practice on Voluntary Dispute Resolution and the Industrial Relations (Amendment) Act 2001.

4. The following measures were agreed for this purpose:

- the introduction of an indicative overall time-frame targeting 26 weeks – with provision for up to a maximum of 34 weeks where necessary – for the processing of cases under the Voluntary Dispute Resolution Code and the 2001 Act to the point of issuance of a determination, save when an extension is agreed by the parties;

- the amendment of Section 2 of the 2001 Act to provide that engagement by the Court could now take place on the basis of a breach of the time-frames within the Code, the exhaustion of the time-frames or the indication at any time by the Labour Relations Commission that it is unable to assist the parties; these provisions to be substituted for the existing Section 2(1)(b), while preserving the remainder of the Section;

- the amendment of Section 3 of the 2001 Act so as to allow the Court to combine both
the preliminary and substantive hearings, where it considers this to be appropriate;

- the removal of the provision in the Act for the Labour Court to review a determination, prior to seeking enforcement of a determination by the Circuit Court, by deleting section 9 and amending section 10 to provide for an entitlement for the trade union or excepted body to apply to the Circuit Court for the enforcement of a determination immediately – or on expiry of whatever implementation period is provided for in the determination;

- the development of transitional provisions to allow for the processing of cases in current disputes where access to the Code of Practice on Dispute Resolution as at the date of agreement is not available;

- the introduction of a new Code of Practice setting out the different types of practice which would constitute victimisation arising from an employee's membership or activity on behalf of a trade union or a manager discharging his or her managerial functions, or other employees and the amendment of the Act to provide that the Labour Court should have regard to breaches of this Code and where appropriate should provide for redress when making its determination.

5. In April 2003 the Minister for Enterprise, Trade and Employment requested the Commission under section 42(1) of the Industrial Relations Act 1990 to prepare a draft

Enhanced Code of Practice on Voluntary Dispute Resolution pursuant to the provisions of Article 8.9 of the Sustaining Progress Social Partnership Agreement 2003 – 2005.

6. In advance of the Minister's request the Department of Enterprise, Trade and Employment chaired discussions over a five-week period between trade union and employer organisations on the enhancement of the existing procedures (Article 8.11 of Sustaining Progress). The outcome of these discussions was communicated to the Labour Relations Commission in May 2003.

7. When preparing and agreeing this Enhanced Code of Practice, the Commission consulted with the Department of Enterprise, Trade and Employment, ICTU, IBEC, and the Labour Court and took account of the views expressed to the maximum extent possible.

8. The major objective of the Enhanced Code is to provide an improved framework that has the full support of all the parties for the processing of disputes arising in situations where negotiating arrangements are not in place and where collective bargaining fails to take place.

2 – PROCEDURES

Where negotiating arrangements are not in place and where collective bargaining fails to take place, the following process would be put in place with which management and unions should fully co-operate in seeking to resolve the issues in dispute effectively and expeditiously:

1. The procedure will last for a period of 6 weeks from the date of receipt by the other party of a written invitation from the Labour Relations Commission to participate in the procedure. The referring party may copy the original Labour Relations Commission referral to the other party at time of referral. The 6 weeks to include 2 weeks to arrange meetings and commence discussions on the issues in dispute and 4 weeks for substantive engagement on the issues in dispute. In the event that the parties are making substantial progress toward a resolution of the dispute this time frame can be extended by agreement (see paragraph 5 below).

2. In the first instance, the matter should be referred to the Labour Relations Commission in the prescribed format (see Appendix). An Advisory Officer will be appointed by the Commission to facilitate the procedure.

3. On receipt of the referral in the prescribed format the Advisory Officer will issue a written invitation (by registered post) to the other party to the dispute to participate in the voluntary dispute resolution procedure. Failure by the other party to indicate to the Advisory Officer (in writing) their willingness to participate in the procedure within 2 weeks (during which a reminder will issue) will be deemed to be a breach of the time frame. During this two-week period the Advisory Officer will seek to arrange a preliminary meeting with the other party.

4. On receipt of written confirmation (within 2 weeks) of the other party's willingness to participate in the procedure the Advisory Officer will work with the parties in an attempt to resolve the issues in dispute over a period of 4 weeks.

5. If progress is being made it may be agreed by the parties to extend the time frame. In this context the parties will seek the views of the Advisory Officer as to the likelihood of progress being made through the Labour Relations Commission intervention in the event of any such agreed extension. During any such extension an agreed cooling-off period can be put in place and the Advisory Officer will continue to work with the parties in an attempt to resolve any outstanding issues. The Labour Relations Commission may engage expert assistance throughout the procedure, including the involvement of ICTU and IBEC, should that prove helpful to the resolution of any differences.

6. If after the six-week period or following any agreed extension, including any agreed cooling-off period, all issues have been resolved, the Advisory Officer will disengage and the procedure will be deemed to be completed. Before disengaging, the Advisory Officer may make proposals to the parties for the peaceful resolution of any future grievances or disputes.

7. In the event of issues remaining unresolved the procedure will be deemed to have been exhausted and the Advisory Officer will then make an immediate written report to the Labour Court on the situation.

Appendix

Prescribed Format for Referrals to the Labour Relations Commission

The referring party must ensure that the following details are made available to the Labour Relations Commission at the time of referral and that all referrals are addressed to the **Director of the Advisory Service, Labour Relations Commission, Tom Johnson House, Haddington Road, Dublin 4.**

- Name and address of union official and contact number/fax/email address.
- Name and address of company, contact person, number/fax/e-mail address and details of any representative organisation where known (IBEC, CIF etc.)
- Category of members i.e. general operatives, admin., production, technical etc.
- A description of the issues in dispute.
- Any correspondence or dialogue entered into with other party by the initiating party.

GIVEN under my hand, 13th January 2004.

Frank Fahey

Minister of State at the Department of Enterprise, Trade and Employment

INDUSTRIAL RELATIONS ACT 1990 (CODE OF PRACTICE ON VICTIMISATION) (DECLARATION) ORDER 2004

SI No 139 of 2004

WHEREAS the Labour Relations Commission has prepared under subsection (1) of section 42 of the Industrial Relations Act 1990 (No 19 of 1990), a draft code of practice on victimisation arising from an employee's membership or activity on behalf of a trade union or a manager discharging his or her managerial functions, or other employees:

AND WHEREAS the Labour Relations Commission has complied with subsection (2) of that section and has submitted the draft code of practice to the Minister for Enterprise, Trade and Employment;

NOW THEREFORE, I, Frank Fahey, Minister of State at the Department of Enterprise, Trade and Employment, in exercise of the powers conferred on me by subsection (3) of that section, the Labour (Transfer of Departmental Administration and Ministerial Functions) Order 1993 (SI No 18 of 1993), (as adapted by the Enterprise and Employment (Alteration of Name of Department and Title of Minister) Order 1997 (SI No 305 of 1997)), and the Enterprise, Trade and Employment (Delegation of Ministerial Functions) Order 2003 (SI No 156 of 2003), hereby order as follows:

1. This Order may be cited as the Industrial Relations Act 1990 (Code of Practice on Victimisation) (Declaration) Order 2004.

2. It is hereby declared that the code of practice set out in the Schedule to this Order shall be a code of practice for the purposes of the Industrial Relations Act 1990 (No 19 of 1990).

SCHEDULE

1 – INTRODUCTION

1. Section 42 of the Industrial Relations Act, 1990 provides for the preparation of draft Codes of Practice by the Labour Relations Commission for submission to the Minister, and for the making, by him/her of an order declaring that a draft Code of Practice received by him/her under section 42 and scheduled to the order shall be a Code of Practice for the purposes of the said Act.

2. Paragraph 9.22 of Partnership 2000 for Inclusion, Employment and Competitiveness established a High Level Group on Trade Union Recognition. The High Level Group, involving the Departments of the Taoiseach, Finance and Enterprise, Trade and Employment, the Irish Congress of Trade Unions (ICTU), the Irish Business and Employers Confederation (IBEC) and IDA-Ireland, considered proposals submitted by the ICTU on the Recognition of Unions and the Right to Bargain and took account of European developments and the detailed position of IBEC on the impact of the ICTU proposals. As a result of these deliberations a set of procedures were put in place in the Code of Practice

on Voluntary Dispute Resolution (SI No 145 of 2000) and the Industrial Relations (Amendment) Act 2001 .

3. Article 8.9 of Sustaining Progress Social Partnership Agreement 2003-2005 provides for the further development of employee representation. It was agreed by the trade union and employer organisations that there was a need to enhance the effectiveness of the existing procedures put in place in the Code of Practice on Voluntary Dispute Resolution and the Industrial Relations (Amendment) Act 2001.

4. Among the measures agreed for this purpose was the introduction of a new Code of Practice setting out the different types of practice which would constitute victimisation arising from an employee's membership or activity on behalf of a trade union or a manager discharging his or her managerial functions, or other employees.

5. In April 2003 the Minister for Enterprise, Trade and Employment requested the Commission under section 42(1) of the Industrial Relations Act 1990 to prepare a draft Code of Practice on Victimisation pursuant to the provisions of Article 8.9 of Sustaining Progress Social Partnership Agreement 2003-2005.

6. When preparing and agreeing this Code of Practice, the Commission consulted with relevant organisations and took account of the views expressed to the maximum extent possible.

7. The major objective of the Code is the setting out of the different types of practice which would constitute victimisation arising from an employee's membership or activity on behalf of a trade union or a manager discharging his or her managerial functions, or other employees.

2. PURPOSE

1. The purpose of this Code of Practice is to outline, for the guidance of employers, employees and trade unions, the different types of practice which would constitute victimisation.

2. Victimisation in the context of this Code of Practice refers to victimisation arising from an employee's membership or nonmembership, activity or non-activity on behalf of a trade union or an excepted body, or a manager discharging his or her managerial functions, or any other employee in situations where negotiating arrangements are not in place and where collective bargaining fails to take place (and where the procedures under the Code of Practice on Voluntary Dispute Resolution have been invoked or steps have been taken to invoke such procedures).

3. DEFINITIONS

1. For the purposes of this Code, victimisation is defined in general terms as any adverse or unfavourable treatment that cannot be justified on objective grounds (objective grounds do not include membership of, or activity on behalf of, a trade union) in the context referred to at Clause 2 above. It shall not include any act constituting a dismissal of the employee within the meaning of the Unfair Dismissals Act 1977 to 2001, where there is a separate recourse available. For the

avoidance of doubt, "employee" in this Code includes any person in the employment concerned, the duties of whom consist of or include managing the business or activity to which the employment relates.

For the purposes of this Code none of the following
    (a) the employer,
    (b) an employee, or
    (c) a trade union or an excepted body,

shall victimise an employee or (as the case may be) another employee in the employment concerned on account of
    i. the employee being or not being a member of a trade union or an excepted body, or
    ii. the employee engaging or not engaging in any activities on behalf of a trade union or an excepted body, or
    iii. the employee exercising his/her managerial duties, where applicable, to which the employment relates on behalf of the employer.

2. Examples of unfair or adverse treatment (whether acts of commission or omission) that cannot be justified on objective grounds may in the above contexts include an employee suffering any unfavourable change in his/her conditions of employment or acts that adversely affect the interest of the employee; action detrimental to the interest of an employee not wishing to engage in trade union activity or the impeding of a manager in the discharge of his/her managerial functions.

3. The legal definitions of employer, employee, contract of employment and trade unions shall be as set out in Part III of the Industrial Relations Act 1990 . A trade union shall be taken to mean any authorised trade union as defined in the Trade Union Act 1941 .

4. AVOIDANCE

1. Where there is a dispute in an employment where collective bargaining fails to take place and where negotiating arrangements are not in place, no person, be they union representative, individual employee or manager, should be victimised or suffer disadvantage as a consequence of their legitimate actions or affiliation arising from that dispute. The positions and views of all concerned should be respected and all parties should commit themselves to resolve issues in dispute expeditiously and without personal rancour.

5. PROCEDURE FOR ADDRESSING COMPLAINTS OF VICIMISATION

1. A procedure for addressing complaints of victimisation is set out in the Industrial Relations (Miscellaneous Provisions) Act 2004 . Section 9 of the Act provides that a complaint may be presented to a Rights Commissioner.

GIVEN under my hand,

6th April 2004.

Frank Fahey

Minister of State at the Department of Enterprise, Trade and Employment.

DRAFT PLEADINGS
(CASE I)

Statement of Facts

The Effective Medicine Company manufactures pharmaceutical products at a very substantial premises. It recognises and negotiates with a number of trade unions including the Maintenance Workers Union. The Maintenance Workers Union is the principal union to a nationwide agreement registered pursuant to the provisions of the Industrial Relations Acts in respect of employees in a number of industries but *not* including pharmaceutical manufacture. The Effective Medicine Company is not bound by the terms of the registered agreement and indeed its rates of pay, terms and conditions and benefits of employment are generally better than those provided for in the national agreement. The Effective Medicine Company, however, does utilise external contractors, some of whose employees are members of the union and who are a party to the national agreement.

By reason of a dispute in relation to the implementation of the national agreement, the union has placed pickets on a nationwide basis. These pickets are not only at the premises of employers governed by the agreement but also the union have selectively placed secondary pickets at a number of high-profile employers' premises, including at the manufacturing premises of the Effective Medicine Company. The union have been called on to desist from the picketing at the premises and have refused, and the company has initiated proceedings seeking interlocutory injunctive relief.

PLEADINGS

THE HIGH COURT

Record No. ....

BETWEEN:

THE EFFECTIVE
MEDICINE COMPANY

Plaintiff

– AND –

THE MAINTENANCE
WORKERS UNION
AND
[NAMED PICKETERS]

Defendants

PLENARY SUMMONS

GENERAL INDORSEMENT OF CLAIM

THE PLAINTIFF'S CLAIM AS AGAINST THE DEFENDANTS IS FOR:

1. An injunction restraining the Defendants, and each of them, whether by themselves, their servants or agents or otherwise, or any person acting in concert with them or any person having notice of the making of any Order of this Honourable Court, from watching and besetting and/or picketing and/or trespassing at the Plaintiff's premises situate at .... in the County of ....

2. An injunction restraining the Defendants, and each of them, whether by themselves, their servants or agents, or otherwise, or any person acting in concert with them or any person having notice of any Order of this Honourable Court from interfering with access to and egress from the Plaintiff's premises situate at .... in the County of ....

3. An injunction restraining the Defendants and each of them, whether by themselves, their servants or agents or otherwise, or any person acting in concert with them or any person having notice of the making of any Order of this Honourable Court, from representing, whether by way of the erecting or carrying of placards, distribution of documents and/or leaflets or posters or otherwise, that there is in existence any trade dispute involving the Plaintiff and/or any of its employees.

4. An injunction restraining the Defendants and each of them, their servants or

agents or any person acting in concert with them or any person with the knowledge of the making of any Order of this Honourable Court, from inducing, procuring or persuading employees of the Plaintiff or employees of their contractors or sub-contractors to break their contracts of employment by striking or engaging in any industrial action or in any other manner by failing or refusing to co-operate with the Plaintiff.

5. An injunction restraining the Defendants and each of them, their servants or agents, or any persons acting in concert with them or any person having notice of the making of any Order by this Honourable Court from inciting, instructing, inducing, procuring, persuading, organising, financing or, in any manner whatsoever, facilitating picketing of the Plaintiff's premises situate at …………… in the County of …………

6. An Order requiring the Defendants and each of them, their servants and/or agents and any persons acting in concert with them or with the knowledge of the making of any Order of this Honourable Court to forthwith withdraw any direction, instruction, inducement, advice, finance or other encouragement given, whether directly or indirectly to the employees of the Plaintiff or to any employees of any contractor or sub-contractor of the Plaintiff or to any other person to do any act in breach of their contracts of employment with the Plaintiff and/or its contractors or sub-contractors or to threaten to do any such act or to interfere with the contracts made between the Plaintiffs and its employees or made between the Plaintiff and its contractors or sub-contractors or otherwise howsoever to interfere with the business of the Plaintiff or otherwise howsoever to picket the Plaintiff's premises.

7. Damages for unlawful watching and besetting, unlawful picketing and unlawful interference with access to and egress from the Plaintiff's premises.

8. Damages for inducing breach of commercial contracts.

9. Damages for interfering with the Plaintiff's lawful activities and commercial relationships.

10. Damages for causing loss by unlawful means.

11. Damages for trespass.

12. Damages for conspiracy.

13. Such further and other relief as to this Honourable Court shall deem meet.

14. Costs.

A BARRISTER BL

Signed: _____
A Solicitor
Solicitors for the Plaintiff

THE HIGH COURT

BETWEEN:

Record No. ....

**THE EFFECTIVE
MEDICINE
COMPANY**

Plaintiff

– AND –

**THE MAINTENANCE
WORKERS UNION
AND
[NAMED PICKETERS]**

Defendants

NOTICE OF MOTION

TAKE NOTICE that Counsel on behalf of the Plaintiff will apply to this Honourable Court sitting in the Four Courts in the City of Dublin at the sitting of the Court at 11am on the forenoon on ... day of .... for the following Orders and reliefs:

1. An interlocutory injunction restraining the Defendants, and each of them, whether by themselves, their servants or agents or otherwise, or any person acting in concert with them or any person having notice of the making of any Order of this Honourable Court, from watching and besetting and/or picketing and/or trespassing at the Plaintiff's premises situate at .... in the County of ....

2. An interlocutory injunction restraining the Defendants, and each of them, whether by themselves, their servants or agents, or otherwise, or any person acting in concert with them or any person having notice of the making of any Order by this Honourable Court, from interfering with access to and egress from the Plaintiff's premises situate at .... in the County of ....

3. An interlocutory injunction restraining the Defendants and each of them, whether by themselves, their servants or agents or otherwise, or any person acting in concert with them or any person having notice of the making of any Order of this Honourable Court, from representing whether by way of placards, documents, leaflets or posters or otherwise that there is in existence any trade dispute involving the Plaintiff and any of its employees.

4. An interlocutory injunction restraining the Defendants and each of them, whether by themselves, their servants or agents or otherwise, or any person acting in concert with them or any person having notice of the making of any Order of this Honourable Court, from interfering with the Plaintiff's business interests and economic relations and restraining the Defendants and each of

them from breaching or inducing breaches of the Plaintiff's commercial contracts.

5. An interlocutory injunction restraining the Defendants and each of them, whether by themselves, their servants or agents or otherwise, or any person acting in concert with them or any person having notice of the making of any Order of this Honourable Court, from engaging in industrial action of any type whatsoever against the Plaintiff at its premises situate at .... in the County of ....

6. Such further and other relief as to this Honourable Court shall deem meet including such interim relief as is appropriate and including, if necessary, an Order abridging time for the service of this Notice of Motion.

7. Costs.

AND TAKE NOTICE THAT THE SAID APPLICATION will be grounded upon the proceedings already had herein, the Affidavit of P Manager sworn on ... day of ...., the exhibits referred to therein, the nature of the case and the reasons to be offered.

Dated this .... day of ....

Signed: _____
                       A Solicitor
                  Solicitors for the Plaintiff
To: The Maintenance Workers Union
             [address]
And To: Named Picketers

THE HIGH COURT

Record No. ....

BETWEEN:

**THE EFFECTIVE
MEDICINE
COMPANY**

Plaintiff

– AND –

**THE MAINTENANCE
WORKERS UNION
AND
[NAMED PICKETERS]**

Defendants

<u>**AFFIDAVIT OF PATRICK MANAGER**</u>

I, **PATRICK MANAGER**, Engineering Manager of .... in the county of
.... aged 18 years and upwards make oath and say as follows:

1.   I am the Engineering Manager employed by the Plaintiff at its premises at
.... in the County of .... and I make this Affidavit for and on its behalf
and with its authority from facts within my own knowledge save where
otherwise appears and where so otherwise appearing I believe the same to be
true and correct.

2.   I say that the Plaintiff Company manufactures human medicines for treatment
of critical illnesses at a very substantial plant situate at .... in the County of
...... The entire site and the production process are subject to strict regulation
by the Irish Medicines Board and by other regulatory authorities throughout the
world. The company employs approximately 500 persons at its plant in ....,
including 50 persons who are employed in the engineering and maintenance
departments. The company also engages contractors from both within this
jurisdiction and from overseas to supply, install and repair equipment and those
contractors employ a significant number of engineering and maintenance
workers.

3.   I am aware that a trade dispute exists between the Maintenance Workers Union
(the first named Defendant) and employers' organisations representing
maintenance workers in certain named industries. I believe and am advised that
agreements between the first named Defendant and those employers are

324

governed by the terms of an Employment Agreement registered with the Labour Court pursuant to the provisions of the Industrial Relations Acts.

4. The Plaintiff Company does not have any persons in its employment who are subject to the terms of the registered employment agreement. The company does have in its employment a significant number of employees who are members of the first named Defendant, however the Plaintiff negotiates directly with the trade union for the purposes of agreeing terms and conditions, remuneration and other benefits which are applicable to its employees and it has never been the case that the union has sought to rely on the terms of the Registered Agreement referred to heretofore. It is my belief that all of the remuneration and other benefits and terms and conditions of employment of maintenance workers employed directly by the Plaintiff are superior to those provided for in the Registered Agreement.

5. The Plaintiff company has not been advised by the Defendant trade union that that trade union is in dispute with the Plaintiff, no notice of industrial action has been served on the Plaintiff and there is in fact no dispute currently existing between the Maintenance Workers Union and the Plaintiff or any of its associated companies.

6. I say that at approximately 9 am on Wednesday ... day of ...... a group of six individuals arrived at the entrance to the Plaintiff's premises and staged a picket. I say that each of the six individuals carried placards identifying themselves as acting on behalf of the Maintenance Workers Trade Union. The individuals, whilst they were not known personally to your deponent are not employees of the Plaintiff and are not, as far as I am aware, and never were employed to carry out any work on behalf of any contractor or subcontractor on the Plaintiff's premises. From inquiries undertaken by me I am now satisfied that the six persons involved are the second to seventh named Defendants in these proceedings.

7. I say that the picketing had an immediate adverse effect on the Plaintiff's business. A number of employees of the Plaintiff and a number of employees of contractors and subcontractors refused to pass the picket and goods and services were not delivered. I say that a supply of a critical raw material was not delivered because the driver of the truck involved refused to pass the picket. I say that notwithstanding the existence of the picket sufficient members of staff of the Plaintiff company continued to attend at work however by reason of the fact that a number of persons had not attended and in particular by reason of the fact that raw material supplies were at risk, it was necessary, in the interests of safety and security, for the Plaintiff company to take a decision to immediately cease production.

8. I say that shortly after the picket commenced I telephoned Mr James Secretary, who I know to be the General Secretary of the Defendant union and during the course of a telephone conversation with him I asked him to instruct his members who were picketing the Plaintiff's premises to cease forthwith. Mr Secretary informed me that as far as he was concerned his union was involved

in a legitimate trade dispute on behalf of its members. I informed Mr Secretary that none of his members in the employment of the Plaintiff were affected by or had their terms and conditions governed by the registered employment agreement. He advised me that it was his union's policy to take whatever steps were necessary to bring their dispute to a satisfactory conclusion and that in all of the circumstances the picketing would continue.

9.   I have very serious concerns that if the picketing continues the Plaintiff will suffer serious immediate and irreparable adverse affects and in particular I believe that given the uncertainty about raw material supplies that the Plaintiff company will not be in a position to resume manufacture of its products unless and until the picketing ceases. I believe that a cessation of manufacturing will result in immediate adverse affects not only on the Plaintiff company but also on its employees and could result in immediate and critical shortages of important medical supplies to patients.

10.   I say that following my telephone conversation with the trade union official I instructed ...., solicitors for the Plaintiff, to write to the trade union calling on them to undertake to desist from engaging in any trade dispute and/or picketing on their own behalf and asking them to take appropriate steps to ensure that no further picketing took place. I believe that that letter was sent by courier and email at approximately 12 noon on the ... day of ...... and I also believe it was delivered by hand to the trade union Defendant's principal offices at .... in the city of Dublin.

11.   I say that at the time of the swearing of this Affidavit no reply has been received to that communication. I beg to refer to a copy of the said letter upon which pinned together and marked with the letters "PE1" I have endorsed my name prior to swearing hereof.

12.   I say that the Plaintiff's solicitors also prepared letters addressed individually to the second to seventh named Defendants calling on them to immediately cease their activities. I say that I personally handed those letters to each of the picketers. I beg to refer to a copy of each of the said letters upon which pinned together and marked with the letter "PE2" I have endorsed my name prior to swearing hereof.

13.   I say that notwithstanding the personal delivery of the said letters to the second to seventh named Defendants the said Defendants continued to picket the Plaintiff's premises.

14.   I have been advised as to the undertaking as to damages which must be given to this Honourable Court in the course of an application such as envisaged herein and I say that that undertaking has been fully explained to me and I am authorised on behalf of the Plaintiff company to give to this Honourable Court an appropriate undertaking as to damages.

15.   In the premises, I pray this Honourable Court for the relief sought in the Notice of Motion herein.

SWORN by the said **PATRICK MANAGER**
On the   day of
At
In the City of Dublin before me a Commissioner for
Oaths and I know the Deponent.

COMMMISSIONER FOR OATHS
PRACTISING SOLICITOR

This Affidavit is filed this ... day of .... by

DRAFT PLEADINGS
(CASE II)

Statement of Facts

The plaintiff company, Fashion Retailers Limited, operates a chain of six retail shops, three of which are located in Dublin and three in other towns and cities. The company has decided to close down its Main Street premises in circumstances where the lease has expired and it does not intend to renew that lease. Some three months ago, the employer entered into negotiations with the Garment Workers Union, who represent all of the staff in all of the shops, in respect of redundancy payments. Agreement was not reached and the matter was referred to the Labour Relations Commission and ultimately was the subject of an investigation and recommendation by the Labour Court. The Labour Court recommended the payment of enhanced redundancy payments at the same level as the company had paid some two years ago when it closed a shop in Cork. The company rejected the Labour Court recommendation and has advised the trade union and its staff that it is not in a position to pay any sum greater than statutory redundancy having regard to its current trading difficulties. The company served on all of its employees, Notice of Termination of Employment by Reason of Redundancy some six weeks ago, which notices are due to expire on Friday, 23 April. The union has conducted a secret ballot and has served upon the employer two weeks' notice of industrial action, up to and including strike action, with effect from close of business on Thursday, 22 April. During the afternoon of Wednesday, 21 April, company management accompanied by external contractors removed substantially all of the stock in the Main Street premises and advised the staff that they were to sell the remainder of the stock at 90% discount. During the course of Wednesday morning, all of the computers and cash registers were disconnected and the staff were advised that all transactions were to be done manually thereafter on a cash-only basis, and credit and debit cards were not be accepted. Following the closing of the premises on Wednesday evening, three members of the staff refused to leave the premises and have blockaded themselves in an upstairs office. It is believed that they have been joined by a trade union official and an unknown number of members of their immediate families.

PLEADINGS

THE HIGH COURT

Record No. ....

BETWEEN:

FASHION RETAILERS LIMITED

Plaintiff

– AND –

GARMENT WORKERS UNION AND [TRADE UNION OFFICIAL] AND [THREE NAMED EMPLOYEES]

Defendants

PLENARY SUMMONS

GENERAL INDORSEMENT OF CLAIM

THE PLAINTIFF'S CLAIM AS AGAINST THE DEFENDANTS IS FOR:

1. An injunction restraining the Defendants, and each of them, or any of them, whether by themselves, their servants or agents, or otherwise, or any person acting in concert with them or any person having notice of any Order made by this Honourable Court from interfering with access to and egress from the Plaintiff's premises situate at ... Main Street in the City of Dublin.

2. An injunction restraining the Defendants, and each of them, or any of them, whether by themselves, their servants or agents, or otherwise, or any person acting in concert with them or any person having notice of any Order made by this Honourable Court from trespassing upon and/or occupying the Plaintiff's premises at ... Main Street, in the City of Dublin.

3. An Order directing the Defendants and any person having notice of the making of such an Order by this Honourable Court to vacate forthwith the said premises at ... Main Street, in the City of Dublin.

4. Damages for unlawful interference with access to and egress from the Plaintiff's premises.

5. Damages for trespass.

6. Damages for forcible entry and unlawful occupation.

7.   Damages for inducing breach of commercial contracts.

8.   Damages for interfering with the Plaintiff's lawful activities and commercial relationships.

9.   Damages for causing loss by unlawful means.

10.   Damages for conspiracy.

11.   Such further and other relief as to this Honourable Court shall deem meet.

12.   Costs.

A BARRISTER BL

Signed: _____
                          A Solicitor
                  Solicitors for the Plaintiff

THE HIGH COURT

Record No. ....

BETWEEN:

**FASHION RETAILERS
LIMITED**

Plaintiff

– AND –

**GARMENT
WORKERS UNION
AND [TRADE UNION
OFFICIAL] AND
[THREE NAMED
EMPLOYEES]**

Defendants

NOTICE OF MOTION

TAKE NOTICE that Counsel on behalf of the Plaintiff will apply to this Honourable Court sitting in the Four Courts in the City of Dublin at the sitting of the Court at 11am on the forenoon on the ... day of ...... for the following Orders and reliefs:

1. An interlocutory injunction restraining the Defendants, and each of them, or any of them, whether by themselves, their servants or agents, or otherwise, or any person acting in concert with them or any person having notice of the making of any Order of this Honourable Court from interfering with access to and egress from the Plaintiff's premises situate at premises at ... Main Street, in the City of Dublin.

2. An interlocutory injunction restraining the Defendants, and each of them, or any of them, whether by themselves, their servants or agents, or otherwise, or any person acting in concert with them or any person having notice of any Order of this Honourable Court from trespassing upon and/or occupying the Plaintiff's premises at ... Main Street, in the City of Dublin.

3. An Order directing the Defendants or any person having notice of the making of any Order to this effect to forthwith vacate the Plaintiff's said premises at ... Main Street, in the City of Dublin.

4. Such further or other Order as to this Honourable Court shall deem meet, including such interim relief as is appropriate, and if necessary, an Order abridging time for the service of this Notice of Motion together with, if necessary an order providing for the mode of service of these proceedings and Order of this Honourable Court.

5. Costs.

AND TAKE NOTICE THAT THE SAID APPLICATION will be grounded upon the proceedings already had herein, the Affidavit of Oscar Wilde sworn on ... day of ...., the exhibits referred to therein, the nature of the case and the reasons to be offered.

Dated this .... day of ....

Signed: _____
                              A Solicitor
                    Solicitors for the Plaintiff
To: The Garment Workers Union
            [address]
And To: Named Picketers

THE HIGH COURT

Record No. ....

BETWEEN:

**FASHION RETAILERS
LIMITED**

Plaintiff

– AND –

**GARMENT
WORKERS UNION
AND [TRADE UNION
OFFICIAL] AND
[THREE NAMED
EMPLOYEES]**

Defendants

AFFIDAVIT OF OSCAR WILDE

I, **OSCAR WILDE**, Company Director of ...., in the City of Dublin, aged 18 years and upwards make oath and say as follows:

1. I am the Managing Director of the Plaintiff company and I make this Affidavit for and on its behalf and with its authority, from facts within my own knowledge save where otherwise appears, and where so otherwise appearing I believe the same to be true and correct.

2. I make this Affidavit for the purposes of grounding an application for interim and, subsequently, interlocutory relief before this Honourable Court arising out of the unlawful occupation of the Plaintiff's premises situate at Main Street, in the City of Dublin.

3. I say that the Plaintiff company operates a chain of six retail stores throughout Ireland, retailing ladies' fashion garments. Three of the stores are located in Dublin and three in other towns and cities throughout the country.

4. The Plaintiff company holds a lease on a retail premises situate at Main Street in the City of Dublin and I say that the said lease is due to expire on or about the 1st May next. I say that the Plaintiff company has decided that it will not renew the lease and has decided to cease trading from that location.

5. The Plaintiff company recognises and negotiates with the Garment Workers Union in respect of all of its staff at all of its retail outlets.

6. I say that in anticipation of the closure of the Main Street premises negotiations were entered into between the Plaintiff company and the union on behalf of the workers. The union sought, during the course of those negotiations, for the

payment of very substantially enhanced redundancy payments whereas the Plaintiff company was only willing to pay statutory redundancy payments. I say that following the failure of the negotiations the matter was referred by the Trade Union to the Labour Relations Commission and in circumstances where further discussions under the auspices of that body was not successful the matter was referred to the Labour Court. The Labour Court issued a recommendation dated the 10th day of April recommending that the Plaintiff company pay enhanced sums at the same level which it paid some years ago when it closed a shop in Cork. I say that the Plaintiff company has decided that it is not in a position, by reason of trading difficulties, to make such payments and has accordingly rejected the Labour Court recommendation.

7. In accordance with the individual employees' contracts of employment and in compliance with the terms of the Minimum Notice and Terms of Employment Acts the Plaintiff company served, on all of its staff at the Main Street premises, Notice of Termination of employment by reason of redundancy some six weeks ago. All of the staff's employment is due to end by reason of redundancy with effect from Friday next, 23rd April. I beg to refer to a copy of the Termination Notices served on the third, fourth and fifth named Defendants herein upon which pinned together and marked with the letters "OW1" I have endorsed my name prior to swearing hereof.

8. I say that the union conducted a secret ballot among the members of staff of the Plaintiff employed at the Main Street premises and have served upon the company a written notice of industrial action "up to and including strike" to take effect from close of business on Thursday next, 22nd April. I beg to refer to a copy of the union's notification of strike action upon which pinned together and marked with the letters "OW2" I have endorsed my name prior to the swearing hereof.

9. I say that in anticipation of the closure of the store the Plaintiff company took appropriate steps to make its stock safe by removing a substantial amount of stock from the Main Street premises on the morning of today Wednesday, 21st April. I say that the Plaintiff company also arranged for the disconnection of computers, cash registers and other point of sale electronic equipment and advised the staff to sell off the remaining stock at substantial discounts on a cash only basis.

10. I say that when the retail shop closed at 6 pm, in normal course, this evening 21st April, three members of staff, being the third, fourth and fifth named Defendants remained in the premises. I believe and am advised that they were immediately joined by the second named Defendant who is an official of the Garment Workers Union and also by an unknown number of members of their families and perhaps other unknown persons. From observations made I believe that there are now approximately 10 persons in occupation of the premises. I say that immediately following the occupation the persons in occupation have pinned placards and notices to the inside of the windows proclaiming that they are engaged in industrial action and they have also placed a large quantity of furniture and other materials so that the door to the premises cannot be opened.

11. I say that I attended at the premises at approximately 7 pm this evening, Wednesday 21st April, I sought admission and same was refused by the third named Defendant who is known to me. I say that I then had a telephone conversation by mobile phone with the third named Defendant and I called on her to vacate the premises and she stated that she would not do so and that she would stay there as long as it took to get the company to agree to the payment of the Labour Court recommendation.

12. I say and believe and am advised that the second, third, fourth and fifth named Defendants are in unlawful occupation of the Plaintiff's premises and I believe and am advised that such occupation is not protected by virtue of the provisions of the Industrial Relations Acts.

13. I say that the building is now wholly occupied by persons with no authority to be present and I believe that the Defendants do not intend to vacate the said premises and in the circumstances I believe that unless directed by this Honourable Court the said occupation will continue indefinitely.

14. I have been advised as to the undertaking as to damages which must be given to this Honourable Court in an application such as is envisaged herein and I say that I am authorised on behalf of the Plaintiff company to give such an undertaking and I do so.

15. In the premises, I pray this Honourable Court for the interim and interlocutory relief sought in the Notice of Motion herein.

SWORN by the said **OSCAR WILDE**
On the   day of
At
In the City of Dublin before me a Commissioner for
Oaths and I know the Deponent.

_____
COMMMISSIONER FOR OATHS
PRACTISING SOLICITOR

This Affidavit is filed this ... day of ……….. …. by

DRAFT PLEADINGS
(CASE III)

Statement of Facts

Abe Lincoln & Partners is a firm of business consultants. They do not provide accountancy or professional legal advice but they do advise businesses in relation to such matters as human resource management, recruitment, out placement, safety audits and other similar services. Thomas Jefferson & Company, which provides a similar range of services, has recently ceased trading on the retirement of the principal, Mr Jefferson. Thomas Jefferson & Company made all of its staff, 20 in number, redundant and agreed with the Trade Union representing those workers that they would pay enhanced redundancy payments and that they would also circulate full details of its employees' skills and experiences to other companies engaged in similar business. Abe Lincoln & Partners immediately offered employment to all of the redundant staff on condition that each member of the staff of Thomas Jefferson would use his best endeavours to bring over the former clients of Thomas Jefferson to their new employer. The employees were remarkably successful in this action and it is believed that more than 90% of the former clients of Thomas Jefferson have signed on with Abe Lincoln. Thomas Jefferson & Company previously recognised the Clerical Workers Union as representing all of its employees.

About three months after the recruitment of the former Thomas Jefferson employees, their new employer advised them that 10 persons were to be made redundant and they were individually served with one week's notice of termination and advised that they were not required to work out that period of notice and that they should leave the premises immediately.

The Clerical Workers Union immediately sought a meeting with Abe Lincoln & Partners to discuss the following matters:

- the unfair dismissal of 10 of their members;

- the failure of Abe Lincoln & Partners to recognise the rights of the new employees under the Transfer of Undertakings Regulations;

- the failure on the part of Abe Lincoln & Partners to pay salaries and other benefits, in particular pension contributions, at the same level as previously applied in Thomas Jefferson & Co; and

- union recognition.

Abe Lincoln & Partners refused to enter into any discussions with the Union. Some four days later, the Union advised the employer that it had conducted a secret ballot of its 20 members and that it intended to engage in industrial action 'at such level as might be determined by the General Secretary of the Union up to and including strike action'. The employer was given two weeks' notice of the intended industrial action and it was invited in the interim to refer the matter 'through normal procedures' to seek a resolution.

No efforts were made by Abe Lincoln & Partners to seek a resolution of the dispute during the period of notice and accordingly picketing commenced this morning, Monday, 1 June.

Abe Lincoln & Partners have their offices in a substantial office building which is occupied not only by that company but also by a number of businesses, engaged in entirely different types of work, but which are either owned wholly or in part by Mr Lincoln. The picketing has taken place at the front entrance to the building and has involved all 20 former employees of Thomas Jefferson & Co, including the 10 dismissed workers, and they have been accompanied by a number of trade union officials, together with a group of unidentified supporters, so that the total picket consists of about 30 persons. The picketers are walking up and down the public footpath carrying placards making it clear that the action is directed against Abe Lincoln & Partners. However, one of the dismissed workers is carrying a homemade placard with the words 'Abe Lincoln – abuses his workers' written on it.

Abe Lincoln & Partners are seeking interlocutory injunctive relief and in the proceedings have named the Union, four named union officials and 20 employees as defendants.

PLEADINGS

THE HIGH COURT

Record No. ....

BETWEEN:

ABE LINCOLN & COMPANY

Plaintiff

– AND –

CLERICAL WORKERS UNION

first named Defendant

[FOUR NAMED UNION OFFICIALS]

second to fifth named Defendants

[TWENTY NAMED EMPLOYEES]

sixth to twenty-sixth named Defendants

PLENARY SUMMONS

GENERAL INDORSEMENT OF CLAIM

THE PLAINTIFF'S CLAIM AS AGAINST THE DEFENDANTS IS FOR:

1. An injunction restraining the Defendants, and each of them, their servants or agents or any person acting in concert with them or any persons having knowledge of the making of any Order by this Honourable Court from engaging in industrial action against the Plaintiff at the Plaintiff's premises situate at ....

2. An injunction restraining the Defendants, and each of them, their servants or agents or any person acting in concert with them or any persons having knowledge of the making of any Order by this Honourable Court from watching or besetting or picketing the Plaintiff's said premises or any part thereof.

3. An injunction restraining the Defendants, and each of them, their servants or agents or any person acting in concert with them or any person having knowledge of the making of any Order by this Honourable Court from interfering with access to or egress from the Plaintiff's said premises or any part thereof.

4. An injunction restraining the Defendants, and each of them, their servants or agents or any person acting in concert with them or any persons having knowledge of the making of any Order by this Honourable Court from portraying or communicating, whether by recourse to pickets or posters, placards or leaflets or otherwise that they are engaged in a trade dispute with the Plaintiff.

5. An injunction restraining the first to fifth named Defendants, and each of them, their servants or agents from inciting, instructing, inducing, procuring, persuading, organising, financing or in any manner whatsoever facilitating picketing of the Plaintiff's premises.

6. An Order directing the first to fifth named Defendants and each of them to forthwith withdraw any direction, instructions, inducement, advice, finance or other encouragement given, whether directly or indirectly to the sixth to twenty-sixth named Defendants or to any other employees of the Plaintiff to do any act in breach of their contracts of employment with the Plaintiff or otherwise howsoever to interfere with the trade or business of the Plaintiff or otherwise howsoever to picket the Plaintiff's premises.

7. In the alternative an Order limiting any picketing of the Plaintiff's premises to no more than two persons at any time.

8. An injunction restraining the Defendants, or any of them, their officers, servants or agents, from carrying any placard or displaying any leaflet or notice defamatory of the Plaintiff or any of its officers, servants or agents.

9. A declaration that there is not in existence any valid trade dispute as between the Plaintiff and the Defendants or any of them.

10. Damages for unlawful watching and besting, unlawful picketing and unlawful interference with access to and egress from the Plaintiff's premises.

11. Damages for causing loss by unlawful means.

12. Damages for interfering with the Plaintiff's lawful activities.

13. Damages for trespass.

14. Such further and other relief as to this Honourable Court shall deem meet.

15. Costs.

A BARRISTER BL

Signed: _____
A Solicitor
Solicitors for the Plaintiff

THE HIGH COURT

Record No. ....

BETWEEN:

ABE LINCOLN & COMPANY

Plaintiff

– AND –

CLERICAL WORKERS UNION

first named Defendant

[FOUR NAMED UNION OFFICIALS]

second to fifth named
Defendants

[TWENTY NAMED EMPLOYEES]

sixth to twenty-sixth
named Defendants

NOTICE OF MOTION

TAKE NOTICE that Counsel on behalf of the Plaintiff will apply to this Honourable Court at the sitting of the Court at 11 o'clock in the forenoon in Court No ... in the Four Courts in the City of Dublin for the following Orders and reliefs:

1. An interlocutory injunction restraining the Defendants, and each of them, their servants or agents or any persons acting in concert with them or any persons having knowledge of the making of any Order by this Honourable Court from engaging in industrial action of any type whatsoever against the Plaintiff at the Plaintiff's premises situate at ....

2. An interlocutory injunction restraining the Defendants, and each of them, their servants or agents or any persons acting in concert with them or any persons having knowledge of the making of any Order by this Honourable Court from watching or besetting or picketing the Plaintiff's said premises or any part thereof.

3. An interlocutory injunction restraining the Defendants, and each of them, their servants or agents or any persons acting in concert with them or any persons having knowledge of the making of any Order by this Honourable Court from portraying or communicating whether by recourse to pickets or posters or

leaflets, placards or otherwise howsoever that there is in existence a trade dispute between the Plaintiff and the Defendants or any of them.

4.   In the alternative, if necessary, an injunction restraining the Defendants, and each of them, or any person acting in concert with them or any person having knowledge of the making of any Order by this Honourable Court from engaging in any picketing of the Plaintiff's premises situate at .... in circumstances where there are more than two persons engaged in such picketing at any time.

5.   An interlocutory injunction restraining the Defendants, and each of them, from carrying or publishing any placard or leaflet which is defamatory of the Plaintiff or any director, officer, servant or agent of the Plaintiff.

6.   If necessary an Order abridging the time for the service of this Notice of Motion.

7.   Such further or other orders as to this Honourable Court shall deem meet including, if necessary, orders for substituted service of this Notice of Motion and any order made by this Honourable Court.

8.   Further and other relief.

9.   Costs.

AND TAKE NOTICE THAT THE SAID APPLICATION will be grounded upon the proceedings already had herein, the Affidavit of Abraham Lincoln sworn on ... day of ...., the exhibits referred to therein, the nature of the case and the reasons to be offered.

Dated this .... day of ....

Signed: _____
                            A Solicitor
                   Solicitors for the Plaintiff
To: The Clerical Workers Union
            [address]
And To: Named Picketers

THE HIGH COURT

Record No. ....

BETWEEN:

ABE LINCOLN & COMPANY

Plaintiff

– AND –

CLERICAL WORKERS UNION

first named Defendant

[FOUR NAMED UNION OFFICIALS]

second to fifth named Defendants

[TWENTY NAMED EMPLOYEES]

sixth to twenty-sixth named Defendants

AFFIDAVIT OF ABRAHAM LINCOLN

I, **ABRAHAM LINCOLN**, Business Consultant of ...., in the City of Dublin, aged 18 years and upwards make oath and say as follows:

1. The Plaintiff is a Partnership of business consultants consisting of your deponent and four Partners. The main business of the Partnership is the provision of business consultancy and advice particularly in the areas of human resources management. The Partnership is not a firm of accountants or solicitors.

2. The Plaintiff firm has in total approximately 100 employees, including 10 employees who were previously employed by Thomas Jefferson & Company.

BACKGROUND

3. The Plaintiff Partnership is a very successful consultancy business and I am personally extremely well known in business circles both by reason of my involvement in the Plaintiff firm and also because of my involvement in a wide range of other businesses in which I am either principal or substantial shareholder. Many of these businesses share office space in the building where the Partnership carries on business. I am personally the owner of that premises.

4. I say that approximately four months ago I became aware that the long standing firm of Thomas Jefferson & Company intended to cease trading on the

343

retirement of the principal of that business. Mr Jefferson who was well known to me forwarded to me the curriculum vitae of all of his employees and advised me that as they were about to be made redundant they would all be available to be recruited and he gave glowing references in respect of each of the office employees.

5.   I say that on receipt of Mr Jefferson's communication I, on behalf of the Plaintiff, offered each of the former employees employment with the Plaintiff company and I advised each of those employees, during the course of interviews, that they would be expected to use their best endeavours to bring clients and customers with them. It is my belief that about 80% of the former clients of Thomas Jefferson & Company are now clients of the Plaintiff firm.

6.   About three months after the recruitment of the former employees it became clear that much of the work which they were doing could be absorbed by existing employees of the Plaintiff firm and accordingly I advised 10 of the new employees that they were to be made redundant with immediate effect. In this regard I complied with their contractual entitlements giving them each one week's notice in accordance with the provisions of the Minimum Notice and Terms of Employment Act. I did not require the employees to work out their period of notice.

7.   I say that immediately following the service by the Plaintiff of the Notice on the employees a communication was received from the Clerical Workers Union who asserted that they represented those employees and they sought negotiation on a number of matters, including, what is referred to as, the unfair dismissal of its members, union recognition and it also demanded application of rights which it asserted its members were entitled to by virtue of the Transfer of Undertakings Regulations. I beg to refer to a copy of the Union communication in this matter upon which pinned together and marked with the letters 'AL1' I have endorsed my name prior to swearing hereof.

8.   I say that I replied to the Trade Union advising that I would not engage in negotiations, that I did not recognise it as representing any of the employees of the Plaintiff and that I would not take any steps whatsoever in relation to the matters. I say that some four days later I received a further communication from the Trade Union advising that it was serving two weeks' notice of industrial action 'up to such level as may be determined by the General Secretary of the Union including strike action'. The Union further advised that it had a unanimous decision of all of its members employed by the Plaintiff in support of such action and it again called on the Plaintiff company to engage in negotiations. I beg to refer to a copy of the said letters upon which pinned together and marked with the letters 'AL2' I have endorsed my name prior to swearing hereof.

THE PICKETING

9.   I say that this morning, 1st June, at about 7 am a large number of people assembled at the entrance to the Plaintiff's premises. The group consisted of 20 employees including the dismissed 10 employees together with 4 union officials

who are known to me and a group of other persons who are unknown. In all the group consisted of approximately 30 people, the vast majority of whom were carrying placards printed with the name of the union and the words 'Official Strike on Here'. One former employee, the sixth named Defendant, carried a large placard handwritten with the words 'Abe Lincoln – abuses workers'.

10.   I say that the entire group of picketers commenced walking extremely slowly in close-knit file backwards and forwards along the public footpath so that at any given time the entrance to the building was virtually blocked. The group also engaged in regular chanting of 'strike on here'.

11.   I say that as a result of the activities of the Defendants a number of employees of the Plaintiff have not attended at work and I believe that they feel intimidated by the pickets. Employees of other companies whose offices are in the building have passed the pickets but I have been informed by the managers of those businesses that those employees also feel intimidated. The usual deliveries of newspapers made by a local newsagent to the offices has not occurred this morning.

THE ISSUES

12.   I believe and am advised that the activities of the Trade Union and the other picketers is unlawful and that there is not in existence a valid trade dispute and I am further advised by my solicitor that the union has not acted correctly and in accordance with the law in relation to balloting and notification of the trade dispute.

THE BALLOT

13.   I have been advised by members of the Plaintiff's staff that the ballot was limited solely to the group of employees of the Plaintiff who previously worked for Thomas Jefferson & Co and that none of the other employees of the Plaintiff were invited to partake in that ballot. I am advised that in that regard the union have failed in their duty to ballot all persons likely to be effected by the industrial action.

THE TRANSFER ISSUE

14.   The Plaintiff company did not acquire the business or assets of Thomas Jefferson & Co and accordingly there was no transfer of an undertaking within the meaning of the relevant regulations. I am advised in those circumstances that it is not open to the union to make a claim for the payments of terms and conditions and benefits attributable to the employees' former employment and that in those circumstances there is no valid basis for the present industrial dispute.

THE DISMISSAL ISSUE

15.   The 10 employees were validly dismissed by the Plaintiff company by reason of redundancy and in those circumstances are no longer employees of the Plaintiff

company and have no right in law or otherwise to engage in picketing of the Plaintiff's premises.

THE PREMISES

16. The Defendants are not only picketing the Plaintiff's premises but by picketing the building they are in effect picketing other businesses, admittedly businesses in which I have an interest, which are also occupiers of the building. I say that in those circumstances the picketers are not entitled to engage in their present unlawful activities.

17. The activities of the picketers are excessive, intimidatory and not peaceful. The placard being carried by the sixth named Defendant is clearly defamatory of me, your deponent, and implies that I am guilty of physical or sexual abuse of persons. I further say that the chanting by the picketers is generally intimidatory and the number engaged on the picket line is excessive. I believe that any number greater than two unreasonably restrains access to and egress from the building.

18. My solicitor has explained to me the undertaking that I must give to this Honourable Court when making an application for an interlocutory injunction of the type sought in these proceedings and I am happy to give that undertaking to the court.

19. In the premises, I pray this Honourable Court for the relief sought in the Notice of Motion herein.

SWORN by the said **ABRAHAM LINCOLN**
On the   day of
At
In the City of Dublin before me a Commissioner for
Oaths and I know the Deponent.

_____
COMMMISSIONER FOR OATHS
PRACTISING SOLICITOR

This Affidavit is filed this ... day of ………... …. by

THE HIGH COURT

Record No. ....

BETWEEN:

ABE LINCOLN &
COMPANY

Plaintiff

– AND –

CLERICAL
WORKERS UNION

first named Defendant

[FOUR NAMED
UNION OFFICIALS]

**second to fifth named
Defendants**

[TWENTY NAMED
EMPLOYEES]

**sixth to twenty-sixth
named Defendants**

AFFIDAVIT OF GEORGE WASHINGTON

I, **GEORGE WASHINGTON**, Union Official of ...., in the City of Dublin, aged 18 years and upwards make oath and say as follows:

1. I am the General Secretary of the Clerical Workers Union, the first named Defendant in the above entitled proceedings and I make this Affidavit on behalf of all of the Defendants and with their respective authority, from facts within my own knowledge save where otherwise appears and where so otherwise appearing I believe the same to be true and correct.

2. I make this Affidavit in reply to the Affidavit of Abraham Lincoln sworn herein on the 1st June, which Affidavit was sworn for the purposes of grounding that Plaintiff's application for interlocutory relief.

3. By way of general reply to that Affidavit of Mr Lincoln I say that the industrial action, including picketing of the Plaintiff's premises currently being undertaken by the Defendant's herein is lawful and I further say that that the Union and its officials have at all material times acted in full conformity with the Union's own rules and in compliance with the provisions of the Industrial Relations Acts.

4. I say that much of what is set out in paragraphs 3 to 8 inclusive of the Affidavit of Mr Lincoln is incorrect and I say that his brief history of the matter is lacking in many material respects.

5. I accept that the Plaintiff partnership is a very successful consultancy business and I accept that Mr Lincoln is very well known. I believe however that Mr Lincoln prides himself on his anti trade union stance and I believe that his conduct in refusing to even meet with your deponent or other representatives of the first named Defendant union in relation to very serious matters discloses an uncompromising attitude on his part. I believe that his application to this Honourable Court to seek to restrain, by way of injunction, lawful activities of a Trade Union is an excessive response and wholly unnecessary in a trade dispute which could be resolved if there was adherence to normal good industrial relations practice by the employer.

6. I believe that Mr Lincoln has been less than forthright in relation to the takeover by the Plaintiff of the business of Thomas Jefferson & Company. I have been advised by many of the former employees of that company who are now employees of the Plaintiff company that it was made abundantly clear to each of them by Mr Lincoln that their recruitment was wholly dependent on them bringing with them the customers and clients that they had previously dealt with when employed by their former employer. I am advised by the union members involved that essentially all, except a few minor clients, have transferred their business to the Plaintiff company. I believe that in those circumstances, notwithstanding what is said by Mr Lincoln, there in fact was, in law, a transfer of an undertaking within the meaning of the Transfer of Undertakings Regulations. I am advised by the individuals who are members of the Plaintiff trade union that they were offered jobs by the Plaintiff company on terms and conditions substantially less favourable than those which they enjoyed when in the employment of Thomas Jefferson & Company. I believe that salaries are of the order of 10%/20% below those previously enjoyed, no pension contributions are made by the employer and there has been a significant reduction in relation to other benefits such as holiday entitlements and sick pay schemes.

7. The first named Defendant union had a Collective Agreement with Thomas Jefferson & Company which provided, *inter alia*, that that company recognised the Defendant union for the purposes of negotiating pay and conditions of employment of all of the employees of that company. The Union regularly met with the management of Thomas Jefferson & Company, agreed rates of pay and other terms and conditions and regularly updated the Collective Agreement and agreed alterations in the Thomas Jefferson Employee Handbook. I beg to refer to a copy of the most recent version of the Collective Agreement and the Employee Handbook upon which pinned together and marked with the letter 'GW1' I have endorsed my name prior to swearing hereof.

8. I say that it became clear, immediately following the recruitment of the former employees of Thomas Jefferson & Company, that the Plaintiff company was acting to absorb into its systems and procedures all of the customers and clients of the other company. I have been advised by the union members that within

days they were instructed to transfer management of their individual clients to existing employees of the Plaintiff company. I believe that thereafter the former employees of Thomas Jefferson & Company were assigned mundane tasks and I believe that same was planned for the purposes of making them susceptible to being dismissed by reason of redundancy. Mr Lincoln has failed to bring to the attention of this Honourable Court my first communication with his company where I complained about his treatment of the new employees, advised him of the existence of the Collective Agreement and asserted an entitlement to protected benefits by reason of the Transfer of Undertakings Regulations. I beg to refer to a copy of my letter dated 1st April upon which pinned together and marked with the letters 'GW2' I have endorsed my name prior to swearing hereof. I say that I at no stage received a reply to that communication.

9.   I accept that immediately following the notice of termination I wrote to the Plaintiff company calling on them to enter into negotiations on a number of matters including the unfair dismissal of the union members, union recognition and related matters. Mr Lincoln has exhibited the exchange of correspondence at Exhibits AL1 and AL2 to his Affidavit and I say that it is clear from the contents of that correspondence that Mr Lincoln had adopted an uncompromising position.

10.   The Union organised a secret ballot conducted in accordance with the Union Rules of all of its members in the employment of the first named Defendant. The union membership was limited in fact to the 20 employees who had transferred in from Thomas Jefferson & Company. That ballot was conducted properly and resulted in a unanimous decision authorizing industrial action up to and including picketing of the Plaintiff's premises. I beg to refer to a copy of the ballot paper used in the said ballot and a copy of my communication to the union members who had balloted setting out the results of the secret ballot upon which pinned together and marked with the letters GW3' I have endorsed my name prior to swearing hereof. I reject out of hand the contention contained in paragraph 13 of the Affidavit of Mr Lincoln that the ballot was invalid in some way and I say that the union's obligation was only to ballot its members who were likely to be affected by the industrial action and I say the Union has complied with that. There is no requirement in law or otherwise for the Union to ballot employees who are not members of the Trade Union.

11.   I believe that there is in existence a valid trade dispute between the parties and the issues are:

(a)   unfair/wrongful dismissal of ten employees;

(b)   refusal to recognise the Trade Union for the purposes of collective bargaining; and

(c)   breach of the Transfer of Undertakings Regulations.

12.   I believe and am advised by the Union's solicitors that these matters constitute a valid trade dispute and that in the circumstances, where the Union has complied with its rules in relation to balloting and has given appropriate notice to the

employer, that its activities, including the picketing activities, are valid and lawful and enjoy the protection of the Industrial Relations Acts.

13.   In relation to the picketing I say that same had been conducted in a lawful and peaceful manner. All of the employees who are on strike are entitled to picket the premises and I believe that all of those employees, together with Union Officials, are entitled to engage in picketing and carry appropriate placards and banners. I further say that the chanting of slogans and the other activities of the pickets, including your deponent, are solely for the purposes of communicating information to employees of the Plaintiff company, members of the public and employees of other businesses associated with Mr Lincoln for the purposes of encouraging them to support the picketers in their action. I reject the allegations of intimidation contained in the Affidavit of Mr Lincoln and I say that it is important for this Honourable Court to note that despite having every opportunity to do so the Plaintiff company have not filed Affidavits sworn by any of the alleged intimidated employees.

14.   I accept that other businesses are located in the premises used by the Plaintiff company however I say that all of those other companies are associated with or owned by Mr Lincoln. I am advised by members of the Union that there are considerable linkages and interaction between Mr Lincoln's various businesses and it is often very difficult to ascertain who is the employer of any individual person working within the building.

15.   I believe and am advised that the Plaintiff has not in the instant case raised a fair issue to be tried such as would warrant this Honourable Court restraining the Defendants from exercising their lawful rights to engage in industrial action and picketing of their employer's premises and in all of the circumstances I pray this Honourable Court to refuse the relief sought by the Plaintiff in these proceedings.

SWORN by the said **GEORGE WASHINGTON**
On the   day of
At
In the City of Dublin before me a Commissioner for
Oaths and I know the Deponent.

_____
COMMMISSIONER FOR OATHS
PRACTISING SOLICITOR

This Affidavit is filed this … day of ……….. …. by …………………………..

INDEX

[all references are to paragraph number]

Acquiescence
trade disputes, and, 9.12–9.13

Affray
picketing, and, 10.34

Agreement or combination between two or more persons
conspiracy, and, 5.11–5.12

'All-out' policy
picketing, and, 10.81

American Cyanamid **principles**
injunctions to restrain, and, 11.05–11.06

'Blacking'
industrial action, and, 3.07

Bona fide belief
trade disputes, and, 9.07–9.11

Breach of contract
economic torts, and
See also **Inducing breach of contract**
breach, 6.56–6.72
damage, 6.83–6.85
elements, 6.05–6.09
generally, 4.07–4.12
inducement, 6.29–6.55
intention, 6.26–6.28
introduction, 6.01–6.04
justification, 6.73–6.82
knowledge, 6.10–6.25
OBG Ltd v Allan, and, 4.06
proper plaintiff, 6.86
single tort, as, 4.13–4.25
statutory immunity, 6.87–6.96
strikes, and, 3.09–3.11

unlawful means conspiracy, and, 5.45

Breach of the peace
picketing, and, 10.30–10.33

Causing loss by unlawful means
constitutional rights, and, 7.38
damage, 7.39
historical development, 7.05–7.16
independent actionability, 7.30–7.37
intention, 7.17–7.22
introduction, 7.01–7.04
motive, and, 7.22
nomenclature, 7.01
OBG Ltd v Allan, and, 4.06
statutory protection, and, 7.40–7.46
unlawful means, 7.23–7.38

Closed shop
freedom of association, and, 2.23–2.25

Commission of Inquiry on Industrial Relations report (1981)
generally, 1.29–1.33
strikes and contracts of employment, 3.01

Communication of grievance
trade disputes, and, 9.12–9.13

Conflict of constitutional rights
introduction, 2.37–2.38
right to strike or take industrial action, 2.39–2.52

'Connected with'
trade disputes, and, 9.04

Conspiracy

agreement or combination between two or more persons, 5.11–5.12

conspiracy to do unlawful act or use unlawful means

acts contravening a penal statute, 5.44

breach of contract, 5.45

generally, 5.24–5.26

introduction, 5.08

knowledge, 5.29–5.33

tort to agree a tort, as, 5.27–5.28

unconstitutional acts, 5.39–5.43

unlawful means, 5.34–5.45

conspiracy to injure

generally, 5.14

good motive, 5.18–5.20

intention, 5.15–5.17

introduction, 5.08

justification, 5.18–5.20

mixed motives, 5.21–5.23

motive, 5.15–5.17

damage, 5.13

generally, 4.26

injury must result from the combination, 5.13

introduction, 5.01–5.07

picketing, and, 10.22–10.23

rationale, 5.08–5.13

'simple' conspiracy

generally, 5.14

good motive, 5.18–5.20

intention, 5.15–5.17

introduction, 5.08

justification, 5.18–5.20

mixed motives, 5.21–5.23

motive, 5.15–5.17

statutory immunity

action contrary to outcome of secret ballot, and, 5.52–5.55

'actionable', 5.49–5.50

generally, 5.46–5.47

one-worker disputes, and, 5.51

scope of protection, 5.48

unlawful means conspiracy

acts contravening a penal statute, 5.44

breach of contract, 5.45

generally, 5.24–5.26

introduction, 5.08

knowledge, 5.29–5.33

tort to agree a tort, as, 5.27–5.28

unconstitutional acts, 5.39–5.43

unlawful means, 5.34–5.45

Conspiracy and Protection of Property Act 1875

generally, 1.13

Constitution

causing loss by unlawful means, and, 7.38

conflict of rights

introduction, 2.37–2.38

right to strike or take industrial action, 2.39–2.52

freedom of association

balancing collective and individual interests, 2.10–2.12

enforcement of a closed shop, 2.23–2.25

generally, 2.05–2.09

human rights, and, 2.34–2.36

individual contracts of employment, 2.31–2.33

recognition of trade unions, 2.27–2.30

secret ballots, 2.26